CELTIC: THE AWAKENING

Alex Gordon is a former *Sunday Mail* sports editor and chief sports sub-editor of the *Daily Record*, and has also worked as a columnist for *World Soccer Monthly* and as the Scottish correspondent for *France Football* and *L'Équipe*. He has co-authored a number of sports books, including *A Bhoy Called Bertie* with Bertie Auld, *The Quiet Assassin* with Davie Hay and *Seeing Red* with Chic Charnley. He lives on the outskirts of Glasgow with his wife.

Celtic

The Awakening

From East End Misfits
to European Masters

MAINSTREAM
PUBLISHING

EDINBURGH AND LONDON

First published in Great Britain in 2013 by

MAINSTREAM PUBLISHING COMPANY

(EDINBURGH) LTD

7 Albany Street

Edinburgh EH1 3UG

ISBN 9781780575896 (Hardback edition)

ISBN 9781780576350 (Trade paperback edition)

A catalogue record for this book is available
from the British Library

Printed in Great Britain by
Clays Ltd, St Ives plc

1 3 5 7 9 10 8 6 4 2

To Gerda, my wee rock

ACKNOWLEDGEMENTS

The author would like to thank the following for all their kind assistance, for making themselves available for interviews and for their invaluable input and insight: Billy McNeill, Bertie Auld, Jim Craig, John Clark, Willie Wallace, Stevie Chalmers, Bobby Lennox, Davie Hay, George Connelly, Danny McGrain, Mike Jackson, John Hughes, Lou Macari, Tommy Callaghan, Davie Cattenach, Harry Hood and Evan Williams. Thanks also to the many others who chipped in, and to Pat Crerand for permission to quote from his book *Never Turn the Other Cheek*.

I would especially like to say a massive thank you to Tommy Gemmell. We've spent the best part of a year talking about this book and putting it together, and his guidance has been wonderful and well received. He brought the old times to life with his vibrant storytelling. Happy days.

Thanks also to my dad, John, for introducing me to the delights and delirium of the Jungle in the '60s.

I would also like to thank Bill Campbell, director of Mainstream Publishing, for some of his extremely astute observations. Greatly appreciated, Bill. The book was enhanced by your influence and assistance. Thanks also to Graeme Blaikie, editorial coordinator, for all his invaluable help and editor Claire Rose for all her sterling work above and beyond.

Finally, I would like to show my appreciation to Big Joe and Jack at The Ferry, Clydeside, to Gary and Jemma at the Birds and Bees restaurant in Stirling and to Michael and Jamie at the Old Bridge Inn, Bridge of Allan. They made Tommy Gemmell, my wife, Gerda, and me most welcome on our frequent visits to their establishments as we put some things together for this book. Thanks, folks!

CONTENTS

PREFACE 9

INTRODUCTION: TWO FOR THE ROAD
   – BILLY McNEILL AND BERTIE AULD 12

1. PARADISE LOST 25

2. JOCK VERSUS CELTIC 42

3. RUMBLE IN THE JUNGLE 54

4. THE STUFF OF NIGHTMARES 64

5. THE NEARLY MEN 77

6. SILVER SERVICE – AGAIN 86

7. DREAM ON, CHAMPIONS! 101

8. LET THE GOOD TIMES ROLL 118

9. MAGIC AND MAYHEM 137

10. JOCK VERSUS RANGERS 163

11. TROUBLE IN PARADISE 190

12. WHAT PRICE SUCCESS? 216

13. MIXED FORTUNES 230

14. FAREWELL TO THE LIONS 239

15. A TIME OF CHANGE 261

16. PARADISE REGAINED 274

APPENDIX: THE HONOURS LIST 285

PREFACE

Everyone has the right to pursue a dream no matter where it may lead them. In the early 1960s, Celtic Park was a bleak place where dreams went to die.

During these grim times, the Celtic support trudged wearily along a one-way route to the graveyard of hope and aspiration. Football fans, by the very nature of their calling, are doomed to suffer. But some poor souls suffer more wretchedly than others. Watching Celtic at the start of the 1960s was more often than not an unbearable ordeal for even the most resolutely loyal supporter. Parkhead had become a monument to misery. The football club teetered on the precipice, peering gloomily into impenetrable darkness. Where once there had been fields of splendour, there was now a wasteland of mediocrity.

Celtic were entrenched among Scottish football's have-nots. Ambition had drained from the heart of a proud old club that had become impoverished of imagination and bereft of leadership. There was little or no pleasure to be derived from following a team ponderously dragging along the path of failure, lacking ingenuity on the field and enterprise off it. It was an excruciatingly painful combination. To many, it appeared starkly unlikely that the formidable history of the club would ever be matched by a triumphant future. The wicked, chill winds that signalled the descent of another winter barren of expectation provided their own obbligato of despair and disenchantment during those black days.

In the first five years of the '60s, Celtic's participation in the First Division Championship, the Scottish Cup and the League Cup was a mere irrelevance. Pitifully, the club wasn't even equipped to aspire to second-rate. Supporters, compelled purely by loyalty, made their way to Celtic Park on match days in the full awareness that enjoyment had been replaced by endurance. The players often left the field to a din of derision, the regular requiem for serial underperformers.

The main and persistent problem in the early years of the '60s was the supporting cast. While Charlie Tully, Bobby Evans, Willie Fernie, Bertie Peacock and Bobby Collins could consistently produce outstanding moments in the glare of the spotlight, they found themselves surrounded by honest, earnest individuals whose only flaw was that they were simply not good enough to perform in the manner expected of a Celtic footballer. It would be tantamount to flattery to say that the contributions of such individuals could be rated as ordinary. Their intentions were laudable, but, sadly, they did not possess the gifts required to deliver on promises. Their lack of expertise was usually exposed long before the final curtain came down. The void between the two extremes was routinely exploited by ruthless opponents.

The dawning of the '60s offered little cheer to those of the Celtic persuasion. There was no positive reason for optimism. All logic pointed unwaveringly and unhesitatingly to sustained sorrow. Yet, from these joyless depths, something utterly unexpected was about to emerge: success at a level that even the most relentlessly optimistic among the support would not have imagined. The side's dull-grey performances changed gradually to a faded black and white, then, wonderfully and magically, halfway through a defining decade, erupted into glorious, vivid technicolour. Celtic's resurgence was pure theatre in the East End of Glasgow. Celtic Football Club went from B-listers to the star attraction in the space of five memorable, mesmerising years.

The story of Celtic's trip through the momentous '60s and '70s is a thrilling, multilayered one. From the doldrums to delirium. From rubble to riches. From excruciating lows to exhilarating highs. From bit-part players to the best in Europe. The cloak of lethargy was shed, vision recovered, guidance restored, magnificence sustained. The club arose from dreary desolation to discover once again the direction, fortitude, hunger, ability, drive and desire that became trademarks of a football team loaded with masterful characters quite comfortable parading their ostentatious talents centre stage. It was a team rightly acclaimed as one of the best in the history of world football, a collection of personalities whose skills were avidly appreciated and enthusiastically admired.

In the absence of a bloke called Merlin, it is a source of wonderment that a football team that had toiled and struggled against the most mediocre of opposition, some of them part-time, in front of their own legions at Celtic Park came within a short space of time to rule Europe with a pizzazz and elan that set them apart from pretenders to the throne. With skill, authority and wondrously fluent creativity, Celtic had launched themselves to an enchanting new level. This was a team of indisputable charm and exceptional panache. To the neutral onlooker, they became the best team on the planet and, if fair play had won the day, they would have had the silverware to prove it in 1967.

Before Billy McNeill headed in the Scottish Cup winner in the 3–2 victory over Dunfermline at Hampden in 1965, Celtic had gone eight dismal years without a trophy success. Celtic played Rangers 20 times in a variety of domestic competitions in the first half of the '60s. They won twice. In the second half, they faced their old foes 21 times. They won ten of those matches and, importantly, three were cup finals. The decade kicked off with a drab 1–0 defeat from Rangers. Highlighting the startling transformation, the '60s ended with an overwhelming 8–1 triumph over Partick Thistle. In between, there had been five league championships, three Scottish Cups, five League Cups and, of course, a European Cup.

From the awfulness of those early years of the '60s, when Celtic were adrift, a ship in distress without a steady hand on the tiller, someone, somehow, had found the way to football's Utopia. Celtic's journey through two unforgettable and significant decades was one of epic proportions. The magisterial ascent of the East End side to exalted grandeur, as beguiling as it was bewildering, was an apparently impossible dream come true. This book examines how that near miracle came about.

INTRODUCTION
TWO FOR THE ROAD – BILLY McNEILL AND BERTIE AULD

Billy McNeill and Bertie Auld were the only two players who took part in the first game of 1960 and the last one of 1969 during a decade of exaggerated metamorphosis. (Auld, of course, had a four-year interlude at Birmingham City between 1961 and 1965.)

McNeill, the majestic captain and leader of men, was still around as manager in 1988, when he led the celebrations in the club's centenary year with a league and cup double. Fate, somehow, had determined the occasion.

Auld, a vitally important player and an inspirational figure in the Jock Stein era, epitomised the bold new Celtic that evolved in the mid-'60s. He was the cheeky chappie who, along with the equally creative Bobby Murdoch, became the choreographer-in-chief of a revitalised, rejuvenated team.

Auld and McNeill both have extraordinary tales to tell about life at Celtic in the '60s and '70s. Here they talk to the author about their experiences.

ALEX GORDON: Could either of you have foreseen the revolution that was around the corner when you played and lost in the 1960 New Year's Day game against Rangers?

BILLY McNEILL: There was no leadership and it was obvious mistakes were being made at the club, but we lived in hope. Remember, we weren't just Celtic players, we were Celtic fans, too. The club meant everything to us and, although we weren't getting much joy on the field, we still wore that jersey with pride. If the supporters were hurting, you better believe we were, also.

BERTIE AULD: Yes, those were obviously frustrating times for everyone connected with the club. There seemed to be no rhyme or reason to a lot of the decision-making. For instance, I had hoped to play against Rangers in the League Cup final in 1957, but I was dropped and missed the 7–1 victory. I had played in six successive ties leading up to the final and had scored three goals, too. But, without a hint of an explanation, I was chopped from the Hampden squad. There was no man-management. I was out and no one bothered to sit down with me and discuss the situation. I was only 19 years old at the time and, naturally, I was bitterly disappointed to miss the big game. You might have thought that, after I'd played in the previous six ties, I'd have at least got a seat in the stand. No chance. I was packed off to play for the reserves against Queen of the South in Dumfries on the same day. Mind you, Neilly Mochan came in, had a stormer and scored two goals, and we gubbed them, so there were no complaints afterwards.

However, even today, it is difficult to comprehend that I was transferred in 1961, four years after that final, had another four years at Birmingham City, returned to Parkhead and the club still hadn't won a solitary trophy in that period. You didn't expect such a barren run at a club like Celtic.

McNEILL: The club should never have allowed Jock Stein to leave in 1960. That was a huge error of judgement on someone's part. Jock was in charge of the reserves and the players really enjoyed working with him. Not once did I hear anyone question his methods. I'm not just being wise after the event, because I said it back then. Jock was always going to be a huge success as a manager. He was light years ahead of his time. I was close to Jock, of course. I suppose he was a bit of a mentor to me. I think it helped that he had played in my position, at centre-half, and could work on that with me and pass on his knowledge.

AULD: Everybody on the playing staff admired Big Jock for his football knowledge. Even experienced first-team players, guys who had played alongside him, listened when he spoke. He was immersed in the game and very enthusiastic. He thought about it constantly, even down to the most minute of details. Jock would work on free kicks, corner kicks, even throw-ins. Everyone knew what was expected of them when he was in charge. He was always on the ball and never missed a trick. He realised he had a dressing-room full of Celtic fans. If a guy he brought into the club wasn't a Celtic fan, it didn't take too long before he became one.

The supporters won't know this, but when they were singing their songs out on the terracings before a game, the players were singing them too, in the dressing-room. When they put the music on the tannoy and gave it pelters with 'Hail! Hail! The Celts Are Here', we were giving it big licks as we prepared to go out on the pitch. Jock made sure our dressing-room window was always open on match day. It was high up near the ceiling and the fans couldn't see through the frosted glass. It didn't matter if it was sub-zero temperatures, that window remained open. As the supporters made their way along Kerrydale Street and were bashing out their songs, we were listening to every word and singing along with them. We didn't realise it at the time, but it was a fabulous bonding experience between the players and the men on the terracing.

McNEILL: Jock was a great seeker of knowledge. He would travel all over the place taking in games and, more often than not, paying out the cash from his own pocket. I know he went to Wembley in 1953 to watch the Hungarians play against England. They were the emerging nation and Jock wanted to see them for himself. Nowadays, you can flick a switch and get games beamed into your living room from anywhere in the world. Obviously, that wasn't the case back then. Jock watched a team that possessed the great Ferenc Puskás take England apart, winning 6–3. The English still thought they were the best in the world, so a result like that really shook up football. Jock must have taken a lot of notes that day. He noticed that Hungary deployed their centre-forward, Nándor Hidegkuti, in a deep-lying role and that England didn't know how to react to this tactic. Jock was so impressed that he bought one of those old-fashioned movie projectors, probably state of the art back then, obtained film of the entire 90 minutes and pored over it time and again at home. God knows how many tapes of that Wembley game he must have wiped out!

AULD: That was the man's style, Billy. He could take in a top-flight international one night and then pop in to watch a junior game a couple of days later. He always insisted you would pick up something from every game if you watched properly and concentrated. By the way, I have to say the English goalkeeper that day against the Hungarians knew his football. It was Gil Merrick who signed me for Birmingham City!

GORDON: How popular was Jock with the players?

McNEILL: I know I was seen as his blue-eyed boy, but that was never the case, believe me. Possibly because I was captain, he rarely gave me a doing in front of my colleagues in the dressing-room. But I knew what to expect afterwards when he said, 'Billy, can I have a word?' Then he would let me know what he thought of my performance. I think if you gave him 100 per cent all the time and cared deeply about the club, he was a great ally. If you stepped out of line, he was down on you like a pile of bricks.

AULD: Jock never courted popularity among the players. He never saw that as being part of his remit. All he ever wanted to do was get the best for Celtic. He treated individuals in different ways. There were some who would sulk and retreat if he gave them a verbal blast. He knew these characters would respond better to an arm around their shoulder and a quiet word in their ear.

He was full of surprises, though. I recall a game I had against Rangers in a Glasgow Cup tie at Ibrox in 1966. I had a stinker. Virtually nothing I tried that night came off. After the match, he came over and congratulated me for a pass I had hit that set up a goal for Bobby Lennox. I was expecting a hammering. Mind you, it probably helped that we won 4–0!

GORDON: How did it feel making the breakthrough to the first team back then?

McNEILL: Nerve-racking! No, I just went out to do my absolute best in every game. I knew what the Celtic supporters looked for in a player. They wouldn't accept someone they spotted not giving it their all – and you could be sure they would clock a player not performing at his utmost. I think they made allowances for young lads such as myself and gave us great encouragement.

Their backing at such a crucial stage in the club's history was absolutely vital. Even when we weren't playing too well, and that was the case for far too long, we were still getting crowds of 20,000 to 30,000. That was an awful lot of people making an effort to get along to Parkhead on match day to see a team they knew beforehand probably wouldn't excel. But they still turned up, thankfully.

AULD: In those days, the players could actually socialise with the fans. There weren't the huge barriers there are today, when the gulf between the working man and the player is widening by the minute. They are not on the same planet these days. I loved the rapport with those supporters. Still do. They knew their football, that's for sure. No one talked down to them. If they had a grievance, they knew they could talk to you about it. They could sidle up to you in the pub and have a word. Big Jock constantly drummed into us that these guys were the lifeblood of football and deserved to be entertained. 'Football without fans is nothing,' he would often say. He was right, too.

McNEILL: Although Celtic hadn't been too successful in picking up any silverware, we still tried to put on a show for the man on the terracing. The team had a lot of colourful characters the fans could identify with. Those personalities played in what became known as 'the Celtic Way'. It may not have brought in the trophies, but it was certainly watchable. We scored a lot of goals. Mind you, we shipped in a few, too!

AULD: Billy, I can remember a funny story when you were beginning to make an impact in the reserves and were looking at breaking into the first team. Bobby Evans, who became a great friend of mine, used to pick me up after training in the afternoon and give me a lift in his car to Glasgow city centre. A few other teammates – guys such as Paddy Crerand and Mike Jackson – would catch a lift, too. We would congregate in an Italian restaurant called Ferrari's in Sauchiehall Street and we would talk non-stop about football. Bobby would drop us off and then drive on to his newsagent's shop elsewhere in the city, where he would put in a shift until closing time, around 6 p.m. Could you believe that? He was the captain of Celtic and Scotland, and there he was selling newspapers and cigarettes to the punters! Do you know, no one thought that unusual back then? Today's players don't know they're born. The point of the story, though, is that Bobby was a wee bit anxious about your arrival. You were getting noticed in the reserves and he knew you were a centre-half and that was his position. He had played in the old right-half berth earlier in his career because he was such a fine passer of the ball and he also had a good engine. But he had settled in at number 5 and he enjoyed playing in central defence. However, there was a young whippersnapper on the scene and he was under pressure.

McNEILL: If I remember correctly, I was pushing for a first-team place at the start of the 1958–59 season, but Bobby, who I must say was always an inspiration to any budding centre-half, played in the first league game, against Clyde. Celtic lost 2–1 at Shawfield.

AULD: I recall that game, Billy, because I scored our goal. However, to be honest, we didn't play well that day.

McNEILL: We played Clyde three days later in the League Cup at our place and a few changes were made to the line-up. I made my debut and

I was in at centre-half and Bobby was left out. We won 2–0 and I believe you scored again. We had already beaten them 4–1 at Shawfield in the opening game in the tournament. Do I remember you scoring that day, too, Bertie?

AULD: As a matter of fact, I did score in both those games. I had no idea I was such a goal machine!

McNEILL: We were due to play Rangers at Celtic Park in the league at the start of September and I wondered if I would be selected again. Obviously, I really wanted to play in that one, but no one could have blamed Celtic if they'd gone for experience and reinstated Bobby. I was only 18 years old at the time, after all. However, I was delighted to keep my place and we drew 2–2.

AULD: I didn't score in that one, Billy. My wee pals Eric Smith and Bobby Collins were the men on target that day. 'The Wee Barra', as Bobby was known, was a fabulous player. He was a real dynamo. Bobby made me feel so welcome at Celtic right from the start. I remember him giving me his Adidas boots from the 1958 World Cup finals. They were slightly big for him – his feet were tiny – but they were my first major manufacturer's pair. I had been making do with all sorts of inferior models until then. I was the envy of all the younger players at the club. I thought it was a marvellous gesture and he was a major influence on me. He realised the reserves of today were the first-team players of tomorrow.

McNEILL: Bobby was a great source of inspiration to us all, Bertie, as we were coming through. Unfortunately, I didn't get much time with him in the first team because he moved to Everton that season. Bobby Evans also left for Chelsea. That was a pity, because you can learn so much from such individuals.

AULD: I know I did. The Wee Barra was a winner. He was physical and a bit robust, but he was not a dirty player. And when you were struggling in a game or if you made a mistake, he would be the first to offer suggestions. You could not help but admire him.

McNEILL: Like I said earlier, we might not have won too much during that period, but we did have some wonderful individuals. There was the Wee Barra and Bobby Evans, for a start, but there were others such as Charlie Tully, Willie Fernie, Neilly Mochan, Bertie Peacock and yourself,

Bertie. Goodness knows how a team with that sort of talent didn't wipe the floor with their opponents. That will remain a mystery forever.

AULD: Well, we didn't have much direction, Billy. We had precious little in the way of tactics, if any. If someone had taken more time in training to work with us, things could have been a whole lot different. I'm sure of that. For instance, I came into the team as an outside-left and God forbid if I ever came in from the wing. My job was to get down the flank, fire over crosses and leave it to others to try to put the ball in the net. Any sort of improvisation was frowned upon.

McNEILL: That's right. The defenders were there to defend, the midfielders, known as half-backs, were there to run, fetch and pass, the wingers were there to put over crosses and the central forwards were there to score goals. There was precious little variation in our play. Everyone knew how we would line up and our style of play.

GORDON: Who was to blame?

McNEILL: It would be impossible to lay the blame at any individual's door. Clearly, that wouldn't be fair. Jimmy McGrory was the manager and he was a lovely man, a true Celtic legend as a player. But a manager back then wasn't really the team boss. Others would have the final say in team selection and suchlike. Jimmy McGrory would be asked to do all sorts of tasks: taking care of players' wages, match tickets and other menial duties. We never saw him during training. I never saw him in a tracksuit. He was always immaculately attired and spent all of his time in his office, no doubt carrying out all sorts of duties that should have been left to other people. We were so naive back then.

AULD: I agree with you. Jimmy McGrory was a wonderful, warm man, but he wasn't cut out for management and I don't mean to be disrespectful when I say that. Simply put, he was from another era. It was the same across the road at Rangers. Their manager was Scot Symon and no one ever saw him in a tracksuit. Big Jock changed everything. I recall Hal Stewart, the Morton chairman, saying something along the lines of, 'We were all getting along fine until that upstart Stein came on the scene!' I know he was only joking – in fact, he and Jock were big pals – but I think that just about summed up the situation. Big Jock came into football management with the force of a hurricane. Cobwebs were blown away at Celtic, training changed dramatically, innovative tactics suddenly came into play and we started to perform in a different manner. Others were forced to follow.

McNEILL: His motto was 'Play to your strengths and disguise your weaknesses'. Simple enough advice, but then Jock never complicated anything. He never once asked a player to do something that was outwith his capabilities. There was no use asking me to play at centre-forward, for instance. He never put John Clark at outside-right. He knew the strengths of individuals and he instinctively knew how to get the absolute best out of them.

We had flair players such as Jimmy Johnstone and sometimes Jock would let him off the leash. Jinky had all the ability in the world – I know what he did to our defence in training! Jock would see him taking the mickey, sticking the ball through your legs for the umpteenth time, and he would bellow from the touchline, 'Right, Johnstone, that's enough of that!' Thanks, Boss.

AULD: Aye, Wee Jinky was a genius, but he did sometimes overlook the fact that training was for all of us. Maybe we should just have given him a ball to himself and everyone could have got on with taking care of business. We used to play a little training game where you could only take three touches before passing the ball on. Jinky would prefer to play about and maybe take some extra touches. Jock would spot this. I think we ended up playing two-touch football just to make sure Jinky would release the ball at some stage. I loved the Wee Man; he was special.

McNEILL: You can say that again, Bertie. Remember the day he threw his shirt at Jock when he substituted him in a game against Dundee United? Jinky wasn't too pleased at having to go off early and, with that hair-trigger temperament of his, actually chucked his jersey at the dugout on his way up the tunnel. Big Jock's limp meant he wasn't the quickest on his feet, but he moved that day. He raced after Jinky, who later told me, 'Billy, I thought about running straight through the main gates and heading for Parkhead Cross. I was sure Jock was going to stiffen me. I locked myself in a room and he was banging on the door. "Johnstone, get out here!" Eventually, I said, "I'll open the door, Boss, if you promise not to hit me." Everything went silent and then I could hear that unmistakable shuffle of his feet as he headed back to the dugout. I swear I could hear him laughing!'

AULD: I remember the first time I saw Jinky. This wee lad with the big red curls turned up one day for training. I thought he might be a fan.

There wasn't an awful lot of him at the time – a wee, frail figure. He sat in the dressing-room and said nothing. He actually looked somewhat embarrassed to be mixing with some of the players. Well, that was until he got onto the pitch and then we all knew who Jimmy Johnstone was. What a talent! He was like a rubber ball. Defenders would bowl him over and he would just keep bouncing back to his feet. After he started to make a name for himself, you could see the fear in the eyes of our opponents when they looked at the Wee Man. That fear was a real compliment to Jinky. There was no disguising it, either. Those opponents knew they were in for a torrid time.

McNEILL: Wee Jimmy left us with so many good memories. You could talk about him forever and a day. Actually, I believe we are very fortunate that there is so much wonderful footage of the Wee Man in action during his playing days. Film has captured all those marvellous images of Jinky doing what he did best: entertaining the fans. Those supporters were always so important to him. He loved it when they sang, 'Jimmy Johnstone on the wing,' and he would just keep playing away, ensuring they didn't stop! When people who haven't been fortunate enough to witness the Wee Man playing in the flesh see film of him in action, they will understand why so many folk rave about him.

Jinky was a Celtic man – that's the beginning and end of the story. He was a genuine working-class hero and I don't think for a second he would mind me making that observation. Like I said earlier about a lot of the players back then, he was a Celtic fan who played for Celtic. He was one of the lads and success and adulation never went to the Wee Man's head. Do you know he was actually a ball-boy at the club when he was a kid? Jinky played in an era where there were an awful lot of skilful players, talented individuals and remarkable characters. But Jimmy Johnstone was the king of them all.

AULD: Tommy Gemmell's got a great story about the Wee Man. Jinky was as proud as punch when he bought his first Jaguar car. We all got a chance to walk round it and look inside – 'That's real leather, no' any o' yer plastic!' – and he loved to drive it all over the place. One day, he and Big Tommy were going for a wee bit of fishing and he picked up TG before heading off for some place in Perthshire. Tommy was giving Jinky instructions and at one point said, 'Straight through the roundabout, Wee Man.' Jinky took it literally, drove up through all the flowers and stuff and came down the other end! 'Fuck's sake, Wee Man!' shouted Tommy. Jinky answered, 'Well, you said straight through.' You had to watch when he was around.

I thought it was fitting that the supporters should vote him the greatest-ever Celtic player in their millennium poll. Do you know he was surprised? He thought the award would go to Henrik Larsson. So typical of the Wee Man.

GORDON: We discuss the European games, the World Club Championship final and other situations elsewhere in the book. So, going back to the beginning, what was it like in those Old Firm games when Rangers were undoubtedly top dogs?

McNEILL: We realised these games meant so much to our supporters and we all felt as though we had let them down when we didn't produce a good result. To be fair, Rangers had a very good team back then, with some very useful players. You didn't have to look at anyone other than Jim Baxter to see the class players they had at their disposal. I got on well with Jim, and he, myself, Paddy Crerand and Mike Jackson were great mates off the park. The Rangers hierarchy frowned on one of their employees associating with Celtic players, but Slim Jim didn't give a stuff. He liked our company and that was the end of it. On the park, though, he was immense. That left foot of his could open up any defence.

Mike Jackson recalls a great story about Jim no one would have believed. Certainly it couldn't happen today. Jim had been out for a wee drink with some of the Celtic players before an Old Firm Glasgow Cup tie, which was due to take place the following evening. Now, as we all know, Jim liked a beverage and slightly overdid it that particular afternoon, which turned into evening. Eventually, Jim got a bit tipsy. No one had a spare bed, so Mike took the Rangers player to his mother's place in Govanhill, where Jim crashed out on the sofa in the living room. Now, Mike's mother just happened to be very religious and the front room was packed with holy pictures and statues. Jim must have wondered where on earth he was when he came to! Actually, religion never came into it when Jim was mixing in our company. On the day of the Glasgow Cup game, he got cleaned up, had a bite to eat and Mike came over to pick him up in a taxi to take him over to the game. As my pal recalls it, Jim had a blinder that evening against Celtic. Only Slim Jim could get away with that.

AULD: Jim was at Rangers only for a matter of months after I returned from Birmingham City in 1965. Just as well for him or we would have seen who had the better left foot! Only joking – the lad could play, all right. He came back from England, after spells with Sunderland and Nottingham Forest, in 1969 and the only time we were ever in opposition was in a League Cup tie at Ibrox. I got on as a substitute that night, but we lost 2–1. The newspapers raved about Jim's return the following day. However, we turned the tables and beat them 1–0 at Parkhead to get through eventually to the final, where I scored the only goal to beat St Johnstone 1–0. So I never really got the opportunity to pit my wits against Slim Jim. I would have looked forward to it, let me assure you.

McNEILL: Some of the results in the early '60s were difficult to accept. The 3–0 defeat in the Scottish Cup final replay against Rangers in 1963 is still one that rankles. We had played well enough to get a 1–1 draw in the first game, but, unaccountably, we just didn't turn up four days later. We were two goals down early on and, sad to say, it was game over. Jim was exceptional that evening. We never got to grips with him and the match just passed us by. That was a sore one.

It's hard to believe, but three of that team – myself, Bobby Murdoch and Stevie Chalmers – would win European Cup final medals four years and ten days later. We would have had you certified if you had predicted that in the Hampden dressing-room that night!

AULD: I loved Old Firm occasions. I was confident enough to believe we could win every one of these games, even when we were struggling. Some players don't want to know in these games and they're quickly found out. They are so intent on not making a mistake that they don't produce anything worthwhile. The ball is passed around like a live hand grenade; they can't get rid of it quickly enough. There was a fair bit of banter between the players before these confrontations. John Greig was talking to me in the tunnel one day and said, 'Bertie, we're picking up £60 per week at Rangers these days. What are you on at Celtic?' I replied, 'Just a little bit short of that, John, but then we get win bonuses and you don't!' Then we would go out and kick lumps out of each other.

I revelled in the tension, the electric atmosphere, the tribal rivalry between the two sets of supporters – och, the lot. Mind you, it was even better when we won. It would be fair to say I enjoyed these occasions a lot more in the second half of the '60s than I did at the start!

GORDON: You kicked off the decade with a defeat against Rangers and ended it with an 8–1 victory over Partick Thistle. Does that just about sum up the see-saw '60s?

McNEILL: It would have been difficult to envisage us having a seven-goal winning margin in the early period. As I've said, we were more than capable of sticking the ball in the opposition's net, but they scored against us, too, with far too much regularity. In my first 12 league games of season 1958–59, we netted 26 goals, which is a fair ratio. Balancing that, though, we conceded 23. We scored three against Falkirk at Parkhead and lost four. We got three against St Mirren and they got three against us. Hibs, at Easter Road, were another team to hit three into our net, as they beat us by the odd goal in five. I missed a game against Stirling Albion in Glasgow when the lads up front did the business, scoring seven. Our keeper, Dick Beattie, conceded three, though. I think early on I realised that life was never going to be dull at Celtic!

But those scorelines at the start and end of the decade do emphasise a shift in how we played. We could still attack, but now we knew we could defend, too. It took us a while to get the balance right, but we got there in the end.

AULD: Spot-on, Billy. During your debut season, I got well into double figures in goals, which wasn't bad for a guy who was supposed to be stuck out on the left wing. But the opposition certainly knew the route to our goal. We had players in the team back then who never helped out in defence. Charlie Tully was a special talent, a real maverick, but I don't recall him doing too much backtracking. He always wanted the ball at his feet and he would go off on a mazy dribble. That was his forte; heading balls off his own goal line clearly wasn't! The team always seemed better geared to attack, and shutting the back door wasn't a priority.

That was Celtic's style, though. It was drummed into us that we needed to put on a show for the fans. It appeared we were entertainers first and foremost and professional footballers second. I can tell you the board back then didn't even like you going in hard on the opposing players. Our directors had an almost puritanical approach to football. God help you if you actually injured an opponent. Your 'reward' would probably be a lengthy spell in the stand. Jock changed that outlook, too. If the ball was there to be won, he expected you to win it. He was never specific on how he wanted you to go about winning the tackle, he just expected you to emerge with the ball. 'Win the battle and you'll win the war,' was another of his favourite sayings. Thankfully, we did that more often than not during his reign.

GORDON: It's been a pleasure talking to you, fellas. Thanks for the memories, Billy and Bertie.

McNEILL: I'm always happy to talk about the good old days. It brings back so many wonderful memories.

The fans, too, deserve massive credit for the way they stuck by the team. Certainly, I'll never forget the way they treated me. It might have been a bit rocky at some points, but hopefully we gave them some memorable moments along the way. I know they gave me plenty.

AULD: Aye, those supporters are brilliant; they're the best in the world. No matter where I go, I tell everyone that. When things weren't going too well, they were our 12th man. Those fans were our substitute before substitutes were allowed in football. You might have been struggling in some games, toiling to get things going, and then suddenly you would hear 'Hail! Hail!', look up at the terracing, see those magnificent fans and then the adrenalin was pumping again. How could you let those guys down? Great days shared with great people.

1

PARADISE LOST

As 1960 made its debut, with the cruel wind shrieking and wailing to herald the advent, a pall of despair had already been in evidence in the East End of Glasgow for some time. Celtic Football Club welcomed the New Year in much the same manner as an overindulging late-night reveller relishes a thumping hangover. The decade got into motion with the traditional 1 January game against Rangers at Celtic Park and, with total predictability, the Ibrox men went home with the points, as they had done in their previous two league visits to the ground where in years gone by they had been tested to the limit. On this occasion, Frank Haffey, 6 ft 2 in. of goalkeeping enigma, offered hope with a swooping save from a Johnny Little penalty kick. It was merely a stay of execution, the sufferings of thousands temporarily held in abeyance. A last-minute goal from Jimmy Millar sent the green-and-white legions into a state of grief that afforded no room for the merest hint of optimism, with four months of the season still to play.

The Celtic support must have been getting used to the lack of festive cheer in these fixtures; Rangers had triumphed in the previous five encounters and you had to go back to 1954, when Neilly Mochan got the only goal of the game, to discover a Celtic success. However, the latest loss was only one of thirteen defeats from thirty-four games that the club would suffer in a thoroughly miserable 1959–60 league campaign. There were nine draws and only twelve successes in an era when you got two points for a win.

Manager Jimmy McGrory saw his team finish ninth in the eighteen-club formation of the old First Division with a total of thirty-three points, failing even to achieve a point-per-game ratio. They had won only six of their previous eighteen outings before the New Year's Day defeat. They were non-starters in the championship race. The club was a catastrophic 21 points adrift of eventual title winners Hearts. Kilmarnock (50), Rangers

25

(42), Dundee (42), Motherwell (40), Clyde (39), Hibs (35) and Ayr United (34) could also look down on Celtic. Third-bottom Airdrie were only five points away from matching the total of a team evidently in steep decline. The process of disintegration of a famous old football club was as painful as it appeared irreversible.

Any hopes of early-season success in the League Cup were rendered redundant after the first three group ties – defeats against Raith Rovers (1–2), Partick Thistle (1–2) and Airdrie (2–4). The once-mighty, once-feared, once-powerful Celtic were being propped up mainly by their faithful support as oblivion beckoned. But even the most devoted fan was getting more than a little frustrated with the lack of initiative displayed by what he perceived to be an apathetic and unambitious board of directors and a faltering football-playing staff. The resources of enthusiasm to be found in the heart of even the most fervent follower are not limitless. Hearts and Rangers were the two best-supported teams in Scotland, drawing a remarkable 70,000 spectators to Ibrox when the Edinburgh men won 2–0 in October 1959. Celtic were a poor third, often playing in front of estimated gates of some 20,000. Where some supporters swore allegiance, others simply defected. The pain of watching 11 men in green and white hoops in turmoil on a consistent basis was too much to accept for some. Only 10,000 bothered to attend a November fixture against Ayr United at Parkhead and they witnessed a dismal performance in a 2–3 defeat. The alarm bells were sounding. Was anyone bothering to listen?

When Willie Fernie swept a last-minute penalty kick beyond a static Rangers goalkeeper, George Niven, for the seventh goal in a momentous 7–1 League Cup final triumph over their oldest rivals at Hampden on 19 October 1957, no one could have predicted that Celtic would have to wait another eight years before they won meaningful silverware again. From glory days to grim times was a transformation Celtic effected with worrying ease. Those were eight long and arduous years even for the most steadfast of supporters to endure. There's an old saying that goes along the lines of 'When you don't have anything, you take what you can get'. That just about summed up the outlook of the suffering fans who dipped into their often-meagre wages for the privilege of standing on the terracing in all sorts of conditions and watching their favourites, with uninspiring predictability, toil against even the most indifferent opposition.

In 1959–60, three separate games against a distinctly average Partick Thistle critically exposed the deficiencies of a team in freefall. The Firhill side eased to a 4–2 triumph at Parkhead in April for their third success against their more exalted and bigger Glasgow brother. They had beaten

Celtic 3–1 at Firhill earlier in the league and picked up another win bonus in their 2–1 League Cup victory. This, remember, was a Maryhill outfit that contrived to finish below Celtic in the league that season. There was pandemonium within Paradise as the entire club blundered and stumbled along a well-worn path strewn with mismanagement, misjudgement, miscalculations and monumental mistakes.

It was obvious to all that Jimmy McGrory was not being allowed to manage. Chairman Robert Kelly would ask McGrory to submit his team sheet at the Thursday night board meeting and then make what he believed to be the 'appropriate' adjustments. It has been said by many that McGrory was 'too nice to be a manager'. Never once did he complain about being abruptly overruled and his decision-making questioned before being dismissed for the evening.

The power that Kelly wielded over team selection was highlighted in a farcical moment in October 1960. Bertie Auld recalled the incident. He said, 'We were travelling on the team coach when Kelly spotted Willie Goldie, our third-team goalkeeper, standing at a bus stop. He was wearing one of those old woolly Celtic scarves. That was enough for Kelly to order the driver to stop and pull in. He gestured for Willie to come onto the coach. Presumably, Willie thought he was merely getting a lift to Broomfield where we were due to meet Airdrie. John Fallon, who had played in our first four league games of the season, had been chosen to turn out again. Kelly, though, was so impressed at Goldie making his own way to the game that he immediately told him he was playing. We knew he wasn't joking; Robert Kelly rarely did humour. Poor John Fallon! He just sat there for the remainder of the journey with a bemused look on his face after his kit had been handed to Goldie, who had to borrow boots, as well. But this was Celtic in 1960 and you came to expect the unexpected. Anything could happen. And often did.'

Alas, there was no happy ending to this tale. Willie Goldie made his first-team debut for Celtic – and never played again. He dropped two clangers, Airdrie won 2–0 and his career at the club he loved ended with the final shrill of the referee's whistle. Kelly's decision might have been hilarious, but it was also completely unprofessional. John Fallon, an innocent in all of this, seems to have been caught in the crossfire. He never played another league game during that campaign, with the unpredictable and unconventional Frank Haffey coming back into the side.

Mike Jackson, a thoughtful right-sided midfield player signed from junior side Benburb in 1957, can tell a similar tale about the selection process at Celtic. 'It was a Wednesday night league game at Celtic Park during the time of the Home Internationals and Paddy Crerand was with the Scottish squad, so I half-expected to be playing in his position at right-half. I arrived at the park just after 6 p.m. and was met by my old schoolteacher John Murphy, who was instrumental in boys from Glasgow's Holyrood School going to Celtic. He sent me and others such as Paddy, John Kurila and Charlie Gallagher to the club. I think he acted as an unpaid scout, and for years he did the public-address work at Parkhead. Anyway, I met Mr Murphy – I could never call my former schoolteacher John – and he had just received the team to announce for the game. Sure enough, I was pencilled in to play at right-half. At 6.45 p.m., Bob Rooney, our physiotherapist, came into the snooker room where all the lads congregated to relax and get ready before a game. According to Bob, I was now at inside-right, but at least I was playing, so I went in to get ready for the game.

'I did all my usual preparations, had my rub-down with the oil and liniment and was knocking the ball about in the shower area. Then Bob reappeared. He told me to go and have a bath. I wasn't playing now, there had been another change made to the team. So, at 6.30 I was right-half, at 6.45 I was inside-right and at 7.15 I was out of the team altogether. I had given my dad a ticket for the game and told him I was playing. He was in the stand and wondered why there was no sign of his son when the team ran out. He thought I had taken ill. Honestly, that is a true story and that sort of thing was all too commonplace during the years I was at Celtic. Other players could tell you similar tales.

'I can remember another bizarre situation back on a Monday night in September 1962 when we were due to play Real Madrid, the most glamorous team in the world and the side that had won the European Cup five times in the previous seven years. It was a match for the Blue and White Cup, would you believe, which was inspired by the colours of the Israeli national flag. The challenge match was the brainchild of Max Benjamin, a well-known Glasgow businessman and huge Celtic supporter. All proceeds were to go to the Jewish National Fund Charitable Trust and would help refugees from Europe and North Africa. I believe something like £10,000 was raised and that was a lot of money back then. Having the soccer aristocrats of Real Madrid in town guaranteed a 72,000 all-ticket sell-out at Parkhead. The last time the magical Spaniards had been in Glasgow was two years previously, when they memorably thumped Eintracht Frankfurt 7–3 at Hampden to win the European Cup. For weeks before the game, our supporters were going on endlessly about the prospect of watching Di Stéfano, Gento and Puskás in the flesh. Hey, as a player I could hardly wait to get on the same pitch as those guys.

'The ground was packed long before the evening kick-off and the Celtic players assembled in the snooker room as usual. We all wanted to get the opportunity of facing the fabled Real Madrid; that would be something to tell the grandkids. However, none of us took a place in the starting line-up for granted. We had been told that each club could name three substitutes for the game, which was highly unusual in those days. Remember, Celtic won the European Cup in 1967 and were only allowed to name goalkeeper John Fallon as substitute, with no outfield players on the bench. Would you believe our chairman, Bob Kelly, was against the idea of substitutes that night? However, he relented when Real insisted on naming three extra players who would get an outing at some stage in the evening.

'It was getting fairly close to kick-off time and all the players were standing around in our civvies wondering who would get the nod. Bob Rooney popped in with a sheet of paper and said, "Right, lads, get ready to strip. It's Frank Haffey in goal with Dunky MacKay at right-back. Jim Kennedy, you're at left-back. The half-back line is Pat Crerand, Billy McNeill and Billy Price." Then Bob got ready to leave. "Hey, Bob, you've only named six players. What about the rest of the team?" I asked. Our physiotherapist looked over his shoulder and replied, "Oh, we haven't picked the forward line yet. I'll be back later." So six of the guys could get prepared for the game while another ten or so of us were left milling around with our hands in our pockets. Crazy, I know, but so typical back then. Eventually, Bob returned with not a lot of time to spare. "Right," he said, "we've got a forward line now." He continued, "Bobby Lennox, you're outside-right, Charlie Gallagher is at inside-right, John Hughes is at centre-forward." Then came my big moment. "Mike Jackson, you're inside-left and Frank Brogan will be outside-left." There was a pause before the other guys were told who would be stripped as substitutes. "Stevie Chalmers, Bobby Carroll and Alec Byrne, would you like to get ready, too?" And with that Bob was gone.

'Actually, it turned out to be a really memorable night. I recall they went two goals ahead with efforts from Puskás and Amancio, and I swear our own support were cheering on our opponents. Our fans were just so thrilled to see such a team performing at Parkhead and it turned out to be the forerunner of some fabulous European evenings in the East End of Glasgow. I believe we played quite well, but our defence had no answer to the breathtaking pace of Gento on their left wing. He raced away to plonk the third behind Big Frank around the hour mark, although we pulled one back almost immediately through Stevie Chalmers, who had come on for Bobby Lennox. With about 15 minutes to go, Stevie looked as though he had got another, but it was ruled out for some earlier infringement. Now, if that had stood, we would have been in for a very interesting finale to the contest. Alec Byrne and Bobby Carroll also came on for Frank Brogan and John Hughes in the second half in a very exciting and entertaining game.

'We lost 3–1, but the capacity crowd greeted the full-time whistle as though we had just won the European Cup itself. They were ecstatic. We went back to the dressing-room and prepared to get cleaned up. Bob Rooney came in and said, "Guys, the fans are demanding a lap of honour. They're not leaving until you go back out there." So, some of us without socks and others in their stocking soles grabbed any sort of jersey or someone else's discarded shorts to go and take a bow in front of the support. I've got to say, I think that might just have been the first lap of honour by a Celtic team at Parkhead. Certainly, it was the first ever taken by a side that had just lost 3–1!

'And it wasn't over even then. Thousands of fans discovered we were having a post-match reception at the Central Hotel in Glasgow city centre. By the time we and the Real Madrid players had scrubbed up and reached the hotel, our supporters were already there, singing and dancing and chanting our names. The Spanish players must have wondered what the hell was going on. If this was how the Celtic fans reacted when their team lost, how on earth would they celebrate when they actually won?'

Jackson added, 'I have no doubt, though, that Celtic took liberties with their players. They knew we would play for nothing if we could afford it. I'm sure they would have taken us up on an offer like that. In 1958, while the World Cup finals were taking place in Sweden, the club took the players who weren't involved in the Scotland international squad on a two-week tour of Ireland. Naturally, we were all excited and looking forward to the flight, because not too many of us had been on a plane before. Then we were told to assemble down at the Broomielaw in Glasgow because we were getting the night boat over to Larne. By the time we got to Ireland, we were all seasick. At that time, I was earning £7 a week in the reserves and £10 in the first team. Basically, all the players on the trip were skint. Eric Smith was made captain, with Bobby Evans in Sweden. We asked him if he could see Bob Kelly about giving us some expenses so we had some cash to spend over the next 14 days. Eric put the proposition to the chairman and came back to tell us he would stretch to £45. Now there were 15 of us on that trip and that worked out at £3 each – *for a fortnight*! The players held a quick meeting and decided to return the £45; we would manage somehow. Do you know the Celtic chairman took it back and stuffed the cash in his jacket pocket?

'It was laughable what went on back then. Sad but laughable. In 1961, I had played through the pain barrier for the club. I had picked up a really bad knee injury, but I soldiered on until I could hardly walk, never mind run. Celtic sent me to the Victoria Infirmary for a check-up. I was told I urgently required a cartilage operation. Back then, after such an op, you were stuck in hospital for about two weeks. Nowadays, with keyhole surgery, you're out in a couple of hours. So I was laid up in hospital for a fortnight before I was allowed home. I continued my rehabilitation by walking around Govanhill and Queen's Park with the aid of walking sticks. After about two weeks, I'd gradually built up the strength in the knee, and I returned to Parkhead to collect my wages. You used to get paid in readies on a Tuesday in a wee room at the side of the stand. I went to the window, as usual, and Jimmy McGrory spotted me. "Mike," he said, "I've got a month's wages here for you. Where have you been?" Would you believe he hadn't a clue I had been sent for a cartilage operation? No one bothered to tell the manager of the football team he would be without one of his players for a month. Utterly astonishing!

'Another ridiculous story from back then came when I went out to have a look at the pitch before a game. It was winter and I wanted to test the firmness of the ground. It was flint hard, so I knew screw-in studs would be useless in those underfoot conditions. Celtic had taken a supply of moulded-sole boots from a manufacturer. Nowadays, you would get hundreds of the product, but, all those years ago, you would be lucky to get ten. I went to the boot room to ask for a pair of moulded soles. A guy called Willie Johnstone was a trainer at the time and I told him I wanted to change my boots.

'"Oh, ye cannae hae the moulded wans, Mike," I was informed.

'"Why?" I asked, logically.

'"Because you're only a laddie," was the reply.

'When I was at Benburb, they gave their players brand-spanking-new Adidas boots. When I was leaving to go to Parkhead, one of the bosses asked me to leave the boots behind, because I was sure to get something special at Celtic. Something special? I was handed a pair of something called Mansfield Hotspurs. They looked like the type of footwear you might have seen Frankenstein's monster wearing. They would have come in handy for a deep-sea diver. You could have dropped a boulder on your toe and not have felt a thing. I went along to Greaves sports shop in Gordon Street in Glasgow and bought a pair of Adidas with my own money. A couple of days later, I was getting ready for a game and Willie

Johnstone was going round checking things, as he usually did. He saw my new boots. "Naw, laddie, ye cannae wear those," he said. I looked up and replied, "Aye, I can – they're my fuckin' boots!"'

Jackson had a run-in with Johnstone in another illustration of how ridiculously badly organised Celtic were in 1960. 'We were due to meet Rangers in the Scottish Cup semi-final replay and I didn't think I had a chance of playing. The night before the game, I trained for fully two hours at Celtic Park. I was running round the heavy track and I was shattered by the end of the session. No intelligent person in the football world would ask a player to go through that sort of routine if they thought they would be involved in a game 24 hours later. I was actually standing in the tunnel at Hampden on the evening of the game. It was about half an hour before the kick-off when Desmond White, one of the club's directors, approached me and told me he thought I was playing. No one had told me! I raced off to the dressing-room and got a row from Willie Johnstone for being late. I tried to protest, but I was simply told to hurry up and get changed into my strip. I played and we lost. No wonder there were no cups in the trophy cabinet back then. The board hadn't a clue.'

The supporters craved any kind of reasonable signing during the summer of 1960. They practically begged the board to buy players of experience and substance. Celtic parted with a paltry couple of hundred pounds to sign a chunky centre-half called John Cushley from junior club Blantyre Celtic. The player's dad, Ned, was friendly with some of the backroom staff and had pointed them in the direction of his son. At the same time, Rangers were unveiling the elegant Jim Baxter, signed from Raith Rovers for a Scottish record transfer fee of £17,500, a colossal amount of money in those days. The Ibrox side could also afford to pay Airdrie £12,000 for their bulky central defender Doug Baillie. It was yet another indication of the gulf between the two clubs. What once had been a crack was a chasm by July 1960.

Through all this mayhem and misery, one man remained unmoved and unshakeable in his beliefs: Robert Kelly, who had become chairman in 1947. Infuriatingly stubborn, opinionated and single-minded, he often appeared removed from the concerns of the man on the terracing. Apart from a shared passion for the football club, there seemed to be little in common between the man in the camel-hair coat in the directors' box and the bloke in the bunnet in the Jungle. Kelly always had Celtic's best interests at heart, but how he went about forwarding them rarely won the approval of the fans. To be fair, the paying customers were denied information back then, and there was little, if any, communication between board and fans. Without a doubt, Kelly, son of Celtic's first captain, James, who went on to become chairman, was more into politics than posturing, unlike many of the megalomaniacs who run clubs in the present era. However, there remained something of a simmering distrust among an element of the support.

In 1958, there was talk that Celtic had sold Bobby Collins to Everton against his will for the handsome fee of £23,500. As well as being an energetic and intelligent midfielder and a current Scottish international, the pocket dynamo – all of 5 ft 4 in. – had also scored 81 goals in 220 league appearances for the club. He was a popular figure with the fans and they could identify with a Glaswegian who had grown up supporting Celtic. So, of course, there was a public outcry at the removal of this authentic crowd-pleaser. The transfer money, it was suggested, was being set aside to help pay for the new floodlights that were soon to be installed at Celtic Park. The consensus among the support was obvious – they would have preferred to have had the man nicknamed 'The Wee Barra' illuminating play on the pitch rather than any aid from artificial sources.

Unfortunately, information was in short supply back then. Otherwise, the Celtic fans would have discovered the truth. In David Saffer's 2004 biography, *Bobby Collins*, the player revealed:

Behind the scenes, things weren't ideal. Jock Stein, Billy McPhail and Sean Fallon had retired and Willie Fernie and Charlie Tully would soon depart. The Celtic team I was an integral part of was breaking up. We'd had our swansong in the 7–1 League Cup final win and I felt I needed a new challenge. I'd been fortunate to play for such a great club because not everyone gets such an opportunity.

It was clear, then, that Collins had reached a crossroads in his career and, far from being transferred unwillingly, he was actually fairly keen to move on.

In almost Dickensian prose, Kelly attempted to reassure the fans in an official Celtic book:

I, for my part, will do everything possible to make the players happy and contented in order that they may give of their best because nowadays only the best will do. For their part, the players who are honoured to wear the green and white, made famous on so many historic fields by their gallant predecessors, must realise the great traditions they are asked to uphold. Competition in modern football grows keener every day and only those who are prepared to work hard and attain the maximum of physical fitness can hope to get to the top and stay there.

All very fine, but, in reality, those were not the words to soothe the furrowed brows of a weary support. While Kelly waxed eloquent, Celtic were still being humiliated on the pitch, losing 5–1 and 4–1 to Rangers in the league and Scottish Cup, humbled 4–3 in front of their own fans by Hearts and hammered 4–2 on two occasions, by Third Lanark and Airdrie. Bertie Auld once famously observed, 'Most of our goalkeepers back then thought the net behind them was merely to stop the ball.' Unfortunately, the rigging behind Celtic's custodians was in use far too often in the early '60s. In season 1959–60, an astonishing total of 82 goals were crammed into the Celtic net in 47 games (34 league, 6 League Cup and 7 Scottish Cup).

Still the chairman refused to dip into the coffers to buy the sort of quality Rangers had just invested in. A story persists that shortly after the turn of the decade Leeds United offered Celtic a young Scottish player for a token fee. Apparently, the lad had become homesick and, being of the Celtic persuasion, would have been only too delighted to move to Parkhead. Kelly said no thanks. And so the club missed out on Billy Bremner, later to captain Scotland in the 1974 World Cup finals and be selected to honour his country on 54 occasions. Kelly appeared interested only in encouraging youth from within and buying serviceable performers who would join for a modest fee – and, in the main, prove to be a complete waste of money. It wasn't just the Celtic support who weren't enamoured of Kelly's stance. The *Daily Record* observed:

> Celtic are suffering from outdated thought. Traditionally, they are a club which reared their own players and won honour after honour. But today it is near impossible to achieve success by full dependence on home-reared material. In the face of disappointment after disappointment, they have gone on their way believing they could fulfil their promises, a belief shown to be a fallacy. The time has come to discard their policy of team-building from scratch.

Kelly took no notice. He had a distrust of the press and even had a rebuke for them when he wrote the foreword for *The Celtic Story*, an official history of the club published in 1960. He thanked author Dr J.E. Handley for his efforts in putting together the tome and declared:

> I am sure everyone who reads the book will agree he has produced a very readable and interesting tale. It was a great handicap to him that many vital records and books were lost in the fire that razed the old pavilion. Dr Handley had to rely on newspaper reports for much of his material,

and, as we well know, writers then, as now, could be something less than neutral.

In all honesty, you would have been forgiven for believing he had enough to contend with trying to sort out an ailing football team.

One of Kelly's home-grown players who did produce results was an energetic teenager who made his first-team debut against Third Lanark in the opening game of the 1960 League Cup campaign. John Hughes netted the first of well over 100 goals for the club, with veteran Neilly Mochan adding the other in a 2–0 win. It got better for Hughes, only 17, as he proved to be unstoppable when, against all odds, Celtic won 3–2 over Rangers at Ibrox in another League Cup tie.

The man affectionately known to the fans as 'Yogi', after the popular TV cartoon character Yogi Bear, recalled, 'I knew I would be up against Doug Baillie, who had arrived with a big reputation in the summer. That meant little to me, to be honest. I had been scoring goals for Shotts Bon Accord only the previous year and I thought I could continue to do the same with Celtic. I enjoyed scoring a goal in that game. It was a wonderful experience.'

The *Glasgow Herald* was suitably impressed by the powerfully built centre-forward:

> Celtic have produced, almost from the playground, one big fellow of great potential. Hughes, who is only 17 years old, caused havoc in the Rangers defence even when, for the greater part of the second half, he was the only Celtic forward in position to threaten Rangers' goal, so committed to defence were his colleagues. The even bigger, heavier Doug Baillie, the home centre-half, was time and again confused as his much more nimble opponent beat him for speed and for control of the ball.

Hughes was sensational in the opening ties, but, when it mattered most, Celtic faltered. They lost their last two qualifying games and Rangers, after a 2–1 win at Parkhead, qualified. They eventually went through to the final and claimed the trophy with a 2–0 triumph over Kilmarnock at Hampden.

Jimmy Millar, only 5 ft 7 in. but an exceptionally aggressive centre-forward, often terrorised the Celtic defence in those days. He once admitted: 'My fellow forwards, players such as Ian McMillan, Willie Henderson and Ralph Brand, never really wanted to get involved in the more physical stuff, so I took on that role. Some might say I was a better boxer than footballer.' Billy McNeill probably agreed.

However, searching for positives, the performances of the giant John Hughes had stirred the Celtic support. Five goals in six games made for a more than decent introduction to the top side, particularly when you consider the lack of guidance or leadership given to Hughes when he joined in October 1959. 'It was a nightmare. I was there as a big, raw laddie and, basically, you didn't get any help at all,' he revealed. 'I made lots of mistakes and no one said anything. Players at the age of 17 are commonplace these days, of course, but back in 1960 it wasn't the case. Most teenagers were waifs and needed built up. I was playing centre-forward in a bad Celtic team and scored thirty-one goals in my second season. I got one hundred and thirteen in my first five years. I often feel that if I had been given some advice in the early years I would have been a far better player. I've been told I was inconsistent, but a lot of that was because no one was saying, "You'll need to work on that," or, "How about trying it this way?" That didn't happen. You were just told to get out there and get on with it. There was little or no help offered. Believe me, I would have welcomed advice and I would have acted upon it. But none was forthcoming.'

Given that Jimmy McGrory scored a phenomenal 468 goals from 445 appearances in his playing days in the '20s and '30s, you might have expected him to pilot Hughes through the penalty-box pitfalls, to help him realise his full potential and advance to the highest level with a bit of one-on-one work on the training ground. Hughes, though, chorused what the football world has been saying for years: 'Jimmy McGrory was too nice to be a manager. He couldn't order you, "Just get this done," or, "This way is better." He just wasn't that kind of man. Sean Fallon, the first-team coach, would lock him out at team talks and not let him in. Jimmy McGrory didn't contribute.

'Looking back, you can see it was very amateurish. There was no real thought going into things. When I got into the first team, I was getting around £7 per week and the others were getting £12. I went to see the manager about the discrepancy. He explained, "I know, John, but you're just a boy." I said, "But I'm doing the same job as them." He replied, "I know, but you're too young to get that sort of money." That was the kind of thinking that was around at the time. It was an absolute shambles.'

Hughes had another startling admission to make: 'Initially, Paddy Crerand didn't want me in the team. He said he didn't rate me. He told me I used to run away from him. He would get the ball in midfield, look up and all he could see was the back of my head. I was playing the way I had always played in the juniors. Paddy, though, wanted me to come short sometimes and play in someone else. No one had ever told me to perform in this manner. It was totally alien to me and no one had taken the time to give me some advice. I'm not bitter, but you can't help but wonder how your career might have panned out if there had been someone who had actually worked with you on the training ground. But no one was interested. You were told to run around and, if you were lucky, you might get some ball work.

'Bertie Auld didn't fancy me, either. He would only pass the ball to me when he had no alternative. I spoke to Bertie and Jock Stein about the situation. But nothing was done. Naturally, that didn't do much for my confidence, either. Funnily enough, Bertie, when he was manager of Partick Thistle, wanted to sign me after I returned from Sunderland in the early '70s. I had picked up an injury that meant I couldn't play at the top level again. When I came home, though, I kept fit by playing in the Old Crocks' games. Bertie saw me score six goals in one match and pulled me aside. "Yogi, you've still got it," he said. "Why don't you think about playing for Partick Thistle? I think you could still do a job." I told him I didn't fancy it. Frankly, I didn't believe I could perform at that level. "Look, Yogi, I'll just put you on for the last half-hour or so," said Bertie. I still knocked him back. My playing days were over. A bounce game every now and again was my stretch.'

In Eugene MacBride's book *Talking With Celtic*, Frank Haffey backed up Hughes' theory that McGrory was 'too nice'. He said:

> In the early '60s, I was just coming back from injury and had played a couple of reserve games. Jimmy McGrory asked to speak to me in his office and he told me Celtic were cutting my wages. I was dumbfounded. I hadn't been married long, I had recently bought a house and we had just had a baby. I asked the manager what about all the good years I had given, especially the good performances against Rangers. He broke down and cried. He said it wasn't his idea, it was Bob Kelly's.

Haffey eventually left for Swindon Town in 1964 – 'to maintain my family's standard of living' – but Hughes would stay another 11 years. He was prepared to fight on. So, was the Celtic support's search for a new hero finally over? Was the teenage John Hughes the answer? As ever, there were some bewildering team selections. Hughes led the line in the opening league fixture, a 1–1 draw at Kilmarnock, but for the next game, against Rangers, he found himself, for the first time, at outside-left. You can only wonder at the thought process. Hughes had given the Rangers centre-half Doug Baillie a torrid time in the League Cup victory at Ibrox just three weeks previously. Now he would be up against the uncompromising right-back Bobby Shearer, to whom subtlety was a stranger. He was nicknamed 'Captain Cutlass' and it was a moniker that sat well on his stocky frame.

In *Talking With Celtic*, midfield player Charlie Gallagher testified that it was not beyond the Rangers man to threaten a broken leg to any opponent who ran past him. 'And I was his friend,' said Gallagher. 'Off the field, Bobby was one of the nicest men you could ever meet. On it, though, he was an animal. But that was because Bobby was slow and he could only intimidate people.'

The Celtic fans at Parkhead that afternoon wondered if the new-look attacking formation would pay off. Ninety minutes later, they got their answer. Rangers triumphed 5–1, with Stevie Chalmers getting the home side's consolation goal in the last minute to prevent the Ibrox team's most emphatic victory over Celtic in the twentieth century.

Bertie Auld said, 'I missed the game against Rangers, but, although I wasn't involved in the action, it still hurt like hell. To get turned over on our own ground in two successive weeks in front of our own fans by Rangers was just awful. Sickening. Who could blame the supporters for being unhappy? They took it badly and so did we. You can't hide in Glasgow. Everywhere you go there are Old Firm supporters. Some will smile at you and others will snarl. No one likes to be second best in any sport. Clearly, we were rattled. We were struggling and we knew we had to turn it around quickly or we would be out of the title chase by December or January. And that was something that was happening far too regularly for comfort.'

For whatever reason, and you are invited to draw your own conclusions, John Hughes sat out the whole of October and November, missing eight games, before returning to score Celtic's goal in the 1–1 draw with Dundee United at Parkhead on 10 December. Despite that, he wasn't required for first-team duty for the remaining three fixtures of 1960. At least Hughes could console himself with the fact that, at the age of seventeen, he had reached double figures for appearances, ten in all, with six goals thrown in.

Billy McNeill recalled, 'We realised our best chance of silverware success would probably come in one of the cup competitions. We never achieved the consistency required to push for the championship, although, at the start of every season, that was our number-one target. More realistically, though, we stood a better chance in knockout competitions. We had the individuals to turn any game in our favour over 90 minutes in one-off situations.'

A lot of Celtic's expectations lay with Irishman John Colrain, who was a centre-forward well respected by his teammates, not least Bertie Auld: 'He had it all, I really mean that. He was well built, maybe a bit on the slow side, but he possessed a ferocious shot. There was one snag, though. He may have been about 6 ft, but he rarely headed the ball. I don't think he liked to mess up his hair!' Mike Jackson added, 'Colly was a super player. A bit of a maverick. When he put his mind to it, though, he was as good as anyone on his day.'

The genial giant led Celtic's charge towards Rangers keeper George Niven in the Scottish Cup semi-final in April. As usual, it was a tense encounter, and, once the dust had settled at the grey old national stadium, the game would have to be replayed. Stevie Chalmers scored, with Jimmy Millar replying to bring about a 1–1 stalemate. The roof caved in on Celtic in the second game, with Rangers running amok, winning 4–1. It was their fourth victory in six games against their Glasgow rivals in 1960. In the process, they had helped themselves to fifteen goals to Celtic's more modest seven.

Colrain would play three more league games for the team before being sold to Clyde. Disenchanted, he returned to Ireland to become player-manager of Glentoran at the age of 29, a superb player removed from the mainstream of football. 'He should have contributed so much more,' added Auld. 'And, by saying that, I mean absolutely no disrespect to my many friends in Ireland. Colly was a much sought-after youngster when he was emerging as a genuine talent. Celtic signed him on a provisional form in 1953, when he was only fifteen years old, and I believe he went full-time in 1957, two years after I had arrived from Maryhill Harp. Huge things were expected of him, but, for whatever reason, it never worked out.'

Mike Jackson took up the story: 'It was criminal that Colly didn't get the chance to make it big with Celtic. We knew back then that the board didn't like their players socialising with each other. Colly, myself, Bertie, Paddy and Big Billy went around together and were known as "the Rat Pack" after the original Hollywood gang that was led by Frank Sinatra and consisted of actors and singers such as Dean Martin, Peter Lawford, Sammy Davis Jr and Cesar Romero. I was nicknamed "Dino" after Martin because, although the boys will still tell you differently, I could belt out a song or two. Billy became "Cesar" after Romero, who apparently drove Sinatra and co. everywhere. Billy was the only one who had a car among us, so that's where he picked up his nickname. Of course, it was changed later to the more respectful "Caesar". Wee Bertie became "Sammy D" after Sammy Davis. Terribly politically incorrect today, of course, but it was because Davis was black and Bertie had this dark growth and had to shave about twice a day. Paddy just stayed as Paddy and Colly became known as "Oceans". Sinatra got the title role in a movie called *Ocean's 11* about a mob of guys plotting to rob a Las Vegas casino. Sinatra was Danny Ocean and it stuck with Colly. Of course, a certain Jim Baxter came around every now and again to join in. We used to go to the Locarno Ballroom in Glasgow's Sauchiehall Street on a Tuesday or Saturday or, if we were flush, both nights.

'I lost count of the times Bertie, Colly, Paddy and myself were asked to go to the manager's office on a Monday morning. Apparently, there had been reports about some players enjoying wild nights. Don't make me laugh. It only took a couple of lager and limes to get the lot of us pissed. Anyway, these were the days when they rolled up the pavements in Glasgow at ten o'clock. We were often asked to explain ourselves. We had been seen boozing in public. "The four of you were spotted drinking," Jimmy McGrory would say. To be fair, he never looked too comfortable going through the interrogation process. Obviously, he had been put up to it by someone else. Big Billy was never mentioned. "Who were you drinking with?" How about the blond, six-foot-plus captain of the club? Billy was spared these regular Monday morning meetings. Maybe he wore an invisible suit on a Saturday! But, stage by stage, the board got rid of myself, Bertie, Colly and Paddy. I think we were seen as expendable; my big mate Billy wasn't.'

Colrain's experience sends echoes reverberating around Celtic Park. So many talented teenagers made their way to the club, with unpaid scouts – such as Mike Jackson's John Murphy – up and down the country and beyond unearthing potential gems and pointing them towards the East End of Glasgow. In the late '50s and early '60s, a whole array of eager youngsters made first-team appearances for Celtic: Dan O'Hara, Tom Mackie, Robert Paton, Ian Lochhead, John Kelly, Jim Sharkey, Mike Conroy, Malcolm Slater, John Curran and Bobby Jeffrey. Their top-team outings came to a meagre total of 42. Coincidentally, there was also another Goldie who performed for the club around that time, right-back Peter. He fared marginally better than his namesake Willie; he played in two games. Add John Kurila's input of seven and you get to fifty-one games shared among twelve young players. You must wonder why so many lads failed. Were the training facilities inadequate? Was there a lack of supervision? Was there no direction? No guidance? If John Hughes, as a teenager, failed to get the proper attention as a first-team player, then there were obviously problems. Undoubtedly, some nuggets were cast adrift, discarded as worthless. The conveyor belt of talent, thankfully, would start rolling again some time soon.

The two youngsters who were thought most likely to make the grade were wingers Matt McVittie, signed from Wishaw Juniors, and Jim Conway, who arrived from Coltness United. McVittie turned out thirty-four times and scored ten goals, one of them in a rare Scottish Cup win against Rangers in 1959, and Conway netted nine times from thirty-two outings. McVittie was 17 years old when he made his league debut against Rangers in the New Year's Day game in 1958, which resulted in a 1–0 loss. He left in November 1959 for English lower-league outfit Cambridge Town. Bertie Auld remembers him as being 'a frail lad'. Conway was also 17 when he took his top-team debut in the opening league game of the 1957–58 season, a 1–0 win over Falkirk. Apparently, he grew disenchanted with life at Celtic while attracting the attention of a certain Jock Stein, manager of Dunfermline at the time. A move to Fife didn't materialise, however, and the player signed for Norwich City in 1961 for a reported fee of £10,000, a bid Celtic would have found impossible to resist.

The latter half of 1960 had been good for one prospect, though, in the shape of John Hughes, raw and ready to go. The New Year's Day fixture against Rangers was now just around the corner. Could Celtic hurl themselves into 1961 with a long-overdue victory and avenge six consecutive painful reversals in this historic fixture? A crowd of 79,000 was at Ibrox Stadium to find out.

2

JOCK VERSUS CELTIC

Rangers 2, Celtic 1. A new year, same old sinking feeling. Under gunmetal-grey skies, the Celtic fans filed into Ibrox Stadium, preparing for the kick-off on the chilly afternoon of 2 January and wondering what 1961 would bring. They left in silence, hardly inclined to view the future favourably. The thin whine of the wind failed to obliterate the taunts rolling down from the opposite terracings. Strong ale was required to dull the memory of abject failure – again – against their old foe. Johnny Divers scored, but goals from Ralph Brand and Davie Wilson inflicted Celtic's second Glasgow derby league loss of the season, following the 5–1 drubbing in September. The championship flag hadn't fluttered over the Parkhead stand since 1954. It was evident to even the most defiant among the Celtic support that it wouldn't be observed in 1961, either.

Four significant events occurred at Parkhead in 1961. Celtic reached the Scottish Cup final, where, despite being overwhelming favourites, they contrived to lose in the replay against Jock Stein's Dunfermline; the legendary Bertie Peacock left the club after twelve years; and two young men who were to have a major and dramatic say in the remarkable and unexpected turnaround in the fortunes of the club signed provisional forms: Jimmy Johnstone and Tommy Gemmell.

The history books tell us Gemmell signed on 25 October from Coltness United while Johnstone joined from Blantyre Celtic on 11 November. However, Gemmell, after many years, was adamant someone got the dates mixed up. 'I can guarantee you we signed on the same night,' said Gemmell. 'I have vivid memories of that evening. Who wouldn't? I was there with my dad and Jimmy turned up with his father. The four of us were ushered into the boardroom, situated to the right of the main entrance of the stadium. Jimmy McGrory was sitting there at this enormous table that is still there to this day. He was puffing on a pipe, which was something I came to witness quite a lot over the years. The first thing that hit me, though, was the wall-to-wall trophy cabinets. "Wow," I thought to myself. I had never seen such silverware. I took a walk around on my own while my dad talked to Jimmy McGrory and some other officials. I had just celebrated my eighteenth birthday nine days earlier, on the 16th and, as I learned later, Jimmy was a year younger.

'The actual signing of the forms was a bit of a blur and, basically, was left to our dads. Jimmy and I were just happy to put pen to paper when we were called over and the forms were pushed in front of us. Signing what was known as a provisional form meant you would be allowed to return to the juniors if you didn't make the grade at senior level. That was far from my thoughts at that moment in time.

'Money? Coltness would have received some sort of fee and, as was the tradition in those days, I think I received a farewell bonus of £40 from them and something in the region of £25 from Celtic. There was no haggling or anything like that. Cash was not important; that was way down my list of priorities that October evening. I was getting a chance to do something at the world-famous Glasgow Celtic and, boy, was I excited. I had arrived!

'Another reason I remember that Jimmy and I signed on the same date was the fact that we got the same bus home. It was the No. 240 to Lanark. The both of us, with our dads, walked from Celtic Park to Parkhead Cross. Jimmy lived in Viewpark, in Uddingston, and I stayed in Craigneuk, in Motherwell. Funnily enough, I had met Jimmy before. We were at Burnbank Technical College in Hamilton at the same time. I was about 17 and was training to be an electrician while Jimmy was taking a course in welding. We would go there a couple of times a week on a release course. Along with the other lads there, we would get the tennis ball out at dinner-time and have a kickabout in the playground. Even back then, the Wee Man was untouchable. No one else got a kick at the ball for about an hour. He ran rings round me, I must confess. Little did I know what the future held in store for me and my wee pal.

'Actually, I had been brought up a Motherwell fan. My dad used to take me to Fir Park every now and again when I was a kid and I had an afternoon free and wasn't actually playing the game. I dreamed of wearing that claret-and-amber shirt. Dad would rarely take me to a game when Celtic and Rangers were in town, but I do recall being at a match where Well played Celtic. For whatever reason, my dad must have relented on that occasion. I've checked back to see if I can pinpoint the date of the first time I saw those green and white hoops close up and I think it must have been 8 April 1959, when 'my' team won 2–0. I recall Celtic had a player called Matt McVittie in their line-up and that's the only time I can see that he played against us at Fir Park. If I'm right, that was also my first sighting of two blokes who were to become great mates, Billy McNeill and Bertie Auld. If memory serves correctly, we would have a wee celebration in Lisbon some time in the future.'

There wasn't much to get excited about at the start of the year, though, with yet another blow inflicted by Rangers, at Ibrox. Five days after that, Third Lanark won 3–2 at Parkhead and all Celtic had to look forward to in terms of trying to win silverware for the first time in four years was the Scottish Cup.

Bertie Auld remembered, 'The national trophy was a big deal in those days. The league title was the priority, obviously, but winning the Scottish Cup wasn't a bad second. There was a lot of prestige in lifting the cup at Hampden on the last day of the season. It sent the players and the fans home happy and they could spend their summer knowing their team had at least won something. That would have made the entire season worthwhile.'

Auld and Celtic were on target as the Scottish Cup campaign kicked off with a 3–1 win at Falkirk, while Montrose, from the Second Division, offered scant resistance in the next round. John Hughes, reinstated to the first team, underlined his potential once more with two strikes in a 6–0 triumph. The draw took Celtic to Fife to face a Raith Rovers side struggling at the foot of the First Division. Their thoughts must have been on survival – which they achieved by winning four points more than Clyde – because they rarely threatened Frank Haffey on that occasion, scoring one goal but conceding four. Hughes was on the mark again. It would get a lot tougher when Hibs came to town for the quarter-final meeting in March.

A crowd of 40,000 – almost double the average gate – was at Parkhead for the visit of the Edinburgh side, who might not have been the force they had been in the recent past but who were still exceptionally dangerous opponents. That fact was highlighted when Bobby Kinloch gave them the lead and the Jungle was silenced. Celtic, urged on by Paddy Crerand from the middle of the park, fought back furiously, but they were repelled by an inspired Hibs goalkeeper, Ronnie Simpson. Even in 1961, the newspapers were calling him a veteran, but he was only 30 years old and clearly still had some mileage left in him.

As the clock ticked down, it looked like another failure was about to be inflicted on Celtic. Six minutes were left when Stevie Chalmers snaked his way through the retreating Hibs defence to fire beyond the man who would become his golf partner in years to come.

Celtic, though, were back on quicksand when they travelled to the capital for the replay four days later. The tie attracted another attendance around the 40,000 mark. The tension was electric; both teams realised their only hope of any trophy success that season lay with the national competition.

Left-half Bertie Peacock, one of Celtic's most famous and respected players of the era, was forced to miss the match after being called up for international duty with Northern Ireland. His non-appearance would have serious repercussions. A youngster by the name of John Clark, who had celebrated his twentieth birthday only two days earlier, took his place. Clark, signed from Larkhall Thistle 18 months beforehand, would remain in place for the rest of the season. Peacock's Celtic career, which had lasted 12 years, was over at the age of 31. He had won a league championship medal in 1954 and had also picked up two Scottish Cup honours, in 1951 and 1954, as well as being successful twice in the League Cup, in 1956 and the following year, the 7–1 rout of Rangers. He was one of only eleven players who picked up a Coronation Cup medal in 1953 as well as being selected thirty-one times for his country. His stock was so high he also played in a Great Britain select against the Rest of Europe in 1955. But it was the end of the road in March 1961 for an iconic Celt who later confided to Frank Haffey, 'Maybe I stayed at the same club too long.'

Clark's arrival could hardly have been more timely. Celtic and Hibs matches were more often than not played at a ferocious, frantic pace, the action sweeping from one end of the pitch to another in the blink of an eye. This was to be no exception. Ronnie Simpson and Frank Haffey were defiant as both goalkeepers were called upon to make gallant and brave saves throughout a goalless 90 minutes. The game went into extra time and that was when Clark made a massive impact on proceedings. Fourteen minutes into the extra half-hour, he surged through the Easter Road mud to lash a twenty-five yard drive at goal. Simpson had no chance. The ball thundered past him and strangled itself in the net low down at his post. Remarkably, Clark would score only another two goals in his next 317 games for Celtic stretching over the next 13 years! Timing is everything in this game.

Clark said later, 'I hardly crossed the halfway line throughout my career, so I was never going to be a goal machine, but that strike against Hibs will always remain special. Actually, I could hardly believe I had scored. I remember it was a heavy night with a muddy surface, but I came forward and just took a belt at the ball. It simply flew into the net with Ronnie too late to get a hand to it. I ribbed Ronnie about it on the odd occasion afterwards, but he would shrug his shoulders and say, "That was another

Ronnie Simpson who was in goal for Hibs that night – nothing to do with me." It certainly looked like my old mate to me.'

As the victorious Haffey shook hands with the vanquished Simpson at the end of a memorable night's football, they couldn't have known what an impact they would have on each other's careers three years later, in 1964. At that stage, Simpson was on the verge of signing for Berwick Rangers after losing his first-team place at Hibs to Willie Wilson. He was 34 and it looked very much like his days in the top flight were a thing of the past. Or, as they say in football-speak, 'his future was behind him'. Jock Stein, by then the Hibs manager, was about to sell the veteran to the Second Division side, desperately seeking a reliable keeper after the team had conceded 84 goals in 36 league games. The deal was just about done, but then, in September that year, Sean Fallon made a timely intervention. A fee was agreed with Hibs ('just sweeties', according to Simpson) and, as he arrived at Parkhead, Haffey was packing his bags to move to Swindon Town in an £8,000 deal.

Reflecting on the aftermath of that Celtic–Hibs match, Auld said, 'Any chance of the league was long gone, but we were now in a position where we were favourites for the Scottish Cup. I recall we beat Airdrie 4–0 in the semi-final, with Yogi getting two goals.'

Intriguingly, Jock Stein had guided Dunfermline to the cup final, too. In 1960, he had left his job as Celtic reserve-team coach, a post he had taken when a persistent ankle injury had forced him to quit playing three years earlier. He took over from Andy Dickson at East End Park with the club striving to stay alive in the top division and only seven games remaining.

As fate would have it, Stein had sat in the dugout as a manager for the first time on 19 March 1960, with Celtic, of all teams, providing the opposition in Fife. That might have been seen as a bit quirky, but what was certain was that Frank Haffey was fishing the ball out of the back of the net after only ten seconds. It had been put there by a raging bull of a centre-forward named Charlie Dickson. There was little finesse about the player, but he was effective. To him, then, fell the honour of scoring the first goal of Jock Stein's managerial reign. By the end of a storming ninety minutes, Haffey had been beaten twice more and two goals from Neilly Mochan couldn't prevent Stein from enjoying a 3–2 debut triumph. The Dunfermline manager's enthusiasm, drive and tactical knowledge had immediately been transmitted to a team that had looked as though it had accepted its fate and was preparing to head through the relegation trapdoor. Astoundingly, Dunfermline won their next six games and finished sixth from the bottom.

Billy McNeill was adamant that Celtic should never have allowed Stein even to contemplate leaving Parkhead. He said, 'I think Celtic made a big mistake when they let him go. Clearly, his burgeoning talents as a coach were not fully appreciated by the club, but we youngsters thought the world of him and benefited greatly from his advice and encouragement. He certainly seemed to have a particular interest in my progress and his departure created a void in my life. If Jock had remained at Celtic Park, that would have allowed the club to blood him as Jimmy McGrory's successor and the eventual transition would have been smoother. Celtic obviously didn't offer him a big enough challenge at the time. However, I'm sure that, had Jock been given certain guarantees concerning his future and a financial inducement to stay, he could have been persuaded to remain where he was.'

Leaving Celtic was not a decision Stein took lightly. Two journalists he confided in were Jim Rodger of the *Daily Record* and John Blair of the *Sunday People*, two excellent scribes of my acquaintance who are sadly no longer with us. Jim Rodger, known to everyone in the trade as 'The Jolly', was football's Mr Fix-It. He had contacts everywhere from Tannadice to 10 Downing Street. He was always well placed to drop a suggestion or two in some football chairman's ear. Might Jock Stein have used him back then when it looked as though nothing was emerging at Parkhead and, coincidentally, Dunfermline were looking for a new manager? It's hardly outwith the bounds of possibility, because one thing of which you could be absolutely certain would be that The Jolly would have known someone in power at East End Park.

Stein wanted to talk things over with Blair, a sportswriter he admired and trusted, so they agreed to go for a walk through Glasgow Green, which isn't as extraordinary as it might seem because Stein, at that time, was not an instantly recognisable figure. It wasn't quite cloak-and-dagger stuff. My old *Sunday People* pal told me about it at length one day.

'Jock was torn,' said John. 'I had never seen him in such a state. Normally, he was so decisive. He may not have started off life supporting Celtic, but he swiftly became immersed in the club and its traditions. The fact that he was of the Protestant faith yet could play for a club steeped in Irish traditions, founded by a Marist priest, meant a lot to him. And yet, although they were happy enough to sign Protestants or players of other religions, Celtic had only ever had Roman Catholic managers. Jock might have seen that as some sort of barrier. I say "might have", not definitely. He liked to explore all avenues. He had a very keen, inquisitive mind, and he wouldn't have overlooked that fact.

'But as we continued walking, his mind was in turmoil. He was going.

He was staying. He was going. He was staying. Suddenly, he turned to me and said, "John, what would you do?" I know you should never answer a question with a question, but I asked, "Do you want to be a manager in your own right?" He didn't hesitate: "Yes." I said, "Take the Dunfermline job then." I don't know if I helped to sway him one way or another, but a couple of days later Dunfermline had a new manager, a guy called Jock Stein.'

So, on a windy day, under leaden skies, Celtic and their former captain and reserves coach had a date with destiny at Hampden Park on 22 April 1961. The teams had 12 days to prepare for the Scottish Cup final. The reason for the extended break was the Home International Championship match being played on 15 April. Celtic had Frank Haffey and Billy McNeill in the Scotland side that faced England at Wembley. You have to wonder what state of mind they were in when they returned a week later to play at Hampden; Scotland were annihilated 9–3. Haffey, especially, must have been traumatised. He had a dreadful game and looked at fault for at least four of the goals. Dave Mackay, then of Hearts but who would later play for Spurs, observed bluntly, 'We played crap, Haffey played double crap.' The keeper would never represent his country again. McNeill also had an international debut he might prefer to forget, but it was Haffey who was the main target for abuse. Rather strangely, no one in the Celtic management team thought it worthwhile to counsel their number 1, known to be erratic at the best of times. That dreadful lack of foresight was to backfire spectacularly.

Goodness knows what was going through Haffey's mind when he ran out onto the pitch at Hampden only seven days after his personal humiliation in front of 97,350 fans at Wembley. Emotionally drained or not, he took his place in a game of colossal importance to Celtic. The bookmakers made the Parkhead outfit runaway certainties to lift the trophy and after half an hour no one would have believed they had been wayward in their judgement. Celtic were in control, smoothly passing their way through the Dunfermline side and peppering their goal with efforts from all ranges and angles. There was only one snag: goalkeeper Eddie Connachan was unbeatable. Connachan had been conceding almost every week in the league and, in fact, by the end of the season would have lost 81 goals, the joint highest amount along with relegated Ayr United. At Hampden, though, he was bold and brave in his resistance. It ended goalless, but it had been an exciting encounter in front of 113,328 supporters.

The *Glasgow Herald* reported:

With such exhilarating goalmouth incidents no match can be dull. Nor was this game bereft of the finer arts of football. We had as intelligent long ground-passing from Pat Crerand as has been seen in Scottish football for many a fine day, some astonishingly clever dribbling by John Hughes and Willie Fernie – and cool, calculated defence by Dunfermline, who, even when their centre-half Jackie Williamson was absent in the last thirteen minutes or playing out on the wing, maintained their studied pattern of play.

There had indeed been some slick footwork on display from Hughes and Fernie, but with little reward. Maybe things would be different in the replay.

It rained all day the following Wednesday, with Celtic little realising the heavens were weeping for them. Willie O'Neill, signed from St Anthony's two years earlier, was rushed into making his debut at left-back in place of Jim Kennedy, who had been taken to hospital after feeling unwell just hours before the kick-off. The significance of this would be obvious as the game developed. Clark had only played nine first-team games and O'Neill, performing directly behind him, was making his debut. Their inexperience would not have been lost on Stein.

This time, there were 87,866 at the national stadium to see if Eddie Connachan could repeat the heroics of Saturday. Unfortunately, for Celtic, he could. Connachan was inspired, even better than he had been in the first game. The conditions were hardly ideal, but his grip was safe and sure in the air and on the ground. Celtic pounded away in the desperate hope that something had to give, that a goal had to come. It duly arrived in the 68th minute – for Dunfermline.

Davie Thomson started and finished the goal that flummoxed Celtic. He swept a pass out to the scampering George Peebles on the left wing. Thomson wasn't picked up by the defence as he followed up into the penalty box and was unmarked to get his head to Peebles' assured cross and send a looping effort over Haffey.

Celtic's fate was sealed two minutes from time when Haffey presented Dunfermline with a second goal. Alex Smith pushed the ball through the middle of the Celtic defence. Charlie Dickson was onto it, but his first touch was bad and he knocked it too far in front of him. It was the goalkeeper's ball. Dickson followed in, more in hope than expectation. Either that or he had viewed footage of Haffey at Wembley and realised anything was possible. Inexplicably, the goalie fumbled the ball, then somehow managed to stumble over it in the most awkward fashion, and the gleeful Dickson simply raced round him and poked the gift into the net. He would never score an easier goal.

Dunfermline had won the 76th Scottish Cup in their 76th year and a white-coated Stein bounded onto the park at the end. He headed straight for his goalkeeper. Connachan had been a miner, just like Stein, and had recently quit his job to concentrate fully on football. It looked a wise choice. The more cynical among the Celtic support wondered if their goalkeeper might contemplate a switch in professions, too, taking the reverse route. Connoisseurs of calamity were in their element when Haffey was performing. Somehow, he had become quite adept at mixing comedy with catastrophe.

Stein, as one would expect, was passionate in his celebrations, yet Willie Cunningham, a player brought to East End Park by Stein and who would eventually succeed him as manager at the club, detected something different in his boss. Speaking to Archie Macpherson for his book *Jock Stein: The Definitive Biography*, the defender said:

> I think he had a special feeling for Celtic. There was most certainly a tinge of affection there. When we travelled through for the game and I heard him speaking to people from the west, I could tell he had a special regard for the club. He wanted to beat them all right, make no mistake about that – he was too professional for anything else – but there was definitely something about Celtic and him.

Robert Kelly, the man who had allowed Stein to walk away from Parkhead the previous year, was in the presentation area at Hampden in his official capacity as president of the SFA, and he watched as his wife handed the Scottish Cup to Dunfermline captain Ron Mailer. Magnanimously, Kelly said later, 'It's no loss what a friend gets.'

Billy McNeill said, 'That was a real sickener. We had most of the play over the three hours and we had absolutely nothing to show for it – not even a consolation goal. It was hard to take. I was never a good loser and, later on, I would realise how much the triumph meant to Big Jock. But at that moment, standing drenched on the Hampden turf and watching Dunfermline's players go up to take the trophy, it was extremely difficult to accept. My only feeling was for my teammates and our fans. Back then, the Celtic end at Hampden was completely uncovered, but our supporters still packed it out despite raindrops as big as golf balls falling on them throughout. They must have been drenched, saturated. But they gave us their backing all the way. They were as desperate as us for us to win something. We were sick. They were sick. You started to wonder if Celtic would ever win anything again.'

Bertie Auld remembered, 'Curiously, Celtic had a reserve fixture arranged that same night against Hearts at Tynecastle. I was told I wouldn't be needed for Hampden, so I was packed off to Edinburgh. Little did I realise that my one and only appearance in the Scottish Cup that year – the 3–1 win in the first round against Falkirk – would be my last first-team outing for Celtic for almost four years. Birmingham City manager Gil Merrick had taken a shine to me and he cornered me after the game in the capital. "I want you to sign for my club," he said, with the minimum of fuss. "You'll hear something tomorrow." I was intrigued when I turned up at Parkhead for training the following morning. As you might expect, it was like walking into a morgue. The players, even those who hadn't played, including me, were scunnered. I had no thoughts of leaving the club, though – none whatsoever. Someone else had other ideas, though.

'I was awaiting the call that the manager wanted to see me. In his normal forthright manner, Jimmy McGrory told me that an English First Division club wanted to buy me. They had offered £15,000 and the directors were willing to accept the bid. To be honest, it was a shattering blow to discover that Celtic were quite content to allow me to leave. I felt sick to my stomach. I found myself in a quandary. What should I do? I didn't want to go, but something within me told me I didn't want to hang around some place where I wasn't wanted. What had gone wrong?

'My old Parkhead chum Paddy Crerand had a theory that might not be too far off the mark. He insisted, "Those in power at the club wanted rid of Bertie at the time. He was a typical Glaswegian and wasn't afraid of answering back. That was to be his downfall at Celtic. Bob Kelly didn't like his style."

'Those were Paddy's thoughts and, yes, I wasn't afraid to let my feelings be known if I thought I had something constructive to say. If I didn't agree with someone, I was hardly going to sit there and nod my approval. I'm not a particular fan of yes-men. I should have known that outlook would have been frowned upon at Celtic. So, with that, I was on my way to Birmingham City. You probably won't believe this, but, deep down, I knew I would be back at Celtic some day. Honestly, I genuinely held that thought on the day I cleaned out my locker, said my goodbyes to my colleagues and headed for the Midlands.'

It was becoming a ritual that Celtic fans would clamour for new faces during the summer. They were increasingly frustrated by continued failure; the team, bereft of leadership, was obviously on the slide. Robert Kelly, though, appeared to be quite content with the squad of players who had finished the previous season in fourth position on thirty-nine points, twelve behind champions Rangers, trailing Kilmarnock by eleven and three adrift of Third Lanark. Kelly liked to be known as a visionary, but perhaps he was a visionary wearing blinkers.

It was obvious to all that Celtic desperately needed a goalkeeper who would bring consistency and stability to the defence. The wonderful/woeful Frank Haffey had played in 29 league games and had conceded 35 goals: not a good ratio. John Fallon had been in goal during the 2–2 draw with Kilmarnock, the 5–1 collapse against Rangers, the 2–0 defeat by Third Lanark and the goalless draw against Aberdeen. Willie Goldie, of course, made his one and only appearance in the 2–0 loss to Airdrie. It was clear that the club had an Achilles heel and opponents were zeroing in on it. As it happened, Haffey missed the start of the 1961–62 season because of a skin infection and Kelly's answer was to kick off with a new goalkeeper: Frank Connor, signed from Blantyre Celtic the previous year.

The Celtic supporters' awe was not inspired. Their sense of foreboding about a lack of new signings would prove to be well founded. The biggest purchase in the summer of 1961 came in the shape of Billy Price, an honest and hard-working left-half from Falkirk. The fee was £1,000. With all due respect, the signing wasn't exactly big box-office material.

However, most football fans are blessed with an irrational and unwarranted sense of optimism at the start of a new season, and those who favoured a team in the East End of Glasgow were no different. As usual, the enthusiasm among the support was palpable and hopes were soaring when the League Cup got under way. It began with a promising 3–2 win over Partick Thistle at Firhill, with Mike Jackson claiming two and John Hughes, beginning to revel in this tournament, adding the other. Frank Connor did reasonably well, although the consensus of opinion among the fans, getting their first glimpse of the custodian, was that he was 'too wee'. Any early-season feel-good factor was wiped out in the next game when St Johnstone won 1–0 at Parkhead. The Saints eventually qualified, with Celtic failing once more. At least the club were consistent: they scored ten goals and lost ten goals. New keeper Connor was consistent, too, in that he failed to keep a clean sheet in each of the six ties.

Celtic had hoped for a good start in the league, because, as Auld accurately pointed out, title ambitions had far too often been heading for the scrapyard around the turn of the year. A tricky trip to Rugby Park to face Kilmarnock was the opening-day hurdle. It was a banana-skin fixture and, sure enough, Celtic didn't miss the inviting object. Johnny Divers and Stevie Chalmers scored, but, unfortunately, the back door was swinging open again and Kilmarnock stuck three past Connor. There was still no sign of Haffey and that was worrying for vaudeville writers always searching for new material. Connor kept his place and claimed his first shut-out in a match in which a goal from Divers undid Third Lanark. Ironically, although he kept a clean sheet for the first time in his eight appearances, that was the end of Connor's Celtic career. A year later, he signed for Irish side Portadown.

Billy Price made his debut in the win over Third Lanark and, like Connor, never quite made the Celtic Hall of Fame. He played another seventy-three games, scoring three goals, before moving to Berwick Rangers in 1964.

It was a dreary pattern that was being played out year after year: cut-price performers who, sadly, did not possess the ability to match up to the expectations of the support, misfits popping in and popping out again. The fans were beginning to wonder if there was a revolving door at the players' entrance.

Haffey returned for the first Old Firm game of the campaign in September. Gag writers swarmed towards Ibrox hoping to exploit the latest in a long-running series of blips and blunders by the goalkeeper, who remained perfectly affable off the pitch despite the snipers firing away at every opportunity. However, they could save their ammunition for another day. An entertaining confrontation ended 2–2.

Would Haffey have the last laugh? He kept his position for the remaining 13 league games in the run-down to the turn of the year as the Parkhead side stubbornly kept in contention. There were nine wins in those outings.

The most intriguing and eagerly anticipated match came in October, when Jock Stein brought his cup-winning Dunfermline to Glasgow. Stein even provoked some grudging applause among the home support. There were no free gifts from Haffey on this occasion, though, as two goals from Bobby Carroll gave Celtic a 2–1 victory.

McNeill and co. had every right to be fairly satisfied with their overall performances as they jousted with old rivals Rangers and Dundee at the top of the table. The turn of the year was upon us and there was more good news for Celtic.

3

RUMBLE IN THE JUNGLE

The New Year's Day derby had become an annual ritual that no one of the green-and-white persuasion anticipated with any particular fondness. But in 1962 the Celtic fans did not have to suffer the pain and humiliation of a seventh consecutive defeat. Winter's icy grip, unforgiving and unremitting, obliterated fixture lists throughout the country, with pitches all over the place deemed unplayable. These were the freezing old days before the advent of under-soil heating. Back then, the ground staff at Parkhead would spread bales of hay on the surface days before the game and then attempt to brush the frost-covered straw off the pitch as close to kick-off time as possible. This action, of course, served to confuse player and fan alike when the markings on the pitch were fairly well disguised. There was also the use of braziers, strategically appointed around the playing area. This was not the most imaginative, innovative or workable of ideas, as the braziers often scorched the grass directly beneath them. So, on this occasion, the conditions were the winners and the Celtic support, for the first time in seven years, was not forced to endure a different kind of Ne'erday hangover.

Celtic had waved a fond farewell to 1961 with a 4–0 success over Raith Rovers two days before Christmas Day. Would 1962 be ushered in with another victory? Alas, no. Kilmarnock were the visitors to Parkhead on 6 January, once the snows had cleared and the thaws had made known their welcome presence. It was a lively encounter, but Celtic and their fans had to settle for a 2–2 draw, with Stevie Chalmers and Bobby Carroll pulling the trigger for the Glasgow side. Four days later, Chalmers, with his ninth goal of the league campaign, was on target again, but once more it ended in stalemate against Third Lanark. Chalmers was a likeable guy off the field, but on it he was a demon; no goalkeeper was safe when Stevie was around. If a goalie fumbled a shot or a header, he knew there was every likelihood Chalmers would be onto it in a flash, taking ball and keeper into the net if need be. The player's route to a career in the hoops was a strange one. He started at junior side Kirkintilloch Rob Roy, then moved to Newmarket Town and on to Ashfield before being spotted by Celtic when he was 23.

When I interviewed him, he shook his head in disbelief and said, 'You know, I signed for Celtic from Ashfield on 6 February 1959 and made my debut just a month later against Airdrie at Celtic Park. Unfortunately, we lost 2–1, but imagine that: one month I was turning out in junior football and the next I was playing for the famous Glasgow Celtic. Couldn't happen today, could it? Possibly not surprisingly, that was my only appearance of that particular campaign. Now you see me, now you don't! But I realised I had been handed a great opportunity by Celtic and I wasn't about to pass it up. I knew I could score goals for this club.'

Meanwhile, it had been a while since the chants from the away fans of 'Ha Ha Haffey' had been heard, but, as anticipated, it was only a matter of time before his alter ego put in an appearance. Big Frank was at his butterfingered worst as Dundee United lashed four behind him at Tannadice on 13 January, but, fortunately, he was bailed out by the blokes in front of him. Mike Jackson (2), John Hughes (2) and Pat Crerand were among his rescue party in a roller-coaster 90 minutes. Jackson said, 'You never knew what you were going to get with Frank. He looked a world-beater on occasion and then he'd perform like a rookie in the next game. In fact, if you were really unlucky, you would get both in the one game. It couldn't have done much for the nerves of our defenders.'

Tommy Gemmell was one of those often harassed defenders. His sense of humour was severely tested on occasion by his erratic teammate. 'I remember one game at Parkhead when we were under a bit of pressure. I can't recall who we were playing, but I do know it was a tight, fraught encounter, where one mistake would undoubtedly prove costly. At one stage, our opponents were mounting an attack and were about ten yards into our half. I just happened to glance over my shoulder and couldn't believe my eyes when I witnessed Big Frank actually swinging on the crossbar going through some sort of gymnastic routine that wouldn't have looked out of place in the Olympics. I almost fainted.

'As I played more and more first-team games, I got to know that this was not out of the ordinary for our goalkeeper. He really was a puzzle. Sometimes when I was playing I was convinced there were three Frank Haffeys in goal for us. Someone would fire in a blistering shot and you'd fear the worst as it zipped past you. A quick look round and there was Big Frank with the ball safely in his hands, making an awkward save look routine. When his eye was in, he was a brilliant keeper. You could say, though, that consistency was not his strongest point. In the next game, you could give him a simple back-pass and your heart would be in your mouth when you realised the other Frank had turned up – the one we used to say had washed his hands and couldn't do a thing with them!'

Around this stage, one of Celtic's most consistent performers was Mike Jackson. 'Before signing up at Parkhead, I had been down at Manchester United for trials and they offered me a contract,' recalled the midfielder. 'I came home to think things over and that's when Celtic got in touch. They were my team and I didn't have to be asked twice. You can't help but wonder how your career could have turned out if you had made different decisions along the way.'

Billy McNeill was among many who would be mystified as to how this talented, versatile and quick-thinking player failed to make the grade at Celtic. The captain said, 'To be frank, several careers were ruined because of the apathy and lack of interest that appeared to pervade Celtic Park. The training facilities were practically non-existent and the kit left much to be desired. The reserve players could easily be identified by the red weals on their necks caused by the rubbing of the coarse jerseys.

'Jimmy McGrory, the manager, was a lovely man, but he was dominated by the chairman, Bob Kelly. Bob picked the team and called the shots. Anyone who dared to stand up to him didn't have a future at Celtic, including my close buddy Mike Jackson. For whatever reason, Mike got on the chairman's wrong side. He was suddenly perceived as being a disruptive influence and, in April 1963, I returned from international duty to learn that Mike had been transferred to St Johnstone. This was also an indication of where the power lay. Jimmy McGrory was the manager, but Bob Kelly was the boss. Had I been around at the time I would have done everything in my power to prevent that from happening. I thought Mike was unjustly treated. He was a fine player who could have done really well for Celtic if he had been given the chance.'

Jackson said, 'It was just bad timing on my behalf that I was out of the club a couple of years before Jock Stein arrived. I got on well with him when he was coaching the reserves and, naturally, I would have loved to have played while he was in charge of the first team. The whole place went to pot when he was allowed to leave.

'Instinctively, he spotted a player's strengths. Bobby Murdoch was actually known as "Bobby Murder" to a lot of Celtic fans at the time. That was cruel because he was playing out of position. He was too far up the field for a guy with a lack of genuine pace. Bobby would struggle to chase down balls thrown forward, but, boy, could he pass a ball. Stein saw that immediately. He put the player into a deeper role, where he didn't have to run about looking for passes. Given that wee bit of time and extra space, Bobby was magnificent. I'm told Bob Kelly told Jock, "Murdoch is an inside-forward – that's his best position." Jock replied, "Watch the game and you'll see that it's not." Bob Kelly never brought up the subject again.

'Jock swept through the team. Stevie Chalmers and Bobby Lennox had been playing as old-fashioned inside-forwards. He took a look at them and said, "You're not clever enough to play in those positions. You're both speedy and you're now playing as strikers." Their previous roles would have entailed putting in some graft in midfield, but, at a stroke, they were freed of these duties to concentrate on scoring goals, something they did rather well. It was the same story with John Clark. He too was playing in a position where he was supposed to contribute something further up the field. Jock thought he was only average in this position, but could read play really well as it came towards him. He had little pace, but his anticipation was excellent. My big pal Billy suddenly had a new defensive partner.

'If anyone could have found my perfect role in that Celtic team, it would have been Jock. I was played all over the place and I would have been only too happy to have got a settled position and worked on it. Sadly, after playing for Jock in the reserves for three years between 1957 and '60, I never got that opportunity.

'One thing that still annoys me is when a supporter comes up to me and says, "Oh, Mike Jackson? You were in that crap team during the early '60s that couldn't play." I feel like screaming. Listen, I scored 33 goals in 79 games playing mainly in midfield. I don't think that's bad going. With guidance from Jock, I would have added to that and, undoubtedly, improved my overall game. Look at Johnny Divers, too. He scored 102 goals. Hopeless? I don't think so. We could play all right, but, without proper preparation and direction, we never got the chance.'

Undoubtedly, Divers, like Jackson, could have thrived under the influence of Stein. One of his admirers was teenager John Hughes. He said, 'I thought Johnny was a very underrated player. He helped me a lot when I first came into the team and he was only a youngster at the time, too. As Mike Jackson points out, he scored more than 100 goals for the club and he was an inside-forward and not a main striker. That's a fabulous total, but he was moved on when Jock decided it was time for him to go. Like so many before him, he could have contributed so much more and his name should have been in lights.'

Bobby Lennox made his debut in March 1962 at Parkhead against championship-chasing Dundee and in front of a crowd of just over 37,000, the majority of whom would go home happy after Celtic's 2–1 victory. Lennox didn't mark his baptism with a goal, but he would make up for it as his career unfolded – 273 times, to be precise. So that was one game down and 570 to go for the man who would become known as 'The Buzz Bomb'. Admittedly, the Dundee team that visited Glasgow that day had lost a little of its verve and venom, with the talismanic Alan Gilzean toiling with injury problems, but they were still a formidable outfit and they had their eyes on winning the title for the first time in the club's history.

Frank Brogan, a speed merchant on either wing who had been signed from St Roch's the previous year, got Celtic's first goal. Once again, you are left to ask, 'What on earth happened to him?' Brogan, whose brother Jim would later play for Celtic too, looked the real deal, with pace to burn, an eye for goal and breathtaking accuracy with cross-balls while running full pelt. His style was hardly complicated. He knew he could skin any full-back with his breathtaking acceleration and didn't overindulge in fancy footwork. Step-overs and the like were not for him simply because he didn't require trickery to leave his opponent in his slipstream.

Why, then, was he allowed to leave Parkhead a year later for Ipswich Town after a total of only 48 appearances? Had the Celtic system failed him, too? Something, somewhere was not right, because Frank Brogan possessed awesome potential and he should have been around for years to entertain the home support and terrify the opposition.

Celtic's winning goal against the Tayside men was provided by Billy McNeill with an unstoppable header from a well-flighted corner kick by the aforementioned Brogan. The goal impressed the *Glasgow Herald*. Their reporter observed:

> The centre-half, McNeill, left his beat as Brogan placed the ball for a corner kick, but he did not invade the penalty area and give Dundee notice of his intentions. As Brogan lofted the ball over, McNeill ran all of twenty yards and, with remarkable judgement of timing and with a leap not one of his forwards could have achieved, got his head above the ball and, McGrory-like, forced the ball down and through a crowded goalmouth.

It would be extremely difficult to comprehend what happened next. Celtic were once again derailed by a club in the relegation dogfight. This time it was Airdrie, who just escaped the drop on goal average at the end of the season. Two of the Broomfield side's points came at Celtic's expense in a startling 1–0 win. Not for the first time, the Celtic support was left aghast at what it had witnessed. A strong and purposeful Dundee team with its eye on the title had been beaten in the previous league encounter, and here was the same side in green and white being turned over by a bunch of stragglers at the other end of the table. It was becoming increasingly perplexing.

One of the reasons for the collapse against Airdrie was, alas, Frank Haffey, so often the whipping boy, but, at the same time, so often guilty as charged. And this time his own teammates turned on him following an unforgivable howler. It was comic cuts stuff as he practically threw the ball into his own net and the players converged on their embarrassed number 1 without any attempt to disguise their disgust in front of the Broomfield audience. It's harsh to single out an individual in what is after all a team game, but there are occasions when you can quite easily detect the turning point in a match, even in a season. Any chance Celtic had of being crowned First Division champions disappeared that day in March with seven games still to play. Deservedly, the title eventually went to Dundee.

The Scottish Cup ended in utter and unexpected embarrassment for Celtic when fans rioted at Ibrox during a 3–1 defeat by St Mirren in the semi-final. The club had gone into the game on the back of an overwhelming five-goal success over the same opponents only the previous week. Aspirations were high for a second successive cup final appearance and, hopefully, better fortune than that enjoyed against Dunfermline. Rangers were due to face Motherwell in the other semi-final at Hampden the same day, hence Celtic playing at the home of their great rivals. The failure of the team against an ordinary Saints outfit was as horrendous as it was unacceptable. After the first forty-five minutes, Celtic players sought the refuge of the dressing-room, having capitulated three times without reply.

With 18 minutes left to play, it was too much for some undesirables. Suddenly there was a pitch invasion. The players were ushered off, bottles were thrown and police were wrestling with hooligans. Unfortunately, a fringe element followed Celtic – other clubs, too, had their own problems – and their insane reactions marked a new low in their behaviour. The game was eventually completed and finished 3–1, with Alec Byrne pulling one back. However, the sickening images of so-called fans swarming all over the pitch appeared in newspapers the following day and the Celtic hierarchy, as you might expect, were mortified. The club warned emphatically against any repeat. A statement read:

If the thugs who profess to support Celtic think that they can influence the result of a match by such behaviour as they indulged in on Saturday, they are very far and dreadfully mistaken. As soon as they tried to influence the outcome of the match we, as Celtic directors, decided the match was St Mirren's.

The *Glasgow Herald* was horrified:

The game will be remembered less for its merit than for the disgraceful scenes on the terracings which led to the invasion of the pitch. It's a sorry state to which senior football as a sport, entertainment and spectacle has been reduced when a referee has to abandon play for the time being because the pitch is black with boys, youths and young men and the police, up against heavy odds, are assaulted as they try to break up brawling groups on the terraces.

The 1961–62 season had delivered little: the league blown with seven games still to play; an inability to qualify from a League Cup section that saw a relegated side, St Johnstone, get through; and a Scottish Cup adventure that ended in chaotic scenes at Ibrox.

That powder-keg situation should have awakened a few at Parkhead; the natives were getting restless. During the season, they had seen their favourites written off when one particularly dull game was described in the *Evening Times* as being 'the worst entertainment in the East End'. That seemed harsh criticism because, appealing or appalling, the individuals in the green and white hoops had, in fact, always attempted to uphold the club's tradition of entertaining football. It was just that they did not possess the quality to deliver to a trophy-winning standard.

There appeared to be very little happening on the player recruitment front in the summer of 1962. Disconcertingly, a general apathy seemed to be settling on the club. Indeed, it would be October before money was spent in the transfer market, with a 27-year-old journeyman called Bobby Craig arriving from Blackburn Rovers for something in the region of £10,000. Apparently, he had also played for Third Lanark and Sheffield Wednesday, but the question asked most by the man in the Jungle was 'Bobby who?' And yet, for all the wrong reasons, his name would be on every Celtic supporter's lips by the end of the 1962–63 campaign.

Most of the usual suspects were in place when the new season kicked off in August with a League Cup tie against Hearts at Parkhead. Frank Haffey was in goal with Dunky MacKay and Jim Kennedy remaining at full-back. The wing-halves on either side of Billy McNeill were Pat Crerand and Billy Price. John Hughes, of whom big things were expected now he was being recognised as a first-team regular, spearheaded the attack and Charlie Gallagher, Crerand's cousin, would be playing immediately in front of him in the inside-right position, with Bobby Murdoch occupying the same role on the left. Bobby Lennox was fielded on the right wing, with Alec Byrne on the opposite flank.

There were still no real tactics in what appeared to be a rigid 2–3–5 formation. Improvisation among the players was a luxury denied them. There would have been apoplexy in the dugout if, for instance, Lennox, without prior permission, wanted to swap wings with Byrne for a spell to freshen things up. And God help the full-back who wanted to cross the halfway line. The prohibition on this stifled the aggressive MacKay, but probably suited the more pedestrian Kennedy. Things would change. Eventually.

Looking back, Billy McNeill said, 'We knew we had good players and we kicked off every campaign wondering if this was going to be the breakthrough season. We always wanted to make an early impact in the League Cup but had failed to do so for too many years. It was the first piece of silverware up for grabs and we all realised the confidence that would come our way if we could win the trophy before the turn of the year. It would have given everyone, player and fan alike, a real lift.

'I recall we started that term with a 3–1 victory over a strong Hearts side who could prove troublesome to anyone on their day. Our failure to display any sort of consistency was evident in the next game, when we lost 1–0 at Dundee. One minute we were up, the next we were down. To be perfectly honest, it was infuriating. Hearts ended with eight points to our seven and that was the end of the League Cup for another year. I have to admit to feeling a fair degree of sympathy for John Hughes. He had scored thirteen goals in the competition since making his debut against Third Lanark three years earlier and had yet to play outside the group stages.'

Rangers travelled across Glasgow for the first Old Firm encounter of the season. Once more, the litmus test had arrived early. The Ibrox side was still smarting after being dismissed by Dundee in the previous season's race for the flag and had made all sorts of threats and promises throughout the summer. It was crunch time for them, too. Could they deliver? Manager Scot Symon had his strongest team at his disposal and, unfortunately, they answered the rallying call, with Willie Henderson, a darting imp of an outside-right, beating Haffey for the game's only goal.

Consistency and this set of Celtic players were never natural bedfellows. The league had barely started, the players still sporting their summer suntans, and already Celtic were playing catch-up. Unfortunately, it was typical of the times.

Had no one listened to Bertie Auld, by now plying his trade with Birmingham City? Celtic looked to be heading once again for championship oblivion and indeed they faded without trace before the turn of the year. Auld recalled, 'I may have been in the Midlands, but I wasn't on the moon. I was still keeping up with things that were happening at Celtic, but I could see a familiar picture unfolding. Points were being thrown away in the most careless manner and that would always come back and bite the team at some stage of the campaign.'

The Old Firm clubs have always shown a 'nosy neighbour' interest in what is happening in each other's camps. They deny it publicly, of course, but that's a lot of hogwash. If someone sneezes at Parkhead, then they want to know about it at Ibrox and vice versa. So, what had been happening across the Clyde during Celtic's abysmal run? Rangers, in fact, were undefeated on their own soil and had dropped only two points out of ten. You can win championships with form like that.

While Rangers dazzled, Celtic, sadly, dithered. Muhammad Ali and George Foreman did not invent the Rumble in the Jungle in Kinshasa, Zaire, in 1974, as anyone who was in the vicinity of Parkhead during the early-season 0–1 defeat by Queen of the South would surely testify. Clearly, the dreadful inconsistency of the team was doing more than just merely irritating the Celtic faithful. It had now reached the level of unsettling a support that felt the need to let its feelings be known.

Nonetheless, the club sailed serenely on, hitting every iceberg possible. Robert Kelly and his fellow board members were regular targets for some vicious verbal abuse as tempers frayed and snapped on the terracing. Jimmy McGrory, it appeared, was immune from criticism, the supporters having too much respect for a club legend. Alas for the chairman and his directors, they didn't fall into that category as far as the fans were concerned.

After the Queen of the South catastrophe, Celtic went on a run of five games without success. The club had barely reached December and any thoughts of unfurling a championship flag at the start of the next season had been shredded and binned. It was like being forced to watch rerun after rerun of the worst movie you had ever seen. In slow motion. There was no respite, and yet emotional ties brought the man with the bunnet back every match day, the proverbial moth to a flame, the glutton for punishment.

An interesting diversion for Celtic in 1962 was their participation in European competition, although fate was hardly kind in the draw. The ballot for the Inter-Cities Fairs Cup paired them with Valencia, who, unfortunately for the Scots, were the holders of the cup after an astounding

7–3 aggregate win over their fellow Spaniards Barcelona in the two-legged final the previous season. Valencia won 6–2 at the Mestalla Stadium and drew 1–1 in the Nou Camp. It would be fair to say they were no mugs.

The first leg was in Spain on 26 September. Billy McNeill recalled, 'We realised they were an absolutely fantastic team, a side with exceptional players and individuals the like of whom we would rarely come up against in our own country. We wanted to do well, though. We had no intention of merely going through the motions. Bobby Carroll scored Celtic's first goals in Europe, but we still lost 4–2. Although we performed reasonably well against Valencia away, that did not lessen the sense of failure when we could only draw 2–2 in the return in Glasgow a month later. Alec Byrne claimed the distinction of being the first Celt to score a European goal at Parkhead and Paddy Crerand got the other.

'Obviously, playing against a side like Valencia broadens your horizons and you can always learn from competing against excellent players and different systems. It was an exciting adventure, all too brief, but it left us wanting to sample some more at that level. Even back then, we really did want to achieve something in Europe. That was incredible when you looked at how we were performing at home. Stevie Chalmers played in both ties, too, and it didn't do either of us any harm, did it?

'In actual fact, I kept my eye on Valencia's results as they defended their trophy. I wasn't one bit surprised that they retained the cup. I recall they beat the Yugoslavs of Dinamo Zagreb 2–1 away from home in the first leg of the final and then completed the job 2–0 in Valencia. They were a very good team and it was just our luck that we drew the holders in our first-ever European tie.

'It was interesting but ultimately disappointing. I can tell you that every single Celtic player who was around at the time wanted to bring success to our club, home and away. We, more than anyone, realised our fans deserved so much better. The way things were going around then was frustrating for us, too, believe me.'

The European excursion was snuffed out at the first hurdle, but it did leave Celtic free to concentrate on matters at home. The league was outwith their reach, but there was no way they would allow Rangers to saunter to the title. The Celtic players readied themselves to begin a dismantling job on their old rivals on the first day of 1963.

4

THE STUFF OF NIGHTMARES

'Can it get any worse than this?' That was the collective thought of the grim-faced, morose, thoroughly disheartened Celtic support as they filtered out of Ibrox Stadium on 1 January 1963. The reason for their plunge into the black hole of despair? Rangers 4, Celtic 0. And the answer to the earlier question was 'Yes. Much worse.' This was to turn out to be the year when allegiances were severely put to the test, the year when only those with the strongest of convictions would make it through to 1964.

It was one of those games in which the Rangers players seemed to spend more time in the Celtic half than the Celtic players. The visitors must have realised it was not going to be their day when defender Harold Davis got on the scoresheet, as he had done at Parkhead two years previously. The effort at Celtic Park had been half his goal tally for that season. He didn't score at all in 1962, and here he was planting another past Frank Haffey in a campaign that he would finish with a modest two goals to his name. Davis must have wished he could line up against Celtic every week; he could have become a contender for top goal-scorer.

Haffey was blameless. The defence in front of him simply disintegrated and Celtic's attack, starved of service, didn't function. 'It was never easy to accept defeat against Rangers,' said Billy McNeill. 'It was never easy to accept *any* defeat, but it was particularly hard against Rangers. Sadly, it was another match where we hadn't turned up. We were all getting sick of it.'

In 1963, alas, Celtic would have to get used to it. And they would have to get used to it without the services of their most creative player and on-field influence, Paddy Crerand. The volatile midfielder had a heated argument with coach Sean Fallon at the interval with the club trailing 1–0 at Ibrox. There were reports of Crerand throwing his jersey at the Irishman and he never played again for Celtic.

Years later, in his book *Never Turn the Other Cheek*, Crerand admitted:

[Bob] Kelly was the main reason why I came to leave Celtic. I never wanted to go, but my situation at the club became untenable. We played against Rangers at Ibrox on New Year's Day 1963; the game should never have been played because it was a brick hard pitch. I argued with the coach, Sean Fallon, with whom I normally got on well, about what kind of tactics we should play . . . In truth, Sean and I differed on our football theories that day and I couldn't hide my feelings any longer. We were trailing 1–0 when we trudged back into the dressing room and the lid came off.

'We need to knock long balls forward,' said Sean in a measured and firm manner.

'No, we need to pass the ball to feet,' I replied angrily. 'The long ball won't work.'

'No, we play long balls forward,' replied Sean, clearly agitated. 'And you, Crerand, don't move so far up the park.'

'I'm not going back on the field if we have to play like that,' I said. 'You don't know what you are talking about.' The toys had well and truly been thrown from my cot.

'You're wrong, Crerand, you're wrong,' Sean replied. I was, especially as there were no substitutes in those days, and after a few minutes I backed down and walked angrily back onto the pitch. Bob Kelly was in the dressing room and witnessed everything. He didn't say a word though. Nor did ten of my team-mates. It was me against the rest.

We were hammered 4–0 anyway . . . I was distraught and very angry when we returned to the dressing room, where I had another stand up row with just about every Celtic player and Sean. I adore Sean . . . But that day at Ibrox I was furious with everyone, especially Sean.

Mike Jackson didn't play but was in the dressing-room that fateful afternoon. He recalled, 'I was well and truly bombed out as far as the first team was concerned, but I went along to watch the game. For no apparent reason, Sean picked on Paddy during the interval. He blamed my mate for everything, including, I think, the sun not shining. It was way, way over the top. Now anyone who knew Paddy realised he would not take such abuse. Constructive criticism? No problem. Shouting and bawling? No chance. Sean eventually ran out of steam. Paddy looked at him and said, "See you, I used to watch you when I travelled on the supporters bus from the Gorbals every Saturday." He paused for a moment. "You were fuckin' useless!" He had just signed his death warrant. Bob

Kelly would come into the dressing-room at half-time in every game. An unusual practice for a chairman, I suppose, but he was an unusual chairman. I clocked him at that moment. He looked glum at the best of times. Now he looked as though he had just been informed his house had been burned down along with all his possessions and someone had nicked his car. I knew how much Celtic meant to Paddy. I said to him, "Watch yourself, pal." Paddy was totally wound up, though. He looked angry. Little did he know he had only 45 minutes left of his Celtic career.

'I knew I would be on my bike shortly, too. Like Paddy, the club and the fans meant the world to me. But, as I have often said, some players were clearly targeted and, for whatever reason, I was among them. I had been with Celtic for six years and had never received any sort of benefit payment. I knew John Hughes, with four years' service, had received something. Good luck to my old mate, but I would dig my heels in as far as being transferred was concerned. St Johnstone, then managed by Bobby Brown, who would become the Scotland international manager, liked me and I knew he was keen to get me. Jimmy McGrory called me into his office one morning to say St Johnstone had made a bid of £7,000, it had been accepted and I was now to talk to them. But I was in no rush to go anywhere. I would be due some sort of payment for agreeing to move to the Saints and eventually I was offered £250. The Perth team gave me £750, making the total £1,000. I think that was the same as Paddy received when he went to Manchester United and, remember, at £56,000, that was the British record transfer fee at the time. I don't know if he got a penny off Celtic.'

Crerand was dropped for the next game against Aberdeen. In *Never Turn the Other Cheek*, he wrote:

> It was obvious to me that the club either wanted rid of me or that I was just not good enough, despite being a Scottish international . . . Then I was dropped for a game against Falkirk. I decided that enough was enough and asked for a move . . . After 120 appearances and five goals, I would never play for Celtic again. Unbeknown to me, Bob Kelly and Matt Busby at Manchester United had an agreement that Matt would have first refusal on me if I ever left Celtic.
>
> . . . Jim Rodger, a journalist from the *Daily Record*, . . . was big pals with Matt Busby and, in later years, Alex Ferguson. He told me [one Sunday] that I was going to Manchester United . . . I went to Celtic Park for training the following morning and trained as normal. Nobody said anything to me and I assumed that Jim Rodger was wrong. Then, after training Jimmy McGrory asked for a word. He told me that there had

been talks between Celtic and Manchester United and that a fee had been agreed for me to move to England.

'That's what I've been told to tell you, Pat,' he said, as though it had nothing to do with him. Jimmy, despite being manager, wouldn't have had a choice whether I was sold or not as he would have been acting on Bob Kelly's orders. There was no room for negotiation, I was going to Manchester United and that was that.

. . . My head was spinning . . . [A] good friend, a bookmaker Tony Queen who was also a great pal of Jock Stein, [advised me,] 'Go to Manchester, Pat. Celtic are going nowhere.' Deep down, I knew he was right.

Crerand therefore witnessed at first hand the differences behind the scenes between Parkhead and Old Trafford. He wrote:

[Celtic] went on a tour of Ireland in the summer of 1960 and I played in every game . . . Billy McNeill had got into the team just before me and there was a feeling that a new wave of home grown Celts were coming through . . .

Some of the press bought it and coined the phrase 'the Kelly Kids'. One journalist even suggested that we would surpass the fame of the Busby Babes . . . You might have thought that with a headline like that Kelly, not Jimmy McGrory, was our manager . . . such was [Kelly's] power at the club that he picked the team, too. And that was the crux of the perennial problem at Parkhead.

Unlike at Old Trafford, Celtic had no Matt Busby-type figure with a long term plan. At Parkhead, there wasn't the quality among the trainers or the ambition from the board to spend money when it was needed. Jock Stein had the talent, but he was looking after the reserves and Jimmy McGrory wasn't really football manager material.

And, while Matt Busby let players serve an apprenticeship and blooded them when they were ready, Celtic did not. Players barely out of junior football were expected to play in Celtic's first team and cover for the experienced men who had left. Worse, they were played in different positions to cover for deficiencies. Jock had done that in the reserves because it made your game better and there was room to experiment. You couldn't take chances like that in the first team, but Celtic did. Billy McNeill played right-half, right-back and centre-half. He was a great footballer, but it was too big an ask for most of the young lads.

Crerand travelled to Aberdeen four days after the New Year derby but took no part in the game. Celtic clobbered their opponents 5–1. John

Hughes thumped a hat-trick beyond John Ogston. The goalkeeper was nicknamed 'Tubby', and if he was looking to lose a few pounds then he got plenty of exercise that afternoon. Bobby Craig netted the other two and the game welcomed Tommy Gemmell into the top team for the first time.

This laughing cavalier of a left-back would bring a brightness and a freshness to the side. He was one of the rare Celtic full-backs who had the desire to actually cross the halfway line. Gemmell said, 'I was an outside-right during my amateur footballing days, would you believe? You start out as a right-sided forward and you end up as a left-sided defender. How did that happen? Yes, it's true certain people in the Celtic dugout tried to curb my attacking instincts. "You're a defender, you're there to defend," I was told often enough.

'Sean Fallon made most of the on-field decisions and he threatened to drop me: "Hey, you, Gemmell! Cross that halfway line again and I'll make sure you're dropped for the next game." So what was I supposed to do? I wanted to remain in the first team, but I was eager to do my best for the club and I could often see opportunities to bomb forward and help out the attack. I thought if I hit the byline it would give, say, Frank Brogan, Stevie Chalmers or John Hughes, who were mainly our wingers back then, the opportunity to get into scoring positions and it could only help our options. I know it's an old cliché, but attack is the best form of defence. No one is going to score a goal from their half, are they? Or they shouldn't, anyway!'

There was also a surprise in store for Gemmell when the train rolled into Aberdeen station. 'There was only one taxi,' he recalled, 'and that was for all our gear. There was space for only two or three passengers, so Jimmy McGrory, Sean Fallon and another of our backroom staff always volunteered for that particular duty. Us? The players were told they would be walking from the railway station to the football ground, Pittodrie, about one-and-a-half miles away. "It'll get the stiffness out of your legs," I was assured. Could you imagine present-day footballers accepting that situation? When I realised no one was pulling my leg, stiff or otherwise, I joined the trek towards the ground. Neilly Mochan, still exceptionally fit, despite retiring from playing a couple of years beforehand, would march on up front. Honestly, we could hardly keep up with him and we would be actually playing in about an hour-and-a-half's time. Fans mingled with us. "How do you think you'll get on today, Big Man?" they asked. "Watch that centre-half of theirs, he's a dirty big so-and-so." We were offered all sorts of advice from our well-meaning supporters.

'I recall, very early in my career, being really excited about doing an interview with a local newspaper; actually I think it was the *Aberdeen Evening News*. It was a midweek fixture and we stayed overnight in a hotel. The night before the game, I was relaxing with the rest of the players when I was told there was a telephone call for me at the foyer. I picked up the receiver.

'"Is that Tommy Gemmell?" I was asked.

'"Yes."

'"Is that Tommy Gemmell of Celtic Football Club?"

'"Yes," I repeated.

'"This is Joe Smith of the *Aberdeen Evening News* and I would like to do a story on you. Are you OK for an interview?"

'I thought for a moment. "I'll have to see the boss, Mr McGrory. I'll need his permission."

'"OK, I'll hang on if you like."

'I sought out the manager and asked him for the go-ahead. He puffed on his pipe and said, "Sure, Tommy, no problem."

'I got back to the phone to tell the reporter, "Sure, that's fine."

'He replied, "Great, I'll see you outside your hotel in an hour."

'I was excited – an interview with the *Aberdeen Evening News*. Maybe he would bring a photographer with him and take a wee picture of me for the paper. I recall it being a very cold night as I stood on the steps outside the hotel. After an hour of shivering and shaking, I wondered what was going on. Another five minutes passed. And then another five minutes. And so on. Eventually, a teammate, I think it was Billy McNeill, popped his head round the door. "Come in, you daft bugger," he said. "You've been set up."

'My heart sank. No exclusive interview in the local newspaper, no picture of yours truly. I was devastated. I never did discover who the culprit was, but it could have been one of around twenty. One thing that did amaze me, though, was the fact that Jimmy McGrory was in on the joke. Thanks, boss!'

Gemmell had another interesting memory of the early days. He recalled, 'Some of the lads used to go back to Celtic Park on a Sunday morning for a bit of voluntary exercise. I suppose it was our version of the warm-down, as it's now called. We didn't think about sticking a label on it back then; it was just a simple way of relaxing the muscles and toning up your body. Most of the boys in and around Glasgow went through this routine, but you couldn't expect, say, Bobby Lennox to come up from Saltcoats to join in. One thing that struck me, though, was the fans cleaning up the ground after the previous day's game. Celtic had three supporters clubs in Bridgeton and these guys would turn up on a Sunday morning to be given these massive brushes. They swept the terracings and were allowed to keep the empty beer bottles. Those were the good old days when a fan could take a crate of ale into the ground on Saturday and no one took a blind bit of notice. It wasn't illegal in the early '60s, of course. Watching football was probably their main entertainment of the week and they came suitably equipped to enjoy their day out. Jock Stein always reminded us of how important these guys were. "You'll be playing in front of supporters who work down mines, on building sites, on buses, up ladders throughout the week – go out and entertain them. They deserve that."

'So these guys were there on a Sunday morning going through their ritual. What a good job they did of it, too. They were working for Celtic Football Club in some sort of capacity and they were very thorough. Their reward was the money they would get back on the beer bottles. I think there used to be a 3d – just over one new pence – refund on them at most pubs, and these blokes would pick up their cash and put it back into their particular supporters club. Of course, Celtic were quite happy with the arrangement; it meant they never had to part with a penny to get their stadium cleaned from top to bottom.'

Gemmell must have ventured forward too often for someone's liking in his Aberdeen debut because there was no sign of him for the next league game, a 3–1 win at home to Airdrie. Jim Kennedy, never keen on adventure, had returned to the left-back position and he seemed quite content to potter around in his own half. That would earn him a gold star in his jotter. Gemmell recalled, 'Jim wasn't the most enterprising type and rarely ventured into the other team's half. He had other strengths, though. For a start, he would kick his granny!'

Gemmell returned for the visit to Palmerston to face Queen of the South a few games later. Again, he figured in a team that scored five goals on their travels, winning 5–2. Bobby Craig claimed the only hat-trick of his Celtic career and John McNamee and Frank Brogan got the others. Gemmell remembered, 'I was thoroughly enjoying the experience of first-team football. It was extremely difficult to hold myself back, though. I would see play developing in front of me and I would be thinking, "I can get forward here, use Frank Brogan as a decoy and get the ball into their box." I couldn't help myself. However, I felt as though if I strayed into enemy territory this giant hook would appear and haul me off the pitch!'

Five goals at Aberdeen and Gemmell was dropped for the next game. Five goals at Queen of the South – would he be dropped again? He would. Kennedy returned to the number 3 berth for the match against

Raith Rovers, in which Celtic eased to a 4–1 victory. 'I was beginning to wonder if I would ever get the opportunity to play in front of the Celtic fans at Parkhead,' mused Gemmell.

Surely he would get his chance after the next match? Kennedy had an absolute nightmare against Kilmarnock at Rugby Park. Haffey was injured and Celtic hurriedly introduced Dick Madden, only 18 years old, as their new goalkeeper. It was hardly the debut he might have selected. Kilmarnock 6, Celtic 0 was the final score and Madden, like Goldie three years before him, would go into the history books as a Celtic goalkeeper who made a solitary appearance for the club. His family won £10,000 on the football pools that week and the players urged him to buy a pub. 'You can call it the Lets Six Inn,' he was told helpfully. Another Celtic debutant that night had a vastly different career path: a wee red-haired outside-right called Jimmy Johnstone.

Billy McNeill missed the debacle through injury and John Cushley stepped into central defence. It wasn't that memorable for him, either. McNeill said, 'I watched the game from the stand and it was a total embarrassment. It was 90 minutes' worth of torture. If any one match summed up Celtic at the time, it was that one. Don't get me wrong, Kilmarnock were a very good and able side, but they shouldn't have been wiping the floor with Celtic.'

Bertie Auld said, 'I was still with Birmingham City at the time and I was watching the news on the Wednesday night. The Rugby Park scoreline flashed up. "That's got to be a mistake," I said to my wife, Liz. "Celtic don't lose six goals to Kilmarnock." I telephoned a friend immediately. He confirmed the scoreline. I said, "Someone will swing for that, Liz." And out went the poor goalkeeper. But everyone knew the real problems lay elsewhere.'

At the completion of another wretched and shambolic campaign, Celtic finished 4th in the table with 44 points, Rangers reclaimed their crown with 57 points. Kilmarnock, with 48 points, took the runners-up place and Partick Thistle, on 46, were 3rd.

If there was despair in the league for Celtic, there was disaster ahead in the Scottish Cup. After beating off the challenges of Falkirk (2–0), Hearts (3–1), non-league Gala Fairydean (6–0), St Mirren (1–0) and Raith Rovers (5–2), Celtic took their place in the Scottish Cup final on 4 May at Hampden. Rangers would be the opponents.

Can it get any worse than this? That was the question posed by the Celtic fans after the New Year thumping, a seven-game failure rate in that fixture interrupted only by Jack Frost the previous year. The green-and-white legions were on the verge of finding out, but, first, there was a shaft of light, a flicker of hope. A crowd of 129,643 crammed into Hampden for the cup final and no one, and I mean no one, could believe what they witnessed.

Frank Haffey, so often a figure of fun, decided to put on a spectacular show that defied Rangers, being beaten only once, by a strike just before half-time from Ralph Brand that was nullified almost immediately by an effort from Bobby Murdoch. Haffey's performance was awesome. He plunged, swooped, leaped and dived this way and that way in a breathtaking display of acrobatics and heroics. The ball became a magnet to his yellow jersey.

Another Celt putting on a mesmerising solo show was little Jimmy Johnstone on the right wing. This bundle of mischief – likened by one newspaper reporter to Harpo Marx, with his head of bouncing, curly red hair – had been introduced for three league games near the conclusion of that campaign. Davie Provan was in at left-back for the injured Eric Caldow and he looked as though he would much rather have been anywhere else than a football stadium situated in Mount Florida as his opponent continually teased and tormented him. The *Scotsman* newspaper noted, 'That little fellow Johnstone was very good and it's difficult to remember him not using the ball well. He seems cut out to be a Hampden personality.'

Everyone knew Celtic's selection process could bewilder even the brightest of intelligences, boggle the sharpest of minds, but what happened next completely beggared belief. Staggeringly, Johnstone was dropped for the replay and the poor wee chap went to his grave never knowing why anyone would make such a preposterous decision. Totally inexplicable, utterly absurd. There is meddling and then there is madness. The two names that should have been first on the team list for the second game were Haffey and Johnstone. No argument. Johnstone later said, 'I felt it wasn't Jimmy McGrory's decision because I don't think he was that influential. Bob Kelly ruled everything. Amazing, but these were the type of decisions that were being made.'

Bobby Craig came into the side at outside-right and Davie Provan, realising he wouldn't have to endure 90 minutes being tortured by a pirouetting prankster, must have heaved a mighty sigh of relief, all his Christmases and birthdays arriving on 15 May. The Celtic fans among the 120,273 crowd trekked to Hampden that Wednesday evening fully expecting to see their snake-hipped wee winger in action again. They didn't have a clue about the line-up until it was announced over the tannoy just before kick-off. Johnstone's name was missing. There was general shrugging of shoulders and mystified looks among the support.

'Johnstone must be injured,' was the chorus. How wrong they were. A perfectly fit Jimmy Johnstone watched from the stand that evening, powerless to help a team that was about to be put to the sword.

Alas, Haffey was unable to reproduce the performance of the earlier game. Instead, he reverted to type, the flawed character who frustrated teammate and supporter alike. He flapped at a right-wing cross, palmed it down in front of Ralph Brand, and the ball was in the net early in the proceedings. Davie Wilson added a second shortly afterwards and it was game over. With 20 minutes to go, Brand tried his luck from 25 yards. It wasn't quite a net-buster, but it was enough to bounce past the collapsing Haffey, and that was the signal for a fair percentage of the Celtic support to head for the exits.

Billy McNeill recalled, 'We couldn't cope with Rangers that night. In truth, we were outclassed. Jim Baxter was in supreme form. He wanted to take the mickey and there was little we could do about it. Of course, I knew him well. I sidled up to him at one stage and said, "Right, Stanley, that's enough of the showboating for the night." He just grinned. Stanley was his nickname, after the comedian Stanley Baxter.'

Tommy Gemmell, who watched the horror show from the Hampden stand alongside Johnstone, recalled, 'It was always difficult to keep a smile off Jinky's face. He made light of everything, nothing seemed to bother him. He knew he had played well in the first game, but there wasn't a murmur from the Wee Man when he was told he wasn't required for the replay. Later on, though, he would look back on that game every now and again. A solemn expression would come across his face. "Tam," he would ask, "remember that cup final? Dae ye think Ah could huv made a difference?" I answered as I always answered, "Of course, Jinky, of course." Then he would smile again.'

Bobby Craig was on the pitch that night, but it would be fair to say he contributed as much as the little bloke with the flaming red hair sitting in Row E. The result was a total embarrassment, the display unacceptable, the team selection unfathomable.

How would Celtic attempt to turn things around during the summer of 1963? Craig never figured in the first team again. Left-half Billy Price would be on his way after only six more appearances. Haffey was shown the door after 17 games and right-back Dunky MacKay would only play 11 more games before being offloaded to Third Lanark. Jim Kennedy, thankfully, never played again at left-back, where his lack of pace had been repeatedly exposed by raiding right-wingers such as Rangers' Willie Henderson. John McNamee, who played alongside McNeill in the cup final replay, was seen in only five more games and Frank Brogan, who played in the first match against Rangers, was shipped out to Ipswich Town after another twelve first-team outings.

Around this time, there seemed absolutely no pattern or planning to what was going on behind the scenes at Parkhead. One minute a player was good enough to feature in an Old Firm cup final and the next he was out the door. In short, Celtic were in a mess, lacking leadership and guidance.

Once more, the fans were left pondering the future. Was there a messiah out there? Morton had attracted a lot of attention in their promotion surge from the Second Division with a fantastic total of 135 goals in their 36 games. Allan McGraw netted more than 50 times in an extraordinary campaign and the scouts flocked to Cappielow, Celtic's among them. McGraw was unstoppable, the man in form. So Celtic bought Irishman Paddy Turner, a neat little right-sided midfielder. He cost £8,000 and didn't quite set the heather on fire. In fact, he played only 13 first-team games, didn't even last a year and was quite happy to move on to Irish side Glentoran. It was yet another illustration of money squandered. Celtic had also been interested in St Mirren's midfielder George McLean earlier in the year, but they beat a hasty retreat when Rangers came on the scene and wrote a cheque for £27,500. There was no way Celtic would even attempt to match that sort of fee.

As luck would have it, Celtic and Rangers were paired in the League Cup sections and the season kicked off at Parkhead on 10 August. The home support must have wondered if they were being forced to watch an action replay of the Scottish Cup final. Celtic 0, Rangers 3 was the scoreline and even the most optimistic home fan among the 60,022 crowd must have realised this was not going to be a memorable campaign. Jim Forrest rattled two past Haffey and the aforementioned McLean rubbed it in with another.

Four days later, Celtic drew 0–0 with Kilmarnock at Rugby Park before the powder keg went up in the most astonishing fashion against Queen of the South in Glasgow on 17 August. Frank Brogan scored in a lamentable 1–1 draw against a team that would be relegated at the end of the season. That game afforded them their only League Cup point and they would go on to concede twenty goals in their six games, ten of them to Rangers. On that particular afternoon, though, the Celtic support decided to stage a demonstration outside the main entrance after witnessing another dreadful display. 'Kelly out!' was the cry. The fans remained for well over an hour before the intervention of police and stewards persuaded them to disperse. It was an ugly incident and there was a frightening mood of revolt in the air. Enough was enough. A week later, Celtic were turned over again by Rangers, 3–0 for the third consecutive occasion. The older fans among the Celtic support reminisced about the good old days when the team had a backbone.

Gemmell recalled, 'It was difficult being a Celtic player at the time. We knew we were letting down the fans, but, no matter how hard we tried, we just couldn't get round that corner. The crowds were turning on us and that didn't help, but, at the same time, you couldn't blame the man on the terracing. Following Celtic was everything to them and, believe me, the players, or most of us, anyway, realised it. I can also remember a day when the fans were gathering outside the main door before a game. It looked like a prearranged meeting among some supporters clubs and they were letting us know what they expected that particular afternoon. There was a popular television show at the time called *Your Life in Their Hands*, and when Bob Kelly appeared in the dressing-room, looking gaunt and apprehensive, he told us, "You've got my life in your hands." He was deadly serious. He was the main culprit as far as the Celtic supporters were concerned. The truth is he was a Celtic man, but I think his main problem was that he thought he *was* Celtic.'

Rangers won 2–1 in the third Old Firm encounter and it was obvious to all it was going to be yet another long, hard season. Then came a crazy encounter with Third Lanark that summed up Celtic perfectly. Goals from Brogan, Lennox, Divers and Turner, his solitary counter in green and white, gave them a 4–0 half-time lead over Third Lanark. The final result? Would you believe 4–4?

Gemmell played that day, and he recalled, 'We were superb in the first 45 minutes. We were striking passes all over the place and every shot seemed to be hitting the Thirds' net. Goodness knows what happened after the interval. We just became a completely different team. Simply put, we couldn't do a thing right.'

The supporters were getting used to league title ambitions being dismantled before the turn of the year, and the nightmare scenario was being played out in front of them again as their favourites faltered. One win in the opening five league games was never going to be good enough to halt the misery. It was tough being a Celtic supporter at that time, very tough. The balance of power had settled in Govan and it would take something or someone special to change the situation. Celtic did not possess that special individual. Not at that stage, anyway.

Mind you, as Billy McNeill has often asserted, it wasn't dull while Celtic were around. They took nine off poor Airdrie in October that year, with good mates Johnny Divers and John Hughes helping themselves to hat-tricks while Charlie Gallagher, Bobby Murdoch and Stevie Chalmers notched singles. There was an amusing moment late in the game when the referee awarded Celtic a penalty kick. The crowd roared for goalkeeper Frank Haffey to take the award and the other players motioned for him to come forward. Sure enough, up stepped Haffey to blaze the ball goalwards, only to see his opposite number, Roddie McKenzie, punch the effort to safety. Years later, Haffey, somewhat proudly, would say, 'Do you know I am the only Celtic goalkeeper in history to take a penalty kick?'

The colourful custodian was coming to the end of a remarkable career at Celtic. The hierarchy could no longer tolerate his outrageous antics and, after a 5–3 success over Partick Thistle, it was all over for Haffey. It was just as well the forwards were on their game against the Firhill side, because Haffey was throwing them in at the other end. He clearly believed one lobbed effort from Ian Cowan was going over the bar and made little attempt to save it. There was a look of horror on his face as the ball dipped and ended up in the net. Chalmers, with a hat-trick, Johnstone and Hughes spared his blushes as they stuck five past George Niven, the same keeper who had conceded seven in Celtic's last silverware success, at Hampden in 1957. Haffey was actually laughing as he came off the pitch that day, but no one in the directors' box saw the joke.

Gemmell said, 'It appeared absolutely nothing could upset Frank. I was told later on by my old chum Denis Law that he was going to drown Big Frank in the bath at Wembley after Scotland had lost 9–3 to England. Denis couldn't believe his ears when he heard someone merrily singing after one of the most embarrassing results in our history. He searched out the culprit. It was Frank, warbling away, apparently without a care in the world. Even worse, Denis told me, he actually wasn't too bad as a singer. What he thought of him as a goalkeeper, though, was unprintable.'

In came John Fallon, unspectacular but more reliable, and the nerves of the Celtic defenders could stop jangling, for the time being, anyway. Rangers were due at Parkhead on 1 January. Would Celtic at long last put an end to the horrible run of New Year's Day failures that had left strong men weeping into their beer? Would 1964 see a change in fortunes? Would the sun be blotted out by flying pigs? All would be revealed.

5

THE NEARLY MEN

The Celtic supporters' annual rendezvous with misery and heartache. Another New Year's Day game. Another New Year's Day defeat. By now, the Celtic fans were ushering in new years with weary emotions, fearful apprehension replacing eager anticipation. Hopes simply faded away like smoke on a nippy January day. A sell-out crowd of just over 65,000 made it to Parkhead on the first day of January 1964 to see if Celtic could buck the festive trend. A goal from Jimmy Millar provided the answer: Celtic 0, Rangers 1.

Tommy Gemmell recalled, 'That was my first Old Firm game and I would have been a lot more impressed if we had actually won. It was a fascinating encounter and I could see why all the old stagers who used to frequent Celtic Park went on endlessly about these fixtures. Remember, these were the days when the attendance was split 50–50. Celtic had their half of the ground and Rangers had the other half. So when they scored there was this remarkable sight of half of the ground singing and dancing and the other half totally silent. It was a weird experience, to say the least. We played well enough that day, as I remember. I'm not being churlish when I say that if there was a break of the ball it went Rangers' way. You get games like that. But it was a hell of an afternoon and I was left wanting more. Somehow I knew we would get the upper hand. Eventually.'

Celtic could still entertain, though. Shortly after the Rangers defeat, they hammered Falkirk 7–0, with Stevie Chalmers notching a hat-trick. A photograph appeared in the newspapers the following day of Falkirk keeper Willie Whigham sitting on his backside, covered from top to toe in mud, the ball nestling behind him in the net for the seventh time. Remarkably, he was smiling; possibly he was in a state of shock.

Billy McNeill said, 'When we clicked, we reckoned we could beat anyone. If we scored one, we wanted a second. If we scored a second, we went in search of a third. I don't recall us ever sitting on a lead back then. We were probably a bit naive, but we always tried to put on a show for our supporters. The sad thing is we weren't doing it in the games that really mattered. Yes, we could take nine off Airdrie and seven off Falkirk, but the Celtic fans were waiting for us to achieve something against Rangers. Those, clearly, were the games that mattered.'

Quietly, and almost imperceptibly, things were changing at Celtic. Gemmell was becoming an automatic choice at left-back, Jimmy Johnstone was getting an extended run at outside-right – without any decisions, verging on the idiotic, to chop and change – Stevie Chalmers was now permanently in from the wing to lead the attack and John Hughes was being utilised as an outside-left. Frank Haffey's perplexing performance in the 5–3 win over Partick Thistle was to be his last in a Celtic jersey. It was somehow fitting that the keeper should say his farewells with another extravagant display of mishaps. Celtic Park would never be the same again. Billy McNeill and co. would sleep more easily at night. Opposition forwards would have to work that little bit harder. Haffey lasted just one year at Swindon Town before packing up altogether and moving to Australia. Some would say it still wasn't far enough removed from the East End of Glasgow.

A week that typified the eccentricities and inconsistencies of Celtic around that time arrived in March. The team fired on all cylinders as they overwhelmed a strong Hibs side 5–0 in Glasgow, but seven days later they were turned over 4–0 by Kilmarnock at Rugby Park. The league was blown early and the Scottish Cup once again represented the club's best chance of silverware. But no one was holding their breath when the quarter-final draw paired Celtic with Rangers at Ibrox in March. It didn't augur well.

Rangers didn't need a helping hand in their encounters with Celtic back then, but the unfortunate John Fallon gave them one anyway. Taking a leaf from the Frank Haffey Book of Blunders, Fallon gifted the opening goal to the club's fiercest foes. A corner kick dropped into the penalty box and Fallon, challenged by Ralph Brand, gave it the bar-of-soap treatment. It fell perfectly for Jim Forrest, smack in front of goal, and he couldn't miss from six yards. It was all over when Willie Henderson scored a wonderful solo goal. The tantalising outside-right, who would eventually be eclipsed by Jimmy Johnstone, raced past three defenders before unleashing a drive from the edge of the box that hurtled past the helpless Celtic keeper. The domestic season ended there and then as the net bulged behind the flapping Fallon.

'Willie was a smashing wee player,' said Gemmell, who faced him that day. 'My best trick was to force him inside and let the other defenders try to cope with him. I did that during that cup tie, but it didn't stop him driving past every tackle. His finishing shot was brilliant, but I never got round to telling him that when I was talking to him after the game. Willie's problem was that Jinky came on the scene a couple of years behind him and I have to admit Celtic's Wee Man was just a shade better than Rangers' Wee Man. Willie has just about admitted as much, but I don't think there is any shame in being edged by the best in the world. It really is just a shame they were around at the same time. I remember when Billy Bremner was captain of Scotland and he went to the international boss at the time, Bobby Brown, and asked if there was any way he could fit them into the same team. Brown, apparently, didn't hesitate. "What? And give them a ball each?" That was fair comment.'

Celtic still had to perform on the European stage, having qualified for the Cup-Winners' Cup as Scottish Cup runners-up, and, rather remarkably, they had reached the semi-finals by the time April arrived. The run had got off to an astonishing start with a 5–1 victory over Basel in Switzerland in September 1963. The headlines in the national press informed us it was a 'Swiss Roll for Celtic'. Hughes became the first Celt in history to score a hat-trick in Europe, with Divers and Lennox delivering the other two. Basel didn't represent much of an obstacle, either, in the return at Parkhead, when they conceded another five without reply.

The wonderful European adventure continued in December with a 3–0 victory over a very good Yugoslav side in Dinamo Zagreb, and Celtic survived a 2–1 defeat in the away leg. Then they faced Czechoslovakian cup-winners Slovan Bratislava, whose line-up included many of the players who had represented their country in the 3–1 defeat against Brazil in the World Cup final two years beforehand. Goalkeeper Viliam Schrojf was one of their biggest names, but he was left powerless when Bobby Murdoch slotted home the only goal of the game via the penalty spot in Glasgow. It was the slenderest of leads, but Celtic doubled their advantage when Hughes scored in the second leg with an excellent solo effort.

There was an extraordinary and refreshing feel to Parkhead during the club's European excursion. The woes on the home front could be shelved while a journey into the unknown was made. Hungary's MTK Budapest arrived in Glasgow for the first leg of the semi-final and it was difficult to comprehend that Celtic could be a mere three hours away from a glamorous European final, to be held in Brussels. It was all very exotic and exciting facing up to players with unpronounceable names. Gemmell said, 'In truth, we didn't know a lot about the teams we were up against.

These were the days when you didn't send scouts to have a look at the opposition. Goodness knows how long it would have taken to get to Hungary in 1964. I'm sure the opposition wouldn't have known an awful lot about Jinky, Yogi, Big Caesar or me, for that matter. It all added to the intrigue.'

Chalmers took his goal haul in Europe to five with two opportunist efforts against MTK Budapest, and Johnstone added another in a splendid 3–0 triumph. The Celtic players disappeared down the tunnel after a memorable 90 minutes, but had to reappear when they were told the joyous 60,000 support had no intention of leaving the ground until they had taken a lap of honour. Fans left Parkhead that night already planning ways to get to Belgium for the final. Could the old Hillman Imp stand the rigours of the journey? Sadly, it was all a bit premature.

What went wrong? John Hughes takes up the story. 'No one knew what to expect back then. Tactics? We never discussed them. We just went out and played our natural game and that was to attack. It didn't matter where we played, home or abroad, that was how we went about our business. You could say we were just a shade naive. Nowadays, if you are three goals ahead, you would probably be told to play it tight, keep the ball and hit on the break. Not in the early '60s, though. After winning the first leg against the Hungarians, we were expected to go all the way. Once again, though, we showed an alarming lack of tactical skills.

'Robert Kelly was our chairman, but he was also in charge of team selection. He told us we had beaten MTK in Glasgow by playing in a good, attacking manner and we could beat them again in Budapest playing the same way. That's how he wanted Celtic to perform, on the offensive all the time. Once more, we went into the game without any sort of defensive plan. We were halfway there after the first match, but we were still chasing the game. The Hungarians couldn't believe it. They must have expected us to erect a defensive wall in front of our keeper, but, instead, we came out and attacked. They took full advantage and won 4–0. Unbelievable. A laudable outlook, but totally unrealistic.'

Gemmell added, 'Yogi's right. We weren't told to contain them in any way. We were actually ordered to take the game to them. Gung-ho stuff. Absolute suicide. That might have been OK if we had had guys like Real Madrid possessed, but we didn't. It didn't take the Hungarians long to twig we were playing with a full complement of forwards who rarely helped out in defence.

'I recall they had a little winger called Sándor and he made my life hell in Budapest. He was very tricky, in the Willie Henderson mould, and just kept coming at me for the entire 90 minutes. We were completely overrun. MTK must have wished they could have played us on their ground every week. They would have won everything in sight.

'We had just thrown away a three-goal advantage in the semi-final of the second most important European trophy and I don't recall anyone getting a telling off. We had gone out playing "the Celtic Way" and the hierarchy didn't appear to be too perturbed. Do that today and there'll be a lynching party waiting for you at Glasgow Airport!'

That was the end of Europe. It was also the end of the season, without a Scottish Cup final to look forward to. In usual Celtic fashion, there had been soaring highs mixed with plunging lows. The positives could be seen in McNeill, Gemmell, Murdoch, Johnstone, Hughes and Chalmers. They were becoming assured first-teamers. But, annoyingly, there was still little or no direction off the field.

The chairman appeared to revel in the club's moniker of 'the Kelly Kids' and when there was criticism he would dismiss it with an oft-repeated phrase: 'Come back in two years.' Sadly, Kelly had been uttering those same words since before the turn of the decade and nothing was happening on the silverware front. It was all very well a young Celtic side gelling together to provide spectacles every now and again, but there was no consistency or scope for long-term optimism. The tide of expectation among the supporters was being repelled time and time again.

Worse still, Celtic's captain, Billy McNeill, was capturing admiring glances from across the border. He revealed, 'I was aware of interest from Spurs. People also mentioned Manchester United and I have to admit it would have been intriguing teaming up again with Paddy Crerand. But the main interest was definitely coming from White Hart Lane and Tottenham's manager, Bill Nicholson. I had no thoughts of leaving Celtic, but I am only human, and you couldn't help wondering if things were going to change. It was no fun going through season after season without a hint of a trophy. Rangers ruled the roost and that was difficult to accept. Money didn't come into it. I'd talked with the Anglos in the Scottish international squads; we all realised there was more cash in England. Genuinely, though, I wanted to do a job for Celtic, but it was becoming more and more frustrating. Was I ever tempted? Of course I was. Something held me back, though, and thank God for that. I always hoped there was something going to happen. And then along came Jock Stein and it was a completely different story.'

The opening game of season 1964–65 again emphasised that all was far from well with Celtic's methods. They kicked off against Partick Thistle in the League Cup at Parkhead and had to settle for a goalless draw. 'Here we go again,' seemed to be the consensus among the supporters as they drifted away after a fairly tedious 90 minutes. And yet better things were around the corner. For a start, not only did Celtic qualify from their League Cup group for the first time in five years, but they got all the way to the final.

East Fife, performing at a mediocre level in the old Second Division, barred the path to the semi-final. Surely this was the start of something good? Celtic could even go into the midweek encounter at Methil after a 3–1 Old Firm success at Parkhead the previous Saturday, 5 September. There was no need for meddling in team matters on this occasion. Celtic put out the same side against the Fifers and promptly collapsed to a 2–0 defeat.

It wasn't the end of the world – or the League Cup – and fans returned to Glasgow that evening still believing that events could be turned around. Stevie Chalmers certainly thought so. He was like a green-and-white tornado as he pierced the East Fife defence time and again with his electrifying bursts of speed. He rattled in five goals and Jim Kennedy, having finally found a compass to direct him to the opposition's goal, netted too, in a landslide 6–0 triumph.

Morton, who were consolidating their place in the First Division after their meteoric promotion of the previous season, were the semi-final opponents at Ibrox on 29 September when Rangers met Dundee United at Hampden.

John Cushley was again in at centre-half instead of Billy McNeill, while Bobby Lennox replaced John Hughes at outside-left against the Greenock side. It proved to be a wise decision by someone – credit where credit is due – and Lennox scored, with Charlie Gallagher claiming the other in a hard-fought and well-earned 2–0 success.

Rangers' young centre-forward Jim Forrest was revelling in the competition and brought his goal total to an astonishing 16, scoring both in the 2–1 win over Dundee United. Rangers, in fact, were only minutes from defeat when Forrest snatched an equaliser and then struck the winner in extra time. Unhappily, Forrest hadn't quite finished with business in the League Cup, as he demonstrated in the 2–1 final success over Celtic at the national stadium on 24 October. A school of thought among what passed for Celtic's management held that Cushley was more mobile than McNeill on the deck, where Forrest did his best work. McNeill, of course, had no peers when it came to aerial work. There were few frills with the Rangers frontman, whose short backswing often took goalkeepers by surprise. That was exactly what happened that dreary afternoon as he outmanoeuvred Cushley on two occasions and slipped a pair of simple efforts beyond the exposed Fallon. Jimmy

Johnstone squeezed one in, but it wasn't to be. Were Celtic destined to be known as nearly men?

'We were all over the place at that stage of the season,' groaned Gemmell. 'It was astonishing that we even managed to reach the final of the League Cup. *Any* cup! Four days after the defeat from Rangers, we took on Kilmarnock at Rugby Park and that wouldn't have been the game of my choice coming on the back of a cup final disappointment. Killie were a really strong team at the time. So you might have thought we would have shored up the defence, believing a point at their place was a point gained and not one lost. The powers that be didn't think along those lines, sadly. Nope. They put in Charlie Gallagher and Bobby Lennox for Johnny Divers and John Hughes, and we were told to attack our opponents. I did as I was told and cracked one in from distance. Charlie added another. Unfortunately, they dumped five behind Fallon. A typical Celtic performance, I suppose.'

The 1964–65 league campaign had begun with the usual staccato procedure of stop, start, stop, start. Chalmers, Murdoch and Lennox shared the goals in the opening day 3–1 victory at Motherwell on 19 August. Rangers were the next opponents and successes against the Govan side were few and far between in the early '60s. Chalmers, however, appeared to enjoy jousts with Ronnie McKinnon during these tense occasions, and he fired two beyond Billy Ritchie. Rangers manager Scot Symon fielded the robust Roger Hynd, normally a wing-half, at right-back in direct opposition to John Hughes on the left wing. It didn't quite work and Yogi scored the other Celtic goal. Davie Wilson got his side's consolation.

It had been an encouraging showing from Celtic, but, true to form, they then drew 1–1 with Clyde, had an identical scoreline against Dundee United and nosedived 2–4 to Hearts at Tynecastle.

They had, at last, overwhelmed their greatest rivals, but they had then carelessly thrown away four points in the next three games. However, Rangers struggled too, and this looked like it could be the season for someone to mount a serious challenge on the championship, won the previous two years by the Ibrox outfit. Sadly, that threat was not going to come from Celtic. There was also the ignominy of a 3–0 defeat by a distinctly average St Johnstone side for the supporters to contend with.

Celtic, as usual, had hardly been active in the transfer market, but they did make a move for Falkirk inside-forward Hugh Maxwell, who had taken the eye back in the League Cup sections in August when he netted four in his side's 5–2 win over Dundee United. Mind you, they were *all* penalty kicks!

The Glasgow team parted with £15,000 for the player and he made his debut in front of a confused Celtic support against Dundee at Parkhead in November. There had been nothing in that day's newspapers about Celtic signing a new player and if you got in late and missed the tannoy announcement you had no idea who the tall, skinny, red-haired bloke wearing the number 10 shorts was. Hugh Maxwell was not a household name, and hardly an instantly recognisable figure. Probably not even in Falkirk, either.

It wasn't a debut to remember. Celtic went down 2–0 and Maxwell hardly got a kick of the ball. You only get one opportunity to make a first impression and sadly for the new boy his had passed him by.

Celtic went through the usual topsy-turvy routine as the turn of the year approached. They beat Partick Thistle 4–2 and then lost 1–2 at home to Dunfermline. The last action of 1964 saw Hughes firing in a couple in a 2–0 victory over Motherwell at Parkhead on Boxing Day. The cry from the terracing at the time was 'Feed the Bear! Feed the Bear!', referring to Yogi, and, it must be said, he rarely disappointed when he got decent service.

Celtic got another taste of European competition in 1964, but the club and the fans saw precious little of the drama that had unfolded in the Cup-Winners' Cup. There was no disgrace, though, in going out to Barcelona before 1965 dawned.

Bobby Murdoch gave Celtic a very creditable 1–1 draw against Leixões in the first leg of their Inter-Cities Fairs Cup tie in Portugal in September and he hammered in a penalty kick, with Chalmers adding two more, in the second game in Glasgow a fortnight later for a 3–0 triumph.

In November, Ronnie Simpson, at the age of 33, made his first appearance for the club, but was powerless to prevent a 3–1 defeat at the hands of Barcelona. It was Hughes who scored, and hopes were high for a surprise in Glasgow. The Spaniards, so flamboyant in front of their own fans in the Nou Camp, showed their other side and shut up shop in the second leg. The match ended goalless, but it was another lesson learned in an exciting arena.

Gemmell observed, 'You had to hope that someone from the Celtic management had twigged that even the great Barcelona knew when to put up the barriers and protect what they had after a first-leg advantage. Well, you had to hope.'

Charlie Gallagher was one of the most consistent Celtic players of that year. Essentially, he was used to pull the strings in the middle of the park, but he was also the possessor of a powerful shot, which he had put to good use since the start of the year, with 12 goals to his credit. That wasn't bad for a player who performed behind the likes of Hughes, Chalmers, Divers and Johnstone. The problem with Gallagher, in the eyes of most supporters, was that he lacked a little bit of devilment, some dig. He wasn't a ball-winner. Celtic would find someone who had those qualities in spades in 1965, and they'd solve a few other problems, too.

6

SILVER SERVICE – AGAIN

Ronnie Simpson, whose father, Jimmy, was a former Rangers player, made his Old Firm debut on 1 January 1965. New goalkeeper, same old outcome, with Jim Forrest claiming the only goal of a fairly drab contest that wasn't helped by the dodgy pitch. Studs crunched on the carpet of frost as conditions deteriorated while the game wore on. The Ibrox playing surface gleamed under the floodlights and managed to look very picturesque. A winter wonderland for Celtic fans it was not. Once again, they had little to enthuse over following a derby reverse at the turn of the year.

Nevertheless, the support were more than a little intrigued by what the club did next, two weeks into the new year. Celtic brought back Bertie Auld, sold to Birmingham City for £15,000 in April 1961. They paid £12,000 for a player who, like his good friend Paddy Crerand, was never slow to voice an opinion in the dressing-room. It was an unusual step for the club, but who was behind the transfer? It was unlikely to have been chairman Bob Kelly, who must have had a major say in Auld, against his wishes, leaving in the first place. Was it Jimmy McGrory, the manager being given his place, albeit belatedly? Was it Sean Fallon, who had more to do with the coaching and running of the first team than anyone else? Or was there the possibility of Jock Stein, still manager of Hibs, laying down some groundwork before returning to Celtic?

Bertie Auld attempted to shed some light on the topic. 'I was at home when I received a telephone call from a guy called Dougie Hepburn, who just happened to be a big pal of Jock Stein. He asked, "Would you like to come back to Celtic?" I didn't hesitate. "When? Tonight?" I said. I have to admit I think it was Big Jock who was behind the signing. The following day, Birmingham City were due to play West Ham in a cup tie and I was overjoyed to see Sean Fallon there with another guy I knew, Tommy Reilly. He had driven Sean down to Upton Park and, as soon as I saw them, I knew it wasn't a wind-up. I was indeed heading home. I recall bumping into Big Jock when he was down in Birmingham to take in an English League v. Scottish League game around about that time. He was accompanied by Bob Kelly. The Hibs manager with the Celtic chairman? I'll let you draw your own conclusions.

'Anyway, Big Jock was quite chatty and said, "How are things going, Bertie? Enjoying yourself?" I answered, "I'm having a great time. I've just become a father, too. Everything is wonderful." Big Jock rarely if ever indulged in small talk, but on this occasion he seemed genuinely interested in what was going on in my life, on and off the pitch. Anyway, history now shows I returned to the club I never wanted to leave in the first place in January 1965. I even agreed to take a £5 drop in my wages, a lot of money at the time. I'm convinced my wife, Liz, must have thought I was going off my head. So, I came back to my spiritual home and Big Jock was to join up formally at Celtic two months later. It could have been a coincidence, but I certainly was not complaining. I sensed some fabulous things were about to happen.'

Auld made his second Celtic debut eight years after the first when he faced Hearts on 16 January at Parkhead. Tommy Gemmell welcomed back a player who would become a lifelong friend with a scorching goal, but the Edinburgh side still won 2–1. A week later, Gemmell, with a shot of resistance-wrecking power, scored again in a 3–3 draw with Morton. Auld had to wait for his first victory – and first goal – which came with only a day of January remaining. It was a memorable occasion. Celtic hammered Aberdeen 8–0 in Glasgow, with John Hughes shredding the Dons rearguard and scoring five. Lennox and Murdoch knocked in the others and Auld, designated the new penalty-taker, showed his prowess by striking one perfectly beyond John 'Tubby' Ogston.

Twenty-four hours later came an announcement that dramatically changed the fortunes of Celtic Football Club: Jock Stein was to become the new manager. He had agreed to succeed Jimmy McGrory, but only after Hibs found a new manager themselves. Bob Shankly, brother of Liverpool legend Bill, got the Easter Road position after leaving Dundee and Stein was officially named the new Celtic boss on 9 March.

The jungle drums had been beating long before the news broke. It's not easy to keep secrets in football, and Glasgow, it must be said, is a wonderful city of rumour. Stein, a well-known punter, played his cards extremely close to his chest. He had, after all, only become the Hibs manager in April 1964. However, the pull of Celtic was to prove irresistible. Stein was originally asked to become joint manager with Sean Fallon. Stein never intended any disrespect towards the Irishman, a former teammate, but clearly it was going to be his way or no way. Fallon had taken over the duties of manager during the reign of McGrory and it had been widely acknowledged within the walls of Parkhead that one day the job would be his. Stein, though, stuck to his guns. News was somehow leaked that Wolves, searching for a new manager, were casting glances in Stein's direction. Jim Rodger, of the *Daily Record*, at work again? Very probably. Kelly, as everyone realised, liked to get things his own way. Stein was prepared for a game of bluff and double bluff. He won in the end, as he knew he would.

'First Protestant Manager of Celtic' blazed the front page of the Scottish *Daily Express*, and history had been made at the club, 77 years after it had been formed by a Marist priest, Brother Walfrid. Jimmy McGrory was appointed head of press relations, Sean Fallon became the official assistant manager and Stein brought old favourite Neilly Mochan back from Dundee United as first-team trainer.

Stein met his new players only 24 hours before a league match against Airdrie at Broomfield on 10 March, but it was obvious that the main target for Celtic was the Scottish Cup. They had reached the semi-final following a real humdinger of a quarter-final tie in the mud of Parkhead four days beforehand. Celtic overcame Kilmarnock 3–2 and suddenly there was a belief about the place, heightened by the imminent arrival of Stein. The new boss had a brief message for his players: 'You work hard for this club and I will work hard for this club. Together we will achieve something.'

Auld said, 'It was as brief as that. I knew Jock, of course, and many of the Celtic players had been in the reserves when he was coaching the second string. For a couple, though, it would have been the first meeting with Jock that morning. I'm sure they didn't know what to expect. Jock kept it simple.'

Stein, of course, was welcomed by most. Billy McNeill admitted that, as soon as the news was confirmed of his return, 'On a personal level, I got a tremendous lift. I knew things would start to happen again at the club.' Ronnie Simpson was less enthusiastic. Stein had sold the goalkeeper to Celtic from Hibs the previous year and, after being told about his former manager's arrival, Simpson is reported to have gone home and informed his wife she should get ready to pack. 'We're on the move again, Rosemary,' he is supposed to have said. Tommy Gemmell, on the other hand, was overjoyed. 'I knew Jock actively encouraged his full-backs to drive forward. There would be no more of this "Don't you dare cross that halfway line" again. Thank goodness. We were going to be given the freedom to express ourselves and I was going to take full advantage. There was no looking back for me the day Jock Stein walked back into Celtic

Park. I clearly recall his very first instruction to me. "Remember, you are a defender and your first job is to defend," he said. "But get up that park as often as you can when you see an opportunity." That suited me perfectly.'

In Stein's first game in charge against Airdrie at Broomfield, Auld slammed in five goals, two penalty kicks among them, in a 6–0 victory. Auld laughed, 'I always thought I had good timing.' Gemmell added, 'The remarkable thing about that display was that Bertie actually played wide on the left. He wasn't playing right up front in the middle or just off the strikers. Forget the two spot kicks, to score a hat-trick from a wide-left berth was an incredible feat. It was only when Big Jock settled into the job that Bertie eventually moved into a midfield role, but against Airdrie that night he played as an orthodox left-winger, actually setting up opportunities for the likes of John Hughes and Bobby Lennox. I was playing right behind him and I can remember thinking, "This guy is class. He's giving us a new dimension." Exciting times indeed.'

Three days later, there was a double disappointment: St Johnstone won 1–0 in Glasgow in front of only 18,000 fans. There was a 3–3 draw with Dundee before the next home game, when, once again, the fans didn't exactly flock to Celtic Park. This time, a crowd of only 19,000 watched Hibs win 4–2, a result that would undoubtedly have wounded Stein. However, he would have been much happier just over two weeks later when Celtic travelled to Easter Road for a league game that had been rearranged after it had been frozen off during the winter. Goals from Auld (2), Stevie Chalmers and Bobby Murdoch gave the club a 4–0 victory.

The focus was the Scottish Cup, of course. It had kicked off in February with a 3–0 win over St Mirren at Love Street, but Celtic made it astonishingly difficult for themselves in the next round, when they had to rely on a Lennox strike to see off the amateurs of Queen's Park. Then came that classic confrontation against an excellent Kilmarnock side, which brought goals from Lennox, Auld and Hughes to win the day 3–2 against stubborn, dangerous opponents.

There was the intriguing possibility of Stein leading out Celtic against Hibs in the Scottish Cup final at Hampden on 24 April. While Celtic were due to play Motherwell in the semi-final at the national stadium, the Easter Road side were preparing to face Dunfermline on the same day, 27 March, at Tynecastle. Hibs lost 2–0 and Celtic struggled to a 2–2 draw with the Fir Park side. Joe McBride, always quick to declare his passion for all things Celtic, stuck the ball past John Fallon twice. Bobby Lennox and Bertie Auld, with another superbly executed penalty kick, scored to ensure a replay four days later. This time, there was no mistake.

Celtic piled the pressure on Alan Wylie, in the Motherwell goal, and swept to a comfortable 3–0 victory, Chalmers, Hughes and Lennox on target.

The fact that the main aim of Celtic's desire was the Scottish Cup was underlined by an awful 6–2 collapse against Falkirk a fortnight after the semi-final replay win. That was followed by a 2–1 defeat at home to Partick Thistle, and the league campaign would come to a close against Dunfermline in a 5–1 flop at East End Park after the two clubs had fought out an enthralling Scottish Cup final four days earlier.

To this day, Bertie Auld is convinced that the 3–2 Scottish Cup final triumph over Dunfermline in 1965 was the most important win of that era. 'Yes, even more so than the European Cup,' he insisted. 'Remember, Celtic had won nothing, absolutely nothing, for eight years. I was at the club when they beat Rangers 7–1 in 1957, eight years earlier. I found it extraordinary that the club *still* hadn't won anything in between. Eight years without a major success? That's a lifetime to a club such as Celtic. Would everything have fallen into place if we hadn't beaten Dunfermline? We took great confidence from that success. For me, that was the game that turned everything on its head. That broke the spell we were under. The club had reached other cup finals during that period but had not delivered. Was this going to be another failure? No, we had to win the cup, simple as that.'

Stein tried to relax his players at a hotel in Largs before the game, making a change from the usual haunt at Seamill. He wanted a fresh outlook and he always paid attention to the smallest detail. Billy McNeill recalled, 'Jock knew what he was doing. We didn't go into this game thinking the end of the world was nigh if we were unsuccessful. He made certain he, and not his players, absorbed the pressure and we could actually enjoy the preparation for the cup final.'

McNeill and his colleagues John Clark, Charlie Gallagher, Stevie Chalmers and John Hughes might have needed the relaxed atmosphere more than their other teammates. All five had been in the Celtic line-up that had been outplayed and outfoxed by Stein's Dunfermline in the final of the same competition four years earlier. Stein had actually told his Dunfermline players, 'This lot aren't as good as they think they are. We're better, so go out and prove it.' McNeill, Chalmers and Hughes were also unfortunate enough to be in the team beaten by Rangers in the replay only two years after that. They could become three-time losers – or first-time winners. If Jock Stein managed to calm these players in the days prior to Hampden, he would have performed a minor miracle.

Stein would sit the players down after the afternoon training session and produce a magnetic board upon which he would illustrate moves he expected the team to follow. John Clark said, 'We had never had a tactics talk of any kind before. This was completely new to us. He would point something out, but he would never repeat himself. You had to concentrate completely, for there were no second chances.' Auld added, 'Sometimes Big Jock would ask for a player's opinion. I would pipe up every now and again and he would listen. Once I had finished, he would just wave that big left paw at me and say, "Naw, naw, we're doing it this way!" This happened all the time. He would invite you in and then slap you down.'

There was the usual guessing game before Jock Stein announced his line-up for Hampden. He went with: John Fallon; Ian Young and Tommy Gemmell; John Clark, Billy McNeill and Jim Kennedy; Stevie Chalmers, Charlie Gallagher, John Hughes, Bobby Lennox and Bertie Auld. A crowd of 108,803 was in attendance.

Gemmell recalled, 'I believe Dunfermline were favourites. On league form alone, that would make sense. They completed the campaign only one point behind eventual winners Kilmarnock, who shaded Hearts on goal average. We weren't at the races, but, at the same time, there was a lot of confidence in the team. Jock Stein had brought a belief with him.

'And we had to show a lot of trust in ourselves, too, when our opponents took the lead in the 15th minute. Any time's a helluva time to lose a goal, but it's so important to keep things tight during that sparring spell of the first 20 minutes or so. And now we had conceded and we had it all to do. Harry Melrose scored for them after a bit of a goalmouth melee when we just couldn't get to the ball to hoof it into the stand.'

Auld remembered, 'Before the match, I looked at my teammates and I realised they felt to a man just like me. "We're going to win this one" appeared to be the unspoken, but unified, feeling. Sixteen minutes later, I was left sitting on my backside in the Fifers' net, but I was not one bit upset; the ball was lying there beside me. I had equalised.

'I remember the goal like it was yesterday. John Clark slid a pass to Charlie Gallagher and he took a couple of steps forward, shaped to play it wide, changed pace and then sent a thunderbolt of a shot towards their goal from about 30 yards. Jim Herriot, the Fifers' extremely competent goalkeeper, who would become a teammate of mine at Hibs later on, threw himself at Charlie's effort, but he failed to divert its course and it thumped against the face of the crossbar. I saw my chance as the ball swirled high into the air. Herriot was on the ground and was desperately trying to get back to his feet as I moved in for the kill. The ball appeared to be suspended by an invisible hand. It seemed to be up there for ages. I was aware of their full-back Willie Callaghan coming in at speed from my right. He was wasting his time – I was never going to miss this opportunity. The ball came floating back down after what seemed an eternity and I launched myself at it to head it over the line. One–one: game on!'

Fallon, in the Celtic goal, surrendered again just a minute before the interval when Melrose rolled a free kick in front of John McLaughlin, who belted it first time from 20 yards. The ball went straight through the defensive wall and eluded Fallon on his right-hand side. Auld observed, 'It looked saveable from where I was standing. Once again, we had it all to do.' Celtic had had to fight back twice against Motherwell to earn a replay in the semi-final. There was no way this side made life easy for themselves.

In his autobiography *Thirty Miles from Paradise*, Bobby Lennox said:

> It was a quiet dressing-room at half-time. I think Jock realised he only had us for a couple of months or so and if he lost his temper and bawled and shouted it might have tensed us up too much. That afternoon would not have been the right time to beef into the players. Jock was the big, friendly bear. On another day and on another occasion he might have savaged us.

Auld remembered, 'As we left the dressing-room, Jock said, "Get that early goal ... get that goal and we'll win this trophy." Seven minutes into the second half, Tommy Gemmell turned the ball to me and I swiftly passed it on to Bobby Lennox on the left. He took off like a sprinter and I chased into the penalty area, hoping to be in the right place at the right time. Bobby couldn't have hit a sweeter pass into the danger area and I arrived on the button to first-time a right-foot shot low past the helpless Herriot. Two-two: we're going to win!'

The spectacle could not have been scripted better, nor the finale more exciting. Nine minutes remained when Celtic won a corner kick out on the left. Gallagher, a gifted striker of a dead ball, trotted over to take it. The midfielder floated in a curling cross that had all the devastating effects of a wrecking ball on the Fife defence. Goalkeeper Herriot hesitated before leaving his line and that was to prove fatal. As he struggled to readjust his shape, Billy McNeill came thundering in with awesome timing to get his blond head to the cross and send the ball thudding into the net between the two helpless full-backs, Callaghan and John Lunn, who were guarding the posts; the area in between was splendidly vacant.

I have heard it said that Hampden was actually silent for a split second as the moment sunk in. I was there that afternoon and I have to say I believe this curiosity could be fact. So many things had gone wrong over so many years and now Celtic were on the cusp of actually winning a trophy. I think a lot of the Celtic support around Mount Florida might just have been brainwashed into believing their team was destined never to be successful. Bertie Auld was right: this victory sent Celtic soaring to a new level.

One of the first things Jock Stein did in the summer of 1965 was scrap the third team at Celtic, allowing almost thirty players to move on. Davie Hay was one of the youngsters who was brought to the club as Stein revolutionised the entire playing system. Hay said, 'I think I might have been Big Jock's first signing for Celtic. After a meeting with Sean Fallon, I couldn't sign those forms quickly enough and I did so at the start of March, just as Jock was coming in.

'It may seem a bit harsh to some observers to free such a large amount of players, but Jock's reasoning, as ever, was sound. He wanted to know the strengths and weaknesses of a smaller band of players. That would give him the opportunity to work with all of them at first hand. There would be no one at Parkhead who hadn't been assessed by him personally, no one who had escaped his attention.

'I remember turning up one Tuesday night and there seemed to be about fifty other players of all ages at our training ground at Barrowfield. Jock had organised a special bounce game and it wasn't to see how good individuals were, it was to see how *bad* they were. I got on for about twenty minutes at one stage and, thankfully, did quite well. If I hadn't performed reasonably OK during that short spell, then God only knows how my career would have panned out. There were a lot of lads at Barrowfield that evening I never saw again. There is little doubt Big Jock could be ruthless. He didn't waste his time on any individual he didn't think could produce for the club. Jock had the ability to assess players very quickly.

'Of course, as a youngster I didn't know any better, but I was continually told by the older pros that it was night and day, Jock's regime and what had gone on beforehand. Jock was a tracksuit boss and that was unusual. No disrespect to Jimmy McGrory, but players back then were telling me they saw him mostly on match days, and only briefly in between. Apparently, they always saw him on a Tuesday because that was the day he handed out the wages! No one witnessed Jimmy without one of his three-piece suits and trademark trilby perched on his head.'

One player who would be beating a hasty retreat was Hugh Maxwell, bought only six months beforehand. Stein fielded him in two games and Celtic lost them both, 2–4 against Hibs and 1–5 against Dunfermline.

Maxwell, after only eight league games, was on his way. A rather cruel observation from one of his soon-to-be-former teammates was 'Hugh would have looked out of his depth in a puddle'. St Johnstone paid £10,000 for him in the summer of 1965. In transfer-cash terms, that meant the lanky midfielder had cost Celtic exactly £625 per game. It didn't represent good value for money and the bean-counters at Parkhead must have lain in a darkened room for some considerable time as a consequence.

A shaft of light, though, was delivered via the £22,000 purchase of Joe McBride from Motherwell in May. If Stevie Chalmers took an unusual route to Celtic, via three junior clubs, it must be said that McBride's path to Parkhead was downright weird. The stocky striker, so often a thorn in the side of his boyhood heroes, was only one month short of his twenty-seventh birthday when he signed but had already played for one amateur team (Kilmarnock Amateurs), two junior clubs (Shettleston Town and Kirkintilloch Rob Roy) and five senior outfits (Kilmarnock, Wolves, Luton Town, Partick Thistle and Motherwell). He might have been perceived as a journeyman forward, but Stein was convinced he was worth the money to become his first major signing at the club. If Maxwell came in with a whimper, McBride marked his first league appearance with a goal in a 4–0 triumph over Dundee United. Coincidentally, both full-backs, Ian Young (with a penalty kick) and Tommy Gemmell, scored after Johnny Divers had hit the breakthrough goal.

McBride sparked to life big-time in the League Cup, hammering in seven goals in five appearances, including a hat-trick in an overwhelming 8–1 quarter-final first-leg victory over Raith Rovers at Stark's Park. Stein took the opportunity of bringing in Northern Irishman Jack Kennedy, a former Great Britain Olympic goalkeeper, for the meaningless second game against the Fifers, a comfortable 4–0 win. Kennedy, despite having a shut-out, joined Willie Goldie and Dick Madden as the third Celtic custodian of the '60s to play one game for the club before disappearing off the radar.

'Jock Stein always had a great distrust of goalkeepers,' recalled Billy McNeill. 'Maybe he had a bad experience with one or two of them during his playing days. It appeared he couldn't get his head round the fact that we were playing *foot*ball and these guys were allowed to use their hands.

'He was tough on them, too. I remember we were down at Seamill taking it easy before one big game when Jock appeared and summoned John Fallon, our keeper, to get changed into his tracksuit and join him out on the lawn. He placed some paint pots on the ground to act as goalposts and then produced this enormous net packed with balls. "Right,

John, we're going to have a wee workout," he said. We were sitting in the hotel, our feet up, reading books, watching TV or playing cards, and there was our unfortunate keeper out there being put through hell. Big Jock walloped balls at him from all angles for what seemed hours on end. John looked absolutely done-in when he returned.'

Stein gave Fallon the nod for the first Old Firm meeting of the campaign at Ibrox in September. Fallon conceded twice, to Jim Forrest and a George McLean penalty kick, in a 2–1 defeat, with John Hughes getting the consolation goal. Johnny Divers, smack in front of goal, missed a pinch in the fading moments, and Stein demonstrated that he could be as uncompromising and unforgiving with his forwards as he was with his goalkeepers. Divers, despite scoring in the opening league triumph at Tannadice and collecting two in the League Cup campaign, never played for the first team again.

Bertie Auld recalled, 'Johnny was a more than useful inside-right with a lot of skill. He started in the first team in 1957, played more than 200 games and scored something in the region of 100 goals. Not bad going at all, but Jock thought otherwise. Johnny has admitted he had a conversation with Jock after the boss's return from Hibs and agreed he might have lost a bit of enthusiasm. Jock immediately said, "Then you're no use to me." Poor Johnny. He played against Rangers and missed a good chance. If memory serves correctly, Billy McNeill nodded the ball down into his path and it looked a goal all the way. Johnny swung his boot at it, but the ball bounced awkwardly and he connected with fresh air. The opportunity was gone and the game was lost. Jock absolutely abhorred losing to Rangers and he was far from impressed.

'It was then, I believe, he had his conversation with Johnny and, there and then, the player could have packed his bags and left the club. He trained with the reserves for about three months and was then injured when Willie O'Neill accidentally stood on his foot. That was his season wrecked. He always insisted he knew his time at Celtic was over when he picked up a newspaper and there was a story informing everyone that he was to be given a surprise free transfer. Well, it would have been more of a shock than a surprise, I would think. There must be better ways to discover you are heading out the door.

'However, that was typical of Jock. Personalities meant nothing to him. He wasn't interested in popularity contests. It was all about Celtic and the players he believed could do a job for the club. You might have questioned his methods, but what wasn't up for debate was his success rate.

'Johnny gave up football altogether shortly afterwards, following a spell at Partick Thistle, where his heart clearly wasn't in it. He went into the car business and John Clark remembers spending part of his £1,500 European Cup bonus on a car from Johnny's showroom in Bearsden!'

Stein always had his reservations about Fallon and, although he was not to blame for the defeat at Ibrox, he played only one more first-team game that season. Clearly, Stein took no prisoners.

A story of the time told of the boss making a surprise appearance at a reserve fixture. One first-team player was performing in the second string at the time and the manager was furious with what he believed to be a lacklustre display from a man still picking up top-team wages. Stein appeared in the dressing-room and said, 'Enjoy the second half – it's the last time you'll ever play for Celtic.' People around the club at the time would agree that such a dramatic action from Jock would not have been unusual.

Ronnie Simpson replaced the unfortunate Fallon a week after the Rangers defeat, for a 7–1 romp against Aberdeen at Parkhead. Simpson, then, had become Stein's third goalkeeper in as many games, and he kept his place for the first game in October, a League Cup semi-final meeting with his former club Hibs at Ibrox, with Rangers taking on Kilmarnock in a sensational encounter at Hampden the same day. McBride and Lennox, in the 89th minute, netted in a thoroughly invigorating two hours. While it was deadlocked 2–2 in Govan after extra time, it was a day when defences took the day off at the national stadium, with Rangers triumphing 6–4 in a breathtaking encounter. The Ibrox side had booked their place in the 23 October final and they had also racked up twenty-eight goals in nine games. Jim Forrest seemed to enjoy the early-season tournament and had claimed ten of the goal tally.

So Celtic knew it was their fiercest rivals they could be facing when they returned to Ibrox for the replay against Hibs. Whereas in the first game the Easter Road men had erected a solid back line in front of Willie Wilson, the keeper who had forced Ronnie Simpson out of the Edinburgh club, they were posted AWOL on this occasion, with Celtic rampaging to a 4–0 success. McBride and Hughes scored within a five-minute period early on, Lennox swept in a magnificent third, with the ball being shuttled from the edge of the Celtic penalty area all the way down the pitch without an opponent getting a touch. Murdoch buried the fourth behind the black-clad keeper and there was a moment of controversy when John McNamee, the former Celtic defender, was ordered off. Petulantly, he kicked dirt in the direction of Jock Stein in the dugout before disappearing up the tunnel.

Celtic and Hibs had protested about Ibrox being the venue for the

CAPTAIN SUPREME: A youthful Billy McNeill looking optimistic at the start of the '60s.

MIDFIELD MAESTRO: Bertie Auld back at Celtic after his four-year 'exile' at Birmingham City.

CELTIC ON TOUR: The line-up that beat Derry City 7–0 in Ireland on 17 May 1958. Back row (left to right): Dunky MacKay, Neilly Mochan, Frank Haffey, Eric Smith and Billy McNeill. Front row (left to right): Matt McVittie, Jim Conway, Bertie Peacock, Mike Jackson, Sammy Wilson and Bertie Auld. European Cup glory was a mere nine years and eight days away for McNeill and Auld.

BUNCH OF FIVES: Celtic's line-up for a 5-a-side tournament at Falkirk. Left to right: Pat Crerand, Billy McNeill, Mike Jackson, Jim Kennedy and Dunky MacKay.

HERE WE GO: The Celtic team that kicked off season 1961–62 with a League Cup tie against Partick Thistle at Firhill. Back row (left to right): Dunky MacKay, Jim Kennedy, Frank Connor, John Kurila, Billy McNeill and John Clark. Front row (left to right): Bobby Carroll, Mike Jackson, John Hughes, Johnny Divers and Stevie Chalmers. Bob Rooney (physiotherapist). Celtic won 3–2, with goals from Jackson (2) and Hughes.

THE LAUGHING CAVALIER: Adventurous full-back Tommy Gemmell in a serious moment, but he was a defender with the ability to put smiles on the faces of the Celtic support throughout a fabulous era.

THE COOL CUSTODIAN: Ronnie Simpson, the veteran keeper known to his teammates as 'Faither', shows a safe pair of hands – as usual.

THIS MAN CRAIG: Right-back Jim Craig rarely hit the headlines but was a dependable and often crucial performer in the Celtic back four.

THE PASS MASTER: Bobby Murdoch, who combined power with panache and strength with skill in the Celtic midfield.

HITTING THE HEIGHTS: Billy McNeill in aerial combat with Hibs number 1 Jim Herriot as Alan Gordon and John Blackley look on. McNeill beat the same keeper with a header in the 3–2 Scottish Cup final triumph over Dunfermline in 1965 to open the silverware floodgates.

HEADS I WIN: John Clark, the sweeper who dovetailed magnificently with Billy McNeill in the heart of the Celtic rearguard.

WEE MR MISCHIEF:
Jimmy Johnstone, the
touchline trickster who
struck terror into the hearts
of opponents.

THE MAN KNOWN AS
WISPY: Willie Wallace,
Celtic's versatile, will-o'-the-
wisp perfomer, bought for a
bargain £30,000 from Hearts
in December 1966.

CUP THAT CHEERS: Willie Wallace drills in his second goal of the afternoon
in the 2–0 Scottish Cup final victory over Aberdeen in 1967. Goalkeeper Bobby
Clark has no chance.

ACTION MAN: Stevie
Chalmers in a typically
determined, no-holds-barred
moment in 1965.

MERCHANT OF MENACE:
Bobby Lennox pauses to pose for
the camera – a rare moment of the
player actually standing still.

HAPPY DAZE: Jock Stein and Bertie Auld have every
reason to look delighted: Celtic have just drawn 0–0 against
Dukla Prague in Czechoslovakia to claim a place in the
European Cup final against Inter Milan in Lisbon in 1967.

SOARAWAY: Mike Jackson heads the ball over Real Madrid's legendary Alfredo Di Stéfano, one of football's first acknowledged superstars. Celtic lost 3–1 on 10 September 1962 in Glasgow – and the fans demanded a lap of honour!

MEN AT WORK: Celtic prepare for the 1962–63 season, with Stevie Chalmers leading Pat Crerand, Mike Jackson, Willie O'Neill and John McNamee in training at Parkhead.

POWERHOUSE: A teenage John Hughes. He stormed into the Celtic first team in the early '60s and swiftly became a huge fans' favourite.

UNSUNG HERO: Willie O'Neill, a utility defender who played in the first four European Cup ties in the victorious 1967 campaign.

THE VELVET TOUCH: Charlie Gallagher, a smooth midfield operator who possessed a ferocious shot.

MR GOALS: Joe McBride. The prolific striker was Jock Stein's first buy for Celtic, at £22,000 from Motherwell in 1965.

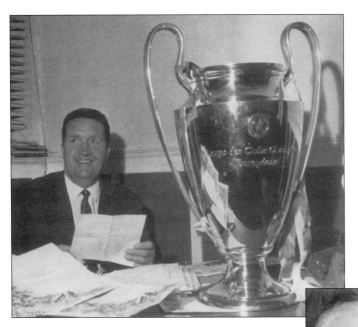

SILVER LINING: Jock Stein opening letters of congratulations, with the newly won European Cup taking pride of place on his desk in the manager's office at Celtic Park.

DREAM-MAKER: Chairman Bob Kelly, who ruled uncompromisingly at Celtic.

CROWD-PLEASERS: Mike Jackson on the ball in a First Division encounter against Stirling Albion at a packed Annfield. It ended 2–2 in November 1959.

replay. Both condemned the quality of the floodlights, their concern being shared by both sets of supporters, who had difficulty following play, particularly in the first game, which was played in a downpour. The Scottish League management committee was approached by the clubs about changing the venue to Hampden Park, which was available for the second game. The supporters associations of both teams also formally sent in their protests, but the committee refused to budge and stuck by their earlier decision. Of course, that meant Rangers getting a considerable fee for the rent of their ground.

Simpson kept his place against Rangers in the League Cup final, and the veteran, known as 'Faither' to his teammates, would remain in charge of the number 1 jersey for the rest of the season.

Auld remembered, 'Of course, we were well up for the Rangers match. I never needed extra motivation for any game, but an Old Firm meeting was always special. As I recall, the bookies had us as slight favourites and that was most unusual around those times for a game against Rangers away from Celtic Park. Maybe people were beginning to cotton on to what was happening at Parkhead.'

Gemmell added, 'I loved those encounters, too. I used to get it in the neck from their supporters. They probably thought I was a traitor because I was a Protestant playing for Celtic. I recall when I was an apprentice at Ravenscraig steelworks and I was about to join up at Parkhead. One of the bosses called me in. "What do you want to join that lot for?" I was asked. To be honest, religion never bothered me and certainly didn't come into any thought process. I answered, "Why not?" He started to splutter, but never finished his sentence. He didn't need to, I knew the script. He was a big Rangers fan and I shouldn't even have been contemplating signing for "the other lot".

'You know, my mum never went back to another football game after a match against Rangers when their fans chanted, "Gemmell's a bastard!" throughout the 90 minutes. She knew better, of course, but she just couldn't accept the way her son was being treated. Me? It didn't bother me one little bit. Let's face it, they weren't ignoring me, so I must have been doing something right. If I had been anonymous, they wouldn't have targeted me. Anyway, I reasoned if they were abusing me they were leaving other players alone so, although they didn't realise it, it was a win–win situation for me.

'Nowadays, I can look back and have a laugh at some of the light-hearted moments in these games. There was a match at Ibrox when a bottle came spiralling towards me from the Rangers enclosure. It dropped at my feet. What was I to do? I picked it up and jokingly went to take a swig. Unfortunately, it was empty. The fans saw the funny side, I'm glad to say. Mind you, a couple of minutes later they were back chanting, "Gemmell's a bastard!"

'There was also a Rangers player, I won't embarrass him by naming him, who continually called me "a big Fenian bastard". To be honest, I doubt if he knew what the word meant and I couldn't be bothered educating him.

'I had some memorable jousts with Willie Henderson around that time. The Wee Barra was a bit special and, although it would probably have been beyond the comprehension of both sets of Old Firm supporters, we were actually good friends off the pitch. In one game I was a bit late with a tackle on Willie – an accident, honest! – and my wee mate went flying, then got up and ran towards me. "Off! Off!" was the raucous cry from the angry Rangers fans wanting my instant dismissal. They might have laughed if they had heard what Willie was actually saying to me. "Where are we going tonight, Tommy?" he asked. I loved the Wee Barra. Still do.'

Celtic returned to Hampden Park only six months after they had blown apart their silverware jinx. There was a genuine belief among the supporters that they were again witnessing the Celtic of old, a team that refused to roll over, a collection of players with a heart for the battle. No cause was lost until the last shrill of the referee's whistle and that had been borne out by the 2–2 League Cup semi-final draw against Hibs. In dreadful conditions, Celtic had relentlessly driven towards the Easter Road side's goal in pursuit of an equaliser, and they achieved it with Lennox's last-gasp effort in the regulation 90 minutes.

Stein sent out this team against Rangers: Ronnie Simpson; Ian Young and Tommy Gemmell; Bobby Murdoch, Billy McNeill and John Clark; Jimmy Johnstone, Charlie Gallagher, Joe McBride, Bobby Lennox and John Hughes. New striker McBride had scored 11 goals in as many games since the start of the season. Like his Rangers counterpart Jim Forrest, McBride was a no-frills frontman. 'When I see the whites of those goalposts, I just let fly,' he said. 'After that, it's up to the keeper.'

A crowd of 107,609 – an all-time high for the competition – turned out at Hampden to see if Celtic, after eight years without a trophy, could claim a second inside six months. It would have been a preposterous thought in the early days of the decade. Rangers had been used to bossing these games, but Celtic put down a marker – almost literally – in the early moments when right-back Ian Young sent winger Willie Johnston spinning with a crunching, but fair, tackle. A bruising encounter ensued, no quarter asked or given by either set of players.

Celtic got the breakthrough goal in the most bizarre of circumstances. A long ball from the Celtic defence was sailing serenely out of play when, for no apparent reason, Rangers centre-half Ronnie McKinnon stuck up a hand to pull the ball down. It was a certain penalty kick and referee Hugh Phillips duly pointed to the spot. John Hughes took it and sent it straight down the middle as goalkeeper Billy Ritchie launched himself to the right. 'I normally hit them to the keeper's right,' said Hughes, 'but on this occasion I had a late change of mind. I saw John Greig having a word with the keeper moments beforehand and figured he was telling him where I would put the ball. I was the designated penalty-taker and, funnily enough, when I left home that morning I thought to myself, "I hope we don't get any penalties!" It was nerve-racking enough in normal games, but an Old Firm meeting, especially a cup final, was something else.'

The advantage was doubled before the first half was over and once more it was another stonewall penalty kick, with even the Rangers players failing to protest. Davie Provan, given the runaround by Jimmy Johnstone in the first game of the 1963 Scottish Cup final, desperately lunged at the winger as he wriggled his way across the 18-yard box. The defender's timing was off and he caught Johnstone just under the knee. Phillips gave the award again without hesitation and Hughes stepped up once more. This time, he did strike it to the goalkeeper's right and he must have taken a sharp intake of breath when Ritchie guessed correctly and got a hand to the ball. Hughes said, 'Thankfully, there was enough power behind the shot to force it past the keeper. I was proud of those goals, because you're under a lot of pressure taking a penalty, especially against Rangers. I was really pleased with myself.'

The Celtic end behind Ritchie once more erupted in delirium. Rangers, as expected, were not about to accept defeat without a fight. They took the game to Celtic after the interval, but the defence in front of Simpson was resolute. There was a fright when Young, panicked by Greig, sent an attempted clearance thumping beyond the helpless Simpson, but Celtic's name was on the cup, won for the first time since the 7–1 victory over the same opponents in 1957. Unfortunately, the historic ritual of parading a newly won trophy before celebrating fans in a lap of honour was sabotaged by a pitch invasion from the Rangers end.

Gemmell said, 'We were presented with the trophy and, as we had done after beating Dunfermline in the Scottish Cup final, we were about to take it over to our supporters. There's no way we would have been going all the way round the pitch, that's for sure. Unfortunately, we didn't even get the opportunity to show it off to our own fans. A photograph of me pulling over a scarf-waving Rangers supporter appeared in the following day's newspapers. Ian Young had been knocked to the ground and a clearly bewildered Billy McNeill was just standing there holding the League Cup. We had earned that trophy and we had earned the right to parade it in front of our loyal support. Sadly, we never got the opportunity. The police eventually arrived on the scene and all the players were ushered down the tunnel. It was an unfortunate ending to a memorable Old Firm occasion.'

The European crusade, now an annual event, had started quietly enough in September, but would end in uproar and controversy in April the following year. As far as the remaining league games of 1965 were concerned, Celtic were on a roll and won eight of their nine encounters, with their only falter being a 1–1 draw with Partick Thistle. It was phenomenal football. Celtic reached the turn of the year having scored 55 goals in 15 league games. Joe McBride had been brought in to score goals and he wasn't disappointing, claiming fifteen in his fourteen appearances while rattling in seven in seven League Cup ties. He added another two from three Cup-Winners' Cup ties. Twenty-four goals in his first four months playing for the club he idolised. Now he was on the receiving end of hero worship.

McBride had scored against Dunfermline, Aberdeen, Hearts, Dundee, Stirling Albion, Partick Thistle, St Johnstone, Hamilton, Kilmarnock, Hibs and Morton in the league and Dundee United, Dundee and Raith Rovers in the League Cup. One name was missing: Rangers. He would get the opportunity to rectify that on 3 January 1966.

7

DREAM ON, CHAMPIONS!

Hallelujah! Celtic 5, Rangers 1. The Celtic supporters could have been forgiven for believing they were hallucinating, especially after Davie Wilson had thumped the Ibrox side ahead in only 90 seconds. It remained that way until the interval. Then John Hughes had a brainwave. For a big, powerfully built specimen, Hughes was extremely nimble on his toes. However, his dainty forays down the left wing on 3 January 1966 – Celtic had beaten Clyde 3–1 on New Year's Day – often ended with him scudding around on his backside, such were the treacherous, flint-hard underfoot conditions. At half-time, Hughes discarded his normal boots for training shoes with suction pads instead of studs. Rangers' Danish right-back Kai Johansen hadn't been unduly troubled by his immediate opponent in the opening 45 minutes. He was to leave the Parkhead pitch totally demoralised after being on the uncomfortable receiving end of an unstoppable force that turned the game completely and sparked off a remarkable goal feast.

Hughes in full flight was indeed a sight to behold – a juggernaut with the balance of a balletic performer. He possessed a deftness that defied comprehension. Stevie Chalmers, a prolific penalty-box predator, was the main benefactor of Hughes' virtuoso performance that chilly afternoon, with gusts of icy air swirling around the East End of Glasgow. Chalmers, chasing down every lost cause, was in the faces of Roger Hynd, Ronnie McKinnon and John Greig for the full 90 minutes. If goalkeeper Billy Ritchie fumbled the ball, Chalmers was in on top of him immediately. He was a frontman who fed on scraps but had a great awareness even when things were in chaos around him, with bodies, arms and legs flying around with great abandon. Chalmers, like Hughes, possessed breathtaking acceleration. He recalled that day fondly, saying, 'Everything changed rather dramatically after the interval. I scored three and Bobby Murdoch and Charlie Gallagher pitched in with two thundering long-range efforts.

'It's a huge understatement to say I enjoyed knocking in three against our oldest rivals, but can you imagine my surprise the following day when all the headlines were given to John Hughes! I score three and Yogi gets the praise – it's just not fair. Seriously, though, Yogi was immense in the second half of that game and I think he actually set up all my goals after some fabulous runs down the left flank. He changed his boots at half-time and put on sandshoes. That was highly unusual in those days, but Yogi was complaining about the slippery surface and decided to change his footwear, casting aside the more traditional boots. It worked a treat.

'I had a quiet chuckle as I left the ground afterwards, making my way to my car. A Rangers fan was talking to a Celtic supporter and I heard him say, "Whit did ye think o' that?" Then he added, "Two bad lots!" Well, he got it half right!'

Astoundingly, Chalmers' hat-trick that day is a record that will stand for all time, with 'old' Rangers going into liquidation in 2012. He added, 'I still find it hard to believe that I will be the last Celtic player to score three goals in an Old Firm league game. Records are there to be broken, and previously I had urged the players to get out there and do the business for Celtic. There have been a few close calls, of course, since then. Willie Wallace, Kenny Dalglish, Charlie Nicholas, Brian McClair and Henrik Larsson have all claimed two, but no one hit a hat-trick. I find that simply incredible. Mind you, my wee pal Bobby Lennox continually reminds me he scored three in a Glasgow Cup tie at Ibrox in 1966 and Harry Hood also managed a trio against Rangers in the League Cup in 1973. But, as far as the league is concerned, I will be the last guy to achieve that feat. What a wonderful feeling!'

Something else that might have been perceived as incredible was the fact that Joe McBride did not get on the scoresheet when the goals were raining into the Rangers net. What's more, McBride's record shows he never scored against the Ibrox side while wearing the green and white hoops.

Celtic were on the receiving end in strange circumstances when they lost 3–2 to Hearts at Tynecastle at the end of January. The Parkhead team had been delayed in their return from a 1–1 draw with Dynamo Kiev and arrived back in Glasgow late on the evening prior to the game. The Cup-Winners' Cup tie had been switched from snowbound Kiev, where the ground was unplayable, to Tbilisi on the Wednesday. Celtic prepared to leave the following morning, but atrocious weather conditions saw them marooned in Tbilisi and they were further delayed before getting a flight to Moscow. 'We were stuck on that plane for hours,' recalled Tommy Gemmell. 'The entire party was getting pretty bored, so there was only one thing for it – I put on an impromptu one-man show.

I was singing, telling jokes, and at least it helped to while away an hour or so. I even got a round of applause afterwards. Showbiz's loss was football's gain!'

Conditions relented and Celtic were eventually allowed to fly out of the Russian capital. There followed the strange sight of Celtic players training at Parkhead under floodlights on Friday at 11 p.m., 16 hours before kick-off. The club had asked for the match in Edinburgh to be postponed, but the Scottish League, in its infinite wisdom, refused their more than reasonable request and ordered them to play the following afternoon. It was an understandably leg-weary Celtic team that faced Hearts and it was no surprise that they lost 3–2, with Willie Wallace scoring two of the Hearts goals. Jim Craig, sent off against Kiev, was missing and Billy McNeill took over the right-back role, with John Cushley deputising at centre-half. It was a disjointed performance from a jaded outfit and goals from McBride and Hughes couldn't save Celtic from a narrow defeat.

McBride hit a hat-trick in the 6–0 victory over Falkirk, on target for a fourth successive league game. But the wheels came off in the most alarming and unexpected fashion when a goal from George Peebles gave Stirling Albion a 1–0 victory at Annfield in February. 'Big Jock was raging,' recalled Auld. 'He hit the roof after that one. In truth, we should have wiped the floor with Stirling, but we couldn't get into our natural rhythm that day. I remember the muddy pitch cutting up really badly. I'm not making excuses, but that can be a great leveller in terms of teams' abilities. Back then, we were aware that some clubs didn't bother rolling their pitches when they were due to play Celtic. They would leave them rutted and, of course, that didn't help our passing game. Others watered their pitches to the extent they were virtual swamps and we would turn up at these places and wonder if it had been raining all week in that part of Scotland. Jock always wanted the ball being moved around on the carpet and that particular afternoon against Stirling it was impossible to play in that manner. It was a day for back-to-front football, the ball being belted from one end to another, but, of course, that was not the Celtic way.

'The dreadful conditions cut us absolutely no slack with Jock. We had all seen him angry, but he went up like a volcano after that defeat. "Totally unacceptable" was what he kept repeating. Then he would break off to berate an individual. He never thought twice about giving anyone a dressing-down in front of his teammates. I was on the receiving end of a few, I can tell you. Big Jock got his message across to us loud and clear. He wanted that league championship. The Scottish Cup and the League

Cup victories were all well and good, but the title was the big one and Jock had his sights on it.'

In the next match, Celtic thumped Dundee 5–0, with McBride slamming in another hat-trick, his fourth of the season. The pursuit of the flag was interrupted by Scottish Cup action and the following Saturday Celtic were involved in a dramatic 3–3 quarter-final draw with Hearts at Tynecastle. Goalkeepers Ronnie Simpson and Jim Cruickshank were the busiest men on the pitch as both forward lines opened fire with verve and gusto. Four days later, the clubs locked horns again in the replay at Parkhead and this time Celtic made no mistake. The result was a 3–1 triumph.

Gemmell remembered, 'Those two games against Hearts probably won't feature too prominently in Celtic's history, but they were two very important fixtures for us. Hearts were an exceptionally good team at the time and had been unfortunate the previous season when they missed out on the league title on the last day of the season. Kilmarnock went to Tynecastle that afternoon knowing they required a 2–0 victory to clinch the flag on goal average. Hearts, at home, were favourites. It was unthinkable that they would fall at this hurdle in front of their own fans. That was exactly what happened. Killie got the 2–0 winning margin they needed and the title was on its way to Rugby Park. Hearts had put so much into the season and had ended with naught. So it was fairly obvious they wanted something from this campaign, and their players, including Willie Wallace who would become one of my best mates, were right up for it. Our 3–3 draw could have gone either way; it was that sort of game. And we had to be at our best for the second meeting.

'I recall both those ties being packed with incident and I can also remember two excellent displays from Jimmy Johnstone. We all knew he was a brilliant wee player and he could skin any full-back when he put his mind to it. Believe me, I know what I'm talking about, because I faced him often enough in training. The only thing he lacked was consistency, but that was something he was achieving on a match-by-match basis under Big Jock. He drilled it into Jimmy that there was little point in skipping past three players if there was no end product.

'Before Jock, Jinky would beat a defender and then double back to beat him again. He would even do it a third time and, of course, the fans lapped it up. He was pure entertainment, but it must have been a wee bit frustrating for the likes of Stevie Chalmers, Joe McBride and the others queuing up in the penalty box, jostling for positions waiting for the ball to be finally delivered. Sometimes it arrived, sometimes it didn't. Jock worked hard with Jinky to get him to realise football was not all about flicks and tricks; it was about putting the ball in the opposition's net. Once the penny dropped with the Wee Man, he became a far better and more consistent player. His must have been one of the first names on Big Jock's team sheet on match day. Along with mine, of course!'

St Johnstone provided the opposition in the next league encounter on 12 March in Glasgow and they gave Celtic a fright with an unexpected attacking formation. At this stage, Jock Stein's side had become used to teams arriving at Parkhead and trying to shut up shop in front of their goalkeeper. Gemmell said, 'It became normal for the opposing right-winger to mark me rather than the other way around. A few of them would say, "Take it easy on me today, Tommy." I lost count of the outside-rights who didn't even come into our half when we were playing them.'

The Saints, beaten 4–1 at home by the same opponents earlier in the campaign, decided to have a go at Billy McNeill and co. It ended 3–2 for Celtic, but after an exhausting 90 minutes the home side realised they would face a stern test in their quest for the championship. Clearly, Rangers also had their eye on the main prize and had spent heavily in bringing in Alex Smith, from Dunfermline, and Davie Smith, from Aberdeen. The Smiths, not related, cost a combined fee of £100,000, a colossal amount of money at the time.

There was a hiccup along the way for Celtic when they faltered in a goalless draw against Hibs at Easter Road – only the second occasion they had failed to score in a league game during the campaign. Then Lennox and Johnstone, great friends off the field, shared the goals in a 2–0 victory over Morton at Cappielow, and the pair staged an action replay the following Wednesday in a 2–1 win against Dunfermline at home. On the same evening in Glasgow, Rangers wound up their league season with a 4–0 triumph over Clyde, their seventh league victory on the trot. They had racked up 55 points, the same total as Celtic, who would play their last league game against Motherwell at Fir Park on 7 May.

Jock Stein's men were already as good as champions. They had netted 105 goals and conceded 30 against Rangers' 91 for and 29 against. It would have taken the most unbelievable, unthinkable nosedive in Celtic's history to allow the Ibrox men to claim the crown. It didn't happen. In the last minute, Bobby Lennox turned in a right-wing cross from Jim Craig past Peter McCloy, who would later sign for Rangers, for the only goal of the game. After an absence of 12 years, the flag was heading back to the East End of Glasgow.

Craig recalled, 'Like Big Tommy on the other flank, I loved to get forward. He took most of the headlines, of course, because of his thunderous shooting power and his spectacular goals, but I would like to think I contributed to the cause, as well. The Motherwell game was a case in point. We knew the league was in the bag and there was only a minute to go, but I still wanted to get down the wing and keep the pressure on our opponents. When I got forward late on, I looked up and there was Bobby Lennox, as usual, in a great position. His speed of thought kept pace with his legs and he was unmarked at the near post. I knocked it across and he got in before the Motherwell defence knew what was going on. He only had to touch it into the net from about two yards. Bobby was deadly from that range!'

'The goals were spread around the team and the side did not rely on me to score,' remembered Lennox, whose goal against Motherwell was his 15th of the campaign. 'With the exception of Ronnie Simpson in goal and John Clark as our defensive rock, everyone was capable of getting a goal or two. Tommy Gemmell, to my mind, was an exceptional left-back. He revolutionised that position in our team. Funnily enough, for a guy who was principally a defender, he used to admit he couldn't tackle too well. He didn't have to, as other teams used to fear him as he bombed forward, threatening to use that mighty right peg of his. I could go through the entire team: Jim Craig might not have claimed many goals, but he certainly set up his fair share; Bobby Murdoch could score goals from distance; Billy McNeill was known to get the odd headed goal or two; Bertie Auld knew where the opposition's net was; Jimmy Johnstone, Stevie Chalmers, Joe McBride and myself were always good for double figures and Willie Wallace would add to that goal threat when he arrived from Hearts. There was a lot of pace about the side, too. Just look at the forward line that won the European Cup a year later. It was Johnstone, Wallace, Chalmers, Auld and myself. All of us had played as out-and-out wingers at some stage of our careers. Back then, you had to possess a fair turn of speed to occupy that position.'

Gemmell recalled, 'That was a fabulous day. As I have already said, I would have loved to have signed for Motherwell, my home-town team. That was my dream until Celtic came on the scene. So winning our first league championship since 1954, when I was 11 years old and still at Craigneuk Public primary school, at the ground where my dad used to take me when I was a kid was simply wonderful. When you consider what Celtic had been through during the barren years, this was an unbeatable feeling. We didn't require champagne that night to get high. In just over a year, the club had won the Scottish Cup in 1965 and the league and League Cup in 1966. Phenomenal stuff. When Wee Bobby stuck that one into the Motherwell net, I wasn't even thinking about us playing in the European Cup the following year and what all that would entail.'

Celtic had become fixated on the championship crown, especially after losing 1–0 to Rangers in the Scottish Cup final replay a couple of weeks earlier. Jock Stein's men had been huge favourites to lift the trophy for the second successive season by the time the final rolled round. Kai Johansen, the right-back destroyed by John Hughes in the New Year walloping, must have gone into the tie feeling a fair amount of trepidation. The Celtic team, in 4–2–4 formation, was: Ronnie Simpson; Ian Young, Billy McNeill, John Clark and Tommy Gemmell; Bobby Murdoch and Charlie Gallagher; Jimmy Johnstone, Joe McBride, Stevie Chalmers and John Hughes. Seven of that line-up would be good enough to become part of the first British team to claim the European Cup, against Inter Milan a year later, but on this occasion they rarely pressurised Billy Ritchie or his defenders.

The infamous Hampden swirl, an unseen menace hardly conducive to accurate passing, was in full force on Saturday, 23 April. The nearest Celtic came to scoring was a header from skipper McNeill that saw the ball clatter off the face of the crossbar. There was a heart-stopping moment, too, when Simpson left his line to claim a harmless-looking left-wing cross. In normal circumstances, this would have been meat and drink to the veteran. The ball, however, was held up in a gust of wind; Simpson's timing was slightly off and he fumbled the cross right at the feet of Jim Forrest, so taken aback by the unexpected gift from the normally reliable custodian that he failed to react and the keeper scooped the ball away at the second attempt.

That miss cost Forrest his place in the replay four days later, with George McLean taking over at number 9. Stein dropped right-back Young and midfielder Gallagher, recalling Jim Craig and Bertie Auld. Lennox missed both games through injury and he was in the Hampden stand the evening the Ibrox side won 1–0 with a late whizz-bang effort from right-back Johansen, enjoying a better ninety minutes than he had had almost four months earlier. Lennox said, 'I thought my teammates outplayed Rangers in the first match and not too many people gave our old rivals much of a chance in the replay. However, Johansen's goal removed the cup from our trophy cabinet and that was a sore one to take. That was one of those games that comes along every now and again where you know fate is against you. I could never be called a defeatist, but I have to admit there are occasions when you instinctively know things will not run your way.

'I remember Celtic storming straight back at Rangers in that game after Johansen's goal. If I recall correctly, big John Hughes ran down the left wing and pitched over a peach of a cross. In the busy penalty area, Joe McBride was first to react and thumped in a ferocious header. Their keeper, Billy Ritchie, hadn't a clue where the ball was. As it happens, it struck him on the shoulder, flew upwards, came down, gently ran along the top of the crossbar and, with what looked like half the Celtic team queuing up on the goal line to knock it in, suddenly veered in the wrong direction, as far as we were concerned, and flopped on top of the roof of the net. That just about summed up Celtic's luck in both those matches.'

Dame Fortune wasn't smiling on Celtic, either, on the European Cup-Winners' Cup front. It all started brightly enough with a runaway 6–0 triumph over Go-Ahead Deventer in Holland. Ian Young played at right-back in the first leg, but Jock Stein brought in Jim Craig for his debut in the return game. Craig recalled, 'I still chuckle when I look back at the day I made my first appearance. I remember it well. Big Jock, as thoughtful as ever, had a habit of selecting games in which younger players could get a chance without too much pressure on them, and he chose well in this one, with Celtic six goals ahead. The evening before the home tie, I was told I would be playing. I was 22 years old at the time and still doing my dentistry studies while playing part-time. Excited? You can bet on it.

'I will always remember waiting in Argyle Street for a bus to take me to the East End of Glasgow, the No. 64 to Auchenshuggle, along with a bunch of Celtic supporters. I was sitting among these guys and they were talking about who might be playing for Celtic that night. No one took a blind bit of notice of me. I was totally unknown. I felt like telling them I would be turning out at right-back for their favourite team, but they probably wouldn't have believed me. A Celtic player on a bus? Just an hour or so away from kick-off? Don't be daft! However, I did indeed make my first appearance in those famous hoops, and a single goal from Joe McBride gave us a rather emphatic 7–0 aggregate triumph. I would like to say I played my part in that victory! I must have impressed Big Jock – I was promptly put back in the reserves, with Ian Young returning to the number 2 berth for the next game, a 5–2 win over Hearts.'

Celtic were drawn away from home for the first leg of their second-round tie against Denmark's Aarhus in November. McBride was on the mark again with a typical effort in a 1–0 win, but Stein was impressed with the Danish keeper, Bent Martin. McNeill and Johnstone stuck two past him in the return match in Glasgow, but Martin was agile and athletic, and shortly afterwards the number 1 signed for Celtic. Stein saw him as a successor to Ronnie Simpson, but the 30-something was in no hurry to don the cardigan and slippers and look out the pipe. Martin, in fact, played only one competitive first-team game for Celtic – in a Glasgow Cup tie – and, after a year, moved to Dunfermline.

The excellent Russians Dynamo Kiev were the quarter-final opponents, with the first game at Parkhead. Celtic turned in a masterclass in front of their own supporters, winning 3–0 with goals from Murdoch (2) and Gemmell. The buccaneering left-back remembered, 'Big Jock actively encouraged everyone to shoot on sight. He was very much of the mind that your shot might not go in, but it might be deflected in the direction of, say, Stevie Chalmers, Bobby Lennox, Joe McBride or Willie Wallace, and nine times out of ten they would tidy things up. The amount of goals we scored from about six or eight yards back then was unbelievable.'

Gemmell sizzled in another unstoppable drive in the return leg, giving Celtic a 1–1 draw and a decisive 4–1 aggregate triumph. Next up were Liverpool, managed by Stein's great friend Bill Shankly. 'Big pals, yes,' said Gemmell, 'but massive rivals, too. They were both former miners and they talked the same language, but friendship went out the window over those two games, especially the second leg at Anfield. I think it would be fair to say we annihilated them 1–0 at Parkhead. We absolutely hammered them and, to this day, I'll never be able to understand how we didn't manage to win 5–0 or 6–0. They hardly came into our half all night. We just went straight at them. I don't think they had ever been on the receiving end of the kind of punishment they took that night. But it was amazing that we had to settle for just one strike from Bobby Lennox to give us a 1–0 advantage. Honestly, if that had been a boxing match the referee would have stopped the fight before half-time. We tore them apart and, to a man, they all looked mightily relieved when the referee blew for full-time, I can tell you. It was one of those games where shots were just inches off target, flying over the bar or sweeping past the post. We had won, but we weren't celebrating because we knew we should have scored so many more to put the tie out of sight. Liverpool remained in the competition and still in with a chance when they should have been well out of contention.'

Billy McNeill recalled, 'We went to Anfield for the return leg and I can tell you we were not one bit afraid. We reasoned we had played them off the park in Glasgow and we could do something similar on their own patch. Everything seemed to be going OK until they were awarded a free kick on the hour mark, about 30 yards out. As I recall, it was a filthy night on Merseyside. Tommy Smith stepped up to take the kick. He fired the ball goalwards and, unfortunately for Ronnie Simpson, it took a wicked bounce off the muddy pitch. Ronnie looked as though he had it covered, but it actually seemed to pick up momentum as it hit the turf in front of him and flashed low into the corner of the net. We couldn't believe it. They were level with us. They had contributed so little over the two and a half hours of play and they were drawing with us. It got worse five minutes later when Geoff Strong got up really well to power an unstoppable header away from Ronnie. There was nothing flukey about that effort – I would have happily claimed it as one of my own. However, the real controversy was just around the corner.

'Near the end, Bobby Lennox turned the ball wide of their keeper Tommy Lawrence and left-back Gerry Byrne on the goal line and into the net. A goal, surely? Alas, not according to the man who mattered, the Belgian referee Josef Hannet. He ruled it out for offside, which was a fairly strange decision when you consider they had a defender behind their goalkeeper. In actual fact, there is absolutely no way the goal shouldn't have counted. We didn't get any consolation much later when Hannet admitted, after watching reruns of the incident, that he had, in fact, got it wrong. Thanks, ref.

'That was just another for the growing collection of Bobby Lennox injustices. Wee Bobby was so quick off the mark that he was too fast for a lot of linesmen. I wonder how many legitimate goals my wee pal scored that were ruled out. He could probably have doubled his goal tally.

'On that occasion in Liverpool, we were furious. So too, unfortunately, were our supporters and a few bottles were thrown onto the pitch. I would never condone such actions, but their frustrations were understandable. They had just seen a perfectly legitimate goal ruled out and their team was out of Europe. What made it all the more galling was the fact that the European Cup-Winners' Cup final was to be played at Hampden Park that year. Can you imagine the scenes if we had played in that game? Dear old Hampden would have been rocking to its foundations. As it turned out, Liverpool took our place and I think they must have used up all their luck against us in the previous two games.

'They lost 2–1 in extra time to the West Germans of Borussia Dortmund and, ironically, the winning goal came from Ron Yeats, who was one of my main challengers for the centre-half slot in the Scottish international team at the time. I remember a Borussia Dortmund player, a guy called Reinhard Libuda, lobbing Lawrence and the ball hitting the crossbar. Yeats, running back in an effort to clear off the line, couldn't get out of the way of the rebound and the ball came down, struck him and bounced over the line. Trophies are won and lost in such bizarre moments.'

So the 1965–66 season was completed with the league championship and League Cup in the Celtic trophy room and successes in the Scottish Cup and European Cup-Winners' Cup just eluding the side. However, Celtic were about to embark on a wonderful voyage and it all kicked off far from home shores.

Bobby Lennox believes the summer tour of North America was another turning point in the continuing Celtic success story. The likeable and laid-back Saltcoats-born lad said, 'I have often stated that Celtic really gelled and came together on that trip. It was a masterstroke by someone at Celtic to take us away for about five weeks. The players got to know one another even better than is possible when you are just turning up for training and, of course, playing on match day. We all enjoyed the experience, but we also knew we were there to work. This was no holiday and Jock Stein was still getting to really know the squad of players he had inherited. We all wanted to impress him and I think I did well enough – I managed to score 19 goals in 11 games! OK, we did play a few select teams from Bermuda, New Jersey and St Louis, but we also took on Spurs three times. The London side were a really top outfit at the time and they went on to win the FA Cup in 1967, beating Chelsea 2–1 in the final.

'I think they were a bit annoyed that they couldn't put one over on us. We beat them 1–0 and then 2–1 before we played them for a third time and they managed to get a 1–1 draw. These were important games for us. They were taking us to another level and it didn't do our confidence any harm, either.

'Tommy Gemmell pestered Big Jock into letting him play at centre-forward in one of our games – I think it was against the Hamilton select – and the boss eventually let him lead the attack. As I recall, Big Tommy did well enough, netting a hat-trick in an 11–0 triumph. Thankfully, though, he accepted that left-back was his best position and the experiment was never tried again!'

Gemmell said, 'Yes, it's true, I did fancy myself as a bit of a goal-scorer because, remember, I did play as an attacking outside-right in my amateur career. I thought the guys up front got it easy. We did all the hard work at the back to set them up with chances and they got all the glory when they scored the goals! I wanted some of that. I had said to Big Jock to give me a chance up front, but I have to admit I knew I was better at the back, where I could come forward and hit shots at goal from long distance.

'I was two-footed, but my right was the stronger. When I played at right-back, I often found myself getting to the byline and simply sending over crosses. I rarely came inside to have a shot with my left foot and, anyway, more often than not, I had Wee Jinky in front of me and he was totally unpredictable. I could cut inside at the same time he decided to do likewise. When Big Jock moved me to left-back, he encouraged me to come in on my right foot and have a dig. I enjoyed my game against the Hamilton select, but Bobby Lennox, Stevie Chalmers and co. were never under any serious threat from me for a position in the front line.'

Lennox added, 'That pre-season tour of the States should never be underestimated in regard to what it meant to the club. There was a real sense of camaraderie among the players and I still believe that's what made that period so memorable. I used to look around our dressing-room at the time and see Big Billy preparing for a game. Then I would look at the Wee Man. Then Big Tommy. Then Bobby Murdoch. Then Wee Bertie. I just looked around the entire dressing-room and thought, "Who can beat us?" We were afraid of no one. We went out onto that pitch expecting to win. It was a great attitude. We really were a good team.'

Gemmell chipped in, 'I'm not being disrespectful to our opponents back then, but when we were discussing the game in the dressing-room before kick-off it wasn't about players asking, "Can we win?" It was more a case of "We should score three, four or more goals against this opposition." That's not meant to be conceited or big-headed, it was just a fact. Genuinely, we believed we could score a barrowload in most matches and, I agree with Bobby, when you looked around the place and saw the players you would be lining up with that day, then who could blame us? It was all about confidence and we had loads of that priceless commodity.'

Joe McBride was in stupendous striking form when Celtic kicked off their defence of the League Cup in the 1966–67 season. The uncompromising frontman claimed thirteen goals in the first five games, including four in an 8–2 romp against St Mirren, five in two games against Clyde and four in two ties against Hearts. Gemmell remarked, 'Joe McBride was an absolutely brilliant goal-scorer. Joe didn't bother with any of the niceties of football or the Fancy Dan stuff. He just wanted to hammer the ball into the net as often as possible. He didn't care how he scored. It could have gone in off his backside and it wouldn't have mattered to him. He had fabulous strength, too. He was burly and impossible to knock off the ball. You would see defenders bouncing off him when he got into his stride. Joe wasn't tall – around 5 ft 9 in. – but he was superb in the air. He threw himself at everything that came into the box. He was totally fearless and goodness only knows how many goals he would have scored for Celtic if it hadn't been for the knee injury that derailed his career. I think he would have given Jimmy McGrory a run for his money.'

As Celtic headed for a League Cup quarter-final date with Dunfermline, they met Rangers in the second league game of the campaign. After a mesmerising start to the game, Celtic were two goals ahead by the third minute. Johnstone flashed over a right-wing cross in the first minute, McBride took a fresh-air swipe at the ball and Auld followed up at the back post to fire it beyond Billy Ritchie. Moments later, Murdoch hit a sublime second, featuring the exquisite finish that was his trademark. The masterful midfielder was just outside the penalty box when he looked up and opted to go for precision instead of power. He neatly dinked the ball over the defenders in front of him and it soared high into the top left-hand corner of the net. Rangers couldn't come back from that startling double blast and the game finished 2–0.

Celtic were on fire and McBride, confrontations with a certain team from Govan aside, couldn't stop scoring. He netted ten as the club racked up twenty-eight goals in a scintillating six-game winning run. They took seven off Stirling Albion, six off St Johnstone and five each against Hibs and Ayr United. They had to be content with three against Airdrie and two against Dundee. After the bleak early '60s, the Celtic fans were thoroughly enjoying themselves.

On the afternoon of 5 November at Parkhead, St Mirren's unconventional goalkeeper Denis Connaghan – later to sign for Celtic, his boyhood idols – was in defiant mood. The extrovert custodian had one of those days when the ball was sticking to him. Peter Kane scored for the Paisley outfit, but another long-range effort from Gemmell, playing at centre-half in place of the injured Billy McNeill, gave Stein's side a point. It was to prove a mere blip.

A fortnight later came one of the most remarkable Celtic matches in living memory, against Dunfermline at East End Park. The Fifers were leading 4–2 with 15 minutes to play. A guy called Alex Ferguson was making life difficult for the Celtic back lot. Ferguson's natural style was that of a bustling, energetic frontman and he wasn't afraid to put himself about. As a matter of fact, he had the distinction of having a Celtic supporters club named after him. During his days at St Johnstone, the centre-forward netted a hat-trick in a remarkable 3–2 victory at Ibrox. He was immediately rewarded by Celtic fans looking for a name for their new club. Presumably, they changed it in 1967 when Ferguson actually joined Rangers! The player was up for the encounter with Celtic, though, and had put two past Ronnie Simpson, with the home side looking to inflict the first league defeat of the season on the Parkhead outfit.

Then, in a truly memorable grand finale, Celtic, who had scored earlier through McBride and Murdoch, launched an unforgettable and furious fightback. Johnstone and Auld scored to pull it back to 4–4, but, even more astonishingly, Celtic then went for the winner. The game was in its fading moments when Dunfermline centre-half Roy Barry conceded a clear-cut penalty kick when he took off Superman-style to fist away a cross that was arrowing in on McBride's head. East End Park held its breath as McBride stepped up to take the award. The revival was complete when he belted the ball high into the net.

Gemmell, who played right-back that afternoon, said, 'What a game that was. I think it emphasised the fact that this Celtic team never knew when it was beaten. This was a line-up comprised of winners; we were never going to accept second best. Dunfermline played really well that afternoon in, as I recall, fairly awful conditions. It was a stamina-sapping playing surface after some heavy rain, but we just kept going. Aye, a lot of teams might get it back to 4–4 and think that was good enough. Not us. We wanted to win. There was still a minute or two left to go and we were on a roll, so we probably fancied our chances.'

December opened in the most unusual of fashions: with a goalless draw against Kilmarnock at Rugby Park. It was a strangely lethargic performance from a Celtic team that was unrecognisable from the one that had stormed to a sensational victory over Dunfermline. Bobby Ferguson became the first goalkeeper to shut out Celtic in the league in season 1966–67, and Aberdeen's Bobby Clark became the second four months later in another scoreless confrontation. Normal service was resumed with an emphatic 6–2 win over Partick Thistle. Willie Wallace netted two, his first goals for the club after his £30,000 transfer from Hearts a fortnight earlier.

Wallace's move to Celtic came as a bit of a surprise because many thought he was destined for Rangers. He revealed, 'I had been in dispute with Hearts and just wanted a transfer. Newcastle United and Stoke City were showing an interest, so it looked as though I would be packing my bags and heading across the border. Then Jock Stein came on the scene and he didn't have to try too hard to sell Celtic to me. As soon as I realised there was a chance of going to Celtic Park and working alongside Big Jock, there was no choice to make. Newcastle and Stoke City, without any disrespect, had no chance of getting my signature on transfer forms.

'Let's try to clear up a few mysteries that have followed me around for 40 years or so. I was not, and never had been, a Rangers supporter. The story goes that I was poised to sign for the Ibrox side until Big Jock made his move. There was a tale that the Celtic manager waited until Rangers were out of town and playing in a European tie before he quickly sealed a deal with Hearts. Sounds like a good yarn, but it simply didn't happen that way.

'I don't know if Rangers were ever interested in me at all. OK, my whole family were Rangers fans and they would have loved for me to sign for them, but I was overjoyed when I got the opportunity to move to Celtic. Yes, some of my family didn't share my enthusiasm for all things Celtic back then. Actually, I admit I did see a lot of Rangers in the '50s because my uncle Jim just happened to be the president of the Kirkintilloch Rangers Supporters Club. However, I spent more time watching Falkirk at Brockville, which was just up the road from where I lived in Larbert. But I am a Celtic fan now, you can be certain of that. Once you have mixed in that company, you couldn't be anything else.

'I live in Queensland in Australia these days, but I still bump into hundreds of Celtic supporters. They are everywhere and that fact simply underlines the worldwide appeal of the club. I have to say I was always made welcome at Celtic right from day one. I was aware of the religious divide that existed in the west of Scotland, but it never bothered me and, anyway, Celtic had always signed Protestants. Big Jock, for a start. And there was me, Tommy Gemmell, Ronnie Simpson and Bertie Auld among the Lisbon Lions. I may have gone to a Proddy school, but, after they came knocking at my door and took me to Glasgow, I was Celtic through and through. Still am to this day.'

It is a general misconception that Wallace was bought to replace McBride after his dreadful injury at Aberdeen on Christmas Eve. Not so. Wallace actually played three times alongside the unfortunate McBride, who, despite missing the rest of the season after the Pittodrie game, completed the campaign as the country's second-top scorer with thirty-five competitive goals – one behind teammate Stevie Chalmers. It was devastating finishing from a player thoroughly enjoying performing in the hoops.

Bertie Auld said, 'It was an absolute travesty what happened to Joe against the Dons. He just couldn't stop scoring and then along came that knee injury. Everyone felt so bad for Joe. We knew this was going to be a massive season for us and Joe was eager to play his part. To score so many goals before the turn of the year was simply sensational and you can only hazard a guess as to what he would have finished up with if he had stayed clear of injury.'

McBride's season ended abruptly in the 1–1 draw at Aberdeen and Lennox took on the mantle of goal-scorer. It's difficult to say if the Celtic players suffered a reaction to such a popular player being sidelined for the rest of the season, but they didn't hit top gear a week later in their first defeat of the campaign, losing 3–2 to Dundee United at Tannadice. It was certainly an off-colour performance from Celtic. Oddly, Jock Stein's side were to lose only two league matches during that campaign, both 3–2 against the Tayside outfit.

So 1966 drew to a halt with an unexpected loss, but there had been something to celebrate in October when Rangers were beaten again in a second successive League Cup final. Celtic were unstoppable in the competition and won all ten of their ties while collecting thirty-five goals, with McBride notching fifteen of the total. They simply scorched through to the Hampden final, the 6–3 triumph over Dunfermline at Parkhead in the quarter-final first leg being the most memorable tie.

Auld scored two that night and recalled, 'Big Jock was forever telling me my right foot was only good for standing on. I used to say to him, "Look, Boss, when you've got a left peg like mine you don't need a right." So I was particularly happy that night to score with a right-foot shot from about 25 yards. I looked up, saw my opportunity and simply hit the ball sweetly. It flew high into the net and then I made a beeline for the Celtic dugout to wave my right foot at Big Jock. The fans must have been wondering what that was all about!'

Celtic eased past Airdrie, winning 2–0 in the semi-final, to set up another October date with Rangers. Auld recalled, 'Old Firm matches, of course, were always special, although they weren't always classics. They could be enjoyable, they could be exasperating. And, yes, they could be explosive. Celtic fans would be coming up to you days before the game and imploring, "Beat them for us, Bertie," or, "Don't let us down, please." So, no pressure there, then. If you weren't prepared mentally and physically for those 90 minutes of combat, they could overwhelm you. There was a genuine rivalry among the players, but a lot of us were friends, too, off the park. We would bump into each other at so many functions and we always got on well.

'Sadly, I was involved in a sickening collision in one of the games that left their defender Davie Provan with a broken leg. It was a pure accident as we both went for a ball down the wing. I was shaping to cross it over when Davie threw himself into a tackle. Neither of us could pull out, unfortunately. Davie, in fact, was a player I had a lot of respect for. I watched him play against Jinky Johnstone on countless occasions and never once did I see him try to kick our player. It must have been frustrating facing up to Jinky when he was in the mood, but Davie never lost the rag or tried to boot our wee winger. In fact, I rated the Rangers lad so highly as a person as well as a professional that I gave him a job on our backroom staff when I was manager of Partick Thistle.

'Davie once reminded me of how he reckons he saved Jinky's life! Some nutcase managed to get onto the pitch at Ibrox and made straight for our player. Davie is convinced the yob was carrying some sort of object in his hand. You could be certain he wasn't about to make a presentation to Jinky to congratulate him on another fine performance. However, as he raced past, Big Davie did a quick bit of thinking and grabbed the would-be assailant. He wrestled him to the ground and the police eventually frogmarched the intruder off the pitch and up the tunnel.

'Actually, there could be a fair bit of banter in those tussles as well as a lot of tension. John Greig, the Rangers captain, also revelled in the derby matches. On one occasion, he went over to the Celtic end to fetch the ball for a throw-in. A voice from the crowd exclaimed, "Hey, Greigy, I didn't realise you were such a dirty bastard." Quick as a flash, Greig replied, "Have you not been watching me all season!"

'Underlining what I said about Davie Provan, Greig was once involved in a tackle on Bobby Lennox that snapped our player's ankle. Bobby was the first to say it was an accident. These things happen in a contact sport.'

Auld came into the Celtic first team when Rangers ruled the roost in Old Firm encounters. He added, 'Between September 1958 and January 1960, I played four league games against them and didn't win one. We drew the first 2–2 at Parkhead with goals from Eric Smith and Bobby Collins. The next was the New Year's Day game in 1959 at Ibrox and, while we got a goal from Bertie Peacock, we went down 2–1. The next came in September the same year and we lost 3–1, with Mike Jackson getting our consolation effort. And the misery continued in the next clash when I played inside-right in a team beaten 1–0 at home. Around that period, Rangers regularly beat Celtic and you can't dispute that they were the better team with better players. They were also well organised, which certainly wasn't the case at Parkhead until Big Jock arrived to turn everything upside down.'

Come the 1966 League Cup final on 29 October, with 94,532 cramming into Hampden, Celtic were favourites after winning the opening league game of the season with a fair degree of ease, those two early goals from Auld and Murdoch enough to see off the Ibrox outfit. Once again, the game was settled fairly early when Auld pinged in an inviting cross and McBride back-headed the ball down to the inrushing Lennox; totally unmarked, the lightning-swift forward lashed an unstoppable drive beyond the exposed Norrie Martin. That solitary effort was enough for Celtic to retain the trophy.

The European adventure had kicked off the previous month with home and away wins over Swiss side Zürich, and Celtic followed those up with back-to-back wins over Nantes of France. That saw Celtic playing in soccer's premier tournament after the turn of the year. What did 1967 have in store? Could the fans dare to dream?

8

LET THE GOOD TIMES ROLL

Tommy Gemmell has, like most of us, been forced to overcome the obstacles that fortune and fate so often scatter across our path through life. So when the smile on that beaming Danny Kaye face of his lights up even the darkest place, you realise this character is far removed from someone with the merest hint of a pessimistic outlook. Tommy has always been respected for his forthright honesty. On occasion, that quality can jar with some people, but that will never stop a genuine footballing legend telling it like it is. Candid as ever, he told me, 'I can't see Celtic ever emulating what they achieved in 1967. There is every likelihood that will remain the greatest year in the club's history.' Then he grinned and, offering hope to today's Celtic legions, added, 'Never say never, though.'

It was the year when the jigsaw came together spectacularly. How could a team that had been soundly hammered 6–2 by Falkirk, humbled 5–1 by Dunfermline, destroyed 5–2 by Kilmarnock and embarrassed 3–0 by St Johnstone two seasons previously ever expect to achieve the honour of being crowned the best side in Europe, the first British club to conquer all and win the European Cup? It was a completely unexpected and stunning turnaround in Celtic's fortunes. On that extraordinary day of 25 May 1967, instead of being humbled by some nondescript opposition, Billy McNeill, in that wonderful Caesar-like pose, was standing in sun-kissed Lisbon, on what appeared to be a podium in an ancient coliseum, holding aloft the most glittering and sought-after trophy European football had to offer. Has there ever been a more iconic image?

The honour of scoring Celtic's first goal in the European Cup fell to Gemmell and only his blistering effort in the Portuguese capital some eight months later would better it. The club's first sortie as Scotland's ambassadors at football's top table kicked off against Swiss side FC Zürich at Parkhead on 28 September 1966. It was an anxious evening, a blanket of tension settling on proceedings.

Gemmell said, 'Our Swiss opponents weren't quite as revered as the giants of Europe, such as Real Madrid, the Milan sides, Inter and AC, or the Benfica of Eusébio's era. We discovered, though, that they were a well-drilled, workmanlike outfit who, it must be said, made life somewhat uncomfortable for us that night. Although we had played in the European Cup-Winners' Cup and the Fairs Cup in previous years, and had a taste for the game at that level, this was the first time we had taken on the actual champions of another country in competitive encounters.

'We could only guess at the standard of football in Switzerland. They didn't possess a lot of individual star names, but it should be remembered that the Swiss international side had played in the World Cup finals in England just that summer. Those were the days before the influx of foreigners plying their trade all over the place. Therefore, it could be reasoned that a fair percentage of the FC Zürich side, their nation's title-winners, would have been included in their international squad. We knew they would be no mugs and they were impressive in the tidy manner in which they went about their business. Big Jock had warned us of their speed while hitting on the break. We were desperate to win at our place, but under no circumstances could we allow opportunities to be presented behind us. We realised that would have disastrous consequences.'

Nerves were jangling among the fans when the hour mark passed and there was still no breakthrough goal. The Swiss defenders were doing an excellent job of blunting the main menace of Joe McBride and Stevie Chalmers. Wingers Jimmy Johnstone and John Hughes were offered no encouragement by two pacy full-backs to advance down the flanks. The skills of Bobby Murdoch and Bertie Auld were suffocated in a congested midfield. Cometh the hour, cometh the man, however, and up stepped Gemmell. As the clock ticked round to the 64th minute, John Clark thwarted a breakaway attempt and flicked a neat ball out to Gemmell, playing at right-back with Willie O'Neill on the left. Gemmell, a few yards inside enemy territory, nodded the ball down and must have been pleasantly surprised that there was no posse of Swiss defenders swarming around him as he prepared to surge further forward. You got the impression immediately that something special was about to happen. The opposition clearly didn't know about the awesome shooting power of the full-back. The defenders backed off and Gemmell, as the whole of Europe would soon get to know, never needed to be asked twice about having a pop at goal.

Celtic fans held their breath in collective anticipation. Gemmell assessed the situation developing around him in an instant, composed himself and then thumped in a mighty right-foot effort from about 25 yards. The ball was a mere blur. Goalkeeper Steffen Iten, safe and sound all evening, didn't move a muscle as the missile zeroed in on its target before smashing into the net at his top left-hand corner. It was hit with such frightening pace that the Zürich number 1 probably did himself a huge favour by not going anywhere near it. Jock Stein, only a few days from his 44th birthday, bounded out of the dugout to acclaim the barrier-breaking goal.

Gemmell said, 'Most of the statisticians timed the goal at 64 minutes – just 60 seconds off my effort in Lisbon. So that might just give you a hint as to why we were successful. We were extremely fit, very fast and every single individual possessed a wonderfully resilient, never-say-die spirit. Big Jock always had us primed for 90 minutes, and indeed another 30 if extra time might be required. There were no slackers in that 1967 squad. If there had been, they would have been right out the door. There was no messing with the manager. Jock insisted that you could possess all the talent in the world but if you couldn't ally that to fitness then you were wasting your time. Teams must have loathed playing us back then because they knew they would have to put in a full shift. There would be no wee rest periods while both sets of players took a breather.'

It got better for Celtic only five minutes after Gemmell's counter when McBride netted with a low drive from the edge of the box. The game ended on a controversial note that saw 47,604 supporters rather perplexed as they streamed out of the stadium. 'What was the final score?' they were asking. 'Was it 2–0 or was it 3–0?' McBride had left Iten helpless again with a typical poacher's goal. It certainly was not offside and the tannoy announcer must have been as puzzled as everyone else, because there was no information coming from his vantage point in the main stand. It later transpired that an over-fussy match official had blown for time up just before the ball had hit the net.

In the end, it didn't matter. Celtic won 3–0 in the second leg, with Gemmell adding two more, one a penalty kick, and Stevie Chalmers claiming the other. Gemmell revealed, 'Big Jock told us it would be easier for us in Zürich than it had been in Glasgow. He reasoned we would have more space to work in and they would have to leave gaps as they searched for goals. And so it proved. He was bang on the money yet again. The Swiss weren't as disciplined as they had been in Glasgow and, in truth, their heads went down when I got the opener. Then Stevie got on the end of a Bobby Lennox flick from a corner kick to fire under the keeper's body and make it an uncatchable 4–0 aggregate. I was delighted to get the third from the spot and become the first Celtic player to get a European Cup hat-trick for the club. OK, it wasn't technically a hat-trick, with the goals spread over two games, but you wouldn't take that away from me now, would you?'

The French champions, Nantes, were the next to fall, on a 6–2 aggregate in the second round. Both ties finished 3–1. France's finest were convinced that the Scots would not be celebrating St Andrew's Day on 30 November at their Malakoff Stadium. They gave Jock Stein's men a fright by taking the lead through Francis Magny in the twentieth minute, but the response was instantaneous and McBride levelled four minutes later. Jimmy Johnstone had already won over the home support, who christened him '*La Puce Volante*' – 'The Flying Flea' – as he shredded his direct opponent, the unfortunate Gabriel de Michele. The outside-right was a darting threat as he put on a solo show for the 15,464 crowd. The Celtic players had superior stamina and fitness and Stein told them to kill off their opponents after the interval. Bobby Murdoch picked out Bobby Lennox with one of his trademark through passes and the speedy raider was onto it in a flash to wallop in the second. Late in the match, Chalmers fired in the third.

The second leg was in Glasgow only a week later and Stein promised the fans, 'We may be 3–1 ahead, but we are committed to attacking, entertaining football, and I can assure everyone that again will be the case on this occasion.' *La Puce Volante* decided to stage an encore and got the opening goal in the 13th minute. Gérard Georgin equalised, but after the interval Chalmers headed in a Johnstone cross and it was déjà vu for the French when the little winger skipped down the right again and sizzled in a low cross that was tucked away by Lennox from close range. Celtic could now take a breather in the competition until March 1967, when they would meet Yugoslavia's Vojvodina Novi Sad in the quarter-finals.

The league continued at the turn of the year and icy conditions meant a postponement of the traditional New Year's Day fixture. After dropping three points in the last two games of December, drawing 1–1 with Aberdeen and then losing 3–2 to Dundee United, Celtic got back on track on 7 January with an excellent 5–1 triumph over Dundee in Glasgow. The club gleefully romped to another five successive triumphs, with Stevie Chalmers scoring eight of his side's nineteen goals. He was dovetailing nicely with Willie Wallace as the attack's spearhead in the absence of the injured Joe McBride. Stirling Albion, on their own trim little Annfield pitch, halted the green-and-white juggernaut for the second successive season with a 1–1 draw. It was another scrappy performance on a playing surface that left a lot to be desired.

Bertie Auld told me, 'Yes, I played that day, too. In fact, ten of the team that faced Stirling Albion at their place would play in the European Cup final, with the curious exception of John Hughes, who actually got our goal that afternoon. He was replaced by Bobby Lennox, of course, against Inter Milan. It's just as well they didn't hold the big game in Stirling instead of Lisbon; we could still be playing and trying to win!

'I hated that horrible little ground at Annfield, but I can look back and have a good laugh today at a rather remarkable incident that occurred on that pitch. The playing surface was so close to the terracings that the crowds could just about reach out and touch you, as I once found to my cost. They had a tough full-back by the name of George Pettigrew, who always tried to intimidate opponents. He was a big bloke and thought nothing about giving you a wallop if you came anywhere near him. It didn't matter if the ball was in the other half of the field, either. One day I had had enough of being battered all over the place and he became the recipient of some retribution. The referee missed it, I'm glad to say, but someone in the crowd didn't. I was running down the wing when I felt this almighty whack on the back of my head. Down I toppled. I looked round and was sure it must have been Pettigrew, but he was nowhere to be seen. Then a voice came from the terracing. It was a woman and she yelled, "Don't you dare hit my man again!" It was the Stirling Albion player's wife and she had just cracked me over the skull with her handbag! God knows what she must have had in there, but it felt like at least a half-brick!'

After the stalemate in Stirling, Jock Stein read the Riot Act to his troops once more and they responded with six consecutive successes as they homed in on their second title triumph in a row. The surge shuddered to a full stop in a goalless draw against Aberdeen in Glasgow. The Pittodrie side's manager Eddie Turnbull – who, as a player for Hibs, had regularly faced Stein – was as ruthless as his counterpart in aiming to achieve success for his club. He was a committed character who, it must be said, would never become a close confidant of the Celtic boss. They would go head to head at Hampden again in the Scottish Cup final ten days later and the dour Turnbull, who never required a second invitation to scowl, would not leave the national stadium the picture of sweetness and light. Stein made sure of that.

However, there was a fright along the Hampden trail. Tommy Gemmell recalled, 'We were all on a high after beating Vojvodina Novi Sad to book our place in the European Cup semi-final. Three days later, we played Queen's Park in the Scottish Cup at our place. The fans, including Sean Connery, James Bond himself, rolled in to see goals galore and they got one in the first minute from me. Unfortunately, I placed the ball behind Ronnie Simpson. Oops! I'm glad to say I made amends by hitting the equaliser and then Stevie Chalmers, Willie Wallace, Bobby Murdoch and Bobby Lennox, in that order, I believe, took over as we won 5–3. Queen's Park really surprised us that afternoon by getting in about it. At the end of the day, we had played three Scottish Cup ties, had scored sixteen goals and were in the semi-finals.'

Billy McNeill added, 'The Queen's Park tie was a game that hammered into us the fact that, if we were to do anything in football, concentration would have to be our watchword. It acted as a wake-up call.'

Celtic were then held to a goalless draw by Clyde in the semi-final but won the replay 2–0 with efforts from Lennox and Auld. Things were getting quite hectic around this period. The European Cup was rolling along in nerve-shredding manner, and the Scottish Cup final was due on 29 April, by which time the club had cemented their place in Lisbon. As far as the league was concerned, Celtic had three games left to play, against Dundee United, Rangers and Kilmarnock, all in Glasgow.

The pressure must have been getting to Rangers, too, in the run-in. They had lost 1–0 at home to Dunfermline, scraped a 1–0 win at Stirling Albion and then had two 1–1 draws with Clyde and Dundee.

Unexpectedly, though, Celtic lost again to Dundee United by 3–2, the same score as the December game at Tannadice. Celtic were leading 2–1 with ten minutes to go before their stunning collapse. On 6 May, the Glasgow team travelled to a rain-lashed Ibrox Stadium – where they were watched by Inter Milan's cunning manager Helenio Herrera – with a game in hand over their rivals and in the knowledge that a draw would be good enough to crown them champions of Scotland for a second successive season.

Gemmell once more takes up the story: 'The performance from Wee Jinky that afternoon was simply unbelievable. Helenio Herrera's first act when he left his seat in the stand afterwards must have been to change his trousers! The pitch was an absolute sea of mud and there was our five-foot-nothing outside-right terrorising the Rangers defence. That surface plus the fact that the heavens opened up from start to finish made it difficult for even big guys such as myself, Jim Craig and Billy McNeill, all six-footers, to wade through the quagmire. It was exhausting stuff, I can tell you. Old Firm games were always difficult enough, but Rangers, who were a very good team back then, were doubly determined that we would not win the league on their ground. To emphasise the enormity of the task we faced, you only have to note that our old foes had also won through to the final of the European Cup-Winners' Cup and would face Bayern Munich in Nuremberg only a week after we had played Inter

Milan. Imagine that – both the major European trophies could have ended up in Glasgow in 1967. The Ibrox lads lost 1–0, but they took an excellent Bayern team to extra time before they were beaten.

'So all guns were blazing when we turned up that day. The league was their last hope of domestic success because, after beating us 1–0 in the Scottish Cup final replay the previous year, they had crashed out 1–0 at the first hurdle to Berwick Rangers. After that game, I recall the Ibrox chairman John Lawrence saying, "There are individuals who will never play for this club again." Front players Jim Forrest and George McLean, in fact, never turned out for Rangers again. A bit harsh, you might think, but, once again, it just showed how determined Rangers were to topple Celtic. Failure wasn't an option for a club that had got used to being the nation's top side.

'They might have thought they were on their way to avenging that season's league and League Cup defeats when Sandy Jardine lashed an unstoppable shot high past Ronnie Simpson. But their advantage was nullified minutes later when Bobby Lennox struck the post and Wee Jinky skipped through the rain and glaur to prod the rebound past Norrie Martin.

'Into the second half and the conditions continued to be miserable, the rain still teeming down. And yet, in this impossible situation, Wee Jinky conjured up a magical moment that is still as vivid today as it was back then. Our wee winger weaved his way in from the right. Their left-back Davie Provan seemed quite happy to see our winger meander across the pitch as opposed to attacking him down the flank. Jinky was on his "weaker" left foot and the defence didn't come out to meet him. They must have wondered who he was going to pass to. Then the Wee Man took aim from about 25 yards and sent a scorching left-foot drive high past Martin into the roof of the net. I have absolutely no idea where he summoned up that energy or power from. It was extraordinary. The wee chap was soaked through, his jersey was flapping outside his shorts, his socks were round about his ankles and he still managed to dredge up that fabulous feat of strength. Herrera must have felt sick! Rangers got a late equaliser through Roger Hynd, but the game remained at 2–2 and we celebrated the title on the ground of our oldest enemy. Happy days!'

Celtic went through the formality of completing their league commitments on 15 May, when they beat Kilmarnock 2–0, with Wallace and Lennox on target. A concerned Inter Milan slipped another spy into the stand, and he must have been confused to see John Fallon taking over from Ronnie Simpson in goal, an unknown in John Cushley playing at centre-half and skipper Billy McNeill turning out in the number 8 shorts. All kidology from Big Jock, of course. It worked, too.

The Scottish Cup had been claimed against Aberdeen the week before Wee Jinky dazzled in the downpour in Govan. The Pittodrie side had been impressive in getting to Mount Florida. Celtic had reached the final by claiming 18 goals while their opponents had scored 16. A fine game was in prospect. There might even have been the flicker of a smile on the countenance of Eddie Turnbull. Well, before the game, anyway. Jock Stein went with the line-up that would make history just under a month later in Lisbon. A goal in each half from the prolific Wallace gave Celtic a 2–0 triumph in a cup final that was a lot more comfortable than the club might have anticipated.

So the league championship, the Scottish Cup and the League Cup had all been won in the 1966–67 season. The players very graciously also threw in the Glasgow Cup, with three successive 4–0 wins over Rangers, Queen's Park and Partick Thistle. Now all eyes were on Portugal.

However, let's turn the clock back to a freezing cold evening in the old Yugoslavia and a European Cup quarter-final collision with Vojvodina on 1 March. Billy McNeill said, 'I know the manager and the lads all rated the Slavs as by far the best team we met that year, including Inter Milan. They were superb technically but were also quite adept in what you might call the not-so-fine arts of the game. There were some memorable mind games going on off the pitch, too, between the boss and their manager Vujadin Boskov, who went on to coach at some of the biggest teams in Europe, including Real Madrid.

'Big Jock clearly wasn't impressed by Boskov's pre-match prediction. The Slav boss stated quite clearly and emphatically that he believed Vojvodina would win by "at least two goals". Jock countered, "Oh, really? We'll see about that." When they won the first leg by a solitary effort, Boskov came out again and declared he hadn't been too impressed by Celtic and he fully expected his team to win in Glasgow. Now, if Boskov was trying to get Jock fired up for the return, he couldn't have done a better job. "We'll be ready for them," Jock said. He went public, too, in the Yugoslav press, saying, "Vojvodina are a very good team, but we are better and, take my word for it, we will win in the second leg." There was a little element of bravado there, because we all knew how difficult the Slavs would be in Glasgow.'

Boskov and his team turned up at Celtic Park the night before the match because they wanted a workout on the pitch under the floodlights. It was normal practice for teams to go through this routine, as it made a lot of sense for them to get a feel for the conditions they would encounter 24 hours later. Boskov, then, wasn't best pleased when Big Jock informed him that neither he nor his team would be placing a foot on the pitch at Celtic Park. Jock told him, 'Sorry, there's been too much rain recently and we can't take the chance of the pitch cutting up.'

McNeill recalled, 'To be honest, the weather hadn't been too kind to Glasgow around the time of the game. But Boskov was far from convinced. He made all sorts of protestations. "I'll take it up with your chairman," he threatened. Jock waved it away in his usual fashion: "You can train at Barrowfield and I'll make sure the lights are switched on. Off you go." No wonder my wee pal Bertie Auld would often insist, "When Jock Stein was in town, the foxes fled for the hills!"

'To say Boskov was not amused would be putting it rather mildly. They were fizzing, but at least Boskov and his boys got the drift that Jock Stein was indeed the man in charge at Celtic. As far as football matters went, there was no higher power. Vojvodina, who had beaten a strong Atlético Madrid team to reach the quarter-finals, warned us they would have the last word on the matter at Celtic Park during the game. We gave them credit for being an extremely talented and resilient outfit, but we knew they weren't slow to hand out a wee bit of retribution every now and then. If they were trying to scare anyone at Celtic, though, they were wasting their time.'

Gemmell had accepted most of the blame for the first-leg defeat when, in dodgy conditions, he tried a pass-back that fell between Murdoch and Clark 20 minutes from time, just when it looked as though the Yugoslavians were running out of ideas about how to get through a resolute Celtic back lot, with McNeill and sidekick Clark in imperious form. Gemmell remembered, 'I didn't make any excuses then and I'm certainly not going to do so now, but I underestimated two things that night: the flint-hard surface and the pace of a player called Svemir Djordjic. The pass might have looked like a lost cause to the Slav, but he didn't give it up and his sheer acceleration defied the elements. He got to the ball first, squared for Milan Stanic and he thumped it past Ronnie, who was helpless. I got an earful from my goalkeeper and I put up my hands. "Sorry, lads," I said, "My fault." I felt dreadful. One slack pass and we were smack in trouble – all our good work had gone for precisely nothing. I knew we would be up against it in Glasgow.'

As everyone knows, Celtic Park can be a special place on European nights, with the stadium heaving, throbbing and rocking, the ground packed to the rafters as a dramatic, breathtaking spectacle unfolds before your very eyes. Could there ever have been one more memorable than the fraught, nail-biting encounter with Vojvodina on the evening of 8 March? It was a game that had everything. Even that cinematic genius and master of suspense Alfred Hitchcock couldn't have scripted that 90 minutes with more skill or cunning. It was a bitterly cold, frosty evening in the East End of Glasgow, but no one of the Celtic persuasion was complaining.

Gemmell said, 'How could I rectify my first-leg mistake? Simple, really – I had to play out of my skin in Glasgow and, as usual, give my everything. I wanted to bomb forward at every opportunity, but Big Jock had drilled into us the need for discipline and concentration. We were up against a team with the ability to pick us off with laser-beam passes if we left any gaps at the back. Vojvodina were excellent at possession football and every outfield player looked comfortable with the ball at his feet, even in the tightest of situations. I remember we were reaching the hour mark in the tie and, to be honest, it was getting a bit exasperating. No towels were being thrown in, but we were beginning to wonder where the goal would come from. Then I saw a chance to use John Hughes as a decoy. Yogi came inside, taking a defender with him, giving me the opportunity to travel down the flank. I took a quick look up, saw Stevie Chalmers lurking with intent, as ever, and I fired over a cross. Their keeper, the highly rated Ilija Pantelic, tried to cut it out, but Stevie was as brave as a lion, got in a challenge and then swiftly banged the ball over the line as the Vojvodina defence, for once, froze. Obviously, they had expected their goalie to deal with the danger, but they reckoned without the fearlessness of our striker. There were 69,374 fans crammed into Celtic Park that evening and you might just have heard my sigh of relief above the din.'

Celtic saved the best for last. Billy McNeill said, 'I've always been a great believer that the best time to get an important goal is as near to that final whistle as possible. You can get off to a great start in a game and score in the first minute, but, logically, that gives your opponents another 89 minutes to hit back. God knows Celtic gave away enough early goals to the opposition back then, but, to a man, we thought, "There's still 80-odd minutes to go and plenty of time to turn things around." It's in the history books now that I headed the winner against Vojvodina in the last minute, but I have been told that the referee blew for time up two seconds after the restart following that effort. Now that is a late, late goal.

'At 1–1 on aggregate, I'll always recall Big Jock waving us all up for one final assault on Pantelic when Charlie Gallagher raced over to take a right-wing corner kick. In those days, there was no extra time, so if we wanted the job done in Glasgow, it was now or never. The game would have gone to a replay and I believe it would have taken place in Rotterdam. Anyway, I think Charlie was about to take a short corner kick, but changed his mind. Thank goodness!

'There was the usual barging and jostling as I made my way forward. The Slavs had marked me very well at set pieces and I hadn't really had a sniff at goal. On this occasion, though, my timing was absolutely spot-on. Charlie swung it in, I kept my run going, the ball hung in the air, I got a good leap and made superb contact. The next thing I saw was the effort soaring high into the net. Pantelic had strayed a bit – I think Stevie blocked his run – and they had a defender on the line who did a fair impersonation of goalkeeper as he tried to paw the ball away with his left hand. He was wasting his time – that was a goal all the way as soon as it came off my napper.'

Bobby Lennox recalled, 'People often ask me what was my favourite goal in that European Cup run. Well, it wasn't one of mine. As it happens, I scored only two – in both legs of our 6–2 aggregate win over Nantes – and neither, I have to say, was particularly spectacular. Big Billy's against Vojvodina was something special altogether. Naturally, I was overjoyed for all the obvious reasons, but I was doubly pleased because we had stuck two past Pantelic. I would like to believe I am a fairly easy-going type of guy, but I really hated that bloke. I know making a comment like that is way out of character for me, so please allow me to explain why I had bad feelings towards Vojvodina's number 1. In the first leg, I made a challenge for a 50–50 ball, as I was quite entitled to do. I did it every week in Scottish football and no one complained. Pantelic didn't like being disturbed, though.

'I slid in, my momentum took me forward and the keeper collapsed on top of me as he collected the ball. It certainly wasn't a foul, but Pantelic wasn't too happy. He got to his feet and went to help me get up, too. It all seemed very sporting, but, if anyone had bothered to take a closer look, they would have seen that the Slav had a handful of my hair as he "helped" me back up off the ground. I've got a sense of humour, but that was no laughing matter. Mind you, I should get in touch with him just in case he still possesses a clump of my hair – I could do with it now!

'When the second leg came round, all I wanted to do was stick one or two behind Pantelic to welcome him to Glasgow in no uncertain fashion. Alas, I didn't get my wish, but we still beat them and that was the main objective all along. However, if you see footage of our first goal by Stevie Chalmers, have a look at what I'm getting up to. I'm right in the keeper's face and giving it "Yahoo!" Normally, I wouldn't dream of doing such a thing, but I was willing to make an exception in Pantelic's case. Sorry, I just had to do it – I couldn't help myself.'

The elegant Josef Masopust and his talented Dukla Prague teammates now stood between Celtic and their date with destiny. The Czechoslovakian international captain had been voted European Footballer of the Year in 1962, but it was a bloke who used to play for Kilsyth Rangers, Stenhousemuir and Raith Rovers who took the spotlight in two very different semi-final encounters. Willie Wallace, playing in his first-ever European Cup tie, was on target twice in the 3–1 triumph in the first leg at a highly charged Celtic Park on 12 April. It was a still evening in Glasgow, the wind a mere whisper, when Billy McNeill and Josef Masopust led their teams out of the tunnel onto the park to be greeted by 74,406 expectant fans. Supporters who had worried about League Cup ties against Queen of the South only a few years beforehand were being catapulted into a new stratosphere of excitement.

Stein brought back Bertie Auld in place of Charlie Gallagher. Curiously enough, Gallagher's last kick of the ball in European Cup football that season was to set up Billy McNeill's winning goal with his astute corner kick in the match against Vojvodina. Wallace recalled, 'I was in the Parkhead stand for that game. Apparently, I hadn't been registered in time with UEFA after signing from Hearts in December. I had been sitting alongside the injured Joe McBride. The atmosphere was electric and I thought, "Wispy, this is the place for you!" I was well up for the Dukla game. I had anticipated it for weeks and just hoped I would get the nod from Big Jock to play. Thankfully, I got my wish and everything went so well for me that night. We won 3–1 and I scored two goals. OK, it would have been nice to have claimed a hat-trick, but I wasn't grumbling. I came close, you know. I actually hit the crossbar near the end.

'Big Jock told us beforehand, "Get a two-goal advantage and I'm sure we'll get through." My first goal came just before the hour mark when Tommy Gemmell launched the ball downfield. It might have been a clearance, but he has always assured me it was an inch-perfect pass. I'll take my big pal's word for it! Anyway, suddenly, I had a bit of freedom in the Dukla penalty area and managed to flick the ball with the outside of my right foot and it carried past their keeper, Ivo Viktor. About five minutes or so later, Celtic Park just went crazy when I scored again. It was all down to the cunning antics and quick thinking of Bertie Auld. He stepped up to take a free kick, paused, bent down, put his hand out and looked as though he was about to recentre the ball. I knew what was coming next, though. Bertie merely slipped the ball to the right and I was coming in from behind him to hit it first time. The ball flew through their defensive wall and was in the net even before Viktor could move.

'It looked like an impromptu bit of skill from Wee Bertie, but, take my word for it, that little bit of trickery came straight off the training ground. We practised that move every day. It was an idea by Big Jock, who was always looking at ways of developing free kicks and corner kicks to take opponents by surprise. He always urged us to put variety into dead-ball situations and Wee Bertie seized the moment against Dukla. The Czechs were startled. They just didn't see it coming. Their defenders started pointing to Stevie Chalmers and claiming offside. Stevie had followed my shot into the net, but there was no way he was off. It was just his speed getting round the back of the wall that got him into that position. When I connected with the ball, I can assure everyone that Stevie was well onside. I should know what I'm talking about – I've only watched the video replay of that goal about five million times!'

Chalmers did get the ball in the Czechs' net early in the game after heading in a cross from Johnstone at the near post, but the referee cut the cheers short within seconds when he ruled the Celtic winger's boot had been too high when he'd collected the original pass from Chalmers. There and then, everyone witnessing the spectacle realised the match official was certainly no 'homer'. Johnstone, however, had the answer in the twenty-eighth minute when he netted one that did stand. It was a goal that started with a kick-out from Simpson. The keeper thumped one down the middle, Chalmers, busy as ever, got a flick and it fell for Auld, who teed it up for Wallace. His shot deflected off a defender into the path of the onrushing Johnstone and, ignoring the menacing advances of Viktor charging from his goal line, he gleefully lifted the ball over the keeper's head and into the net. Celtic Park was bedlam, but the home support was silenced when, most uncharacteristically, the defence gifted Dukla a goal right on the stroke of half-time.

The Celtic back lot got into a real muddle on their own 18-yard line. The ball bounced around, boots were swung at it, but that spherical object stubbornly refused to leave the danger zone. Stanislav Strunc, a beanpole striker who always looked menacing, with his unorthodox style, pounced, dragged the ball wide to give himself a clear shooting chance and stroked it low past Simpson. The veteran number 1 was known to have a healthy sense of humour, but it deserted him at that moment as he berated the men in front of him. Heads were bowed as Celtic, having had so much of the play, headed for the dressing-room level at half-time.

Gemmell said, 'We got the usual pep talk from Big Jock, but right before the interval is a horrible time to concede a goal. You must not dwell on it; you have to concentrate fully on what is still to come. "Just play like you did in the first half and we'll win," urged the boss. Actually, we were already thinking along those lines anyway. I know I was.'

In the end, Celtic took a 3–1 advantage to Prague, but, really, the tie could have been out of sight, as a relentless second-half onslaught swept down on the exhausted Viktor and the men in front of him in Glasgow. Dukla were pinned back and, following Wallace's second goal, Celtic went for the jugular. Chalmers slashed one just past the upright, Wallace missed by inches, Murdoch sent a left-foot sizzler just over the crossbar, with Viktor well beaten, and then Wallace knocked one against the bar after some great work by Chalmers. Jock had asked for a two-goal first-leg lead and his players had responded. Celtic, though, could have carried a more handsome advantage with them for the return leg a fortnight later.

The Celtic manager took everyone by surprise with his tactics for that game. Celtic, even the bad Celtic teams of the early '60s, were always adventurous, a free-attacking force. They had scored sixteen goals from seven games – six away from home – in their run to Prague, but for the one and only time in his life, the manager ordered his players to defend in depth. He was shutting up shop with Lisbon only 90 minutes away. A European Cup final was a temptation that proved too irresistible to ignore. Celtic did not go to Czechoslovakia to entertain.

Willie Wallace, two-goal hero in Glasgow, said, 'Big Jock pulled me aside before the game and gave me my instructions: I was to stick like a limpet to Masopust. Where he went, I went. An early goal for them in front of their own support could have made all the difference. Big Jock just wasn't prepared to give them that opportunity. Hence he took me aside and told me about my new role in the side. He assured me it was a complete one-off and I was happy to hear that. At the same time, I was also determined to get the job done properly. Masopust was clearly the key figure in their side, their inspiration. By the time the kick-off came around, I was ready for the challenge.

'I think I did fairly well, even if I do say so myself. Masopust had a quiet game with me at his side throughout. I could sense he was getting frustrated as the game wore on. I must have done OK, because he refused to shake my hand at the final whistle. I shrugged my shoulders and walked away. To be fair, this wonderful footballer did come into our dressing-room afterwards to apologise, and he offered me his hand and wished us the best of luck in the final. I think that proved him to be a true gentleman and sportsman. He was in his mid-30s by then and he must have realised he would never get the opportunity to play in a European Cup final again.

'And, to their credit, the Czechs put a lot into that encounter. We had surrendered possession as we picked up their forward players and, consequently, they had a lot of the ball. However, we were determined they were not going to make good use of it. Ronnie had a couple of super saves in the first half, which helped settle the nerves. In Prague, it was all about getting the job done. I recall Ronnie screaming at his defence after a rare lapse in concentration by someone. There was only about a minute to go, but our keeper wasn't going to tolerate anyone switching off at any time.'

The game, of course, ended goalless and the man with the most thankless role in the line-up was without question Stevie Chalmers, told to play up front as a one-man forward line. Chalmers recalled, 'That was the solitary occasion I was banned from coming back into my own team's half of the field. Big Jock laid it on the line. "Keep busy, Stevie," he said. "Let them know you're out there." OK, Boss! I was never afraid to put myself about and, as I recall, a few of their players bumped into my elbows that afternoon. It's a man's game, after all. I just kept going for the entire 90 minutes and the Dukla back lot weren't pleased. It was one of the hardest shifts I ever put in, but we were so close to that final place and if that doesn't give you momentum then nothing will. I got in about their defence to make sure they were stretched. Not the most glamorous role in the team, I'm sure you'll agree, but one that was vital in that game. They liked to build from the back and it was my job to make sure they didn't get too much time on the ball.'

Gemmell remembered, 'We were prepared to give away possession and, obviously, that is a dangerous ploy. You are offering your opponents licence to come at you for the entire 90 minutes and it could have backfired. Thankfully, it didn't. But I remember Jock ordering us to belt the ball down the inside-right and inside-left channels to give Stevie the chance to hare after it. Most unusually, we were told not to support him. Remember, this is Jock Stein we are talking about. He built his reputation on attacking play, but here we were, just half an hour or so before kick-off, being told not to go into the other team's half. We would hold what we had and Stevie would take care of business up front. My God, what a job he did in Prague. It must have been like chasing pigeons.'

There was an amusing moment late in the game, with Dukla realising their European Cup dream was fading fast. Chalmers raced after a ball down the left wing and three frustrated Czechs descended on him. There was a melee and other defenders joined in. Bertie Auld sidled up to Billy McNeill and asked, 'Do you think we should go down there and give him a hand? He looks to be in a bit of bother.' The captain didn't hesitate: 'Naw, he'll be fine.'

Then it was off to Lisbon, a moment in Celtic's history that surely deserves a chapter of its own (see Chapter 9).

The League Cup, as in the previous two seasons, was deposited in the trophy cabinet before October was out. The cup looked as though it was taking up permanent residence in the East End. Celtic recorded nine wins out of ten in the section, the only hiccup coming at Ibrox, where they drew 1–1.

As Tommy Gemmell quite rightly pointed out, Rangers would never be content to be second best to Celtic. As they had done the previous year (spending a joint £100,000 on Alex Smith from Dunfermline and Davie Smith from Aberdeen), they got the cheque book out in the summer of 1967. They paid a Scottish record transfer fee of £65,000 to sign Alex Ferguson from Dunfermline; £50,000 to Dundee for midfielder Andy Penman; £50,000 plus veteran winger Davie Wilson and midfielder Wilson Wood to Dundee United for Swedish outside-left Örjan Persson; and £30,000 to Morton for Danish goalkeeper Erik Sørensen. It was a remarkable splashing of the cash from the Ibrox bosses. 'They were flexing their financial muscle,' mused Gemmell. 'We weren't that bothered.'

'This is a new era for Rangers,' trumpeted the club and, given that it had spent almost £300,000 in the space of 12 months, their supporters believed it. They would get an early chance to prove their point with three Old Firm meetings scheduled in a month.

A goal from Johnstone was enough to get Celtic off to a winning start as they beat Dundee United in the opening League Cup group game before Gemmell drove in a penalty kick in the 1–1 draw at Ibrox. The adventurous left-back was on target again, along with Auld and Lennox, when Aberdeen were beaten 3–1 in Glasgow.

Celtic kept up the good work with a 1–0 victory over Dundee United at Tannadice, with Lennox on target. That set up one of the most exhilarating and exciting Old Firm confrontations in decades when Rangers visited Celtic on Wednesday, 30 August. It is doubtful if there had ever been such a dramatic conclusion to any meeting between the two Glasgow giants during the 79-year feud between the clubs. Jock Stein's men were sitting on seven points while Scot Symon's side had six as they approached what would turn out to be a momentous occasion. The group table was, therefore, finely and delicately balanced. A Rangers triumph would tip the advantage in their direction with only one game left to play for both clubs. Unthinkable? With fourteen minutes to go and with 75,000 fans holding their breath – one section anticipating delight, the other dreading despair – Rangers, a goal ahead after eight minutes from Willie Henderson, were awarded a penalty kick.

Kai Johansen, the Rangers right-back who had netted the Scottish Cup winner the previous year, strode forward to take the kick. He fired it high past Ronnie Simpson and then watched in horror as the ball clattered off the underside of the crossbar and bounced down three yards from the goal line. The Dane then took a rush of blood to the head as he raced forward to nod the ball goalwards. The headed attempt was, of course, null and void because the keeper hadn't touched the ball, and referee Tiny Wharton gave the free kick. The Ibrox players must still have been in a state of shock when Willie Wallace bundled in a left-wing corner kick two minutes later for the equaliser. Parkhead was enveloped in pandemonium as Celtic surged forward, the players sensing blood. In the last seven pulsating minutes, Bobby Murdoch pummelled an unstoppable eighteen-yarder beyond Erik Sørensen, and Bobby Lennox raced through a startled rearguard to slide the third under the keeper. It wasn't a great night for Danes at Parkhead that evening.

'We realised we had been given a reprieve when that Johansen penalty kick struck the woodwork,' admitted Gemmell. 'In fact, goodness knows what might have happened if he hadn't touched it a second time. There was the usual scrum of players charging into the penalty area in pursuit of the rebound. One of their guys might have got there first. We'll never know. What was certain was that we had been given a "Get Out Of Jail Free" card and we were going to take full advantage of the situation. We were actually inspired in those closing minutes. Our fans were roaring us on as we had Rangers on the ropes. Our opponents had played well for most of that evening, but now they were panicking. The entire complexion of the game changed in that instant.

'It was an extremely important victory for us. A defeat could have seen the first of the season's silverware possibly heading for Ibrox and that would have given them a massive boost in confidence. As I recall, they had all four summer signings – Sørensen, Ferguson, Penman and Persson – playing that night, too, and it wouldn't have done them any harm to pick up a winner's medal only a few months into their new careers. Make no mistake about it, that was a big win for us.'

Pat McMahon, Jock Stein's first signing for the club after the European Cup victory, scored in the next game, a 5–1 win over a demoralised Aberdeen at Pittodrie. While Rangers signed huge cheques, McMahon arrived from junior club Kilsyth Rangers as a host of big-name English teams, Manchester United and Chelsea among them, also chased his signature. He was a slender, right-sided midfielder of whom much was expected. In fact, he looked very much like a young Slim Jim Baxter in appearance, but, for whatever reason, he failed to realise his potential and was later sold to Aston Villa. Bertie Auld recalled, 'The lad could play, no doubt about it, but he was very quiet. He used to enjoy reading books and playing his guitar after training.'

Next up were Ayr United in the quarter-final and they were clobbered

8–2 on aggregate. The goals continued to flow against Morton in the semi-final. Old Celtic warhorse Jim Kennedy played at left-back for the Cappielow side that night and, after years of threats from Sean Fallon, showed no interest in crossing the halfway line. Mind you, he had enough to do to contend with the skills of a more mature Jimmy Johnstone, a vastly different player from the one he had witnessed being introduced four years earlier. The finishing touch had now been applied to the touchline trickery. The Parkhead side coasted to a 7–1 victory – a memorable scoreline for many Celtic fans.

There were to be another eight goals scored in the October final against Dundee, just four days before the infamous World Club Championship second leg against Racing Club of Buenos Aires (but that's another story for another chapter). The Tayside outfit had romped to Hampden, claiming twenty-two goals on their journey to Glasgow, seven fewer than Celtic. Bobby Davidson was a referee who never courted popularity with the Celtic fans – 'It seemed to everyone at the club that he had a deep dislike of Big Jock and I'm not sure he liked us, either,' said Tommy Gemmell – and he was put in charge of the League Cup final meeting on a crisp, clear Saturday afternoon. 'Get one goal and go and get another,' Stein would often tell his players. 'Then there's nothing anyone can do to stop you winning. If they pull one back, go and get a third. Always remain in control.'

A crowd of 66,603 turned out at Hampden. The Celtic supporters were keen to wave a fond farewell to their South America-bound heroes while hoping to witness another spectacle. Celtic didn't fail them, and nor did Dundee, for that matter. It was a topsy-turvy encounter, but, heeding the words of their manager, Celtic always remained a couple of steps ahead of their rivals. Goals from Chalmers (2), Hughes, Lennox and Wallace gave the Parkhead side a 5–3 victory in a game they were never going to lose, despite some bizarre interventions by the match official.

On the same afternoon at Ibrox, Rangers were booed off the field after being held to a goalless draw by Dunfermline, a result that was to figure heavily in another dramatic turn of events in Glasgow. On the day Celtic prepared for the game against Racing Club, the Ibrox side ruthlessly sacked Scot Symon and replaced him with an ambitious young track-suited manager, Davie White, who had had a year in charge of part-time Clyde before being appointed assistant to Symon six months before. The Rangers board believed a 34-year-old rookie had the tactical knowledge and all-round nous to take on Jock Stein. They were to be proved wrong, very wrong. Symon had won ten trophies – three league championships, three Scottish Cups and four League Cups – for Rangers during the first five years of the '60s, barren for Celtic. In truth, it was a praiseworthy haul that most at Parkhead, especially the board, had envied.

Rangers defeated Celtic 1–0 with an Örjan Persson goal in the league encounter at Ibrox on 16 September 1967 in front of 90,000 fans, but Symon, who, like his old adversary Jimmy McGrory, was a three-piece suit, shirt-and-tie, hat-wearing manager, didn't get too much time to savour the triumph. He was shown the door precisely 45 days later.

Gemmell, forthright as ever, made no excuses for the stumble at Ibrox. He said, 'There were ten Lisbon Lions out on the field that day – Davie Cattenach was in at right-back for the injured Jim Craig – and we just didn't get started. Possibly there might have been a bit of over-confidence in our ranks and that is lethal in these sorts of games. Often if you start on the back-foot, it's difficult to get back into your stride. It gave us a jolt, though. Do you know we never lost another league game that season? Amazing! Thirty-two games, twenty-nine victories and three draws. I suppose you could say we responded pretty well to that Rangers defeat.'

There was a surprise early Christmas present for the Celtic supporters with the first league start of the season for Joe McBride, against Morton, on 23 December. It got better: McBride fired in a hat-trick almost a year to the day since his career had been put in jeopardy at Pittodrie. Hughes netted the other in a 4–0 romp.

Celtic's league campaign had been a vigorous and relentless surge since the dip against Rangers way back in September. Making it one of the most memorable championship chases in decades, Rangers, with Davie White settling in at the helm, had also embarked on an unbeaten run until 1967 came to a halt. Astonishingly, they had dropped a mere two points from a possible thirty-two, in the draws against Hearts (1–1) and the goalless stalemate against Dunfermline, the result that was to end abruptly Scot Symon's thirteen-year tenure as manager of the club. White came in and, against the odds, produced a winning sequence of eight games. Jock Stein, with his champions trailing by two points, looked forward to ending that run on 2 January in the first Old Firm game of 1968.

However, there is still much of the best – and worst – of 1967 to reflect upon.

9

MAGIC AND MAYHEM

In the euphoric aftermath of an epic triumph, amid the most joyous celebrations ever witnessed in the away dressing-room of the Estádio Nacional in Lisbon, Jimmy Johnstone apologised to his teammates. 'Ah'm sorry,' said Celtic's endearing little character. 'Ah let youse doon.'

Bertie Auld exclaimed, 'I could hardly believe my ears. There was so much going on around me that I thought I had picked up the Wee Man wrong. "What are you saying, Jinky?" I asked. He was an emotional guy and was close to tears as he repeated, "Ah'm really sorry. Ah let youse doon." Celtic had just beaten the famed Inter Milan 2–1 to win the European Cup, the biggest club football prize of them all, and there was Jinky apologising. I knew him better than most and I realised he wasn't joking, that this was no act. He really meant it. He thought he had failed his colleagues on the day we turned in an illuminating, devastating ninety minutes that blew away the defensive-minded Italians, the same team that had won the European Cup in two out of the previous three years and had been crowned world club champions on two occasions during the same period.

'I should have been whooping it up, celebrating with my teammates and here I was consoling Jinky. "What are you talking about?" I said. "You were one of the best players on the pitch. You and Bobby Murdoch were just brilliant." Jinky looked up: "Do ye really mean that, Bert? Ye're no' just sayin' that?" I assured him I meant every word and, even years later, when Jinky and I were on our own, he would still ask, "Me and Bobby, best men on the pitch in Lisbon, Bert? Ye huvnae changed yer mind?" For goodness' sake, we had both been out of football for decades and he was still seeking reassurance!

'That Wee Man was a different class, on and off the field. That day in Lisbon is undoubtedly well remembered for my big pal Tommy Gemmell's spectacular equaliser and Stevie Chalmers' winner five minutes from time, but I thought Jinky was immense in a thoroughly unselfish, totally professional performance. We were all aware of what he could do with a ball. He could take it for a stroll in his early years at the club and no one else would get a kick for about five minutes. Then he would lose possession and leave everyone sucking out their fillings. Against Inter Milan, he put in a wonderfully disciplined display against one of the toughest defenders in the world at the time, a guy called Tarcisio Burgnich, who was also an experienced international. Big Jock had told Jinky to take Burgnich for a walk and drag him all over the place. That would unsettle their defence because he was undoubtedly the rock in their back line.

'Giacinto Facchetti was supposed to be the greatest attacking left-back on earth back then, but I think we all knew who was the real deal, the genuine article, after Lisbon: Big TG, Tommy Gemmell. What a game he had – simply mind-blowing. "Cairney", Jim Craig, was like TG, a complete athlete, and he was getting up and down that right wing as often as possible as we pounded the Italians. Jinky deserved every accolade and so too did my mate Bobby Murdoch. He was a big guy, with that barrel chest of his, but he had the touch of an angel. He didn't kick the ball, he caressed it. He was immense, but, to be honest, we won and lost as a team and we all played our part that day.'

Jim Craig said, 'I don't think Jinky ever received the credit he deserved for his performance against Inter. He didn't appear to be involved in the key points of the game, but, believe me, he pulled their player Burgnich all around the pitch to make openings for others. I'm sure if Jinky had hopped on a bus to take him into Lisbon town centre, the Italian would have gone with him! We, the players, knew what he contributed against the Italians. Wee Jinky was discipline personified and we all realised he was at his happiest skipping down the wing on one of those unbelievable, hip-swerving runs, leaving distraught defenders tackling fresh air. The European Cup final was his stage, it was his platform to produce another glorious performance of stunning variety that would have undoubtedly mesmerised millions watching on the many TV sets tuned into the game throughout the globe. Without any debate, he possessed the individual skills to take the spotlight in the biggest game of his life. However, he sacrificed all that in Lisbon for the cause of the team. No one will ever forget that. Nor will we ever forget him.'

Tommy Gemmell observed, 'I agree with Bertie and Cairney. Jinky really couldn't fathom what he had given the team against Inter. Their manager Helenio Herrera was acclaimed as possessing one of the most tactically astute minds in the game. Unfortunately, their tactics were built mainly on defence. He would have plotted and planned for this game as soon as he knew who his team would be facing in that final. There's little doubt that he believed Jinky would play wide on the right in his usual position throughout the match. No doubt he would still have stuck Burgnich on him and that would have given Facchetti a bit of freedom to gallop up their left side. But Facchetti wasn't afforded the cover his teammate would have given him and he was pinned back in his own half for virtually the entire game. He might have looked for some help from the other central defenders, but they were getting tied up by the movement and interchanging of Willie Wallace, Stevie Chalmers and Bobby Lennox. Jinky was totally unselfish, but so too were those three guys. They were all noted goal-scorers, but, like Jinky, they were asked to perform against the Italians in a different manner to confuse the opposition.

'Jock wanted them to make openings for Bertie and Bobby, supporting from the midfield, and for me and Cairney coming down the flanks. The four of us would pass the ball to feet, take the return and put the pressure on their goalkeeper. Looking at the statistics tells you all you need to know. Believe it or not, we had 35 attempts at the Inter goal, with 19 on the button. I had nine shots on target, Bertie had two, including one that struck the bar, Jinky had two, including a header, and Bobby had four efforts saved by Giuliano Sarti, who was having the game of his life.

'And what about the three guys up front, Wispy, Stevie and Lemon [Bobby Lennox], who had scored nine of our sixteen goals in the competition prior to the final? Stevie had claimed five while Wispy and Lemon had two to their names. As you might expect, I've watched that European Cup final several times now – if I'm being honest, I think I've worn out about a couple of hundred pairs of specs! – and even I have been surprised to discover that Stevie only had one shot on target – the winner! – Wispy drew one save and, astonishingly, Wee Lemon didn't work the keeper at all! So if we are just judging the final through statistics, then Jock's tactics were absolutely spot-on.

'I'll tell you something now that might make you want to ask me to go and lie down in a darkened room for a wee while, like a week or so. It actually helped our cause that day that they were awarded a penalty kick in the seventh minute and Sandro Mazzola scored from it. Before the guys with the white coats arrive, let me hastily explain. With that early goal, Inter were given the licence to retreat into defence and that was something they relished. Their horrible style of defensive football was strangling the game because it was successful and other managers all over the planet were copying it. Somebody needed to change this dire situation and Celtic were just the club to achieve that while the rest of

Europe looked on. I believe we managed that quite successfully and, almost overnight, the entire philosophy of football changed. Other teams started to copy us and that was surely good for the game.

'Inter were on the back foot for about 99 per cent of the match and I have to admit it was one of my easiest European ties of the season, if not *the* easiest. I really mean that. They had a very talented player on the right wing, Angelo Domenghini, who was fine going forward but I got the impression he was one of those porcelain performers who didn't really want to know about getting back to put in tackles. I don't think he came near me all day.'

German referee Kurt Tschenscher pointed to the penalty spot early on after Inter frontman Renato Cappellini went down following a challenge from Craig. To this day, the right-back is adamant that it was never a foul. He says, 'I had been assured Cappellini was all left foot, so when he ran in on goal coming in from the left I assumed that at some point he would want to put the ball to his stronger foot. I decided I would block any attempt to do so, but when the challenge came in, he went down rather like an ageing actor, to my mind, and I believe the referee was completely conned by it.

'Actually, I still laugh at the recollection of Big Jock at half-time. He came over and threw an arm around my shoulder and said sympathetically, "Don't worry, Cairney, that was never a penalty. Never in a million years. Don't worry. Don't blame yourself. Put it behind you. Show them what you can do in the second half." At the end of the game, though, with the trophy safely won, he sidled up to me and said, "What on earth were you thinking about at that penalty? What a stupid challenge! You almost cost us the European Cup with that daft tackle!" That was Big Jock.'

Thereafter, Celtic pummelled the Inter goal, but Sarti, playing in his fourth European final, and surprisingly thought by some to be a weak link, was beginning to look unbeatable. A quick turn and a deft touch from Auld sent the ball soaring over the keeper's flapping arm, but, unfortunately, it smacked against the face of the crossbar and was thumped to safety. Johnstone had a header pushed over after having a low shot turned away. Murdoch fired in a couple and Gemmell might have levelled ten minutes from the break. 'I thought that was in,' admitted Gemmell. 'It was one of those shots that leaves your boot and it feels good, you know you've hit it sweetly. It was a curling volley that was heading for the bottom left-hand corner of Sarti's net and I was astonished he got down at lightning speed to push it round the post. I thought it was an excellent save at the time, but when I saw it later on television I had to admit it was world class. It's still one of the best I have ever witnessed.

That guy didn't deserve to be on the losing team that day, although I confess that wasn't my train of thought at the time!

'As I recall, we were all pretty calm at the interval. Och, there had been the usual shouting and bawling as we went down the tunnel, saying things like, "Imagine a German referee giving an Italian team a penalty kick," or, "That will be you fixed up for holidays in Lake Como for the rest of your life, ref." Mind you, it might not have been put so politely. Big Billy was giving him pelters. Of course, there was no reason to believe the ref was biased in any way. We were just wound up. We were all pretty much incensed, but inside the dressing-room Big Jock calmed us down. By the time we had to go out, we were ready to go again and give the Italians some of the same. I believe we all thought something had to give. Big Jock made a couple of small adjustments, asking myself and Cairney to pull the ball across, say, the 18-yard line when we were crossing into their box and keep it away from the dense, congested area just in front of Sarti. How important that simple little instruction was to prove.'

The one-way traffic resumed, Jinky wandering here and waltzing there with Burgnich, making little or no contribution to the actual football-playing aspect of the game, still on his tail. Shots and headers rained in and Sarti stood firm. The black-clad keeper made an unbelievable save from a Gemmell drive that had actually managed to elude him. Somehow, with gravity-defying athleticism any Olympian gymnast would be proud to possess, he somersaulted backwards to hold the ball right on the line as Chalmers raced in. Then came another outstanding effort when it looked as though Murdoch must score with a six-yard header. Incredibly, Sarti threw out his left arm and held the ball one-handed. It was an extraordinary act of solitary defiance. Gemmell then floated in a cross from the left wing that swirled high and bounced on top of the crossbar and off to safety. Even when Sarti was beaten, it appeared the angels were on his side. It was obvious it was going to take something special to force this guy to surrender. Thankfully, in the 63rd minute, that something special arrived.

Celtic forced a shy 30 yards from the goal line on the left. Wallace shaped to throw it inside, but, confronted by the giant obstruction that was Facchetti, changed his mind and lobbed it back to the ever-available Gemmell, who switched play inside to Clark. The defender thrust it forward to Murdoch in the old inside-left channel some 30 yards from goal. Celtic's patience was commendable, as were the methodical defensive patterns woven by their rivals as they attempted to regroup, cover, pick up an opponent. Murdoch slipped a simple pass out to Craig, galloping in from the right. He took it in his stride as he raced towards the danger zone. Craig took three touches in all before nonchalantly rolling the ball into the tracks of full-back partner Gemmell, the man who had been defied more often than any other by Sarti.

As he headed for the edge of the box at full pelt, there was only one intention in Gemmell's mind. 'I was going to hit that ball like it had never been hit before,' said the raiding defender. 'Everything was perfect. It was a sweet cutback from Cairney. I was aware of one of their players breaking out to confront me. He wasn't going to put me off my stride. I pulled back my right foot and the guy stopped in his tracks and turned his back. If he had kept going, he might well have charged down the shot. I wasn't complaining, though. I gave it a ferocious dunt and it just took off and blasted high into the net. God bless Sarti, he did his best to keep it out. Not this time, son!'

Years later, far from the madding crowd, Tommy, my wife, Gerda, and I were enjoying lunch on a quiet August afternoon in 2011 in a little, rustic restaurant off the beaten track somewhere in Stirling. Tommy, 67 years young and still the possessor of that wonderfully mischievous twinkle in his eye, looked up from his sumptuous sea bass and said, 'You know, Alex, the Celtic Supporters Association voted that the club's greatest-ever goal in their official millennium poll.' He smiled, rightly proud of the achievement more than 44 years after he had almost ripped away the net in Lisbon. Personally, I didn't believe the Celtic supporters would have had to deliberate too long before coming to that conclusion. Tommy looked chuffed when I told him so.

Gemmell laughed, too, when he reminisced about instructions from Jock Stein as the ball was recentred after his stunning goal. 'I heard Big Jock shouting, "Take it easy, lads, we'll get them in extra time." There were 27 minutes left for play and I looked over my shoulder and uttered a very uncomplimentary oath. "Fuck off, Boss," I yelled without thinking of the consequences. "It's 85 degrees out here and we're going to finish it here and now." Thankfully, Big Jock was too preoccupied after the game to mention our little bit of touchline verbals!

'Actually, when you are facing opponents you can sense how they feel, and the Inter players were on their knees. They had been run ragged for over a hour and I'm fairly certain they hadn't encountered this sort of sustained pressure in their domestic league games, where most teams cancelled each other out, one or the other eventually being bored into submission. No, we had them on the ropes and it would have been daft not to apply the killer punch.'

Celtic could even absorb the denial of a stonewall penalty-kick award when Gemmell fired over a cross from the left and Sarti and one of his defenders found themselves on different wavelengths. They got in a terrible mix-up at the far post and the ball broke to Wallace. He was just about to stroke the ball into the empty net when the keeper, on the ground, wrapped his arms around one of his legs and quite deliberately brought him down. There were no ifs or maybes about this one. There was no need for slow-motion replays. It was a legitimate penalty kick and only the match officials will ever know why it was not awarded. Frankly, it was a nonsensical decision when you remember how swiftly the referee pointed to the spot when Cappellini went down after the merest of touches from Craig. Sarti, after bowling the ball out, had the good grace to look at the protesting Wallace and shrug his shoulders in an exaggerated Latin fashion that suggested, 'No, I don't know why it wasn't a penalty kick, either!'

No matter. Five minutes from time, there was no argument about the goal that catapulted Celtic into legendary status and gave birth to the Lisbon Lions. Gemmell, still going strong after 85 minutes of perpetual motion, pushed a pass inside for Murdoch, who let fly from the edge of the box. The seemingly inexhaustible Chalmers materialised six yards in front of goal to side-foot the ball past Sarti, motionless by now, and the European Cup was won. Inter's tired-looking defenders half-heartedly appealed for offside – it was obviously second nature to them – but the referee couldn't help them on this occasion. Chalmers was onside, the goal stood and the trophy was heading home to Glasgow. After the match, the referee commented, 'It was a wonderful game and Celtic fully deserved to win.'

'How did I feel when I scored with five minutes to go? Shattered!' said match-winner Chalmers. 'Cramp was coming on, but that disappeared as soon as the ball hit the back of the net. OK, it may not have been as eye-catching as Tommy's effort, but, for me, it was special because it was part of a routine we worked on day in, day out at training at Barrowfield. Big Jock would get Joe McBride, Willie Wallace, Bobby Lennox, John Hughes and me to line up along the six-yard line and then he would get Big Tommy, Bobby Murdoch, Bertie Auld, Jim Craig and Charlie Gallagher to hammer over crosses from the left and, after that, from the right. Then he would vary the routine, with Big Tommy playing the ball back from the line to, say, Bobby to hit the ball diagonally across the face of the goal from the edge of the box. Then he would do the same on the right, with Cairney laying the ball back for someone else to hit a similar effort into the penalty box. This would go on for hours until you knew off by heart where you were expected to be in the penalty box whenever a move was developing. It was no fluke, believe me, that I was standing there when Big Tommy pulled the ball back to Bobby to thump in his shot. All that hard work certainly paid off in Lisbon.'

Gemmell recalled an amusing incident a minute from the end. 'We were awarded a free kick and I grabbed the ball. Bertie asked me what I was going to do with it. I laughed, "See that seat away up in the back row behind the goal? That's where I'm going to fuckin' put it!" I wasn't taking the chance of Inter getting the ball back and possibly fluking an equaliser. I have to say my aim wasn't too bad. I just about got the ball out of the stadium. Moments later came the final whistle and, within seconds, it seemed half of Glasgow had emptied onto the Lisbon pitch.

'I remember Bobby Lennox shouting to our keeper, "Ronnie, remember my teeth!" Bobby had a couple of false teeth and he always gave them to Ronnie to put in his hat inside the goal, so he could retrieve them immediately after a game and look his best for the inevitable photographs.

'Me? I think I was on the pitch for about another half an hour after exchanging shirts with Sandro Mazzola. As I eventually got close to the tunnel, I spied a vendor still selling ice-cream cones. I had to have one. Thankfully, he had the good grace not to ask me to pay for it!'

Just minutes before the players had left the dressing-room for the kick-off, Stein had implored them to remain true to their natural instincts. 'We have a duty to play the game our way and our way is to attack,' he said. 'Win or lose, let's make this a game worth remembering. It's a tremendous honour just to be involved in an occasion like this. You've done all the hard work just getting here, so go out there and enjoy yourselves. We want to win this cup, but we want to do it by playing the sort of football that is associated with Celtic. We want to make the neutrals glad we won it and glad to remember how we did it.' The players must have been hanging on his every word.

Liam Brady had the distinction of being the only individual to serve both Celtic and Inter Milan (Robbie Keane would later play for both teams, although he was only on loan to Celtic for four months). The former Parkhead boss said, 'It would have been a tragedy if Celtic hadn't won. I have never seen a team dominate a match so much. It could have been 5–1 or 6–1 at the end and no one could have complained. Justice was done. It was a victory for the good guys. It was a victory for football. Everything that Inter stood for was wrong. Jock Stein versus Helenio Herrera was an intriguing contest on a coaching level. Thankfully, Jock's philosophy won the day. Celtic really stopped the domination of European football by these stifling, frustrating, unattractive and unimaginative tactics. They did Europe and football a real favour in Lisbon.'

Bill Shankly, the legendary Liverpool manager, hugged his good friend

Stein in the melee around the dressing-room and rasped, 'John [he never called him Jock], you're immortal.' It was a poignant moment between two individuals who had started out digging for coal to make a living.

The Celtic team that will be forever remembered for its glorious impact on football that day was: Ronnie Simpson; Jim Craig, Billy McNeill, John Clark and Tommy Gemmell; Bobby Murdoch and Bertie Auld; Jimmy Johnstone, Willie Wallace, Stevie Chalmers and Bobby Lennox.

Thirteen days after Lisbon, Celtic provided the opposition for Real Madrid and the legendary Alfredo Di Stéfano in his glittering testimonial match at the Bernabéu Stadium. This was to be no friendly occasion. Bertie Auld recalled, 'Big Jock took me aside and told me, "Real Madrid are desperate to do us. We've just won the European Cup, but they still think they're the best team in Europe. Amancio is their main player – do your utmost to keep him quiet. Keep an eye on him. I want to win this one." John Cushley was reserve centre-half to Billy McNeill at the time and he was one of those rarities, a well-educated footballer! He could read Spanish and speak it fluently, and he told us what Real Madrid were saying about us in the national press. Basically, they were informing everyone that Celtic had merely borrowed the European Cup from Real for a year. Oh, yeah?

'When we turned up at the Bernabéu, the place was a 135,000 sell-out. Everyone in Madrid appeared to want to see the great Alfredo for the last time in that famous all-white kit of Real. He was 40 years old at the time, but still looked incredibly fit. He kicked off and lasted 15 minutes before going off to the sort of hero's acclaim he undoubtedly deserved after such an incredible career. However, when he disappeared up the tunnel, the real stuff kicked in. Now we would see which was the best team in Europe.

'Friendly? After Alfredo said his farewells, I don't recall anyone, and I do mean anyone, pulling out of a tackle. They were absolutely determined to hammer us and, equally, we were just as committed to the cause, to showing we were worthy European champions. Just borrowed the European Cup? It was unfortunate for them we had a bloke who could read the lingo.

'Wee Jinky was unbelievable that night. He was simply unstoppable. It looked as though he wanted to put on a special show for Di Stéfano who, along with England's Stanley Matthews, had been Jinky's idol when he was growing up. The Real players were queuing up to kick our little winger, but he was simply too good for them. They just could not get the ball off him. Even I felt like applauding at times. Honestly, it was an awesome display of talent Wee Jinky provided that night. That wasn't in the script. This was supposed to be Alfredo's big night and here was this wee bloke from Viewpark in Uddingston stealing the show.

'While he was going about his business, Amancio and I were "getting acquainted" in the middle of the pitch. He didn't like the attention I was paying him and we had a couple of wee kicks when no one was looking. Nothing too serious, but enough for him to realise I was there to do a job for Celtic that night. We were still going at it when, suddenly, there was a 50–50 ball and we both went for it. Crunch! There was a bit of a fracas. He threw a punch and I felt the need to return the compliment. The referee was far from amused. If he thought he was turning up that night simply to swan around the place taking charge of a routine friendly, then he was in for a real shock. Here were two teams going at it hell for leather. But they would be doing so without any more input from me or my friend Amancio – we were both sent off. To be honest, it was a fair decision, because we were both as bad as each other. As I walked past Big Jock in the dugout, I looked over and said, "Problem solved, Boss." He had the good grace to laugh.

'It was Jinky's night, though. He was at his elusive best. I recall one of their defenders, I think it was a so-called hard man called Pirri, coming out to the right to give the Wee Man a dull one. He clattered into him and down went Jinky. The Real player then turned his back and returned to the penalty area to take up his position to defend the resultant free kick. He must have been alarmed when he looked round and saw Jinky back on his feet and preparing to take the award. He was irrepressible. Maybe he thought he had to make up for Lisbon, where he stuck to the team plan. In Madrid, though, he had the freedom of the pitch.

'It was apt that we won 1–0 and Jinky – who else? – set up the winner. He took a pass from Tommy Gemmell on the left, skipped past a couple of tackles in that effortless style of his and slid the ball in front of his great mate Bobby Lennox. Bang! Ball in the net. Game over. Even the Real Madrid players must have admitted we were true masters of European football after that exhibition. To be fair to their support, they started to applaud Celtic, and Jinky in particular. He would sweep past one of their own players and the fans would shout, "*Olé!*" It was a night for our wee magician to display his tricks and flicks. He didn't let Alfredo down.'

The serious European business kicked off again on 20 September and Jock Stein fielded the same line-up that had won in Lisbon in the opening match of their defence of the trophy, against the tough Soviets of Dynamo Kiev. Sadly, Celtic made some unwanted history on this occasion, becoming the first holders of the trophy to go out of the tournament in the opening round. It was also Celtic's first home defeat in European competition. The timing that had been impeccable in Lisbon deserted them in Glasgow four months later. When Celtic headed to Kiev, the advantage was already with the Russians.

There was an unusual slackness in Celtic's early play as they faced Kiev at Parkhead that evening. The 55,000 fans, obviously still on a high and anticipating another wonderful European adventure on the club's new-found magic carpet, chanted, 'Attack! Attack! Attack!' for a full 15 minutes before kick-off and continued raucously as the game made its early progression. By half-time, there was silence and concern, with the Soviets two goals ahead through efforts from Anatoliy Puzach and Anatoliy Byshovets.

Gemmell, hero of Lisbon, admitted, 'I don't think we got caught up in the atmosphere or anything like that. We were used to that sort of thing. Aye, we were aware the fans were shouting "Attack" over and over again, but that was the way we always played, anyway. As I recall, I got down the wing in the first minute or so and fired a shot into the side netting. Another couple of inches to the left and who knows? Certainly, it had beaten their keeper. However, we left ourselves open at the back and they took full advantage. Bobby Lennox pulled one back in the second half and we piled forward, still taking risks at the back. It ended 2–1, but I can tell you we were convinced we would get back into it over there. We had already played Kiev in Tbilisi two years earlier, so it wasn't like we were going into the unknown. I'd scored in that game, and we'd got a 1–1 draw and gone through 3–1 on aggregate. We knew we could win in Kiev if we got a break.'

Unfortunately, the bounce of the ball, quite literally, was against Celtic in the return. Bobby Murdoch, so influential and so important in the engine room of the team, was dismissed by Italian referee Antonio Sbardella for throwing the ball to the ground following yet another strange decision from the match official. Murdoch had already been booked in the first half for dissent and, just before the hour mark, Sbardella looked as though he couldn't wait to punish him further as he hastily pointed to the dressing-room. 'Bobby was crestfallen,' recalled Gemmell. 'He burst into tears and was inconsolable for hours afterwards. We reminded him that it was an Italian who had been put in charge and maybe he was an Inter Milan fan. He certainly acted like it in Kiev. Billy McNeill had the ball in the net and it looked OK to everyone, but it was ruled out. Big John Hughes came in for Stevie Chalmers that night and he netted after one of those mazy dribbles of his, but the ref called it back and awarded Kiev a free kick for some unseen infringement. A stewards' enquiry might have come in handy around this time. One thing was certain: most of the 85,000 fans in the ground that night weren't complaining about the ref's performance.'

Remarkably, Celtic went ahead only two minutes after Murdoch's ordering-off, when Lennox levelled the tie on aggregate, snapping a free-kick delivery from Auld beyond a startled Viktor Bannikov. But Celtic still needed another because the rule stating that away goals counted double had been recently introduced by UEFA, so 2–2 would still have seen Jock Stein's men topple out of Europe. The fates were conspiring against them.

With one minute remaining, Celtic, who had dominated even with a man short for half an hour, earned a corner kick. Gemmell said, 'There was nothing else for it but for everyone to pile into their box. At that stage, we knew we were out, so we had nothing to lose. They left one player, Byshovets, on the centre spot as they came back to defend the award. He was on his own. Every Celtic player, barring Ronnie Simpson, of course, was in the Kiev penalty box. The ball came over, was hacked clear and, unfortunately, went straight to Byshovets. Honestly, it could have gone anywhere. But a wild boot out of the box turned into an inch-perfect pass. We all chased wildly back, but it was a lost cause. He tucked the ball behind Ronnie and that was that. I'm not being churlish or unsporting, but, in truth, we had played Kiev off the park for three of the four halves over the two games. Make that three-and-half. They didn't contribute much more than the 25 minutes in the first leg that were to prove so crucial. Yet we were out and they were through. We paid a very heavy price for a wee bit of hesitancy early in the game at Parkhead.

'I remember Big Jock was very positive after the match. He realised he couldn't have asked for anything more from his players in Kiev. The referee there was dodgy, no doubt about it. Whether something untoward was going on or he was just rank rotten, we will never know, but he gave everything to our opponents that night. Jock knew it. We knew it. So, we travelled home at least with the consolation we had not been hammered out of sight by far superior opponents.

'Big Jock also understood he would have to get our heads up for our games against Racing Club of Buenos Aires, with the first leg due at Hampden in a fortnight's time. He said, "If we can't be European Cup winners again, let's be the best team in the world." That uplifted all our spirits. It was an appealing thought.'

Unfortunately, 'appealing' was not the word anyone around Celtic was using after three brutal confrontations against an odious bunch of thugs masquerading as footballers in the Intercontinental Cup. It was the so-called reward for the European champions to meet their South American counterparts to decide who would be acclaimed as the World

Club champions. 'It was the night fitba' went oot the windae' was the way Jimmy Johnstone remembered the shocking first leg against the unscrupulous Argentines.

Those nine little words summed up perfectly that night in Glasgow on 18 October. 'The Wee Man nailed it,' said Bertie Auld. 'No one could have put it better. Listen, I can take someone kicking me. When you've played in Scottish junior football as a teenager, there is nothing left to frighten you on a pitch. As a kid in my short time at Maryhill Harp, I was told by so many hulking brutes that they were going to break my leg. Sometimes it was my jaw or my neck or my arm or my back or my nose. It didn't bother me one bit. As long as they could take it back!

'But I defy anyone to accept someone spitting in your face. Where I came from in Maryhill you sorted out your problems with your fists. No one would ever have even thought of spitting. That would have been seen as cowardly and yet it seemed completely acceptable to the guys who wore Racing Club's colours in our three games against them. I still find it difficult to call them players. They would wait until the ball was 50 yards or so away with the referee and his linesmen following play and they would sidle up and gob in your face. Then they would run away leaving you to wipe their spittle off your face. If they did that to you in the street, you would be after them to sort them out. But they hid on the football pitch, where they were protected by a gullible referee. They were sleekit – yes, that's the word – to disguise what they were doing. The fans would miss the initial action and then spot your retaliation.

'Look, I loved my football, still do, and I thoroughly enjoyed most of it as a player and as a manager, but I never dwell on those encounters. The entire episode from start to finish was just a nightmare. Unfortunately, we couldn't handle it and eventually cracked in the play-off in Uruguay. We were only human, after all, and there was only so much we could tolerate, so many times you can turn the other cheek for some cretin to spit on it.

'Manchester United, following their European Cup triumph the year after us, got the same treatment in their games against Estudiantes. I had warned my pal Paddy Crerand to watch them carefully. He might have thought I had been exaggerating until he telephoned one night after their two meetings with that particular rancid gang of Argentines and said, "My God, Bertie, you weren't kidding, were you?"

'Later on, Ajax, Bayern Munich and Nottingham Forest declined to participate in the competition against their South American opponents. What was the point of seeing the likes of Johan Cruyff, Franz Beckenbauer and Trevor Francis putting their careers on the line to win any title?

'Who was running the show, anyway? FIFA, the world's football governing body, presided over the tournament, but UEFA, the European wing of the organisation, didn't seem to be too involved. I found that strange. We were representing Europe, after all. Certainly, they didn't even have match observers at our three games against Racing in Scotland, Argentina and Uruguay. You can be certain, though, that they would have helped themselves to a hefty percentage of the gate money from the Hampden game.

'Maybe if they had sent a representative along to the first match they might have deemed it wise to lobby FIFA to consider scrapping these crazy confrontations. In 1980, someone took the decision to make the occasion a one-off final at a neutral venue and that format remained in place for decades. I have no doubt that if that had been the situation in 1967 Celtic would have been acclaimed as world champions. No one, by fair means, could have beaten us. We came back from South America knowing we were the best team in the world. Sadly, we didn't have a trophy to show for it.'

What should have been a showpiece spectacle for global football was, in truth, a shambles. Once again, Celtic had to play the first match in Glasgow, and that didn't work in their favour. It meant that if the two legs ended in a tie on points, the play-off would be held in South America. Neither goal difference nor goal average would come into it. The competition worked on a points system based on league formats: two points for a win, one for a draw, zero for a loss.

Racing Club were offered the choice of three referees – an invitation that was also extended to Celtic in Argentina – and, as a Spanish-speaking nation, they unhesitatingly went for an official called Juan Gardeazabal, who happened to be a Spaniard. Sadly for Celtic, he didn't speak a word of English. Auld recalled, 'During the game in Glasgow, we could hear him conversing with their players, but all we got were shrugs and gestures when we tried to query anything. It didn't help much either that he frowned on heavy tackles that were perfectly legal and something we did every match day in Scotland. He understood the Latin style of play and that certainly favoured Racing Club when, on the rarest of occasions, they were quite happy to kick the ball and not an opponent.'

A crowd of 83,437 turned up at Hampden Park to witness what had been billed as the biggest club game ever staged in Scotland. Prime Minister Harold Wilson was in the VIP seats. Stein rarely tinkered with his defence and was satisfied to go with the Lisbon Five: Simpson; Craig, McNeill, Clark and Gemmell. Murdoch and Auld again got the nod to patrol the midfield and do most of the link-up play. The trickery of

Johnstone and the pace of Lennox, Stein knew, would give the Racing Club defence problems if they were allowed to play. That turned out to be a big if. Wallace, who could look after himself, was in too, so it was now a straight choice between European Cup match-winner Stevie Chalmers and John Hughes, with the latter getting the go-ahead.

Stein liked to keep pre-match routines as normal as possible. After going through the tactical work that had been detailed the previous evening at the hotel on the Ayrshire coast, he appeared to be spending an inordinate amount of time as the clock ticked down to the kick-off going over ground he had already covered. As John Clark said, Stein rarely repeated himself. Now, though, he was telling the players for the umpteenth time, 'Don't let them put you off your natural game . . . Don't get drawn into any feuds . . . Don't retaliate – that's what they'll want you to do . . . If you lose your discipline, you'll lose the game . . . Let the world see how to win the Celtic way.'

Auld recalled, 'There was genuine concern from the boss. He must have been exhausted just going through his team talk. Big Jock was meticulous, as everyone knew, but he just seemed a wee bit more cautious than normal on this occasion.'

Within minutes, the Celtic players realised why their manager was fairly apprehensive about what was awaiting them out on that football pitch. Jimmy Johnstone was the target. With just about his first touch of the ball, he was sent spinning into the air after a crude lunge from Juan Rulli. With the outside-right still coming back to earth, he was met with another so-called challenge from Oscar Martín. Johnstone went down in a heap. Auld remarked, 'I thought they were trying to volley the Wee Man over the stand and out of the ground. I looked at the referee and wondered what action he would take. He didn't even admonish either of the villains. My heart sank.'

It seemed that the Racing Club players immediately realised that Señor Gardeazabal was a weak referee. He had opened the door for Scotland's national stadium to become a clogger's dream, a hacker's paradise. The Argentines took full advantage. They set about abusing their opponents from that moment on, with Johnstone feeling the full brunt of their punishment. It seemed their priority was to put the Celtic player in hospital that evening.

Jim Craig observed, 'People often talked about the undoubted skills of the Wee Man. One thing quite often overlooked was his courage. He would be scythed down, bumped, thumped, kicked, punched, elbowed, knocked about like a rag doll, but he always came back for more. Jinky gave you the impression an elephant gun might be required to stop him and keep him down, but I doubt if that would have worked, either. He was unbelievably brave.'

Opportunities were at a minimum against a defence that was happy enough to give away fouls anywhere within a 35-yard radius of their goal. They got a fright, though, ten minutes after the turnaround when Auld slung over a beautifully judged dead-ball effort and Billy McNeill's header bashed against woodwork. The Celtic skipper had better luck when Hughes swung over a right-wing corner kick later on. McNeill had been blocked and jostled any time he had come forward for corners or free kicks. 'That happened in every game and I was used to it,' said McNeill. 'They were a bit more sly or cunning than anything I had encountered in our game at home, but I always kept my concentration. Their aim was to distract you and I wasn't going to let that happen.' Hughes flighted over a ball just off-centre of the goal, about 12 yards out. Unbelievably, McNeill found himself with a yard or so of freedom. He leapt, made solid contact and watched in expectation as the ball almost lazily arced away from stranded keeper Agustín Cejas and high past Jinky's pal Martín into the net.

'We all ran to congratulate Caesar,' said Auld. 'He broke off his own celebrations to have a quick word with Alfio Basile, who would later manage the Argentinian international side. Basile had tried to rough up our skipper time after time and it is to Caesar's credit that he refused to take the bait. Later, I asked my pal, who could actually speak a little bit of Spanish, what he had said to the Racing Club defender. He was the picture of innocence when he replied, "You know, Bertie, I can't quite remember." I assumed he wasn't asking him out for a drink afterwards!'

McNeill, however, did recall Basile's reaction at the end of the game. 'You get guys making all sorts of daft gestures as you head for the tunnel,' he said. 'Most of the Racing Club players were at it. Silly threats that are supposed to be menacing, but it's best to smile at these guys. They hate that. Show fear and you are a dead man in the next match. I remember Basile motioning with an imaginary knife that he was going to cut my throat. And do you know, if he had carried out that threat on the pitch at Hampden that night there is every chance the referee wouldn't even have booked him.'

There was a moment of honesty from left-back Juan Díaz afterwards when he was being interviewed by a South American journalist. He was quizzed about what he thought about playing against Johnstone. He answered in a rush of Spanish. Afterwards, the pressman was asked for a translation by his Scottish counterparts. Díaz had apparently said, 'I tried to tackle him fairly at the start, but I realised this would be impossible for the entire game. I elected to kick him when he came near me after that. He would have destroyed me.' Astonishing, then, that at no time during the game did match official Gardeazabal elect to have a word with Díaz. Even more revealing, in a game riddled with fouls, is the fact that not one single player was booked. Maybe the good señor had left his little black book in Spain. Johnstone, sturdy individual of body and mind though he may have been, was in no fit state to play in Celtic's next game, a 4–2 league win over Motherwell.

The great South American adventure continued with the trip to Buenos Aires, which lasted 21 hours, with stops in Paris, Madrid and Rio. There were the usual obstructions, which Celtic were now coming to expect. The hotel was a wreck, the training facilities were a disgrace and the locals were hostile. Just a year beforehand, England manager Alf Ramsey had branded Argentina's players 'animals' after England's 1–0 World Cup quarter-final win at Wembley. Geography, along with football etiquette, was clearly not a strength in this part of the universe: England and Scotland appeared to be one and the same country according to most of the Buenos Aires populace, and it was a bit too late to argue the case. Eventually, Celtic moved their HQ to the Hindu Club, about 30 miles or so from the city centre. They were greeted by the sight of four policemen carrying machine guns. There were another 20 armed cops with shoulder holsters dotted around the complex and there was a 24-hour watch on the grounds. Auld said, 'Did someone tell them we were there to start a revolution instead of play a game of football? It was all very surreal.'

Auld was forced to miss the game after injuring an ankle in the 5–3 League Cup final victory over Dundee the day before the team flew out. He said, 'I was desperate to play, but I knew Big Jock wouldn't select me unless I was 100 per cent fit. I accepted that wouldn't have been fair to my teammates. As we were driven in our coach through Avellaneda, I have to say I was depressed at some of the sights we passed on the way. Buenos Aires looked affluent enough, but we witnessed an awful lot of poverty and deprivation on the hour-long trip to the ground: crumbling wooden shacks that were home to some poor unfortunates, children wandering around on their own and dogs foraging for morsels of food on the streets. Now we understood why their players would run over children's bodies to get their promised bonus of £1,500 per man for lifting the trophy. That would have been a fortune in that part of Argentina.'

Celtic's coach had to avoid several hundred Racing Club fans with obvious death wishes as they tried to disrupt the journey by putting their bodies in front of the vehicle and pushing, shoving and rocking it from side to side at every set of red lights. The driver, obviously a local who had seen all this before, ignored the obstacles and steered a steady path. If someone wanted to head-butt his bus, that was their problem. Eventually, the coach reached its destination, the monstrous, oval-shaped, grey-walled Avellaneda Stadium. Outside, mounted cops with massive sabres pushed back supporters. There were other policemen carrying leather lashes who weren't slow to use them if they thought the fans were getting a bit too excited, while cops with guns patrolled outside the ground.

Gemmell, like everyone else in the Celtic party, wasn't too impressed. 'It wasn't even close to kick-off and they were already baying for blood,' he said. 'A few stared through the windows of our coach and made all sorts of weird gestures. They were all pulling hideous faces with gargoyle-like expressions. I began to wonder if we were still on earth. I don't suppose they mentioned any of this in their travel brochures!'

Willie O'Neill, a left-back or midfield enforcer, got his pal Auld's position in the team and Chalmers, his speed a vital factor, came in for Hughes from the team that had won at Hampden. Auld took his place in the stand alongside Hughes and Joe McBride. As they settled in, the three thought they felt a slight drizzle of rain. Warm rain. Auld looked up to the tier that ran directly above the Celtic party. 'There was a group of disgusting lowlifes urinating on us. When one was finished, another would take his place. We were stuck right underneath them and couldn't move in a packed stadium. Spat on in Glasgow and peed on in Avellaneda. I was beginning to agree more and more with Alf Ramsey.'

Celtic had also been warned that the Uruguayan referee Esteban Marino was 'not strong'. But just moments after the match official had led the teams out of the tunnel, the occasion seemed as if it could be about to turn into a full-blown riot. Marino might not have a game to control after all. Ronnie Simpson was felled by an object thrown at him as he went out to check his nets before the kick-off. There was a massive wire fence behind the goal and it looked virtually impossible for an individual to throw something over it and down with any degree of accuracy. A more sinister thought was that the keeper had been assaulted by someone posing as a photographer or a character with an official pass hovering around the touchline behind the goal. After treatment, it was reckoned that Simpson had been hit by something heavy, like a metal bar. Yet a search of the immediate area only moments after he went down had failed to discover anything that could have caused such damage. Nothing such as a brick or a bottle could be found nearby. Clearly, whatever it was had been removed. By whom? No one ever did find the mystery object. The trackside security later admitted they had failed to search the photographers' camera cases. You could have got a bazooka in some of those enormous hold-alls back then.

Robert Kelly hadn't welcomed the thought of fulfilling the return-leg obligation after the unacceptable behaviour of the Racing Club players in Glasgow. As you might expect, Auld was rightly concerned, as were the other players stranded alongside him in the stand, far from the Celtic officials. 'If our chairman had called the players off the pitch at that point, then God only knows what would have happened next. I don't scare that easily, but I looked around me and all I could see were these ugly faces screaming and screeching abuse. We might just have made it to the sanctuary of the dressing-room, but I genuinely doubt if we would have got out of that ground unscathed. I have been in the thick of all the emotions that run high in an Old Firm game, but the Glasgow derbies were tea parties compared with this. Everywhere you looked, people were gesticulating and threatening, snarling and spitting. Welcome to hell.'

After a hasty confab between Kelly and the Celtic directors, they agreed, albeit reluctantly, to allow the game to go ahead, 15 minutes late. In those most extreme of circumstances, there seemed little alternative. John Fallon took over from Simpson in goal. Astoundingly, in the midst of all the madness, Celtic were awarded a penalty kick in the 20th minute. Auld said, 'As you might expect, it was an absolute stonewaller. Jinky wriggled through and was sent clattering to the ground by their keeper Cejas. It was a clear goal-scoring opportunity and, these days, would have brought an automatic red card for the keeper. Now that would have been interesting. I still shudder to think how the fans would have reacted to that.'

Gemmell placed the ball on the spot. 'The Racing Club players were, as usual, doing everything they could to distract me. You would never have detected it at the game or on the television, but they were throwing little pieces of dirt or flicking stones at me and the ball. On the run-up, a clump of something or other went scudding across my path. I ignored it. I recall one game where I was about to take a penalty kick and a shinguard was thrown at the ball. Didn't bother me. I scored then and I scored against Racing. I enjoyed giving the ball an almighty whack at the best of times, and here I was only 12 yards from goal with just the keeper to beat. I reckoned if I hit the ball as hard as I possibly could and got it on target then there was a good chance I would score. There was little point in a keeper trying to second-guess me when I didn't know which way it was going either. Seemed a reasonable formula. I took a lot of pens, but I think I only missed two or three, and I believe I hit the keepers with those efforts! I was always confident I would score, so the antics of the Racing players didn't put me off one jot. I hammered it and the effort thundered past Cejas, who had advanced to about the six-yard line by the time I struck the ball. If he had saved it, I wonder if the referee would have been strong enough to order a retake? Doubt it.'

Alas, the lead lasted a mere 13 minutes. Humberto Maschio, a tricky midfield customer, picked out Norberto Raffo, all on his own in the Celtic penalty area, and he looped a header over the stranded Fallon. Sweeper John Clark, who made such an exemplary job of controlling the back four, is convinced the goal shouldn't have stood. 'He was yards offside when the ball was played to him. Not just a shade off, but yards.' McNeill added, 'Blatantly offside. No argument.' Auld said, 'From where I was sitting, I couldn't see how he could be onside. I agree with John, he was in oceans of space and our back lot never afforded anyone that luxury. If you see photographs of that goal, you will notice that Raffo is completely on his own. However, after the referee had awarded us a penalty kick, he was hardly likely to rule out a goal by that lot, was he?'

The winning goal of the evening arrived shortly after the turnaround when Juan Carlos Cárdenas, one of the rarities in this Racing line-up who seemed to genuinely want to play football, thumped one past the diving Fallon. The keeper had no chance. Racing, in front of their howling banshee of a support, then retreated back into defence. For the next 40 minutes or so, they were rarely tempted across the halfway line.

Auld admitted that a thought had suddenly popped into his head. 'What would have happened if John Fallon had been injured and had to go off? You were only allowed a goalkeeper as a substitute in those days and no outfield players. Celtic would have been down to ten and that would have shrunk to nine outfield players if Tommy Gemmell, as our volunteer keeper, had had to take over in goal. How farcical would that have been? Remember, this was no bounce game in the park. On the face of it, the Intercontinental Cup should have been the biggest game in world club football. Yet it was fast becoming a joke – and a sad one at Celtic's expense.

'Here's another thought: what would have happened if Fallon and Simpson had both been injured and out of the third game? We only had two keepers with us. What would we have done for a replacement? I'm not even sure who our third-choice keeper was back then. Some kid, probably. We were due in Montevideo on the Saturday for the decider, so it would have been highly unlikely that someone could have been flown out in time. Obviously, air travel in 1967 wasn't quite as sleek as it is today. I know Big Tommy was a confident chap and had stood in for Ronnie a couple of times and performed very well. In fact, I don't believe he even conceded a solitary goal when he answered the SOS. How crazy would it have been for Tommy to be forced to play in goal in the biggest game in Celtic's history, for goodness' sake? One minute he's scoring in the European Cup final and the next he could have been playing in goal in the Intercontinental Cup decider.

'I suppose Celtic could have refused to play the third game and come home, but you never knew which way FIFA would jump. They might have ended up fining the club a massive amount of cash and UEFA might even have followed up by throwing us out of Europe for a year or so. To say we were all becoming just a bit disenchanted would be a massive understatement. The mood of the camp, as far as I was aware, was just to get things over with and return to Scotland as swiftly as possible.'

Chairman Robert Kelly, in fact, didn't want Celtic to play in the third game. However, Billy McNeill said, 'Yes, we were all sick at the way we had been treated, but, deep down, we knew Big Jock was eager to show everyone we were the best club side in the world. He also believed the players might get better treatment in a neutral country. I think that's what persuaded the board to go ahead with the game.'

Thankfully, Fallon had come through the Buenos Aires experience without any mishap and Auld had recovered from his injury to return in place of O'Neill. Chalmers also made way with Wallace moving into the main striking role and Hughes taking over at outside-left.

Celtic requested the same referee, Esteban Marino, for the third game. It made a bit of sense, considering he was a Uruguayan and would be officiating in his homeland. FIFA disagreed and awarded the game to a Paraguayan referee who was still to blow out the candles on the cake for his 30th birthday. Who was it who said common sense isn't that common? The world's footballing body seemed hell-bent on wrecking their own blue-riband climax to the planet's biggest club competition.

When the rookie referee, who had just turned 29, put the whistle to his lips to signal kick-off at the Estadio Centenario in Montevideo, no one, not even Nostradamus, could have predicted what would happen next. The first 20 minutes passed without any calamity or consternation, although left-back Nelson Chabay, who had replaced Díaz, appeared to want to get inside Johnstone's shirt at times. Díaz the honest man making way for Chabay the hatchet man. Seemed about the norm for Racing's way of thinking.

Unfortunately, the referee didn't twig that the Argentines seemed to have drawn up a rota to kick Johnstone. Chabay would hack him. Next time it would be someone else, who would be replaced by another until it came round to Chabay's turn again. The crowd of around 60,000 weren't quite as animated or intimidating as they had been at Avellaneda and that might have been down to the fact that 2,000 plain-clothes riot police mingled among them. The Uruguayan authorities were resolute in their policing of the game. There would be no trouble on the terracings; pity they couldn't do anything about the events on field. The match official awarded 24 fouls against Celtic in the first half. Auld observed, 'That was about as many as we gave away in an entire season at home!'

The fuse that had been lit in Glasgow burned all the way to Montevideo and was about to ignite another explosion of fireworks. Up it went just eight minutes before the completion of the first half. Astonishingly, the first Celtic player to be sent off was Lennox, the same Lennox who could go through season after season without so much as a word in the ear from a referee. There was yet another melee and, once the torsos of the two sets of players had been disentangled, Basile, the guy who had made the throat-cutting gesture at McNeill, was ordered off. As ever, he protested his innocence as he rubbed his jaw as though he had been punched.

What happened next just about entirely summed up the sorriest chapter in Celtic's history. The match official had a word with the Racing player, Basile pointed to Lennox and the ref went over and signalled for the protesting Celt to leave the field. He had been banished, too. Lennox looked mystified. 'Me? What have I done?' he asked. Either the referee didn't speak English or he was hard of hearing, but he simply dismissed the protestations and walked away. Lennox made his way to the touchline, but was waved back on by Jock Stein. There had to be some mistake. Lennox about-turned and noticed that Basile was also still engaged in 'discussions' with the ref. He pointed at an injured colleague who was lying on the ground. Apparently, he wanted the crocked player to take the blame and go off in his place.

Lennox walked back on; the referee sent him off again. The Celtic player, still wearing a puzzled expression, trudged to the touchline, where he was met by Stein once again. The Celtic manager stopped his player, turned him around and propelled him back onto the pitch. The referee signalled to the sidelines and two soldiers with swords came on. Lennox recalled, 'The soldier was only a couple of feet away from me. He told me to get off. I looked at his sword. I headed back to the touchline. I could risk the wrath of our manager; I wasn't going to argue with a soldier with a sabre. I headed straight for the dressing-room.' The argumentative Basile also thought better of continuing his debate with the match official and beat a hasty retreat when another soldier, armed with a sword, headed in his direction.

Gemmell said, 'I was standing there with my arms folded wondering what the hell was going on. Bobby Lennox sent off? There had to be some mistake. He might have been a *bandido* on the golf course, but he wouldn't say boo to a goose on the football pitch. Around this time, I could see that my colleagues, as well as myself, had had just about enough of this nonsense. We had now had to endure two-and-a-half games – fifteen minutes short of four hours – of the Racing players spitting on us, kicking us, pulling our hair, nipping us – och, basically going through the whole repertoire of dirty tricks. They had picked on the wrong bunch of guys. I looked at Bertie, Bobby, Billy and the rest of the lads. John Clark was a cool customer, but he looked about ready to erupt. We weren't going to accept any more abuse in the second half. We knew we would not get any protection from a decidedly ropey referee. He had lost the plot, probably lost it around the time of the kick-off.

'We were all getting frustrated at the ridiculous treatment of Jinky. The Wee Man could look after himself, but you do feel a bit helpless when you see your colleague being used as a football by a bunch of louts. Soldiers with drawn swords escorting one of our players off the field was not in the script, either. It wasn't what we signed up for when we won the European Cup and then genuinely looked forward to playing against Racing Club. How naive can you get? We thought they might be honourable sportsmen. What a laugh. What a preposterous notion. Mind you, we realised that about two minutes into the game at Hampden when two of their defenders tried to play keepy-uppy with Jinky.'

Shortly after the interval, Johnstone, much sinned-against throughout, was dismissed, again in remarkable circumstances. Martín tried to remove his shirt once more and Johnstone tried to wrestle free. His elbow appeared to hit the defender on the chest, but Martín went down clutching his face. That was enough for the ref to race over and point once again to the dressing-room. Auld said, 'I caught the Racing players looking at each other. They were delighted. They were terrified of Jinky and the referee had come to their aid; they wouldn't have to face him again. To a man, we knew we would not get justice that day.

'On a personal note, I was getting sick and fed up of players spitting on me. I wiped my hair at one stage and it was covered in spittle. You have to be an extraordinary individual blessed with the patience of a saint if you can accept that sort of behaviour from anyone.'

The mood didn't get any better when Cárdenas, who had scored the goal to take the game to Montevideo, rifled in a long-range effort for what turned out to be the winner in the 56th minute. Jock Stein later blamed stand-in keeper Fallon for not saving the 35-yard drive, but Auld jumped to his colleague's defence. 'I don't think he had much of a chance. The ball swerved and dipped before it flew past him. Believe me, like our manager, I was a serial critic of goalkeepers, but I don't think Fallon was culpable on that occasion.'

The game descended into anarchy, with Racing now determined to do anything they had to do to hold on to their lead. The referee, who would probably never recover from this experience, couldn't control the Racing players as they continually put the boot in. John Hughes was next to see red. He followed a pass-back to Cejas, in the days when the keeper could pick up the ball. The Argentine could simply have lifted it, but, to waste time, after a slight nudge from the burly Celt he collapsed on the ball. As he lay there, Hughes tried to kick the object out of his hands. A definite foul, it must be admitted. What happened next, though, should have earned Cejas, who had been fairly theatrical throughout, an Oscar for best actor. He rolled around as though the Grim Reaper himself was in attendance. Off went Hughes and back to his feet got Cejas. A career in Hollywood beckoned.

Years later, Auld could laugh. 'I asked Big Yogi what on earth was he thinking about. He replied, "I didn't think anyone was looking." Just the rest of the world!'

Hughes admitted, 'Aye, I did say that and it has come back to bite me for years. It seemed a reasonable thing to do at the time.'

Unfortunately, the TV cameras caught another incident when play had stalled yet again. There was the usual posse of players from both teams arguing the toss over something when Gemmell came into the director's shot to the left of the screen. Raffo, adept at the sneaky foul, was standing a few yards from the latest melee. The Celtic left-back raced forward at full speed and booted the Argentinian up the backside.

'That was inexcusable, I accept that,' said Gemmell. 'At the time, I wasn't thinking straight. Who would in the midst of all we had gone through? I can tell you that one of their players, I think it was Raffo, went along our back four of Jim Craig, Billy McNeill, John Clark and myself and spat in our faces immediately after the start of the game. We had played these hooligans three times inside two weeks and everyone has a breaking point. Mine came in that moment. I looked at Raffo and he was obviously fairly pleased with himself. He was very clever. He jumped out of every tackle and we couldn't catch him. He had got away with murder and not one of the three referees had even spoken to him. I decided to mete out a little bit of justice myself. Yes, I gave him a dunt up the rear end. It could have been worse – he could have come off that pitch with three Adam's apples!

'It was only when I got home that I realised the entire incident had been caught on the telly. It's a pity the TV editors weren't quite as diligent in capturing the antics of our opponents, but they were a wee bit better in disguising their kicking of us. The game, in fact, was edited by the BBC in their London studios and they seemed to dwell on everything the Celtic players did and ignored what Racing were getting up to. It looked like extremely biased editing – maybe that old Scotland v. England thing – and I can tell you Big Jock was livid when he saw the edited tape. I don't think he spoke to the BBC for about a year, which was a bit harsh when you consider the lads in Scotland had no control over the final film.'

It was long overdue, but even Rulli couldn't escape for three full games and, with five minutes to go and after another foul, he, too, was required to leave proceedings. A couple of minutes later, Auld clattered into one of the many culprits who had been dishing it out and down went the Racing player. The referee signalled for the Celtic midfielder to join teammates Lennox, Johnstone and Hughes in the dressing-room. Auld said, 'I shrugged my shoulders and basically told him I didn't speak Spanish, so I hadn't a clue what he was indicating. I looked him straight in the eye and realised he was in a state of panic, if not shock. He looked genuinely startled. I wasn't arguing with him. I just wasn't going off. I simply refused to move. What happened next surprised even me: he restarted the game with a free kick to Celtic!'

Bobby Murdoch had also been booted around for three games and, years later, I was talking to him in the lounge of his Sportsman's Bar in Rutherglen. He was looking for photographs of himself in action to put on the walls of the pub and a friend of mine at the *Daily Record* picture desk had very helpfully printed about 20 or so large-sized images of Bobby performing for Celtic and Scotland. There was one photograph that intrigued me. It appeared to show Bobby doing his best to get a Racing Club player in a Boston crab, a wrestling hold that was popular at the time. I asked him about it. He laughed. 'Oh, I remember this. Aye, it looks as though I'm giving him a right doing, doesn't it? Who says the camera never lies? Actually, what happened here was that this bloke was lying on the pitch, kidding on he was injured and wasting time. The referee was standing there doing nothing and I just knew he wouldn't be adding on any extra minutes. I thought I could help matters by dragging their player off the field and we could get on with the game. Doesn't look too clever, though, does it?'

Murdoch was surprised to discover that, according to the referee's official report, he had been sent off in the game. 'Aye, that's right,' said Bobby. 'Somehow he got me mixed up with John Hughes. I don't know if Bertie was ever in any report. That incident was laughable. The bold

Bertie just stood his ground and the ref crumbled. Och, that bloody guy couldn't get anything right.'

The misery continued for the Celtic players when they discovered that the board of directors had decided to fine every player £250. 'That was our bonus for our League Cup win over Dundee,' said Gemmell. 'The club said they weren't happy with our conduct and announced they would be withdrawing the cash and giving it to charity. We had been subject to the most degrading stuff from a shower of animals – yes, I agree with Alf Ramsey, too – and now we were being fined for our troubles. It was like all our nightmares had come at once.' Gemmell, with that knowing smile, added, 'Lisbon will live forever, though.'

10

JOCK VERSUS RANGERS

Jock Stein's family were staunch Protestants from Burnbank and his father, George, was a fervent Rangers supporter. The family hoped that Jock, adept at performing at centre-half or left-half, would one day sign for the Ibrox side. That was the aim and wish of his father, that his son should play in the blue, red and white of junior side Blantyre Vics before swapping it for the blue, red and white of Rangers. Jock, though, displayed an independent streak early in life. He was not rebellious and never showed the slightest bit of curiosity concerning the religious divide in a small mining community where the majority, Protestants, would have their meeting place at Burnbank Cross and the Catholics would meet at Glenlee Street at a spot known locally as 'Pope's Corner'. Later in life, however, Jock Stein never made any attempt to disguise the fact that he thoroughly enjoyed beating Rangers.

According to Celtic players, Stein was somewhat irked by the media coverage carved out for Davie White, who had taken over from Scot Symon as Rangers manager in 1967. At 34, White was the same age as Stein had been when a London specialist had informed the Celtic centre-half that his playing career was over, that his damaged ankle would stubbornly resist repair. White had won all of his eight league games, his stock was on the rise, praise was avalanching his way and a new-found status was being carefully cultivated. He was seen as the brash young pretender. Not as sedate and sombre as his predecessor, he was seen as a tracksuited man of the '60s, an image more in keeping with the evolving social values of the time. Stein was not about to be overshadowed and was determined to leave White's so-called new standing in tatters after the Old Firm head-to-head on the second day of the new year in 1968. As ever, he wanted to win this game. More than ever, though, he was eager to triumph while rubbing Rangers' noses in it.

First, though, White's former club Clyde had to be taken care of at

Shawfield on New Year's Day. Celtic made heavy weather of it before scraping a 3–2 victory. Stein rested Jimmy Johnstone, keeping his extrovert winger in mothballs before unleashing him on Rangers 24 hours later. Goalkeeper John Fallon had been told he would be playing, with Ronnie Simpson getting a rest. Stein, without explanation, changed his mind about two hours before kick-off: Fallon was out, Simpson was in. It was a decision that was to have dramatic consequences the following afternoon. Celtic toiled on a difficult surface in Rutherglen, but two opportunist goals from Stevie Chalmers and another from Joe McBride got the job done. Simpson twisted an ankle on a ground that would never be one of his favourites. Stein, though, said he fully expected the veteran custodian to be fit for the following day. The manager's prophecy was cast in stone as far as understudy Fallon was concerned. At the same time, across at Ibrox, White was piloting his charges to his ninth consecutive success, Rangers overcoming Partick Thistle 5–2.

Now it was showtime: Celtic v. Rangers, Jock Stein v. Davie White. Bertie Auld recalled, 'Publicly, Big Jock would inform everyone that a meeting with Rangers was just another game. Privately, the players all knew just how much he enjoyed putting one over on our old rivals. I would go as far as to say he detested Rangers. I don't think that is too strong a word. He really disliked them. We all knew his background, we realised where his roots lay, but we also saw him after a win over Rangers. You would have needed plastic surgery to get the smile off his face. We could beat any other team 2–0, 3–0, 4–0, you name it, and we could still get a rollicking when we turned up for training on Monday. If he had seen something that upset him, irrespective of the winning margin, he would give us pelters. However, we could play awful, get a lucky goal and beat Rangers and we never heard a thing, not a murmur. Lose, though, and life wasn't worth living.

'He rarely, if ever, talked about the sectarian divide. He was a Protestant managing a club with Catholic origins and he had Protestant players such as Ronnie Simpson, Willie Wallace, Tommy Gemmell and myself playing for him. Religion didn't come into it as far as he and Celtic were concerned. It did across the Clyde, though. For long enough Rangers would not sign a Catholic. It was well known that they were put off signing a young player, Danny McGrain, who would go on to become world class, because of his name, from which they assumed he was Catholic. If only they had known! Jock used to insist that if there were two players of equal ability and one was a Catholic and one was a Protestant, he would sign the latter. He would say, "Well, Rangers can't sign the Catholic, can they?" Sadly, that was the case back then. Jock found it extremely distasteful. He was only interested in a guy's playing ability and not the school he had gone to. Maybe that fired him up just that little bit more for games against Rangers.'

Auld also recalled Stein preparing for the visit of Davie White on the second day of 1968. 'I think Jock sensed panic in Rangers' decision to dismiss Scot Symon after his 13-year reign and appoint a much younger man. The press had talked up Davie White as a new breed of manager, one for the future, with fresh, wonderful, innovative ideas, all that sort of thing. So far, though, as the Rangers manager, he hadn't come up against Jock Stein or Celtic. As you would expect, Jock would show every respect and every courtesy to a fellow professional sportsman, but, deep down, we all got the message he was eager for Rangers' new boss to understand what pressure, real pressure, was like. As a footballer at Clyde, White had played against Celtic and, as a manager of the same club, he would also have faced Celtic. Anything he had encountered in the past, though, could only be considered infinitesimal compared with what awaited him in an Old Firm encounter, especially that first one against Big Jock, and we knew the boss was looking forward to the match with even more than the usual enthusiasm he seemed to reserve for these encounters. On this occasion, he didn't just want to dent the younger man's credibility or popularity with his growing admirers among the Rangers board, the Ibrox supporters and the Scottish media – he wanted to obliterate it.'

He might have succeeded, too, if Ronnie Simpson had overcome the ankle injury sustained at Shawfield. John Fallon fully believed the biggest problem he would encounter that afternoon would be fighting off frostbite sitting in the stand; Jimmy Quinn was the designated substitute. 'I was in the table-tennis room when the door was kicked open and in rushed Big Jock,' recalled Fallon. 'He grabbed me. "You're playing," he said, and hurled me through the door. All the other players were stripped and ready to go. The referee, Bobby Davidson, was waiting for me to change and get my boots on, he checked them and we were ready to go. One minute I'm playing table tennis with a couple of reserve players and the next I'm out there in an Old Firm game with 75,000 looking on.' Fallon admitted that, in the expectation that he would not be required to perform anything more strenuous than avoiding splinters in his backside on a wooden seat in the stand, he had had a bit of a late night followed by a huge breakfast before the game: hardly ideal preparation.

It was another severe winter's afternoon in the East End of Glasgow, the Arctic chill invading the very marrow of your bones. Supporters stood on the terracings with stiffened limbs and did their best to get the blood corpuscles moving around their systems. 'It was a day for the wee half-bottle or the hip flask to come into action for the fans,' said Gemmell. 'Lucky beggars!'

Auld had his manager – and the Celtic followers – smiling when he got the opening goal. 'I remember it well,' said the midfield orchestrator. 'We were awarded a direct free kick about five yards from the edge of their box on our right. It was the ideal strike for a left-footed player and, as Big Jock never tired of telling me, I only possessed a left foot. They erected their usual defensive wall in front of goalkeeper Erik Sørensen. Bobby Murdoch stood beside me, but I knew I would be taking it. Sometimes it was good to wait that wee bit longer and crank up the tension. You look at the opponents in front of you and they are wondering what is coming next. You've got the upper hand because you know exactly what's about to happen. The ref blew for the kick to be taken, but I still lingered just that little bit longer. Then I stepped forward, struck it sweetly enough and it took the merest of nicks off a defender and flew into the net. Sørensen didn't even move. The Celtic support went crazy. The Rangers end was silent. We were 1–0 up and, as ever, we would want to add to that as swiftly as possible.'

Fallon then dropped an awful clanger to allow Rangers back into the contest before the interval. The keeper must have anticipated a stronger, hooked shot from Willie Johnston, but the Ibrox striker merely mis-hit his effort from about ten yards. Fallon didn't look comfortable as he tried to scoop the ball into his arms and, to the consternation of his manager, his teammates and the Celtic fans, allowed the ball to trickle through his legs and over the line. It was overcast, with a heavy mist settling on the East End, and it appeared to take the Rangers support, down at the other end, some time to realise that their team had drawn level. A couple of seconds later, though, and it was their turn to go wild with delight. Fallon knelt as if in prayer. Gemmell fished the ball out of the net. 'I felt sorry for John,' he recalled. 'It's the same old story about goalkeepers, isn't it? They make one mistake and it's normally fatal. Outfield performers can make error after error and it won't affect the scoreline. But there is no way back for the poor old goalie. They are rarely remembered for the ones they stop but rather for the ones they let in. At that particular moment, John looked distraught. You had to feel for him.'

With a minute to go, it looked as though Stein would get his wish of a victory over his young managerial challenger. Celtic were ahead again, with a superb curling drive from Murdoch from about 25 yards on the right. Murdoch, like Gemmell, knew how to punch a hole in the net with a shot of devastating power, but he also possessed the extraordinary ability, especially for such a well-built man, to delicately glide the ball around, with a range of stunning versatility. Sørensen, steeling himself on his line for the anticipated thunderbolt, was bamboozled when the midfielder checked slightly before deftly striking the ball. It arced round the keeper at his right-hand side and settled in the net. The Celtic support, behind that goal, rose as one for the second time that day. Fallon, at the other end, breathed a sigh of relief. With 60 seconds remaining, the keeper must have been counting down the clock.

Kai Johansen, who never seemed to be anonymous in Old Firm confrontations, broke from his own half down the right. He peered through the deteriorating conditions before trying his luck from long range. He didn't connect properly and the ball seemed to bounce weakly towards Fallon. He couldn't do it again, could he? The answer came when the Rangers crowd behind him rose in unison with the Celtic fans, one hundred or so yards away, wondering what all the commotion was about, until the horrible realisation dawned that their keeper had blundered for a second time. Fallon had allowed Johansen's effort to crawl under his body and barely cross the line. 'I must admit it was a howler,' said Fallon. 'After the game, Big Jock looked as though he wanted to strangle me.'

'Strangle him? I wanted to string him up!' said Auld. 'He was a dejected figure in the dressing-room and didn't need to be told he had performed miserably. I don't think either of the shots carried enough oomph to even hit the net. At the same time, we were aware that the dropped point could have catastrophic consequences at the end of the season. We were two points adrift and that was the second and last Old Firm game of the campaign. Basically, that meant we could win every game between then and the end of the season and still not win the championship. Rangers could even afford the luxury of a draw in their remaining fixtures. We needed someone to do us a favour, because it was now out of our hands. It's incredible how things swing about in football.

'By the way, John's nickname was "Peter" and at least he had lived up to his moniker that day. Peter? We christened him after a character called Peter Brady who appeared in the popular TV programme *The Invisible Man*. Fallon had that ability to go AWOL at times. Brady used to be swathed in bandages and, after they had been unravelled, there was nothing there. We weren't too pleased with Peter, but we didn't want to see him in bandages. I wasn't too sure about Big Jock, though!'

After all the meticulous planning by Stein, two horrendous goalkeeping mistakes had let Rangers and White off the hook. Celtic were by far the superior outfit on the day; there could be no argument about that. What was also undeniably true was that the new man in charge at Ibrox had left Celtic Park still unbeaten after ten games and with Rangers remaining two points ahead in the race for the championship after overcoming their most difficult obstacle. Neither Stein nor Celtic received too much praise in the following day's newspapers. They had played well, controlled the match for almost its entirety and restricted Rangers to two shots on target. Unfortunately, those both eluded Fallon, who would not be chosen for the remaining 16 league games of the season. 'I was sent to Coventry,' said the keeper.

One of the more cynical among the players in the Celtic dressing-room observed, 'I got the feeling that Big Jock would have preferred to have played himself in goal rather than let John anywhere near the first team again.' It should never be underestimated what this particular Glasgow derby meant to the Celtic manager. Stein was still seething when he left Parkhead hours later that evening. It would have been either a brave man or a fool who wished him a belated Happy New Year.

With Scotland in the icy grip of winter once again, Celtic had to wait until a 20 January trip to face Hibs at Easter Road for their next fixture. It had been a frustrating eighteen days for Stein, especially with Rangers' two games against Falkirk at Ibrox and Hearts at Tynecastle going ahead during Celtic's enforced lay-off. It didn't help, either, that White's team had won in both encounters. So the champions were trailing by six points, an alarming amount, by the time they travelled through to the capital for what was clearly a must-win game. There was no way Celtic could afford to surrender more ground at the top to Rangers. Simpson, to Stein's relief, returned to face his former team and Willie Wallace and Stevie Chalmers, missing from the 2 January line-up, were also back in attack. Hibs right-back Bobby Duncan turned one beyond his keeper, Willie Wilson, and Bobby Lennox wrapped up a thoroughly professional performance with the second. How had Rangers fared that afternoon against Motherwell at Ibrox? Goals from Alex Willoughby and John Greig (a penalty) had given them an identical 2–0 scoreline. The pressure was relentless.

Celtic were given a break from chasing league points when they began their defence of the Scottish Cup against Dunfermline at Parkhead the following Saturday. Stein was confident enough to give Joe McBride a place in his starting line-up. There was little doubt the marksman had lost a little bit of his sharpness, the quickness that allowed him to turn an opponent and rifle an effort at goal. Auld said, 'Joe had taken a terrible injury and, back then, it was career-threatening. Even today, with much more sophisticated technology, a cruciate knee injury is a delicate matter. You had to admire Joe, though. He put himself through it in the gym, did extra training sessions on his own, lapping the track at Celtic Park with no one in sight, and not once did he complain. We had gone into business together and bought a pub not far from Celtic Park, so, as you might expect, I spent a fair bit of time with him away from the ground. All he talked about was returning to full strength, getting back in the first team and continuing where he had left off for most of 1966. There was never any talk of chucking it. He remained completely focused.' McBride didn't know it at the time, but, as he lined up with the Fifers in his sights, he would play only two more games for Celtic before joining Hibs in November that year.

The cup tie against Dunfermline was laced with controversy, especially when it looked as though Celtic had equalised a Hugh Robertson goal for the visitors. Jim Brogan caught the ball sweetly from about 25 yards and his first-time drive left his former teammate Bent Martin motionless as it thumped into the net. Celtic Park erupted and not one Fife player complained, but, mysteriously, it was ruled out. Later the referee, Bobby Davidson of Airdrie, explained that Lennox was in an offside position. That was correct, but it was also accurate to point out that he was in no way interfering with play. He was wide to the left of the penalty box and not even involved in the ruck of players in front of Martin. Celtic protested, but the match official stuck to his bewildering decision. In these enlightened times, that decision would have been pored over and the referee's judgement would have been shredded. Back then, unhappily, you could make such a call in the knowledge that very little would have been done about it.

If McBride's Celtic career was coming to an end that afternoon, that also appeared to be the case for Davie Cattenach, one of the original Quality Street Gang, the young reserves whom Stein was lining up to become the Celtic of the future. Youngsters such as Kenny Dalglish, Davie Hay, Danny McGrain, George Connelly, Lou Macari, Jimmy Quinn and Vic Davidson were being nudged gently along the conveyor belt, awaiting their opportunity to make an impact on the big time. However, for one, Cattenach, the future was hardly bright on that freezing Saturday afternoon in the grim East End of Glasgow. In the second half, a wayward pass from the youngster was seized upon by Dunfermline striker Pat Gardner, Simpson's late rush from goal couldn't avert disaster and the ball was carefully knocked into the inviting net. Cattenach looked on in horror.

'I believe that was the beginning of the end for Davie,' said his teammate Davie Hay. 'Jock didn't say anything after the game. However, I don't think it was ever the same for my pal after that. One bad pass and goodnight, Celtic. Winning wasn't everything to Jock – it was the *only* thing.'

Looking back, Cattenach said, 'I wasn't aware of anything like that at the time. I remember being in the boardroom with the rest of the players the following Tuesday and Jock was clearly unhappy. However, if anything, he was saying I, as a young laddie, should have been given a bit more help by my teammates. I had another four years at Celtic before joining Falkirk, so I was hardly booted out of the club for one mistake. However, I do wish I had made a bigger impact.

'Unlike the other Quality Street Gang members, I didn't start my career with Celtic. I was on Stirling Albion's books when I signed for the Parkhead club in 1963, two years before Big Jock arrived. In fact, I was the youngest player to turn out for Stirling at the age of 15 in the strangest of circumstances. I was sitting in the stand on the night they unveiled the floodlights at Annfield in 1961. We were playing Birmingham City when I got an urgent call to get ready to go out for the second half. One of the players was injured and I was rushed into my first-team debut. I must have done well enough, because Hibs came calling a couple of years later. Stirling's manager at the time was Sammy Baird, the former Rangers player, and he was poised to do a deal with the Easter Road club. Someone at Celtic got wind of it and they made an approach. I remember I signed for £12 per week and I would have got more at Hibs. But when Celtic came calling you could never have said no.

'Like everyone else, I was delighted when Jock took over as manager in 1965. I thought he was brilliant, absolutely different class. He was always looking for fresh ideas and I recall a Glasgow Cup final against Rangers in 1970 when he decided to try something completely original. He played me alongside my good pal Davie Hay as twin centre-halfs, with George Connelly alongside us. That may have surprised some people because Davie and I weren't six-footers and you had to be tall to play in central defence in those days. Basically, Jock had come up with the forerunner to the 3–5–2 system. All the other clubs were playing 4–4–2 or 4–3–3, but Jock, yet again, was attempting something fresh and new. Davie and I were told to use the midfield men in front of us when we were passing the ball out of defence, while George was given the scope to spring forward at every opportunity. It worked a treat. We won 3–1 with Tommy Gemmell, almost playing outside-left, getting two and Jimmy Quinn the other. However, with a dominant centre-half such as Billy McNeill around, the system wasn't used too often.

'I played only 19 games for Celtic before I joined Falkirk on New Year's Day in 1972. I had been at the club for more than nine years and witnessed at first hand the truly amazing transformation in fortunes. I wouldn't have missed it for the world.'

The Scottish Cup trail, like the European crusade, hadn't managed to survive the first test. That bleak January afternoon saw the Dunfermline players celebrate like they had won the tournament and, in fact, they managed that feat late in April when they beat Hearts 3–1 in the final at Hampden on an extraordinary day not only for them but also for Celtic. Rangers had toppled at the quarter-final stage of the competition. They drew 1–1 at Ibrox with Hearts before a goal from Donald Ford ousted them in the replay. Rangers' interest in Europe would also end in March when they lost 2–0 on aggregate to Leeds United at the quarter-final stage of the Inter-Cities Fairs Cup.

That meant that their priority, like Celtic's, was the league championship, both clubs zeroing in on that particular piece of silverware in the hope of having something to celebrate at the end of a somewhat intriguing campaign. Stein's instruction to his side was simple: win every game from now until the end of the season. No doubt White was sending out the same message to his troops in Govan. Who would crack first in this exhilarating pursuit of the flag?

A week after being dismissed from the Scottish Cup, Celtic overcame Partick Thistle 4–1, with Bobby Lennox (2), Billy McNeill and Tommy Gemmell easing some of the pain. Across Glasgow, Rangers huffed and puffed before a goal from John Greig eventually saw off Clyde. Next up for Celtic was Motherwell at Fir Park, while Rangers travelled to Dundee. 'We were playing our games and were then desperately trying to find out what was happening at Rangers,' recalled Gemmell. 'The lines of communication in the '60s weren't quite what they became in the twenty-first century. Backroom staff or some travelling reserves would be footering about with dials on radios with reception next to hopeless. It was almost as nerve-racking after a game as it was during it.'

A goal from John Hughes downed Motherwell. Now all eyes – or ears – were on what had happened at Dens Park. Slowly, the announcer said, 'Dundee 2' – there was complete silence in a dressing-room, with every eye on the little plastic source of information perched on the treatment table – 'Rangers 4.'

Gemmell said, 'Of course we were disappointed, but there was a general shrugging of the shoulders as we went for our showers. "There's always next week" was the cry. But we also realised there would come a time when we couldn't repeat those hopeful words. At the same time, we were confident we could hold our nerve. We had been over the course before; we knew the pitfalls. Rangers had made an awful lot of changes over a period of 12 months or so, not least sacking their manager. They had brought in about six players from other clubs and, basically, that was unheard of. Look at Celtic, for instance. We'd added Willie Wallace in December 1966 and hadn't gone anywhere near the transfer market since then. Could Rangers continue to click? Only time would tell. We concentrated on our own game, of course, but naturally we were more than a little interested in what was happening over at their place. We would look at the fixture list to see who we were playing, but we would also check out who they would be taking on.'

Valentine's Day arrived and with it a visit from Stirling Albion, who had been more of a thorn in Celtic's side than a bouquet of roses in the past. Rangers had a Saturday off, with games being rearranged to restructure the fixture list after the ravages of winter. Celtic had the opportunity to close the gap to four points. A ferocious penalty kick from Gemmell sent the Celts on their way and Wallace doubled the advantage to complete a 2–0 victory.

Both sides of the Old Firm resumed combat in the championship at the start of March, with Celtic travelling to Kilmarnock and their old foes at home to St Johnstone. Could this be a defining moment in the championship? Wallace was on fire as he walloped in four in a runaway 6–0 triumph.

'The way I looked at it, we simply had to win. There were no alternatives,' said Wallace. 'That's what Big Jock wanted and there were no cat-and-mouse situations at the time. We had to go out for an hour-and-a-half and score at least one more goal than our opponents. Not that easy, of course, but that was the battle plan every match day.'

Wallace made life a misery for Kilmarnock keeper Sandy McLaughlan that afternoon as he struck shots from all angles with accuracy and power. Lennox netted, too, and substitute Jimmy Quinn, the great-grandson of the legendary Celt of the same name, claimed his first goal for the club. Stein made a fuss of the youngster as he came off the pitch.

How would Rangers react to the news that Celtic had walloped in six at Rugby Park? It was a fair response: they netted six of their own in a 6–2 triumph over St Johnstone. Coincidentally, one of their players, Alex Ferguson, also collected a foursome that afternoon. The bustling, old-fashioned centre-forward with the flashing elbows was living the dream while making life more than just a little awkward for Celtic. His fourth against the Perth Saints was his fourteenth league goal of the season. The other new boys, Andy Penman and Örjan Persson, had pitched in with 15 between them, and the Ibrox side was congratulating itself on good business in the summer transfer market. A new era or a false dawn? Time would tell.

Celtic, two games behind Rangers, were still playing catch-up when Aberdeen came to Parkhead while White took his side to East End Park to face Celtic's Scottish Cup conquerors Dunfermline. 'We were looking for someone to beat Rangers, or at least take a point off them,' said Wallace. 'We knew how awkward and dangerous the Fifers could be. They were a good team as, unfortunately, they had demonstrated against us in the cup. It was also well known that their manager George Farm was not a big fan of the Old Firm. He was always going on about a "them-and-us" situation and was hell-bent on smashing our superiority. We looked at the fixtures and wondered if this could be the occasion a door might be opened for us.'

A blistering hat-trick from Lennox and a header from McNeill guided the club to a 4–1 win over the Pittodrie side. The game was also notable for the first appearance of a youthful Davie Hay, as a substitute. He was an individual who was to prove to be a winner at the club, as a player and a manager. Once more, the transistor radio became the main focus of interest in the dressing-room. The dial was set, the announcer, in strict monotone, went through the list. 'Celtic 4, Aberdeen 1' – 'Aye, we know that one!' – then silence. A pause and the announcer carried on: 'Dunfermline 1' – more intolerable silence – 'Rangers 2.' Ferguson and Persson had nicked it for the visitors. 'There's always next week.'

In total, Celtic would cram seven league games, two more than their rivals, into a frantic month of March to balance the fixtures. With Kilmarnock and Aberdeen overcome, the remaining five were against Airdrie, Falkirk, Raith Rovers, St Johnstone and Dundee United, two at home, three away. Rangers had a clear Saturday when Airdrie arrived at Parkhead. The Diamonds were never a threat as a hat-trick from Wallace and a single from Lennox overwhelmed them 4–0.

Next up was a trip to Falkirk. Meanwhile, Celtic, reasonably, weren't too excited about the prospect of Stirling Albion doing anything to help their cause at Ibrox. At Brockville Park, Gemmell once more paved the way, with an unstoppable penalty kick, and the lethal double act of Wallace and Lennox added the others in a 3–0 victory. Rangers romped to a 5–0 win over hapless Stirling Albion.

Celtic would score five themselves a week later, dismissing Raith Rovers 5–0, with Wallace claiming another trio and Lennox and Hughes contributing the others. Persson led the charge again for Rangers, scoring the opening goal in a 3–1 victory over Hibs at Easter Road. A couple of days later, Celtic destroyed St Johnstone 6–1 in Perth, with Lennox sticking four past Jim Donaldson.

The Parkhead side had now moved a game ahead of Rangers, with six remaining when Dundee United visited the East End on the day the Ibrox outfit travelled to Broomfield to take on Airdrie. Celtic brought down the curtain on a hugely successful month of March with an excellent 5–0 triumph over the Tannadice side, their seventh successive victory in the space of twenty-eight active days. Lennox (2), Johnstone, Wallace and substitute Cattenach, with the only goal of his Celtic career, were the marksmen.

Once more, the transistor came into play. All that was needed was the atmospheric drum roll. The radio informed Celtic that Airdrie had scored one goal against Rangers, but the men from Govan had hit back with efforts from Willie Johnston and Alex Smith. Something, surely, had to give. Was it possible for the Old Firm to win every game in the league campaign after the 2–2 draw at Parkhead on the second day of January? That was the way it was shaping up. Neither club looked like faltering with the finishing tape in sight.

Rangers travelled to Tannadice for a midweek confrontation with Dundee United while Celtic rested. After this game, the clubs would have five matches each to play during the month of April. Remarkably and unexpectedly, Rangers shed a point in a goalless stalemate on Tayside. It was the first time their forwards had fired blanks since the fateful afternoon against Dunfermline in Glasgow at the tail end of October, the result that saw Scot Symon dismissed.

'I could hardly believe it when I heard the score,' admitted Gemmell. 'I was certain of what we could contribute when the pressure was on, but it looked as though the Rangers lads were coping, too. They had won ten consecutive games after drawing with us and we were running out of matches. You never let your spirits sag, but there comes a time when you have to accept the inevitable and, sad though it may be, you cannot expect to win everything every season. If nothing else, season 1967–68 taught us that. We had retained the League Cup, but the campaigns in Europe and in the Scottish Cup were nothing short of disastrous.'

The way the fixture list panned out, Celtic had been left with six away games from their final nine. Rangers, too, would play away from Ibrox in three of their remaining four, with the last game against Aberdeen due at Ibrox on 27 April, when Celtic had a day off because their scheduled opponents, Dunfermline, would be playing in the Scottish Cup final. It was possible, therefore, for Rangers to go a long way to winning the championship with Celtic idle and powerless to do anything about it.

Celtic travelled to Edinburgh to take on the unpredictable Hearts, who weren't enjoying their best league season, with their focus on the Scottish Cup. Nevertheless, they were dangerous opponents, especially on home territory at Tynecastle. On the same afternoon, Rangers played host to Dundee United, only three days after allowing a crucial point to escape against the same rivals. Lennox and Johnstone took care of business in a 2–0 win in the capital. The question now was: could United stage an action replay in Glasgow? Goals from Ferguson (2), Willoughby and Johnston provided the answer, Rangers winning 4–1.

Four days after the trip to Tynecastle, Celtic were on their travels again, this time to Aberdeen for a midweek fixture, while the Ibrox side could rest until the Saturday. It was tense and tight at Pittodrie, but Lennox settled the nerves with the only strike of the encounter.

On Saturday, 13 April, Dundee visited Parkhead while Rangers travelled to Kirkcaldy to face Raith Rovers, still battling relegation. With so much at stake, the Celtic fans would have accepted a win under any conditions, but they witnessed a fabulous five-goal performance, with Lennox (2), Hughes (2) and an own goal from George Stewart propelling them to an exciting 5–2 triumph. The Ibrox side had to fight all the way for the points at Stark's Park and they scraped a 3–2 victory with goals from Davie Smith, Willoughby and Penman.

They were still in the driving seat and they were winning. They were also conceding goals. It was worrying White, with so much at stake and a mere three games to go. New goalkeeper Sørensen had seen 27 goals stuffed behind him in his 28 games and, to the manager, that didn't look like an impressive ratio. The blond Dane was flamboyant and acrobatic, but at that time White was looking for a steady pair of hands. He was about to make a cataclysmic error of judgement.

On Wednesday evening 17 April, Celtic played Clyde in the Glasgow Cup final and thrashed them 8–0, with a hat-trick from Lennox, two from Hughes, one from Johnstone and two booming drives from Murdoch and Gemmell. However, the events at Hampden were of little consequence; most of the attention was focused on Greenock, a few miles away, where Morton were taking on Rangers. White reinstated Norrie Martin to goal instead of Sørensen. Unless the Dane had a mystery injury, it was an inexplicable judgement call from the Ibrox gaffer. If there was one set of goals that Sørensen would have known better than Ibrox's, it would have been those at Cappielow, where he had spent more than three years. As any goalie will tell you – from amateur to junior to senior – they like to feel at home in a particular goalmouth. Sørensen would have known every clump and divot in both those penalty areas, every angle facing him. Not all pitches are the same, and corners, for instance, can be up to four or five yards shorter or longer than on an average pitch. Those little things mean a lot to a goalkeeper. Martin did not possess the same expert knowledge as his teammate. Amazingly, with 20 minutes remaining, Morton were leading 3–1, with Joe Mason, later to become a coach at Ibrox, terrorising the Rangers rearguard. The Ibrox side retaliated and eventually two goals from Greig and one from Johnston helped them scramble a 3–3 draw.

With two games to go, Celtic were now on top of the table, albeit on goal average. They had scored 102 goals and conceded 22, as opposed to Rangers' 89 for and 30 against. Stein's men had claimed 13 more and conceded 8 fewer. Their goal average was 4.64 compared with Rangers' 2.97. Celtic knew they could afford to win their remaining two games by the slenderest of margins and the championship would be theirs for the third successive season. Rangers could win two and match them on points, but only a miracle would pull things around in their favour as far as goal average was concerned.

Celtic fans applauded the Morton players onto the Celtic Park pitch three days after the Greenock side had done their team a massive favour. No set of visiting players had ever received such a delirious reception. The natives weren't so friendly, though, with a minute to go. The game was deadlocked 1–1 and it looked very much as though a good turn from old Parkhead favourite Jim Kennedy was about to backfire on the team closest to his heart.

Gerry Sweeney, trying to work his way through the Celtic reserves, had been released by Jock Stein in the summer of 1966. Kennedy, by now skipper at Morton, remembered the Renfrew-born youngster and tipped off Cappielow's extrovert chairman Hal Stewart. 'I knew he was a good lad,' said Kennedy. 'Possibly not Celtic material, but certainly someone who could do a job for Morton. I had no hesitation in recommending him.' Sweeney was snapped up and, a month or so later, Celtic also freed his pal Tony Taylor, a winger who rarely got a first-team mention. The soccer grapevine got to work again and, through the influence of Kennedy and Sweeney, Taylor also made his way to Morton. And so it was that the two young former Celts found themselves squaring up to their boyhood heroes on 20 April.

All was going according to plan when Wallace flicked a close-range effort wide of the exposed Andy Crawford in the 14th minute. 'Really, that should have settled us,' said the man known as Wispy. 'Maybe it came too early, but we didn't attack as consistently as we knew we could. The fans sensed it, too. If it remained like that, we only had to beat Dunfermline in the last game and, irrespective of what Rangers achieved, the title was ours. It was difficult to get that thought out of your head.'

Morton rarely threatened until, suddenly and without warning, just on half-time, a gap appeared on the edge of the box. Joe Mason took a touch before drilling the ball wide of the diving Simpson. Hush. Taylor rushed forward to have another boot of the ball as it settled in the net and got himself entangled in the mesh. While he tried to get back to his feet, his teammates were racing around Celtic Park dancing jigs of delight to complete silence. Clearly, this wasn't in the script.

Gemmell recalled, 'To be honest, we didn't see it coming. We had been playing reasonably well, keeping possession, but it was also true that we weren't exactly overworking their goalkeeper. Wispy had taken his goal superbly and with guys like him, Bobby Lennox, Jimmy Johnstone and John Hughes up in attack you always fancied getting a goal or two. I don't remember us being particularly nervous that day, but you will get occasions when the ball refuses to run for you. Without taking anything away from the effort that the Morton boys put in, I think that was their only shot at our goal that entire afternoon.

'At half-time, we weren't unduly worried. Big Jock always did good work during this period. He would make sharp observations, point out a few things. I never once saw him fazed in these situations. He had a sharp eye for detail. And you only needed one look at the quality within our ranks and you could see there was no need to panic. We still had a full forty-five minutes to play against Morton and, to a man, we believed we would get at least one more goal. Every single Celtic player who filtered out of that tunnel for the second half was of that opinion. We had put so much effort into getting ourselves in this position that it was really unimaginable that we would fail now in front of our fans. The advantage had been passed to us and we had no intention of handing it back to Rangers. We realised they were playing Kilmarnock at Rugby Park at the same time, but we didn't even know their half-time score. Nor were we interested. It was all about what we did and not what was happening in Ayrshire.'

The hour mark arrived without Celtic making a telling contribution in enemy territory. There was a lot of effort and endeavour, but precious little guile or craft. Jock Stein and Hal Stewart were big buddies off the field, but their friendship must have been stretched to breaking point during that second half, with Morton refusing to leave their own half, camping in front of the 18-yard box. Of course, there are occasions when teams are simply pinned back and aren't allowed an escape route into the other team's half. This was not one of those occasions. Morton were not in Glasgow to provide a spectacle. Their white-clad players presented a ghostly barrier in front of their keeper, who, obviously under instructions, wasn't kicking the ball long. Instead, he would roll it to someone who would dally on it before passing it back. Crawford, as he was entitled to do back then, would pick up the ball and send it on to a nearby teammate, and then they would go through the entire rigmarole once again. Inter Milan could have taken lessons off this team.

Celtic continued to probe. Suddenly, 75 minutes were on the clock. There was a distinct trace of anxiety creeping into play. Celtic, under Stein, were known as a patient, passing team, but they could play it long, too, and were being forced into this tactic against the stubborn Greenock side, which simply packed the penalty box and refused to budge. Eighty minutes gone and still no breakthrough. Eighty-five minutes gone and Morton were holding firm. Eighty-nine minutes gone and there was still no change.

Suddenly, there were loud groans from parts of the ground where supporters had transistor radios, those founts of all knowledge. Behind the Celtic dugout, someone proclaimed, 'Rangers have won 2–1 at Kilmarnock.' Obviously, it was no hoax. At that moment, Jock Stein turned to Neil Mochan and said, 'That's it, Neil. We've lost it.' The situation could only be likened to winning the Lotto jackpot on a Wednesday and being told there's been some mistake and you must return it on the Saturday.

They must have thought it was all over, too, in Ayrshire. Photographs appeared in the following day's press of Rangers fans cavorting around Rugby Park, scarves held high amid much celebration. Hold on, though. There were 30 seconds still to play in Glasgow. It wasn't an effort fit to grace any Goal of the Season gallery. It wasn't a pulverising Tommy Gemmell special or a Bobby Murdoch moment of improvised magic. It wasn't a Jimmy Johnstone flash of solo brilliance. It wasn't a soaring header from Billy McNeill. Even the players who performed in the green shirts that afternoon have difficulty recalling it clearly. But, and be sure of this, Bobby Lennox's winning goal against Morton in the fading seconds was one of the most important strikes for Celtic in the '60s.

What does he remember about it? 'It looked as though we were about to hand the initiative back to Rangers. As everyone had come to expect from this Celtic team, though, it was never over until the referee blew for full-time. We knew it was very, very close to the end. Suddenly, there was a chance. A ball was floated in, the Morton defence didn't clear properly and it dropped perfectly right at my feet at the back post. I didn't hesitate as I lunged forward to stab the ball beyond Andy Crawford from about six yards out. I watched it go over the line with a mixture of elation and relief. We had won.'

The strength, sturdiness and quality of the foundations of Celtic Park were put to the test in that moment. The place was in bedlam. Players hugged each other, total strangers on the terracing embraced as if they were long-lost cousins and Jock Stein beamed before heading up the tunnel. Of all people, he must have realised how wrong it was to write off this Celtic team.

The championship had ebbed and flowed in a truly memorable campaign. Now there was one game to go. Rangers were due to play Aberdeen at Ibrox on cup final day – 27 April – and faced the genuine prospect of going through the entire league programme, all 34 games, without defeat and still not winning the title. That would have been one for the history books.

Stein was at Hampden that afternoon to watch his old club Dunfermline, the team that had abruptly cut short Celtic's interest in the tournament, face Hearts. Two goals from Pat Gardner and a penalty kick from Ian Lister gave the Fifers a 3–1 triumph. It seemed a lifetime ago that Stein had been congratulating his Dunfermline players after their success over Celtic in the competition; in fact, it was seven years minus a day.

He stood to applaud when a national newspaper reporter gave him the news: 'Rangers have lost 3–2 at Ibrox.' Stein asked, 'Are you sure?' He was told that the Pittodrie side had scored a last-minute winner. Rangers had definitely lost 3–2. Ignoring the limp that had ended his playing career, the Celtic manager tried to bound down the Hampden steps and his ankle almost buckled under his weight. He stumbled, got his bearings and raced off to spread the news. 'This has been a great day,' he said. Who could argue?

Davie Smith and Ferguson had netted for Rangers in front of 50,000 at Ibrox, but a goal from Ian Taylor in the fading seconds sent them hurtling to their first defeat at the final hurdle. Two goals in the last minute a week apart in Glasgow were to have a major say in deciding the championship.

Celtic knew they could now afford to lose against Dunfermline in midweek and still keep their crown. It was to be a joint celebration in Fife – the champions v. the cup winners – and it was the hottest ticket in town. There were those, of course, who didn't bother with the necessities of legal entrance. The game attracted East End Park's official record attendance of 27,816, but it was estimated that some 5,000 more fans crammed into the packed surroundings. Walls were scaled and there were amazing scenes, with hundreds of supporters sitting on the roof of the stand at kick-off time. Urgent police messages for them to come down were ignored. 'Nae chance, pal,' was the consensus from these would-be Sir Edmund Hillarys. Turnstiles collapsed under the sheer volume of supporters determined to witness the climax to a truly remarkable season. Eventually, some sort of order was restored (although the fans remained on the roof of the main stand) and the game got under way.

Bobby Lennox was a genuine, unassuming, down-to-earth character who never luxuriated in the praise that came his way from grand admirers such as Manchester United's Bobby Charlton. He could easily have enticed massive transfer cheques from Arsenal manager Bertie Mee or Newcastle United boss Joe Harvey, two who would have had him across the border at the speed of light to play for their teams. Before the duel with Dunfermline, Lennox had scored in every one of Celtic's previous 11 games, amassing an extraordinary 18 goals in total. He had also scored in the opening 3–0 win over Clyde in September. Now he was about to finish what he had started, and in typical style.

Lennox flashed two beyond Bent Martin in a 2–1 victory, and Celtic did not have to rely on goal average to bring the third successive title back to Parkhead. It was the first time any Scottish club had won the championship three times in a row since 1935. The 63 points they had amassed was a record post-war total for the Scottish First Division; it was to turn out to be Jock Stein's best league performance as manager. Celtic had scored 106 goals, more than Motherwell, Falkirk and Stirling Albion combined. It was also the third successive season they had topped the ton. Rangers could take no consolation from the fact that their total of 61 points would have been enough to have won the flag in any other season but one (that of 1957–58) in the history of the 34-game league. In a way, that merely emphasised the magnificent achievement of Jock Stein's team.

In the spring of 1968, Celtic took their players on a swift trip to North America, where, oddly enough, they faced AC Milan on 26 May, a year and a day after they had defeated the Italian side's rivals Inter to conquer Europe. There had been a power shift in the city and AC Milan were the new champions of Italy. The day before the game, Celtic celebrated the anniversary of their historic triumph with a beach barbecue in Miami, where they had spent the previous six days in recuperation following an exhausting season. However, it was down to business 24 hours later for the game at the Roosevelt Stadium in New Jersey, with a healthy crowd of 25,000 turning out. 'We have had a great time in Miami and it was essential to get a break, but football is our business,' said Stein. 'We've got two matches here against the champions of Italy and I want to use them as stepping stones to another European Cup triumph. These are the sort of matches you need to find out a few things about your players and yourself.' Willie Wallace scored in a 1–1 draw and, six days later, Celtic beat AC Milan 2–0 with goals from Bobby Lennox and Charlie

Gallagher in Toronto in front of 30,000, a record crowd at the time for Canada. The results would become significant in the new season.

As they geared up for another tilt at glory in season 1968–69, Celtic were drawn against Rangers in the League Cup sections for the second consecutive year. Morton and Partick Thistle made up the four-team group. An Old Firm encounter on a gloriously sunny day on the South Side of Glasgow on 10 August welcomed in a new season.

Stein was an enormous admirer of the strolling style of George Connelly, an enigmatic Fifer adorned with all the skill in the world. He had been introduced to the Celtic support during the interval in the Cup-Winners' Cup tie against Dynamo Kiev in January 1966. Stein had bet the youngster five pounds he could not juggle to all four corners of the pitch without letting the ball drop once. Connelly was happy to accept the bet and Stein, a gambling man, must have known he was onto a loser as the boy took off confidently in the direction of the Celtic end, returned to the centre circle, strolled across to the Jungle, back to the centre spot and then off to what was known as the Rangers end, then performed in front of the main stand and came to a halt at the home dugout. Not once did the ball touch the ground. Not once did the youngster even look as though he was struggling to display his special talents. The crowd cheered and, later, Stein coughed up when he was reminded of the bet. Clearly, though, the lad was no circus act.

Stein had introduced Connelly's outstanding range of ball-playing skills on the last day of the season, playing him as a substitute against Dunfermline when the title was won. He was prepared now to unleash his potent weapon on football on a more consistent basis. Connelly came in against Rangers, an enormous vote of confidence in the player by his manager, especially with the match being at Ibrox. He wore the number 7 shorts with Jimmy Johnstone at number 8, but the ploy was simply mind games by Stein. As soon as the whistle went for the start of the game and the campaign, Connelly gracefully sauntered in to the right side of midfield and Johnstone hugged the touchline.

More often than not now, the mobile and aggressive Jim Brogan was playing beside Billy McNeill in the middle of the defence instead of John Clark, a solid, if unspectacular, performer. Tommy Gemmell still alternated between right and left at the back of the defence and was in at number 2 for the opener, with Willie O'Neill, sturdy and dependable, at left-back. Stein went with this line-up: Simpson; Gemmell, McNeill, Brogan and O'Neill; Connelly and Murdoch; Johnstone, Wallace, Lennox and Hughes. Apart from new boy Connelly, it was the usual suspects – tried and trusted professionals who rarely, if ever, disappointed.

Rangers, after the whirlwind of transfer activity in the previous two summers, had been strangely quiet on this front, making no major signings. It would only be a matter of months, though, before they shattered the Scottish transfer record.

It was the first Old Firm meeting since 2 January at Parkhead, when Davie White had dodged defeat courtesy of two gifts from the unfortunate Fallon. Curiously, White dropped goalkeeper Erik Sørensen, with the lanky Norrie Martin taking over. There was talk of Sørensen, back in his native Denmark for a summer break, saying exceptionally kind things about Stein and Celtic in an interview with a local newspaper. Whether that was true or otherwise, Sørensen, bought for £30,000 from Morton in the summer of 1967, never played again for the Ibrox side and was freed at the end of that campaign.

A honed and lean Willie Wallace got away from the Rangers rearguard twice to gleefully place efforts wide of the helpless Martin, and there was no comeback from the Ibrox side. There was much for the away support to enthuse over, not least the elegant performance from Connelly, who strode through the game as though he was a veteran of the fixture.

Wallace also got the first goal of the new season at Parkhead in midweek, as Celtic overcame Morton 4–1. He was unstoppable as he hit all the goals in a 4–0 hammering of Partick Thistle in the next game. Hardly surprisingly, he claimed the only goal of the home game against Rangers, having put them to the sword in Govan only two weeks earlier. Incredibly, Wallace, surely the best £30,000 ever spent by Stein, got the ball rolling in the following match, a 3–0 win over Morton at Cappielow. Bobby Lennox was also beginning to set his sights on goals and he lashed in five in the final qualifying tie against Partick Thistle, a 6–1 win at Firhill.

Six successive wins with twenty goals scored. Celtic had now gone a phenomenal 21 games without defeat since being beaten by Dunfermline in the Scottish Cup in January. They stretched that to 22 when the league season got under way at Shawfield, where Clyde were trounced 3–0.

Four days after that, Celtic went on an amazing ten-goal spree against Hamilton in the League Cup quarter-final first leg at Parkhead, the goals being shared equally between Lennox and Chalmers. More than four decades later, I spoke to both marksmen about this remarkable game. Chalmers said, 'You have to feel a bit of sympathy for the goalie. He probably made a few good saves, too, with the game being so one-sided. As I recall, we started at 100 miles per hour and just got faster as the game wore on. Hamilton didn't stand a chance and it looked like a race between Bobby and myself to see who could score the most. We had a friendly rivalry and we were both ruthless in front of goal. A lot of teams might have eased up if they had gone four or five goals ahead, but not this Celtic team. Big Jock hammered into us to always entertain the fans and I would like to think we managed that against Accies. It was just one of those nights when everything clicked into place.'

Lennox admitted, 'I still smile whenever someone mentions that 10–0 game. It gives me a warm glow. As I remember, it was a thoroughly miserable night in Glasgow. The rain was lashing down all the way through the game. In fact, I think it had been chucking it down all day. Mind you, it must have been even more miserable for their goalkeeper, Billy Lamont. No one wants a scoreline like that on their CV. I agree with Stevie, you've got to feel something for the fella. Losing ten goals can't be much fun for any keeper, but when you're piling on the misery you don't actually think about your opponent's feelings. That wouldn't be too professional. You are there to do a job for your club and that's the end of it. The fans turn out to see you win and score a few goals and that's what we achieved that night. I believe I might have scored with the last kick of the ball to level with Stevie. Ten goals and only two scorers? Amazing! I suppose it's also fairly unusual for a player to score five goals in back-to-back games as had happened with me against Partick Thistle and Hamilton. A lot of unusual things happened around that time.'

Incidentally, Lennox has an interesting take on the League Cup. 'I thought it was a more difficult trophy to win than the Scottish Cup. Maybe not as glamorous, but a lot harder. For a start, back then, you had to play six games in a league format, get through that and then face a two-legged quarter-final and then a semi-final before reaching the final. In the Scottish Cup, you could get lucky and get a few home draws against teams from lower divisions. So, for me, the League Cup was most certainly a competition to be treated with the greatest of respect.'

Did Jock Stein make a fuss of the two goal-scorers after the Hamilton match? 'Not a chance,' answered Chalmers. 'He never did, not with me, anyway. That was just not his style. He always liked to keep you on edge. I never looked for a pat on the back. I just wanted to do my job and cram as many goals into the opposition's net as possible. That's what the Hamilton game was all about. If the match had lasted another ten or fifteen minutes, we would still have been chasing goals. Joe McBride played that night, too, so he would have been looking for a few. It's incredible to note that he didn't score, but he would have made a few, that's for sure.'

That overwhelming victory opened the way for a bunch of the Quality Street Gang to make a collective debut in front of their new fans, all

4,000 who turned up at Douglas Park a fortnight later. Lou Macari, who had played in the first leg, Davie Hay, John Gorman and goalkeeper Bobby Wraith played alongside Pat McMahon, Jimmy Quinn and George Connelly, who had already made a handful of appearances in the first team. Kenny Dalglish came on as a second-half substitute.

Before that, though, was the first Old Firm league confrontation of the new season and, after two victories already over the old enemy, Celtic went into the game reasonably confident in front of their own fans on 14 September. Lennox had what looked like two legitimate goals ruled out as the Ibrox men triumphed 4–2. Wallace scored two, which meant he had netted all of Celtic's five goals in their three games against Rangers.

'That was a strange game,' recalled Gemmell. 'You would look at the scoreline and see that a team had scored four goals against us at Parkhead – when did that last happen? – and you would have been forgiven for believing they had massacred us. Honestly, that was not the case. To be fair, Rangers did play well that day and they put in a lot of effort, but it was one of those occasions when you realise there is no way back only when you hear the referee's final whistle. Right up to that moment, you believe you can achieve something. We were making chances and I had a few long-range efforts myself that were blocked, with the keeper all over the place. I remember both Bobby Murdoch and Bertie Auld weren't playing, and who wouldn't miss their presence in the middle of the park? No excuses, though. We had lost to them in the second game of the previous season and had still gone on to win the title. We would just have to go on another 32-game unbeaten run!'

A week later Celtic were held to a 1–1 draw with Dunfermline at East End Park, where Johnstone scored. A point dropped? Or a point gained? This set of Celtic players was only ever satisfied with victory, but on the coach home from Fife the feeling was that it had been important not to lose a second successive league match, and Dunfermline were very dangerous opponents, still on a high after their Scottish Cup victory and with their vociferous manager George Farm claiming they would build on that success. His priority for the new season, he promised Dunfermline fans, was the league championship.

The midweek League Cup return against Hamilton saw the influx of youngsters Stein believed would usher in a bright new era for the club. He mixed in experienced campaigners Jim Craig, John Clark, Joe McBride and Charlie Gallagher to give them a helping hand. Two goals from McBride and a collector's item from Clark plus one from McMahon eased the new-look Celtic to a 4–2 victory.

Davie Hay was pitched in for skipper Billy McNeill at centre-half that night. 'So, no pressure right from the start, then,' joked the likeable Hay. 'Big Jock used to play individuals in all sorts of varied positions to give them an idea of what they should anticipate from players facing them. For instance, he put me in as a centre-forward for a few games in the reserves. I had never played there in my life, but it was merely to give me the experience of coping with someone defending against me. What would I have done in his situation? Would I look to make space, right or left? Would I come off the defender or would I stick with him? All that sort of stuff. It was invaluable and undoubtedly it helped when you were up against someone in a position where you had gained some sort of experience. You had some sort of idea of how they might be thinking. Big Jock knew my preference would be full-back, probably right, but he wanted to further my football education against Hamilton. It didn't do me any harm.

'Myself and the other young guys went into that game without any pressure on us whatsoever and that was another of Big Jock's great secrets. He would pick and choose the games very carefully before he introduced you. He would even look at a string of forthcoming matches and wonder if it was worth the chance of giving you an extended run in the team as opposed to popping you in every now and again. He was a great schemer and was years ahead of anyone else.'

Whereas Hay, Connelly, Macari and Dalglish went on to have excellent Celtic careers, Bobby Wraith joined the list of '60s one-game goalkeepers. Wraith, who had caught Stein's eye while playing for Largs Thistle in a bounce game against a young Celtic side, took his place alongside Willie Goldie, Dick Madden and Jack Kennedy as now-you-see-me-now-you-don't custodians during that decade of change.

'My God, even I played more than one game in goal for Celtic,' said Gemmell. 'I replaced Ronnie Simpson on two occasions in 1969. The first was in a scoreless Scottish Cup tie against Clyde at Shawfield and the next was a League Cup semi-final against Ayr United, which we won 2–1. Ronnie, of course, had been troubled with a shoulder injury and had in fact been appointed captain for a game against Airdrie only a few days before the Ayr match, to celebrate his 39th birthday. Nine months later this very special guy had to retire. What a career, though!'

After their fourteen-goal two-game blitz on Hamilton, Celtic toiled in the semi-final against Clyde. All the big guns, Lennox, Wallace, Chalmers, McBride and Hughes, were on display, but it took a solitary first-time strike from substitute Connelly to book a place in the final against Hibs. The month of October also saw the team scrape a 2–1 home victory over St Johnstone – goals from Lennox and McNeill – and drop a point in a 1–1 tussle with Morton at Cappielow, where McBride netted his last goal for the club.

Rangers failed to take advantage of Celtic's slip in Greenock, losing 3–2 to Aberdeen at Ibrox, the mirror image of their only defeat in the league the previous season. They immediately invested £100,000 in Hibs' all-action frontman Colin Stein and, a month later, they paid St Johnstone £50,000 for combative midfielder Alex MacDonald. That took their spending to only £50,000 short of half a million pounds in just over two years, a breathtaking amount of money in the '60s.

The European Cup campaign had kicked off in France in September and once again Celtic got an early jolt. 'We had originally been drawn against Hungary's Ferencváros,' recalled Gemmell, 'but because of all the unrest and turmoil in Eastern Europe at the time, Bob Kelly protested to UEFA and, remarkably, they had another ballot and this time we were paired with French side Saint-Étienne. We might have been better off with Ferencváros! We had been warned that Saint-Étienne had this big African named Salif Keïta playing as their main striker. He had been scoring goals galore and great things were expected of him. Sure enough, he lived up to his star billing. He made Big Billy's life a misery that night. Keïta was a powerful giant of a man who had this incredible long stride. When he got going, he took some stopping. He scored both goals as they won 2–0 and, to be honest, his performance in the first leg was as good as anything I had witnessed by an opponent against our skipper in all my time at the club. Yes, he was that good.'

At Parkhead, 75,000 turned out to see at first hand the phenomenon that was Keïta while hoping their favourites could reverse the tie. It was another wonderful European night in Paradise. It was scoreless until moments before the half-time whistle. Celtic had played reasonably OK, but the French were well drilled and, of course, they presented the ball to Keïta at every opportunity. A hush would descend upon Parkhead when he got into that mesmerising stride of his. Billy McNeill wasn't about to be beaten on this occasion, though, and the Celtic captain's timing in the tackle was crisp and accurate. Jock Stein was heading up the tunnel, already preparing his half-time pep talk, when defender Francis Camerini hauled down McBride in the box. Penalty!

Gemmell takes up the story. 'I knew it was a crucial award and I also realised a goal at that stage would, in all probability, turn the game on its head. I had to score. The French went through the usual routine of trying to unsettle me. They were uttering all sorts of oaths and, of course, when I stepped up to take the kick there were the mandatory clods of earth and all sorts of stuff being chucked in front of me. They were wasting their time. I hit that ball as well as I have hit any and it zoomed into the roof of the net. We were back in the game.'

Full-back partner Jim Craig took his lead from his big mate in the second period when he galloped onto a neat pass from Johnstone and thumped a low effort beyond Georges Carnus in the Saint-Étienne goal for the equaliser; it was his only European Cup goal for the club. The volume was pumped up a notch and Johnstone ran the French defence ragged with another invigorating performance of invention and incisiveness. Chalmers turned in a third and McBride made it 4–0 just before the end. Keïta trooped off a dejected and defeated figure at the final whistle. The Celtic players, in stark contrast, whooped it up.

Celtic were obliged to squeeze five league fixtures and two European games into the month of November. 'It was just as well we were an exceptionally fit team,' said Bertie Auld. 'There were no slackers in training at Celtic, which was very important when you saw the fixtures stacking up. Big Jock liked to keep us fresh, of course, but he rarely tinkered with his defence, so that meant guys such as Jim Craig, Billy McNeill, John Clark and Tommy Gemmell were in week in, week out. Up front, Jock would change things around almost on a weekly basis. Sometimes he would bring in John Hughes from the wing and play him right in the middle of the attack, then he would play Stevie Chalmers a bit wider on the right. It kept us ticking over.'

Stein also entered the transfer market to spend £35,000 on left-sided midfielder Tommy Callaghan, a player he knew well from their time together at Dunfermline. Callaghan thrived on hard work. He would go deep to take the ball off the defence and, with a marvellous loping stride that ate up the ground below him, carry the ball deep into the other team's half.

Quietly and effectively, Stein was changing things in Celtic's style of play. In the past, he had relied on the likes of Auld, Murdoch and Gallagher to hit telling, long-range passes from their own half. That was not Callaghan's forte. He was a runner. Celtic fans got their first glimpse of him in an emphatic 4–0 victory over Partick Thistle. Callaghan couldn't have wished for a better debut and even scored, with Hughes (2) and Lennox netting the others against former Rangers goalkeeper Billy Ritchie, who would never have nominated Parkhead as one of his favourite places to ply his trade. The domestic scene for November was completed with another of those spectacular, sparkling clashes against Hibs at Easter Road. These games were becoming high-scoring classics and on this occasion Celtic triumphed 5–2.

It was interesting to look across Glasgow to see how Scotland's first six-figure man was faring at Rangers. Stein had started like a whirlwind, although one that appeared to blow itself out after three hours. He notched a hat-trick against Arbroath and followed that up with another threesome against his old club Hibs. However, St Mirren, with future Celtic keeper Denis Connaghan in fine form, stopped Stein and Rangers in their tracks with a surprise 1–0 win at fog-shrouded Love Street. Rangers had now lost three times as many league games as they had done the previous season.

Alarmingly, Celtic were forced to share the points in three out of their four league games in December. The month began as expected with a 5–0 triumph over St Mirren in Glasgow. There was a hiccup in a goalless draw at Falkirk and it took a Chalmers goal to give Stein's side a 1–1 draw with Kilmarnock. There was another scoreless stalemate at Airdrie to bring 1968 to a halt. The forward line that had provided nineteen goals in five games in November had produced only one in three matches in the run-up to the year's end. However, if goals were in short supply in the league, that certainly wasn't the case in Europe, courtesy of a small, flame-haired gentleman called Jimmy Johnstone. The much-vaunted Red Star Belgrade were routed 5–1 in Glasgow after what was surely the most bizarre deal ever struck between Stein and a player.

'It was well known that the Wee Man was terrified of flying,' said Gemmell. 'I used to joke with him. "Jinky, you think you've got a problem? I don't even like being this tall!" Actually, he had a real scare when he was coming back from our tour of the States in 1966. He and Ian Young, our right-back, were allowed home early because they had already set wedding dates. The plane hit an air pocket and, according to Jinky, "dropped like a stone for miles". That's the way he remembered it, anyway! But the experience did leave him with an unshakeable fear of flying. As I recall, we were drawing 1–1 with Red Star at half-time at Parkhead. Bobby Murdoch gave us the lead, but a bloke called Vojin Lazarević equalised. We all knew Big Jock was brilliant at mind games and psychology. He pulled Jinky aside in the dressing-room and said, "Get us a four-goal advantage and you won't need to fly to Belgrade." Jinky's face lit up. "Dae ye really mean it, Boss?" he asked. Big Jock assured him he would keep his end of the bargain if Jinky produced the goods. The Wee Man played like a man possessed after the interval. Red Star must have wondered what on earth had happened in our dressing-room at half-time. Jinky always gave his best, of course, but he was transformed that evening. He ripped their defence to shreds. There was nothing they could do as he kept coming at them and carving them open. He was racing all over the pitch shouting at his teammates, "Gie me the ba'!" It was a truly memorable performance from my wee pal.'

Johnstone started the fightback with a goal two minutes after the turnaround. Then he set up Lennox for the third before providing Wallace with the fourth. So, four down and one to go. He notched the all-important fifth himself, snaking in from the right, bamboozling a couple of defenders and then sliding a right-foot shot low into the far corner.

Jim Craig recalled, 'Jinky was running away shouting, "Ah don't have tae go! Ah don't have tae go!" Any English-speaking Yugoslav opponent must have wondered what on earth he was going on about. We all knew, though. He had delivered big style and Jock kept his word.'

Gemmell added, 'They got a corner kick in the last minute and Jinky was back telling us, "Noo don't youse dare let them score." The kick came over and guess who cleared? Wee Jinky! I don't think I had ever seen him in our penalty box before at a corner kick.'

A crashing 20-yard drive from Wallace gave Celtic a 1–1 draw in Belgrade and Europe was once again sitting up and taking notice of the 1967 champions.

11

TROUBLE IN PARADISE

The final year of a defining, decisive decade in Celtic's history kicked off with two games within forty-eight hours and, like the preceding nine years, they were graphically lopsided: a 5–0 triumph and a 1–0 defeat.

Tommy Callaghan had endeared himself to the Parkhead faithful right from the start. His awesome work ethic was greatly appreciated by the supporters. Bertie Auld said, 'When I signed for the club first time around back in 1955, my dad, Joe, accompanied me to Celtic Park. Afterwards, Jimmy McGrory gave us a wee tour of the ground. My father took me aside. He waved over at the old Jungle and told me, "Son, if you work hard and give it everything you have got, those supporters in there will love you. They are knowledgeable, they enjoy their football. You won't always be the star man, but if you show a willingness to work, no matter how you are playing, they will back you." My dad was right.'

It appeared that the same advice could have been given to Callaghan, a tireless performer and Jock Stein's most expensive buy at £35,000, from Dunfermline earlier in the season. The player was nicknamed 'Tid', which took a bit of explaining. His brother Willie, who played right-back for Dunfermline, was the older of the two. So Tommy was the tiddler in the family and in time that was shortened to 'Tid'. One thing was for sure, though, he didn't come up short at any time for Celtic. He cut an athletic, straight-backed figure in the green and white hoops. To him fell the honour of scoring the first goal of 1969 for the club, a raking 25-yard drive that hurtled past the helpless Clyde goalkeeper John Wright. He added another in a 5–0 success. I reminded him of his thundering effort for the first goal that day. 'Yes, I remember it well,' he said. 'Do you know, I could still score that sort of goal today!'

Now all eyes were on Ibrox, the following day's destination. Celtic had dropped three out of four points against their old foes the previous season and had already shed two in this campaign. Stein was eager to notch his first league triumph over Davie White at the third time of asking.

The young Rangers manager had experienced some turbulence since the 2–2 draw with Celtic the previous new year. Colin Stein, the £100,000 purchase from Hibs, had scored eleven goals in his first seven games, including back-to-back hat-tricks against Arbroath and Hibs in his first two appearances. He was a potent force and had formed partnerships with Willie Johnston and Alex Ferguson. To say the least, though, his temperament was suspect and he was ordered off three times in his initial season as a Ranger. The powers that be at the club were far from satisfied with the lack of discipline displayed by their centre-forward, whose entire game depended on power, energy and strength. His misbehaviour would cost Rangers dear later in the season.

On 2 January, though, he was in place to lead the attack, alongside Johnston, against Celtic. Jock Stein's side went into the contest with twenty-nine points, four ahead of Rangers. Both teams had scored 39 goals, but the Parkhead men had conceded only 12 to the Ibrox side's 18. Celtic, then, held the upper hand, but things could change dramatically if Rangers clawed the points advantage back to two. John Fallon was still the last line of defence – he had played the previous nine games during Ronnie Simpson's enforced absence – and Stein stiffened up the midfield with the choice of Jim Brogan to partner Bobby Murdoch. Willie Wallace, scourge of the Ibrox side during that campaign, with five goals from three matches, led the attack.

'Honestly, I don't remember too much about the game apart from John Greig scoring from a penalty kick to give them a 1–0 win,' said Gemmell. 'What I do recall is that it was a fairly dour encounter. I think both teams got bogged down in the middle of the park, with the players in there nullifying each other. There wasn't much space on the wings, either, with Jinky and Big Yogi starved of service. I was up against Willie Henderson, but he didn't get much joy that day either, and Jim Craig, over at right-back, had Örjan Persson in his pocket. So neither keeper was called into action too often and it was one of those days when it looked as though a penalty kick or a free kick might settle the issue.

'Unfortunately for us, it was a penalty for them that gave them the points. John Greig must have been taking pointers off me on how to take a spot kick. He fairly leathered the ball and it seemed to just go straight up into the net, with John Fallon taking off to his right. Obviously, Big Jock wasn't in the best of moods afterwards. We had now lost both our league games to Rangers, dropping four points in the process. We had played well enough on both occasions, but had nothing to show for it, and we also realised we had allowed the Ibrox side back into the title race. They were two points adrift, but there were still fifteen games to play and that represented thirty points to be won or lost. It looked as though we were in for another fraught climax to the campaign. We were up for it, though.'

It was imperative that Celtic got back on track immediately, with the ever-dangerous Dunfermline due in Glasgow only two days later. Stein dropped Johnstone onto the substitutes' bench, switched John Hughes from left to right and reinstated Stevie Chalmers to the main striking role. There was also a place in midfield for Callaghan, overlooked for the Old Firm match. The changes clicked and two goals from Wallace and one from Lennox earned the champions a solid 3–1 victory.

Around this time, the end was in sight for the conundrum that was Pat McMahon. He scored in a 3–1 triumph over Dundee United at Tannadice, but Stein seemed hesitant to utilise the youngster's talents on a consistent basis. 'He was such a quiet laddie that no one even swore in his presence,' recalled Gemmell. 'He was different from what we were used to at Celtic.' McMahon's strike against the Tayside outfit brought down the curtain on his brief career in the hoops. He never featured again and left for Aston Villa in the summer. His was a puzzling stay at Parkhead. He was undoubtedly gifted but, as far as the manager was concerned, lacking that certain something that marked out a Celtic player.

The Scottish Cup trail began at Firhill on the last Saturday of January and for one Partick Thistle player it was a memorable encounter. Johnny Flanagan, a fleet-footed frontman in the mould of Bobby Lennox, claimed a stupendous hat-trick. Thankfully, though, Murdoch, Wallace and Hughes responded in a thrilling 3–3 draw to take the game to a replay at Parkhead the following Wednesday.

A behind-the-scenes bust-up between Stein and Auld came close to seeing the player leave the club in controversial circumstances. Auld recalled, 'I had been a substitute in the first game at Firhill. I didn't get on, but the least I expected for the replay was to get a place on the bench again. Big Jock didn't say a thing in training as we prepared for the game and then he pinned up the team on the noticeboard. I couldn't believe it – I had been dropped. I was out of the picture without kicking a ball. How bad can you be sitting on a bench? I was far from happy. In fact, I was raging. He had selected the exact same starting 11, but Stevie Chalmers had now been put on standby.

'I went to see the manager and have it out with him there and then. He never liked to be confronted, but I wanted some sort of explanation. He just waved me away, so I left the ground, jumped in a taxi and headed

PICK IT OUT: Mike Jackson nonchalantly scores Celtic's third goal in a 3–1 Scottish Cup win over Morton at Cappielow in January 1962.

A RANGER IN OUR MIDST: Ibrox legend Jim Baxter was a great friend of Celtic players and is seen here (second from the left) with Billy McNeill, Mike Jackson and Pat Crerand at the wedding of teammate John Colrain to Rosaleen in the early '60s.

LISBON, HERE WE COME: Jimmy Johnstone is hoisted high by Tommy Gemmell after the goalless draw against Dukla Prague. Celtic won the European Cup semi-final first leg 3–1 in Glasgow.

PRIZE GUY: Celtic skipper Billy McNeill is presented with the European Cup after the glorious and historic 2–1 victory over Inter Milan in Lisbon on 25 May 1967.

CONGRATULATIONS: Celtic celebrate with the European Cup. Smiles all round from (back row, left to right): Davie Cattenach, Jimmy Steele (masseur), Sean Fallon (assistant manager), Ian Young, Jimmy Johnstone, Bobby Lennox, Billy McNeill, Neilly Mochan (trainer), John Cushley, Bobby Murdoch, Jim Craig, John Hughes and Bertie Auld; (front row, left to right): Stevie Chalmers, John Clark, Tommy Gemmell and Charlie Gallagher. Curiously, there is no sign of Jock Stein.

RECORD-BREAKER: In 1968, energetic midfielder Tommy Callaghan joined Celtic from Dunfermline for £35,000, the highest fee paid by Jock Stein at that time.

PRINCE OF THE PRECISION PASS: George Connelly, a multitalented individual, alas lost to the game far too early in his career.

THE QUIET ASSASSIN: Davie Hay, later to manage Celtic, shows all the determination and enthusiasm that were typical of him during his playing days. His nickname came from former Scotland international manager Tommy Docherty.

TOP OF THE CLASS: Elegant frontman Harry Hood is thwarted on this occasion by a brave save from Hearts keeper Jim Cruickshank. Hood cost £40,000 from Clyde in 1969 – topping the fee paid for Tommy Callaghan the previous year.

THE GOLDEN BHOYS:
Teenagers Kenny Dalglish
(left) and Vic Davidson, two
of the promising youngsters
who emerged to challenge
the Lisbon Lions for first-
team places.

POINT TAKEN: A fresh-faced
Lou Macari organises his teammates
as he lines up for a corner kick, with
Aberdeen goalkeeper Bobby Clark
for company.

JOY BHOYS: Danny McGrain,
a genuinely world-class right-
back, celebrates with Bobby
Murdoch and George Connelly.

SHAKE ON IT: Jimmy Quinn, grandson of the Celtic legend of the same name, is congratulated by Jock Stein at the end of a game. Jim Brogan will be next for the plaudits from the manager.

FLYING HIGH: Goalkeeper Evan Williams punches clear from menacing East Fife striker Joe Hughes in a First Division clash at Methil in April 1972. Celtic won 3–0.

CHEEKY: A puffed-up Kenny Dalglish tries to squeeze the ball beyond diving Airdrie keeper Roddie McKenzie. He was out of luck on this occasion.

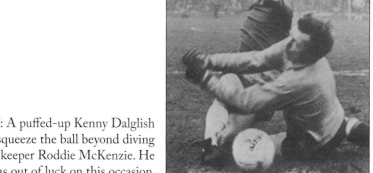

LORD OF THE WING: Wizard Jimmy Johnstone skips past
lunging Motherwell defender Willie McCallum as Joe Wark
races back to cover.

JUST FOR KICKS: Harry Hood hooks the ball goalwards as
Dundee defender Bobby Wilson puts in a full-blooded
mid-air challenge.

PENALTY-BOX PANDEMONIUM: Lou Macari and Billy McNeill combine
to repel a raid from East Fife's Jim Hamilton and John Martis.

AIR RAID: Bobby Lennox soars
high to knock a header past stranded
Dundee keeper Mike Hewitt. Dixie
Deans is poised to pounce on any
rebound – no need on this occasion.

MASTER MARKSMAN: Kenny
Dalglish stretches to slide the ball in
from close range after Partick Thistle's
number 1 Alan Rough has parried a shot
from Lou Macari. The goal was small
consolation for a Celtic team beaten 4–1
by the Firhill side in a remarkable League
Cup final in 1971.

POISE AND POWER: Harry Hood combines the two as he thunders a shot past Aberdeen defender Jim Hermiston to score at Parkhead in a 1–1 draw in November 1971.

WELL DONE, MY BHOY: Jock Stein has a special pat on the head for Jimmy Johnstone after the 6–3 League Cup final triumph over Hibs in 1974. Kenny Dalglish is wearing the number 10 shorts. Johnstone scored one with Dixie Deans (3), Stevie Murray and Paul Wilson claiming the others.

THE GREATEST-EVER CELT: Jimmy Johnstone, later voted the club's top player by the supporters, enjoys the applause after another mesmerising performance. Memories are made of this.

for my favourite restaurant in Glasgow, the Vesuvio in St Vincent Street. I knew the Italian owners – brothers Enzo, Mario and Humberto Romaro – and they were more than a little surprised to see me walking through their door.

"'Ees the game off, Bertie?" I was asked.

"'No, it's on OK, but I'm not involved."

'They saw my mood and left me alone. I realised Big Jock might take some sort of action, but, at that particular moment, I wasn't looking too far ahead. I thought the manager might at least have hinted that I wouldn't be participating. He knew how much it meant to me to play football. I wasn't happy on the substitutes' bench, but I was willing to tolerate it in the hope I might get on at some point and get a kick of the ball.'

All these years down the line, Auld can afford to laugh at the incident, saying, 'Mind you, they didn't seem to miss me – they won 8–1!' Callaghan led the assault on the Partick Thistle goal and collected two goals, with McNeill, Gemmell, Lennox, Hughes, Wallace and Johnstone sharing the others.

If Celtic had made heavy work of their first tussle against the Maryhill outfit, it was nothing to the agony they subjected their supporters to in the next round against Clyde at Shawfield the following month. The game, which finished goalless, signalled the beginning of the end of the glorious playing career of Ronnie Simpson, at the age of 39. He wouldn't play again that season and performed only two more times the following term before calling it a day. Fittingly for such a popular character's swansong, Celtic were victorious in both those games. It was only right and proper that such a fine professional, after a quarter of a century in the game, should leave as a winner. Simpson's game against Clyde ended in the second half when he went down awkwardly on a brick-hard surface saving at the feet of Jimmy Quinn, who, ironically, was on loan at the Shawfield side and still registered as a Celtic player. Goodness only knows why Quinn was allowed to play against his parent club. What would have happened if he actually scored at that fatal moment? Heads would surely have rolled along London Road.

Gemmell got the nod to go into goal, with Auld coming on as a substitute. Gemmell remembered, 'Everyone knew I fancied myself as a striker, but what they might not have realised was that I fancied myself as a bit of a goalkeeper, too. It was sad to see Ronnie go off that day. He was obviously in a lot of pain and we also knew that his shoulder couldn't hold out forever. When I saw him go off in some considerable distress, I wondered if we would ever see him again in Celtic's goal.

'My immediate concern that day, though, was to make sure Clyde didn't score. That would have been a travesty. We were top of the league, we were in the League Cup final and we were also in the quarter-finals of the European Cup. The Scottish Cup was in our sights too, so it was absolutely crucial we weren't on the receiving end of a shock at Shawfield. I had a stint in goal at the end of most training sessions at Barrowfield and I knew it was of the utmost importance not to let your opponents realise that you were in fact a stand-in goalkeeper. I had to act like I had played in goal all my life. We've all seen games where an outfield player goes into goal and that's exactly what he looks like: an outfield player in goal. He doesn't look comfortable.

'So I had to make sure that none of the Clyde players thought they had a hope of scoring from all sorts of ranges or angles. I had to put it into their heads that they would have to work hard for anything they might get against me. They would have to treat me as they would any other goalkeeper. To me, that was vital. If I went for a cross-ball, I had to go with conviction. I wouldn't be seen flapping at the ball and just happy to get a touch. I would want to hold the ball. I wasn't interested in merely palming it away where it could go straight to the feet of an opponent who would stick it in the pokey.

'The guys in front of me did a great job for the remainder of the game, I must say. Clyde did get a chance, though, very late on. Harry Hood got through, but I managed to get down at his feet and smother the ball. Harry, of course, later became a teammate at Celtic and I never tired of reminding him of that moment.'

Fallon came in for the replay and goals from Murdoch, Chalmers and Hughes eased Celtic through to the quarter-final on a 3–0 scoreline. Davie Hay made his second first-team appearance alongside Billy McNeill in central defence and he recalled, 'Naturally, I found it all very exciting. I'd played against Hamilton in the League Cup, but, after winning 10–0 in the first leg, we were already through. This was different entirely. We were facing Clyde on a level basis, with everything to play for. Big Jock was showing a fair bit of belief in me and I was determined not to let anyone down. The more experienced players around me were a great help, too. It was a fairly satisfying evening, with us winning and keeping a clean sheet, as well. That was very important to me.'

Sandwiched in between the Clyde confrontations was a European Cup meeting with AC Milan at the San Siro stadium. The game ended goalless, but it was a victory for Stein and his sophisticated tactics over his counterpart, the impressive Nereo Rocco. Gemmell recalled, 'In the semi-final against Dukla Prague in 1967, we played a blanket defence. On that occasion, Bobby Lennox was told to come back to play just in front of me and Jinky was ordered to do the same alongside Jim Craig. Big Jock wasn't worried if either player even crossed the halfway line that day. The game against AC Milan was different. There would be no gung-ho attacking, but we would try to master the midfield, hold on to possession as long as possible and, basically, try to stay in control. The tie was played in a blizzard, but I remember both teams coping really well with the conditions. There were 81,000 fans in the stadium and I'm told that tie generated record receipts for the home club of more than £135,000, an awful lot of money in those days. Just think – Big Jock could have bought Tommy Callaghan and still had £100,000 left over! The game ended goalless and I would like to think both sets of supporters got their money's worth.'

The much-maligned Fallon pulled off a couple of splendid saves, Connelly looked comfortable patrolling in the midfield alongside Murdoch and in fact Celtic might have snatched the winner late on. John Hughes, who had been sidelined with an injury since facing Partick Thistle in the Scottish Cup replay at the end of January, was pitched in against the Italians. 'I was amazed when Jock told me I was playing,' recalled Hughes. 'He just took me aside, told me I was in and to go out there and do a job for Celtic. Just like that. We could have been playing Alloa and not AC Milan.' Hughes came the closest to scoring when he embarked on one of his astonishing solo sorties, which saw him float past four defenders before he blasted a shot goalwards. Goalkeeper Fabio Cudicini threw up both his hands more in desperation than anticipation and, as luck would have it, the ball crashed against his palms and rebounded to safety. A few inches either way and it would have been a goal.

February in the league saw a positive start, with a runaway 5–0 success over Hearts at Parkhead. Auld, having patched up his differences with Stein, was back in the engine room of the side alongside Murdoch. Hearts had Jim Cruickshank to thank for keeping the score down to five. The overworked keeper was often linked with Celtic, but, despite buying more than 20 shot-stoppers during his reign at Parkhead, Stein was never tempted to move for the player, who was, in fact, a neighbour of his in the King's Park district of Glasgow. That success over the Edinburgh side was Celtic's only league game that month, although the club managed to fit in the two cup ties against Clyde despite adverse weather conditions.

March kicked off with a Scottish Cup quarter-final tie against St Johnstone in Glasgow on the first day of the month. The Perth side maintained the capacity to make life difficult for Celtic. Manager Willie Ormond would often convert his centre-half Bill McCarry – known as 'Buck' – to centre-forward in an attempt to unsettle Billy McNeill. Buck was a hulking brute of a player whose first touch of the ball was rarely first class. He made little pretence of being in any way delicate in the performance of his duties. In short, he was a battering ram. There were a few of his ilk around at the time. Airdrie had Davie Marshall, Stirling Albion possessed Jim Kerray, Morton had Per Bartram and Rangers, of course, could call on Colin Stein and Alex Ferguson. None of them seemed to be interested in the finer arts of the game. However, it must be said they were fearless in their pursuit of goals, and McNeill must have known he was in for another hectic afternoon when he saw the 6-ft-plus muscle-bound frame of McCarry squeezed into the number 9 shirt. It took a goal from the elusive Chalmers to settle the tie 3–2 in Celtic's favour, but it was a distinctly edgy performance against a spirited Saints side.

Stein was already preparing for AC Milan's visit for the second leg of their European Cup tie. Years later, I talked to Bobby Murdoch about his recollection of the game and he had a surprise revelation that gave an interesting insight into the workings of his manager's mind. 'Big Jock knew the Italians would stick a man on me,' said one of the finest exponents of passing a ball it has ever been my privilege to witness. 'He also realised I wasn't the quickest at getting away from an opponent. I had always maintained you should let the ball do the work. I reasoned, "Why run 60 yards with the ball when you can pass it there in seconds?" That was what I put into practice in every game, but Jock worried about me being stifled in this tie. The Italians, of course, were masters at nullifying their opponents' assets. Inter Milan had tried it with Burgnich on Johnstone in Lisbon, but it hadn't worked. Jinky, though, possessed an acceleration I didn't have and could skip away from players.

'Big Jock agonised over what to do. He wouldn't leave me out, that much was certain. So what was the best way to get the most out of me with an Italian breathing down my neck? The ploy he came up with surprised even me. He had the big magnetic board on the wall at the Seamill Hotel again and he pointed to number 4.

"Bobby," he said, "I've got a new role for you for this game. I want you to mark Gianni Rivera."

'The room went quiet. "Pardon, Boss?" I asked.

"If you stick to Rivera, that will take two Italians out of the game. Your guy won't leave you and you won't leave Rivera. What do you think?" Big Jock would often ask for a player's input before waving away their suggestion and saying, "Naw, this is the way we'll do it."

'I said, "I've never marked a player before, Boss. Do you think it'll work?" There was no hesitation from Jock.

"I know it will. The Italians won't realise what's going on until it's too late, take my word for it." And it might have worked, too.'

On 12 March, Stein fielded eight of his Lisbon Lions in this line-up: Fallon; Craig, McNeill, Clark and Gemmell; Murdoch and Brogan; Johnstone, Wallace, Chalmers and Hughes. With a full house of 75,000 looking on, Murdoch, wearing the number 10 shorts, ambled over to a somewhat nonplussed Rivera, AC Milan's main playmaker, at the start of the game. Sure enough, Murdoch's designated companion for the next 90 minutes went with him. Wallace was asked to play a bit deeper to fill the void left by Murdoch, and Johnstone filtered in and out from the right throughout the occasion. It was an intriguing plan. It was blown apart after only 11 minutes, though.

Jim Craig took a quick throw-in midway on the right. Skipper McNeill looked surprised as the ball came in his direction, having obviously thought his full-back was going to heave the ball down the line. Craig thought it better to keep possession and chucked the ball to McNeill. On a slippery surface, the centre-half failed to control it, Pierino Prati, lurking close by, seized on it and, with incredible pace considering the tricky underfoot conditions, sped off in the direction of the Celtic goal. Fallon, without a defender between him and the AC Milan winger, seemed unsure of what to do. Advance or stay put? He came, stopped and Prati put him out of his misery by sweeping the ball past his outstretched right foot.

'That was the ultimate sickener,' said Gemmell. 'All that preparation and the anticipation and one mistake let them in. I believe that was their only effort on target at our place. We had done the hard work in Milan and were then undone in Glasgow. One slip, one goal, one dream kaput. As simple as that. That was the goal AC Milan craved and it gave them the opportunity to retreat into defence for the rest of the game. We tried, my God we tried, but we couldn't get near Cudicini. It ended 0–1 and we were fairly distraught. It was no consolation that AC Milan went on to beat Ajax 4–1 in the final, with Prati getting a hat-trick, and their manager Rocco, a bit of a Jock Stein lookalike, saying Celtic had been his team's toughest opponents during the campaign.'

Gemmell revealed Celtic's European bonus system at the time. 'People were asking me how much that defeat cost me in hard cash. I don't know whether they believed me or not, but I honestly didn't have a clue. I've heard and read that there was a sliding scale of bonuses in Europe, with so much on the table for the first round, then an increase for the second and so on. News to me. As far as I was aware, we got money depending on our opponents. If we played, say, a team from Malta or Luxembourg, then we wouldn't get the same sort of cash as we did for facing a side from Italy or Germany, no matter which round we were playing in. It was as though the board of directors waited until they saw what sort of crowd they had brought in for such-and-such a game before making their decision. I thought that quite odd when you considered that we were just about guaranteed a full house for every European game, irrespective of the opposition. However, that was the way the board went about their business back then. We did have a sliding scale for domestic trophies, but not for Europe. So, how much did it hit me in the pocket for losing to AC Milan? I still haven't got a clue.'

Celtic had to accept that the European Cup excursion was over and it was now all about concentrating on the league. Caviar was off the menu, it was now back to corned beef. Disappointment is always a stern test of character, and Auld, a substitute against AC Milan, was one who would always react well and meet a challenge. He was back in the starting line-up to face Partick Thistle in the next game. Murdoch was freed from his midweek shackles to play his more recognisable role in midfield and Hughes came up with his own ideal response. The effervescent winger scored the only goal of the game for two vital points. Three days earlier, Celtic had stumbled in Europe, but his goal put them back on a reasonable footing on the domestic front.

A week later, Stein readied his troops for a Scottish Cup semi-final against the unpredictable Morton at Hampden. Once more, the Celtic players would have to display strength of character, as the Cappielow side took the lead in only two minutes through Willie Allan, unguarded smack in front of goal. It was obvious that this collection of Celtic players didn't believe in making things easy for themselves. The fears of the fans, though, were allayed when Wallace levelled and then McNeill, playing the captain's part to the hilt, headed in the second. Chalmers added a third and Johnstone a fourth to complete a 4–1 scoreline.

Now for the Scottish Cup final at Hampden, due on 26 April, where Rangers were lying in wait. The Ibrox side had come to life in their semi-final against Aberdeen at Celtic Park, in which they had hammered the Pittodrie side 6–1. It appeared the Govan team had neither forgotten nor forgiven the fact that the Dons had beaten them 3–2 in the last game of the previous season to wreck their unbeaten league record.

Unusually, Celtic now had two cup final dates to look forward to at Hampden in April: the League Cup showdown with Hibs on the 5th – the game had been postponed from its original October date because of a fire in the main stand of the national stadium – and the match against Rangers three weeks later.

Harry Hood, always happy to admit his fondness for all things Celtic, got his long overdue move to the club. Stein parted with £40,000 for the skilful frontman to take him from Clyde and, like McBride, Wallace and Callaghan before him, he looked a shrewd buy. For a total expenditure of £127,000, the prudent Stein had brought in four players who would repay the transfer cash time and again. Hood was quick to get off the mark in a 3–0 success over St Mirren.

Thankfully, there was no April Fool in evidence when St Johnstone – Buck McCarry et al. – returned to Parkhead on league business at the start of the month. Celtic had beaten their Perth rivals twice by the odd goal in the previous meetings and they followed the script by winning this one 3–2. Wallace, Gemmell and Hood, swiftly making up for lost time, were on target.

Celtic broke off from points-gathering to meet Hibs in the League Cup final at a sun-caressed Hampden. Bob Shankly, brother of Liverpool's Bill, one of Stein's great friends, had assembled a stylish outfit that was very easy on the eye. Bobby Lennox dismantled them in a one-sided final, netting a superb hat-trick in a 6–2 triumph. At one stage, with Celtic leading 6–0 near the end, Stein sent on substitute John Clark for Gemmell to lap up the cheers of the support. Hibs scored twice in the fading moments. Clark laughed, 'Imagine that. I was on the field for such a short period of time, during which the opponents score two goals without reply and I pick up a winner's medal. Great game, this football!'

Celtic prepared for the Scottish Cup final with a strangely unsure performance against Airdrie at Parkhead and had to settle for a 2–2 draw, with a goal from Lennox and a penalty from Gemmell gaining the point. 'Maybe we had our eye on the Rangers game,' admitted Gemmell. 'At that stage, we were so close to clinching our fourth successive title and possibly we were a wee bit complacent. That wasn't like us, I must admit. However, we knew we could make certain of the championship when we played Kilmarnock at their place a few days later. We needed a point and I'm glad to report I got the goal that gave us a 2–2 draw and our fourth flag in a row. Frank Beattie had put through his own goal to give us our opener, but the Killie lads, as they always did against us, fought like their lives depended upon it. I joined the attack once again and I remember the ball sitting up nicely and begging to be hit. I wasn't going to disappoint it. I connected and it was a bit of a pulverising effort that zipped past their keeper into the net. Job done, but we would have to put the champagne on ice with the cup final due on the Saturday.'

Worryingly, John Fallon had kept only two clean sheets in nine games leading up to Hampden. Stein, realising Simpson might never overcome his persistent injury, signed Danish keeper Leif Nielsen, who had shipped 68 goals in 34 league games at Morton the previous season. He never got anywhere near the first team. 'People have often stated that if Big Jock had an Achilles heel it was with goalkeepers,' added Gemmell. 'Certainly, he signed plenty, but he never found a long-term replacement for Ronnie, who, of course, he had sold to Celtic in the first place. To be fair, Ronnie was a hard act to follow.'

Rangers had conceded so many points that there were to be no title dreams this time around for the Ibrox support, no heart-stopping run-in to the last day of the season. The bookmakers, those Rolls-Royce-driving gentlemen who favoured cigars the size of rolled-up umbrellas, were rarely wrong in their predictions and, for whatever reason, they had Rangers just a shade ahead of Celtic as favourites to lift the Cup. Possibly, they were swayed by historical events, because the Ibrox side had not lost a Scottish Cup final in 40 years.

Jock Stein would have to do without the skills of Jimmy Johnstone, who was suspended, and the injured John Hughes. Colin Stein, also banned for his onfield indiscretions, would be missing from the Ibrox team. Celtic went with this line-up: Fallon; Craig, McNeill, Brogan and Gemmell; Murdoch and Auld; Connelly, Chalmers, Wallace and Lennox. It was to be Alex Ferguson's last game for Rangers. As Jim Forrest and George McLean had been scapegoated after the 1–0 Scottish Cup defeat by Berwick in 1967, he bore the brunt of the blame for a 4–0 massacre.

Celtic forced a left-wing corner kick in the first minute and Lennox raced over to take it. The Rangers defence was still preparing itself when Lennox floated over a tantalising cross. McNeill, as if on an invisible trampoline, leapt majestically into the air to catch the ball perfectly on his forehead. Time stood still for an instant. Norrie Martin was rooted to his line as the ball kissed the inside of his right-hand post and dropped gently into the net. Davie White had ordered Ferguson to pick up the Celtic captain at dead-ball kicks. The unfortunate Ferguson was left in McNeill's slipstream as he stole forward before launching his header into the net.

Rangers, after only 60 seconds, were in total disarray. A jumbo jet could have landed in the middle of their defence when Lennox – 'I'm sure he was born fast,' Danny McGrain was fond of saying – burst into the open space and drove number two beyond a puzzled Martin. If the keeper was perplexed at that moment, it didn't get any better as the clock ticked down towards half-time. He took a short goal-kick to Greig on the edge of the box. The Rangers skipper was far too nonchalant as he accepted the ball and tried to switch it to his left to McKinnon. Connelly, anticipating the pass, stole the ball, swept away from Greig, strolled past the frantically diving goalkeeper and rolled it into the empty net.

The game was over long before Chalmers powered through on the left, arrowed in on goal, shaped to pass across the box to the lurking Lennox, then, with a deft change of foot, flicked the ball between Martin and his near post. Cue pitch invasion from raging Rangers fans as their counterparts at the opposite end of Hampden danced the afternoon away.

The final score of 4–0 in no way flattered Celtic. Stein, the old fox, had out-thought and outwitted White. It had taken a while, but this was the result he had fully intended to inflict on the Rangers boss on the second day of January the previous year. He realised that such a defeat would leave Ibrox in turmoil. Questions would be asked and answers would be demanded. Ferguson was out, Martin would play only once more, Persson and Mathieson were no longer regulars and White was told there was precious little in the kitty for big-name purchases. Stein, always interested in events across the Clyde, would look back on that Scottish Cup final as a job well done. Rangers endured a second barren season. Now they knew how Celtic had felt at the start of the '60s.

On the Monday after the cup final triumph, Celtic paraded all that season's silverware – the Scottish Cup, the League Cup and the league championship trophy – before their last game, against Morton, at Parkhead. Possibly the players had overindulged in their après-match celebrations following the romp against their Old Firm rivals, because they were dumped 4–2, with the Greenock side's Per Bartram hitting a hat-trick in seven minutes. No one could remember such a feat by an opposing player at Parkhead, even in the dark old days. Wallace and Hood scored for Celtic in a game that didn't really matter.

Stein, though, rounded on his players afterwards. 'He was furious,' recalled Gemmell. 'Big Jock was livid. "You've let yourselves down," he said. "You've let your fans down." There was no use in protesting. That was Celtic's 55th game of a long campaign. A lot of the players were leg-weary. Morton played as though it was their cup final. No excuses, though, we should have done better.'

Celtic did end the season on a winning note, emerging victorious over Dundee at Dens Park. They won 2–1, with goals from Hood and the emerging Macari, and completed the 1968–69 league season with fifty-four points, five more than runners-up Rangers. All things considered, it had been an excellent season. Tommy Callaghan and Harry Hood were shaping as sound investments and the Celtic fans had had their first glimpse of the future in the shape of George Connelly, Lou Macari, Davie Hay, Kenny Dalglish and Jimmy Quinn.

There was the usual whirlwind start to the 1969–70 season, with seven games taking place in August. 'I often wondered if the guys who set out the fixtures at the Scottish League were sadists,' said Gemmell. 'It seemed one minute you were on a beach enjoying welcome sunshine and your pina coladas and the next you were back in your football kit and preparing for another ten months of non-stop action. Summers, back then, seemed to pass so quickly. No one looked forward to pre-season training, I can tell you. Guys such as Bobby Lennox and Stevie Chalmers were lucky. They just seemed to be naturally fit guys. They could go away for two months, enjoy themselves and come back without an ounce of fat on them. Bertie Auld used to say Bobby would chase paper on a windy day! I wasn't one to pile on the pounds, either, but, of course, I always welcomed that summer break and would return for the pre-season with a little bit added on. Actually, I always started a week ahead of everyone else. I would go on long runs on my own until my legs ached. Then, the following day, I would put myself through it again. Big Jock would gather us around him on the first day of training and say, "Right, you've all had a good time. Remember, you're lucky to be footballers and you've got to be fit to do your job. We'll start with the easy stuff." And then he would get Neilly Mochan and the backroom guys to run the legs off you.'

Celtic, drawn against Rangers for the third successive season in the League Cup, opened with a tie against Airdrie in Glasgow on Saturday, 9 August. A packed house welcomed the treble-winners onto the impeccably manicured lawn that was the playing surface at Celtic Park. Stein hadn't bothered dabbling in the summer transfer market. There had been much speculation about Simpson's future and Celtic had been linked with Lennox's old friend Ilija Pantelic, the Yugoslav international goalkeeper of Vojvodina Novi Sad, the team that had made life so difficult in the run to Lisbon. Stein had friends dotted around the press and wasn't slow to drop a story on them every now and again if he didn't think Celtic were getting the column inches they deserved in the national newspapers. It's doubtful if Stein was ever interested in Pantelic, but, once the 'revelation' had hit the newsstands, it gave him the opportunity to come out and say, 'I've got John Fallon here and I know he is the man to do the job for this club. I've got every faith in him.' Fallon's confidence would then be sky high as the new campaign kicked off. 'Big Jock rates me higher than one of the world's best goalkeepers,' Fallon would think. 'I must be good.' If Stein hadn't made it as a football manager, he could have been massive in PR.

'Aye, he was brilliant at that side of things,' said Chalmers. 'He used to con me something rotten. He would leave me out of the side and then come up to me and say, "Why are you not in the team? You're better than that mug. You're a better player than him. Come on, Stevie, give yourself a shake and get into that team. That's where you deserve to be.'''

Hughes backed up his teammate. 'He would put his arm around your shoulders and have a word. "You've got all the ability in the world," he would say. "The fans want to see you in the team. You're one of their favourites." All that sort of thing. You knew he was at it, spinning a line, but you still listened and then went out and played out of your skin for the man, the team and the support.'

Hughes got the opening goal of the new campaign in a one-sided 6–1 victory over Airdrie. He added another as Wallace, Connelly, Hood and Gemmell joined in. It was a welcome way to usher in a new season. Without being fully stretched or required to turn on the afterburners, they had hit six.

Next up was Rangers at Ibrox in midweek. Davie White, still seeking a glimpse of silverware after close on two seasons in charge, had signed only one player in the summer, but it was one who made front-page news. Not even the wily Stein could have kept this one from being the splash story in every newspaper. White had brought back Jim Baxter on a free transfer from Nottingham Forest. He had left the club for Sunderland for £72,500 in May 1965 and moved on to Forest for £100,000 in December 1967 before being allowed to go for nothing in the summer of 1969. He was a throwback to the good old days for Rangers, the first half of the decade, when Celtic had toiled miserably. Baxter at his best was an extravagantly gifted midfielder with a left foot that could carve open the meanest of defences. While Celtic stumbled and fumbled around in the early part of the '60s, the Fifer won an astonishing ten of the fifteen domestic honours that were up for grabs between 1960 and 1965. He had performed in 18 Old Firm games and had been on the losing side only twice. He was perceived as the prodigal son and the Messiah rolled into one when he returned to Ibrox. Everyone was aware, though, that this skilful individual possessed a self-destruct button. Bringing him back was a gamble that would backfire on White and go a long way to him losing his job.

However, on a calm evening on the South Side of Glasgow, Baxter did roll back the years. He inspired Rangers to a 2–1 triumph over a Celtic side that simply underperformed. Baxter, no longer known as Slim Jim, was allowed far too much time and space to captivate his audience once more after an absence of four years. He was even pictured sitting on the ball during a lull in play. The home fans lapped it up. Celtic knew there were another four games to play and nothing had been decided. The League Cup had resided at Parkhead for four successive seasons and no one was going to remove it without a fight.

The second Old Firm game of the campaign arrived the following Wednesday. Baxter was injured and sat in the Parkhead stand. Stein restored Johnstone, missing for the first three games, to the right wing. Defeat would see the end of Celtic's stranglehold on the trophy. Once more, the club stepped onto football's tightrope without a safety net in sight.

Rangers had introduced German keeper Gerry Neef to their line-up, their third custodian in as many years. He hadn't been obliged to do too much in the Ibrox encounter, but this was to prove to be a difficult evening for the blond number 1. Celtic rained shots down on him, with Fallon a virtual spectator at the other end. Something had to give and it did when Neef, clearly alarmed at the activity in his penalty box, allowed Gemmell a chance near the end. 'I wasn't going to miss that one,' recalled the full-back. 'The keeper made a bit of a mistake, fumbling a Bobby Murdoch free kick, and presented me with the opportunity to score with a header from close in, and I tucked it away. I believe justice was done, because we had dominated that match. To be honest, we were still kicking ourselves for letting them beat us at Ibrox the previous week.'

Rangers were rattled. On the day Celtic were coasting to a 3–0 triumph over Airdrie at Broomfield, the Ibrox side were being booed off the field after relying on an own goal from Willie Polland for a 3–3 draw with Raith Rovers at Ibrox. The Baxter feelgood factor had very quickly evaporated. Celtic, a point ahead, were required to beat Raith Rovers in Kirkcaldy to once more advance to the quarter-final stage, dumping Rangers in the process. Stein's men managed the feat, winning 5–2. A crowd of 71,645 had flocked to Ibrox for Baxter's homecoming against Celtic; only 18,000 watched him in action in the 3–0 win over Airdrie in their final League Cup tie.

With Celtic safely in the last eight of the tournament, they switched their attention to the opening encounter in the league, a game against St Johnstone in Glasgow. A capacity crowd of 75,000 turned out to watch the unfurling of the championship flag for the fourth successive season. It was a ritual to which Celtic fans were becoming accustomed. The dismal days of the early '60s had been banished to the dark and distant past.

Once more, St Johnstone boss Willie Ormond threw Buck McCarry into his front line to confront Billy McNeill. 'I was getting used to it by now,' said the Celtic captain. 'Buck and others like him were big, rough guys, but I have to say they were fair. They would barge into you, thump an elbow into your ribcage, that sort of thing, but it didn't bother me so long as they didn't squeal when they got some of the same in return.' It would be wrong to dismiss the Perth outfit as a mere collection of hammer-throwers. They had some excellent ball-playing individuals in the shape of frontman John Connolly, speedy raider Henry Hall, elegant striker Jim Pearson and pacy flankers Kenny Aird and Fred Aitken. They also had former Celt Benny Rooney, son of Parkhead physiotherapist Bob, skippering the club and marshalling his defence. Willie Coburn was one of those stuffy little full-backs Scotland seems to unearth with remarkable regularity. He wasn't Tommy Gemmell and it's doubtful if he ever scored a goal in his life, but he stubbornly stuck to his defensive duties and he never made life easy for any direct opponent, including Johnstone. That turned out to be the case on 30 August when the league campaign got under way; all we needed was a fanfare of trumpets.

Coburn was practically wearing the same shirt as Johnstone and there were precious few opportunities being generated from the Celtic outside-right. St Johnstone doggedly stuck to their task and earned a 2–2 draw, with Chalmers notching Celtic's first league goal of the 1969–70 campaign. Hood added the second. 'St Johnstone always had the capacity to make life extremely difficult for us,' said Gemmell. 'I don't think they ever received the praise they deserved. They always put in a good shift and I had some great duels with their little right-winger Kenny Aird. He was built along the same lines as Wee Jinky and even had red hair. He wasn't in the Wee Man's class, of course, and I don't mean any disrespect by saying that. Our player, after all, was the best in the world, as far as I was concerned. But Kenny was an exceptionally tricky little guy who would try to skin you every time the ball dropped at his feet. He wasn't one of those wingers who hold up play and try to bring others into it. He just got his head down and went straight for you. I had to get my timing just right when I was tackling him. If you missed, you knew he was away.'

Worryingly, the side hadn't started at their usual pace and alarmingly they lost 2–1 to Dunfermline at East End Park in the third league game of the season. Gemmell, who scored Celtic's goal, recalled, 'It looked as though we were very definitely the team to beat. I have no doubt it was a feather in the cap of the opposition if they overcame the side that had claimed the domestic treble the previous season. Whether they deliberately cranked up their effort a notch or two, I don't know, but they had a hell-for-leather approach against us. Fair enough, a bit of competition didn't do anyone any harm. It was just a question of us getting into our stride, but we all realised this would be a big year for the club if we were to remain on top.'

Gemmell's theory is backed up by the result in the next match, a 2–1 defeat at home to Hibs. This was the same Easter Road team Celtic had annihilated 6–2 in the League Cup final only four months beforehand. Johnstone scored, and Stein had seen his team register in all of their ten competitive games – twenty-nine goals in all – but, disappointingly, the defence had now conceded eight goals in only four league games.

'I came in against Hibs,' recalled Hay, 'and it was clear Big Jock wasn't satisfied with the goals the team were giving away. It was difficult to pinpoint the reason. That day, we played reasonably well and then lost what turned out to be the winning goal with virtually the last kick of the ball. It was extremely disappointing. Only one win from our first four games was not what we expected. No one was resting on their laurels, that's for sure, and there was certainly no complacency among the players. Big Jock wouldn't have tolerated that. Sometimes it can just come down to getting into your stride and everything else falls into place. I know that's an easy way to explain things away, but there are occasions when you can't get your passing game quite right for whatever inexplicable reason. The effort and endeavour were still there, the players who were good enough to win everything in Scotland were still in attendance and the training hadn't changed. We just weren't getting good results.'

Celtic, with only three points from a possible eight, travelled across Glasgow to meet Rangers for the last time in the '60s. Those among the Celtic fraternity might have thought back to the first tussle of the decade when a last-minute goal from Jimmy Millar downed the Parkhead side on New Year's Day 1960. Quite a lot had happened since Frank Haffey had to fish the ball out of his net that bitterly cold afternoon in the East End. That was then and this was now.

Rangers, with Baxter in the side, had five points and had looked more than adequate in successive 2–0 victories over Aberdeen and St Mirren. However, there had also been a 2–1 flop against Ayr United at Somerset Park. So Stein and his men arrived at the home of their great rivals in the realisation that while a victory would put them level on points a defeat would open up a four-point gap at this early stage in the season. Once more, it was time to stand up and be counted.

'Big Jock knew Rangers were strong in the middle of the park,' said Hay. 'John Greig was a powerful guy and the Ibrox side would pitch in the likes of Alex MacDonald, Sandy Jardine and Bobby Watson alongside him every now and again. They were all ball-winners and could break up the rhythm of teams going at them. Big Jock had a word with me. "I'm playing you in midfield today, Davie," he said. "Don't let them take control. Let them know you're around." Our manager never once advocated dirty play, but he expected his players to win every 50–50 ball, maybe even those that were 60–40 in the opponent's favour. I didn't have a problem with that. If he wanted me to carry out those duties, then I would do my best in that particular role.

'I remember that game well. Greigy was on the ball when I came in hard to challenge him around the halfway line. The Rangers skipper was solid, but I was made of good stuff myself. I clattered him. The referee gave a free kick and there wasn't a murmur from Greigy. A few minutes later, there was some of the same. The ball was there to be won and I went for it. Now, I'm not too sure how other teams performed against the Rangers captain – that wasn't my concern – but I was going to make sure he wouldn't be given time or space against us. And, while I was at it, I would be doing my best to get forward and put pressure on the Rangers defence. After about the third or fourth clash with Greigy, I could see him looking at me. He seemed to be thinking, "Who is this guy?" I had been given a role by the manager and I was going to see it through, come what may.'

Hay stood his ground, performing with the grit and professionalism that would be associated with him throughout his career. Stein's ploy worked a treat. Denied Greig's ability to push the team forward, Rangers were undone by a flash of elegant brilliance from Harry Hood. Years later, he recalled, 'I remember that goal very well. I was clear in the box when the ball fell at my feet. Out the corner of my eye, I could see Ronnie McKinnon getting ready to launch himself at me. I switched feet, dodged the tackle and placed the ball between their goalkeeper and the near post. It was the only goal of the game and I was really pleased with it.'

Fallon had his first clean sheet of the campaign. At the fourth time of asking, it was Stein's first league triumph over White. The gap had been closed and it was now imperative that Celtic maintained the momentum. Kenny Dalglish made his first start for the club shortly afterwards in a game carefully chosen by the manager. Stein rested Murdoch and put Dalglish in midfield. Celtic eased to a 7–1 triumph over Raith Rovers, with Dalglish fitting in quite snugly.

Celtic turned their attention back to the League Cup semi-final, where they faced a workmanlike Ayr United side, managed by future Scotland international boss Ally MacLeod. The likeable gaffer was known by some as 'Muhammad Ally' or 'The Fastest Gums in the West' for the colourful manner in which he delivered brash promises and made outrageous predictions. He pledged the Somerset Park faithful they would witness 'something special' in the Hampden encounter. He was as good as his word. Alex Ingram, another of the big, bustling centre-forwards of the time, was bumping into everything in sight as he launched himself at every ball that dropped into the Celtic penalty area. This fiercely contested affair ended all square at 3–3. Ayr were applauded for their sterling efforts. 'Aye, and there's more to come,' promised MacLeod. Any individual would have been disappointed in the United manager if he hadn't said something along those lines.

A week later, their interest in the League Cup came to a halt when goals from Chalmers and Hood piloted Celtic, with Dalglish still in the side, to a 2–1 victory. The aftermath was poignant, though, with little in the way of celebrations in the Celtic dressing-room. With only seven minutes left to play, Ronnie Simpson made a daring save at the feet of Ingram to prevent a certain equaliser. The cheers of the Celtic fans in appreciation of his brave stop came to a halt when they witnessed the keeper writhing in pain on the ground. Once more his shoulder had given way and once more Gemmell was forced into action as emergency goalkeeper.

'It was such a shame,' observed Gemmell. 'Ronnie had been acting like an excitable kid in the previous game when he was made captain against Airdrie to celebrate his 39th birthday. It was a nice gesture by Big Jock and Ronnie really appreciated it. I think that was the first-ever time he had led out any team in a career that had started when he was a 14-year-old at Queen's Park. We won that game at Broomfield with goals from Stevie Chalmers and Willie Wallace. Fittingly, Ronnie had kept a clean sheet to mark the moment. Here we were, though, only two days later, playing on a Monday night, and he was being helped off the pitch. A few months earlier, I had wondered if we would ever see Ronnie in action again when I took over from him against Clyde. I couldn't prevent myself from thinking along the same lines that night at Hampden.'

Things were stirring at Ibrox at the same time. White must have sensed he was losing the fan base that had welcomed him so enthusiastically in November 1967. The board were examining his results closely, too. The lustre of White's first season in charge was gone. Baxter, that eccentric, wayward genius, was clearly past his sell-by date. The bravura of his performance against Celtic in his first game back at his spiritual home had very quickly faded from memory. Two goals from Peter Marinello – soon to join Arsenal for £100,000 and become London's so-called answer to George Best – and one from old Celtic favourite Joe McBride gave Hibs a 3–1 victory in Glasgow. Changes were in the wind down Govan way. Celtic, as ever, would monitor the situation from not too far away.

To pile on the pressure, they won the first piece of silverware up for grabs, defeating St Johnstone 1–0 in the League Cup final with a second-minute goal from Auld. The occasion was marred when Chalmers broke a leg in the first half. The sight of the seemingly indestructible striker being stretchered away was a sad one. He wouldn't feature again that season.

The game itself was interesting enough. Things appear to have been even more interesting in the Celtic dressing-room before kick-off. Hay was told he was playing in place of Gemmell, who had been a mainstay in the first team. The fans' favourite had performed in the previous ten games in the competition and had scored three goals, one being the crucial winner over Rangers at Parkhead.

Hay said, 'Genuinely, I didn't have a clue I was about to play in that game. Big Tommy obviously didn't know he was about to be dropped, either. I thought the best I might hope for was a place on the substitutes' bench – you could name one outfield player back then – but I thought it was more likely I would be watching the action from the stand. About an hour before kick-off, Big Jock read out the team: "Fallon, Craig and Hay . . ." Back up there, Boss, did you say Hay? It was quite a surreal moment. I was lost in thought for a moment. I was about to play in my first-ever cup final at Hampden and there was the possibility of my first medal. I had played five times in the competition – all at right-back. Now I was in at left-back instead of Tommy, which was a wee bit baffling. I knew he wasn't injured because I had trained with him for the last few days. Also, there was no sign of animosity between the player and the manager. That was a fleeting thought, though. The main thing was to concentrate on playing in the actual game and making sure Celtic won the trophy.'

'I was fuming,' admitted Gemmell. 'When I was given the news as I stepped into the dressing-room, I just couldn't believe it. I didn't want to make a fuss at the time. Immediately, I went across to Davie Hay, shook his hand and wished him all the best. The following day, though, I was still angry. I knew Big Jock held court with some of his newspaper cronies on a Sunday morning at Celtic Park. I phoned him.

'"Would you like to tell me why I was dropped?" I enquired.

'"Not over the phone," answered Big Jock.

'"OK," I said, "I'll be there in about half an hour."

'I stayed in Kirkintilloch at the time. I jumped into my car and I was at the ground within about 20 minutes. Again I asked, "Why was I dropped?" Jock looked uncomfortable.

'I had been ordered off against West Germany during a World Cup tie in Hamburg the Wednesday before the League Cup final. One of their players, Helmut Haller, tripped me as I prepared to shoot, the red mist came down, I retaliated and, as so often happens in these circumstances, the original culprit got away with it and I was dismissed. I think there was about a minute to go. To make matters worse, Scotland lost 3–2.

'But that wasn't on my mind when I returned to catch up with my teammates as we prepared at Troon for the game against St Johnstone. I had absolutely no reason to believe I would be left out. No one even hinted I wouldn't be playing. I trained as normal and looked forward to the game. I had played in the five League Cup finals before this one and had enjoyed four successes. So when we travelled to Glasgow on the day of the game I still didn't know I wouldn't figure.

'I was normally one of the last guys to get changed. Stevie Chalmers, for instance, was always ready to go about an hour before kick-off, but that wasn't for me. I would greet some family friends and fans at the main entrance at Hampden. I had tickets to pass on and other things to take care of. Then I would go and join the guys in the dressing-room. That's what happened that day. I went up the stairs, got to the door and our former player Jim Kennedy, who did all sorts of jobs around Parkhead, stopped me at the door and handed me tickets for the stand. "What are these for?" I asked. The Prez looked a wee bit embarrassed. "They're for you, Tommy." I stopped and thought for a second. No, it was no joke, for there was Davie getting ready at the left-back berth. I was quite calm and, like I said, I wasn't going to cause a stir before a cup final.

'The following day, though, I was determined to have a showdown with the manager. I wasn't going to accept that sort of treatment. The board wouldn't have liked the fact that a Celtic player had been sent off while playing for his country and I knew Paddy Crerand had been put on half pay for a month after being ordered off playing against Czechoslovakia in a World Cup qualifier back in 1962. But that was in the days when Bob Kelly ruled the roost. It was different this time around. I don't believe for a second the board could have persuaded Jock to drop a player if he didn't want to. I doubt if they would have tried. No, I believe the manager made that decision.

'That being the case, would it have been too much to expect Jock to actually take me aside and give me an explanation? I kept on at Jock. "Why was I dropped?" I repeated. "It can't be my form, so what's the problem?" Jock made the usual noises. I wasn't listening, though. Once he had had his say, I stood up. "You better put me on the transfer list, then," I said, words I never thought I would use. And with that, I left, got into my car and drove up the road. I didn't get any sort of explanation and I still wasn't happy.

'Of course, Jock knew I didn't want to leave Celtic. That was always his trump card. No one wanted to walk away from Celtic and he was aware of that. We were a family and all the lads got on so well with each other. I didn't want to go, but I don't think Celtic had left me with much of an alternative. I was happy for Davie to get his first winner's medal, but I felt a bit humiliated at the same time. I still don't think that is any way to treat a professional. When I was manager at Dundee and Albion Rovers, I never dreamed of doing anything like that to any of my players.'

Stein sent out this side: Fallon; Craig, McNeill, Brogan and Hay; Murdoch and Callaghan; Chalmers, Hood, Hughes and Auld. Johnstone came on as a substitute for Chalmers. The Celtic manager banned physiotherapist Bob Rooney from the dugout because of the emotional ties with his son, the Perth skipper Benny. St Johnstone, as expected, stuck to their task throughout, but their concentration lapsed only moments after the kick-off when Auld, with a close-range right-foot drive, converted a low cross that had eluded keeper Jim Donaldson at his near post.

'That was the start we needed,' recalled Auld. 'St Johnstone were a well-drilled outfit and you had to work hard against them. They had the players to close ranks at the back and they had guys with speed up front who were deadly on the break. You had to be careful against this lot. I have to laugh when I see a photograph of that goal these days. The defender on the goal line doing his best to block the shot is none other than John Lambie, who became a very good friend and was my assistant when I was manager at Hibs. Yes, as I seem to remember, I did mention that goal every now and again!'

October came to a halt with a superb 3–2 triumph over Aberdeen at Pittodrie, Murdoch, Johnstone and Brogan tucking the ball behind Bobby Clark. Hay, continuing to display his versatility, remained at left-back for Gemmell, and also played in the 4–2 win over Ayr United at Somerset Park at the start of November. Hay had now played a handful of first-team games and appeared at centre-half, midfield and right- and left-back. 'I half-expected Big Jock to tell me I was playing in goal one day,' joked Hay. 'To be honest, I was just happy to be in the side. Everything at that stage of your career is a learning curve. You're still getting used to the style of players around about you. But that wasn't too difficult with this set of guys. I already had a fair idea of how they performed before I played a first-team game, but it was interesting to actually play alongside them because that's where you pick up the little things you might miss during training, sitting in the stand or watching on the television. It was a marvellous experience.'

Stein brought Gemmell back for Hearts' visit the following week and also took the opportunity of giving a first league outing to Dalglish, while Macari, too, got a place in the starting line-up. It was a bold move by the manager, but the Edinburgh outfit ruined the day by winning 2–0 in Glasgow. Andy Lynch, who would later join up at Celtic, played outside-left that afternoon and scored one of his side's goals. The nearest Dalglish came to scoring his first goal for the club came in the second half with a pulverising right-foot drive that almost knocked Jim Cruickshank into the net.

Dalglish and Macari were rested for the match against Motherwell at Fir Park a week later. Celtic won 2–1 with goals from Hood and Hughes. Macari was back in harness after another week and claimed his first goal for Celtic, the opener in a 3–0 triumph over Morton at Cappielow. Hood and Wallace also got on the scoresheet, both players going into double figures before December arrived.

If it was relatively plain sailing at Parkhead, it was panic stations at Ibrox. White's two-year honeymoon was over. The manager, under intense scrutiny by the same board that had given him a stunning vote of confidence in the first place, had made one mistake too many. Tales circulated of White socialising with some Rangers players. If true, he was placing himself in a potentially invidious position when it came to decision-making, especially in choosing his team. There were rumblings about a lack of discipline and things came to a head when the players were at Largs preparing for the second leg of the European Cup-Winners' Cup tie against Górnik in November, with Rangers trailing 3–1 from the first game in Poland.

Baxter and Henderson missed training one day and, coincidentally, both claimed they had overslept. White included them in the line-up to face Górnik in Glasgow. Bad idea. The Poles completely outplayed Rangers and triumphed 3–1 for a second time. White was sacked two days later.

After the game, former Rangers player Willie Waddell, who had quit as manager of Kilmarnock to take up sports journalism at the Scottish *Daily Express*, savaged White in an editorial under a banner headline referring to White as 'The Boy David'. It was therefore something of a surprise when Rangers got round to unveiling their new manager: Willie Waddell. To many, it was a bizarre decision; to Jock Stein, it was a welcome one. He had seen off two Rangers managers in Scot Symon and Davie White and he now had Waddell in his sights.

It would be accurate to say Stein and Waddell were not friends. Waddell, wearing his reporter's hat, had written a scathing report on Scotland's 2–1 defeat by Poland at Hampden during their failed 1966 World Cup qualifying campaign. Stein had been boss of the national team in a caretaker capacity at the time. Waddell laid the blame squarely on Stein's tactics. The Celtic manager had never forgotten what he believed to be a personal attack on him. Now he would get the opportunity to go head to head with Waddell where it mattered most to him – on the football pitch.

Stein had realised that Ronnie Simpson's playing days were at an end after the League Cup semi-final replay against Ayr United. The keeper, who allied agility with anticipation, had struggled to command his immediate area as he had not so long ago, although his courage could never be questioned. The Celtic manager saw Fallon concede 20 goals in 15 league games and knew he needed an experienced back-up keeper. He signed former Third Lanark goalie Evan Williams from Wolves for a modest £20,000. 'I took a pay cut to join Celtic,' recalled Williams, 'but I knew it would be worth it in the long run.' Williams, despite the Welsh name, was Scottish, but he never got a look-in at the international side. 'I would love to have played for my country, but Rangers' Peter McCloy got the nod more often than not. On the positive side, though, it allowed me to concentrate completely on performing for Celtic.'

Williams played his first game for the club in a Glasgow Cup tie against Clyde at Parkhead in October. 'I didn't have the best of starts,' he said. 'They scored when I completely misjudged a high ball into the penalty box. My timing was out and the ball sailed over my head into the net. Thankfully, we scored four at the other end to spare my blushes.' Williams, a very underrated number 1 according to most of his teammates, was also chosen for the 2–0 victory over St Mirren at the start of December, with Macari, shaping up nicely as a striker of top quality, netting both.

The unpredictable Fallon returned for the 1–0 win over Dundee, in which Gemmell scored with another explosive penalty kick. 'We didn't play particularly well that afternoon, so it was absolutely crucial that I put that one away,' remembered the defender. 'John had to make a couple of good saves to keep them out. He had fabulous ability as a shot-stopper, you could never take that away from him. I saw him turning in some excellent displays, but he was prone to the odd mishap and Big Jock frowned on inconsistency from any of his players.'

The keeper conceded four goals in the next three league games, but Celtic won them all. St Johnstone were trounced 4–1 at Muirton Park. Wallace (2), Hood and Gemmell were on target. Next up was an incredible nine-goal duel with Dundee United at Tannadice, with Celtic netting seven. Wallace knocked two past the overworked Sandy Davie in the United goal, and Auld, Hood, Hughes, Murdoch and Gemmell also got in on the act. Three days later, Kilmarnock were beaten 3–1, with Hughes notching a double and Gemmell again proving unstoppable at penalty kicks, sending in another howitzer from the spot.

There had been a real scare in the European Cup. After Celtic had eased to a 2–0 aggregate triumph over Switzerland's Basel, with Hood and Gemmell scoring in the second leg in Glasgow, Benfica, with Eusébio still in fine form, visited Parkhead for the first leg of the second-round tie. It looked all over for Benfica after a pulsating 90 minutes – another European night to cherish for the fans.

Auld recalled, 'There had been a bit of a fall-out between Big Jock and Tommy Gemmell around that time, but we all knew TG was a big-game player; the more important the occasion, the better he played. He was absolutely nerveless and a match against the Portuguese champions was one we all knew he would welcome and indeed relish. Jock realised that too, so no one was unduly surprised when TG took the field that night. And what an impact he made, as well.

'I think the game was barely two minutes old when we were awarded a free kick about thirty yards out. I shaped to send it into the box, but tapped it sideways to the left for Tommy. He raced onto the square pass and gave it an almighty clatter. The thing just took off and the keeper hadn't an earthly as it rocketed into the roof of the net. Harry Hood and Willie Wallace got the others. We took a three-goal lead to Lisbon and we thought the job was as good as done. Not quite!

'With Eusébio in devastating form, the Portuguese gave us one hell of a fright. They were 2–0 up nearing the end of a fairly frantic encounter and searching for the equaliser that would take the game into extra time. The minutes were ticking by agonisingly slowly as we tried desperately to keep them at bay. Eusébio had netted just before the interval and Graça piled on the pressure with the second after the turnaround. The game was deep into injury time when Diamantino got their leveller. I have to admit it was deserved. They really put us through it in front of their own fans.

'There were no more goals in the extra half-hour and in those days the tie was settled by the toss of a coin. Big Billy and the Benfica captain were both called into referee Laurens van Ravens' room and asked to make a call. Thankfully, our skipper got it right and, naturally enough, we were elated. We had just been gubbed 3–0 and we were all dancing around the dressing-room. I felt a bit for Benfica, too. They had put so much into the game and, in the end, got nothing because of the flip of a coin. Cruel game football, but I wasn't complaining that evening in Lisbon. I was beginning to enjoy myself in the Portuguese capital.'

McNeill recalled, 'I had the honour – if you can call it that when your insides are churning and you would rather be anywhere else than the referee's room at that moment – of calling first, after winning the initial toss of the coin. Having called heads to earn that right, I stuck with my hunch and shouted, "Heads!" again as the coin was about to land. Thankfully, my luck held. When I asked Jock what he would have done had the coin landed in favour of Benfica, he replied, "I would have kicked the coin before it had even stopped rolling!" I'm sure he wasn't joking, either.'

There was one last league game before the final whistle sounded on the '60s, a truly remarkable decade in the history of Celtic Football Club. Davie Hay summed it up fairly succinctly, 'From depression to delight.' Four words that encapsulated ten years on soccer's roller-coaster. A team that couldn't make an impression in Glasgow had gone on to make an impact on the globe. It had been a fascinating journey. Partick Thistle, who had beaten Celtic twice at Parkhead in 1960, once in the league and once in the League Cup, provided the opposition for that final match. How far the pendulum had swung was shown by the final scoreline: a resounding 8–1 triumph for Jock Stein's side. Fittingly, Billy McNeill and Bertie Auld, the two survivors from the team that had played on the first day of the decade, both scored. John Hughes, who had made his debut in August 1960, celebrated with a hat-trick. Willie Wallace and Auld got two, and McNeill netted with a trademark header.

That was the completion of the '60s, but it was hardly the end of the drama.

12

WHAT PRICE SUCCESS?

Davie Hay has always insisted Celtic would have won at least one more European Cup if the club had managed to hold on to the cream of the Quality Street Gang, the group of supremely gifted youngsters who were eagerly awaiting their opportunity to emulate, and possibly eclipse, the Lisbon Lions. Kenny Dalglish, Lou Macari and Hay were sold, the club cashing in on their talents. George Connelly, disillusioned by football, sadly strayed out of the game. Danny McGrain, a genuinely world-class right-back, remained loyal to the club, but could have done with the company of teammates of a similar stature.

'It was a shame that side was broken up in the '70s,' said Hay. 'If the club had done more to keep us, I have no doubt we would have all been delighted to remain Celtic players for the rest of our careers. For my own part, I had sought the sort of wage I thought I merited. I wasn't being greedy; money has never been my god. I wasn't looking for a fortune, either. I had a family, a mortgage, a car and all the other household bills that can mount up. But my basic wage at Celtic was only £65 per week and I thought I was worth £100. Don't get me wrong, the bonuses were excellent. However, if you were injured, suspended or simply dropped, then you were on the basic. That made life tough. I had gone on a one-man strike [in 1973], but had returned in a 3–1 League Cup semi-final win against Rangers in December before going to play for Scotland in the World Cup finals in West Germany the following summer in 1974. Even if I do say so myself, I had quite a successful tournament and my name was being mentioned with those of some top English clubs. Manchester United and Leeds, I believe, had shown interest. I had even had talks with Spurs boss Bill Nicholson, but I preferred to remain at Celtic.

'When I arrived home after the competition, I had made up my mind I would patch up my differences with Celtic and remain at the club. I had discussed it fully with my wife, Catherine, and I was going to accept what was on offer at Parkhead, buy a pub as a safety net and concentrate completely on getting on with business at the club that was always closest to my heart. There would be no more walkouts. I was, as always, prepared to do my utmost for Celtic and the supporters.

'Big Jock had other ideas. I was summoned to Parkhead on a Sunday morning and, before I could say a word, Jock told me, "I think it's better you move on." Just like that. My Celtic career ended there and then. I wanted to stay, but clearly I was being shown the door and that hurt. Chelsea, I was soon to discover, were willing to pay a hefty fee for me. That would have appealed to the Celtic board back then. I had cost nothing and I was about to be sold for more than a quarter of a million pounds. They had accepted £200,000 for Lou Macari from Manchester United a year earlier. Lou didn't want to go either, but football is a short career and, without sounding mercenary, you have to make the money while you can. Chelsea offered me a basic wage of £215 per week, more than double what I thought I was worth to Celtic. Importantly, they made me feel wanted. I signed for them, and Kenny Dalglish would be the next big-name transfer out of Parkhead when he joined Liverpool for £440,000 a few years later.

'I often wonder what would have happened if we had all stayed and played throughout the '70s. I am utterly convinced we would have conquered Europe again. If the board had invested in the team with a couple of other quality players and paid the going rate in wages, I'm sure we would have remained at the top for years. Without sounding in any way conceited – anyone who knows me will tell you I am not that sort of person – I believe a team with the nucleus of myself, Lou, Kenny, Danny and George would have taken some shifting.

'I was very friendly with George at Celtic and I still am today. He was a big honest laddie, maybe a bit shy of all the publicity and the fuss that was made of a Celtic player. If I had stuck around, who knows what might have happened? Possibly George would have, too, because I was a pal he could always confide in. If there was anything troubling George, he knew where to come. He even came out in support of me and staged his own walkout. Now that's solidarity!

'And what a player he was. There was nothing he couldn't do with that ball at his feet. His passing skills were breathtaking. He would spot a pass two or three moves ahead of anyone else. He had the ability to become a true great. It was football's loss when he decided to call it a day. A measure of his ease with the ball at his feet came in a game against Hibs when I was playing in defence. George must have been bored or something because he simply started playing one-twos with me. I rolled the ball out of defence to him and, despite an opponent breathing down his neck, he effortlessly knocked it back to me. There was nothing on, so I passed it back to him. Immediately, he returned it to me. This happened a couple of times and I suddenly realised he was standing there laughing. He was enjoying himself at my expense. I could hear the punters in the Jungle begin to grumble a bit. They wanted the ball up the pitch, but George thought it would be a bit of fun to keep putting the pressure on me. Eventually, I hoofed it up the park and yelled at my teammate, "What the hell are you playing at?" He just smiled. On the football pitch, nothing fazed him. Off it was a different story.'

Connelly, who at one point was being likened to West German legend Franz Beckenbauer because of his style and poise, opted out at the tender age of 26. I asked him about his monumental decision. In a matter-of-fact manner, this complex character who retains a certain charm, replied, 'I fully believed it was the right thing to do at the time. I had gone up with the team to a game against St Johnstone at Perth and didn't get off the substitutes' bench. Celtic were playing a reserve game at Parkhead that same afternoon and I would have been better off with them. I wanted to play, as it would have helped with my match-fitness levels.

'I was a good trainer, but sometimes all sorts of things got to me and I could vanish into thin air. I felt like a guy from a wee mining community in Fife who was lost in the big city that was Glasgow. I felt uncomfortable in my surroundings and I felt everyone realised it. I was given plenty of motivation by Jock Stein, of course, but if only I could have counted on that sort of backing away from football. Sadly, it wasn't there in my personal life. I knew I could always depend on Davie Hay, though, and I appreciated him going out of his way for me. Of course, I was upset when he was sold in 1974. Yes, I accept there might have been a vastly different twist in my story if Davie had remained at the club. Genuinely, I don't know what might have happened, but he was a bloke I had the utmost respect for. I missed him when he moved on.

'There was also a bit of a row over bonuses at the club at the time. I agreed with Davie that we deserved a bit more in our wage packet. I knew a lot of teams in England gave their players an extra top-up if they were current internationals. They saw it as the individuals bringing a bit of prestige to their clubs and were willing to pay for the privilege. Not Celtic, unfortunately. I was married, had a family, a mortgage and two cars. It didn't seem fair.

'Then one day I returned to the dressing-room from training, got out of my kit, put on my clothes and I was off, never to return. Just like that.

I can hardly express exactly how I felt. I didn't even say goodbye to my teammates. I was out and life would never be the same again. However, it was like a great weight being lifted off my shoulders.

'Actually, I did go back one more time. I had some things to sort out and I wanted to say farewell to Jock. I wasn't there long, though. I knew my old mates would soon start rolling in for training and I wanted out of there as quickly as possible. I didn't want any fuss. A couple of weeks later, I was lagging pipes for a Grangemouth oil refinery company and getting more in my basic wage than I had done at Celtic. Then I worked on the Longannet power station before taking another manual job in Torness. I also went into part-time taxi driving.

'As a kid in Fife, I was allowed to watch Dunfermline's home games because East End Park wasn't too far away. Celtic, though, were my team. I had always supported them. I got the opportunity to sign for Dunfermline back in 1963 when, believe it or not, their manager was Jock Stein! He arrived at my parents' front door one day to tell me he was interested in taking me to East End Park. My dad informed him there had already been interest from Celtic. Jock surprised me and my dad when he told us we should go through to Celtic and see what was on offer. I can look back now and understand where he was coming from. I have no doubt he believed I would go through to Glasgow, a wee boy from Fife, and hate it. I would also see how many players were at the club and the competition I would face if I tried to get into any of their teams. Jock reasoned I would then return and take up his offer. It didn't work out that way. I loved going through those big doors at Parkhead for the first time. I loved everything about the club. I wasn't nervous at all. I saw players I had admired for long enough and I wanted to sign there and then. I agreed schoolboy terms and then moved up to full-time in 1965. I recall Jock coming up our drive at home shortly after our original meeting. I raced out the back door and let my dad handle it. At Celtic, I started off on £12 per week and that went to £14. It jumped to £25, then £35, then £45 and, after getting into the first team, it was £65. It stopped there.

'As I was settling into working in Glasgow, I took every opportunity to go and watch the games, fascinated by the likes of Billy McNeill, Stevie Chalmers, Johnny Divers, Bertie Auld and Jinky Johnstone. I idolised all of them. Then, suddenly, I was sitting in a dressing-room alongside them. I was playing alongside them. But I couldn't allow myself to get friendly with them. I was too scared to mix in their company.

'Of course, I had some good times at the club. There are two games that immediately spring to mind when I am asked the question about special matches. The first is the 1969 Scottish Cup final against Rangers at a sell-out Hampden Park. Jimmy Johnstone and John Hughes couldn't play and I got the nod. A lot of people appear to think that was my first start for the club or at least my Old Firm baptism. Wrong on both counts. I had played in six of the opening League Cup ties in 1968 and two of them – both wins – were against the Ibrox side. So you could say I had a reasonable record against them. It got even better when we won 4–0 in the cup final and I scored the third goal. Now that was enjoyable.

'The other game was the 1970 European Cup semi-final second leg against Leeds United at the same stadium. I had scored when we won the first leg 1–0 at Elland Road and I was picked for the return. It's in the history books that a crowd of 136,505 attended the game and that is still a record for a European tie. Folk who were on the terracings are convinced even more spectators had somehow got into Hampden that night in April. A friend of mine went straight to the game after finishing his work. He didn't have time to get anything to eat, so he just picked up a sandwich on the way. He told me it was so congested where he was standing that he couldn't get his hand into his pocket to retrieve the snack! I could believe him. The atmosphere was simply electric and, after going a goal down, we won 2–1 on the night and 3–1 on aggregate. Two absolutely brilliant football games and the memories will live with me forever. No one can ever take them away.'

Lou Macari, like Hay, had no intention of leaving Celtic. He pointed out, 'Why should I? I was playing for the team I adored and had followed as a lad growing up in Largs. A Celtic supporters bus left the Ayrshire resort every week and, more often than not, I would be on it travelling to home and away games. Sounds like a cliché, I know, but it was a dream to sign for the club. They did mean so much to me and I loved the Celtic supporters, too. I think they recognised me as one of their own who would give everything for the cause.

'I remember being at Hampden when Celtic played Dunfermline in the 1965 Scottish Cup final. I was about 16 at the time and I knew it was such an incredibly important game for the club. I was only eight when they had won their last trophy, the 7–1 League Cup final triumph over Rangers in 1957. I don't know how the Celtic players felt that afternoon against Dunfermline, but I have got a confession to make: I spent the last nine minutes after Billy McNeill's goal refusing to watch what was happening on the pitch. I fixed my gaze on the Hampden car park and wouldn't look round until I heard that final whistle. Then the celebrations could begin, but I was a nervous wreck in those fading moments.

'So, obviously, Celtic meant the world to me and it was a genuine privilege to play for them. I made my debut in 1969 as a 20-year-old and the world was a wonderful place. Without Jock Stein, no one would have heard of Lou Macari. I played for Scotland schoolboys against England and didn't get a kick of the ball. I was just a frail wee boy. It all started to come together at Parkhead.

'And I don't think Jock ever got the credit he deserved for putting together his backroom team. I'm talking about Sean Fallon, Neilly Mochan, Bob Rooney and Jimmy Steele. Each and every one of them played an enormous part in any success that came my way. Jock was the main man, of course, but these guys were very important too. Sean was Jock's assistant, Neilly was the trainer, Bob was the physiotherapist and Jimmy was the masseur. They were a pleasure to be around and made going to work a real joy. Obviously, you could spend a lot of time on the treatment table and get to know these guys very well. They were the life and soul of the place, a genuine driving force. They were the team within the team and they did a wonderful job without ever seeking headlines or adulation.

'I was on £50 per week in my first three years. I thought I did reasonably well and statistics show I scored 57 goals from 102 appearances. One thing Big Jock rarely did, though, was congratulate a player. He never made a fuss of you no matter what you had achieved in a game. These days, managers are quite happy to label their young players "brilliant" or "wonderful", but that wasn't the done thing with Jock. I suppose he wanted all his players to keep their feet on the ground. After three years, I was coming out of contract. I went to see Jock and he offered me an extra fiver. I had already played for the Scottish international team and knew what sort of wages were on offer in England. However, I wanted to stay with Celtic and I was far from being greedy. My father had just passed away, my wife was due to give birth to our first child and I had to help support my mother. A wage of £55 was never going to cover all my expenditure. I was hardly scattering cash around. My first car was a second-hand Audi that cost a couple of hundred quid. But it was obvious Celtic would not budge on their offer. It was a take-it-or-leave-it deal. I had no option but to move.

'I came so close to joining Liverpool before Tommy Docherty stepped in to take me to Manchester United. He offered me £200 per week and a £10,000 signing-on fee. That was a wee bit more than Bill Shankly had initially offered, but it wasn't a bidding war. As was the case with many Celtic fans back then and even today, Manchester United were my English team. I would often see the likes of Bobby Charlton, Denis Law and

George Best on the sports shows on television. The transfer seemed to suit everyone. Celtic got £200,000 from United and that was a record for a player moving from Scotland to England at the time. However, if the wages could have been sorted out, I would never have left Celtic. I read about players seeking new challenges and the like. That's all rubbish. It's just an excuse for wanting to leave a club without saying it's all about money.

'It would have been extremely interesting to see how things might have evolved with that team. Davie Hay was one of the fittest and fastest guys I've ever played alongside and he had so much to offer. I laugh when I hear some of today's players complaining that they have to play in two games in four days or three games in eight. Listen, Davie Hay could have played every night of the week. Like me, Davie didn't want to leave, but, once again, circumstances dictated it. And Kenny Dalglish was coming through nicely at the same time, as well. I often played up front on my own back then with Kenny supporting. The team was shaping up well, but, unfortunately, the wage structure forced a few of the players out.'

Tommy Gemmell recalled, 'My contract was due to end in June 1967, the month after Lisbon. Big Jock would often say to me, "If the club gives you extra cash, then we'll have to give it to the other players, too." My response was always the same: "Well, give it to the other players, then. They're all worth it." Jock used to insist that all the players were on the same wages, but I knew that wasn't accurate. I can now reveal that I was friendly with one of the secretaries at Parkhead. I wasn't married at the time and I liked the lass. She lived in Motherwell and I used to often give her a lift to the ground. Anyway, one day we got round to talking about players' salaries and she let it slip that one of the team was getting an extra £10. Obviously, it was Billy McNeill, our skipper. I confronted Jock. Naturally, I couldn't say where I was getting my information. But Jock once again repeated that we were all on the same wage. I looked him square in the eye and said, "I know there is a player here getting a tenner more than the rest of us. Why is that?" Our manager wasn't normally flustered, but he realised in an instant he had been rumbled. "Oh, that's Billy McNeill. He gets a little more for being captain." I thought for a moment and replied, "The solution is simple, Boss. Make me captain and give me the ten quid!" I was only joking, but I just thought I would let Jock know what I knew.'

The players would often put pressure on McNeill to have meetings with Stein about their salaries. He said, 'I hated it when they urged me to go to talk to Jock. I was told that, as their captain, it was one of my duties. Jock treated Celtic's money like it was his own. He was a real hardliner when it came to these sorts of matters. Anyway, there was one particular day when my teammates were anxious for me to take up their grievances with the boss. Honestly, I knew it would be a waste of time. They were so persistent, though, and eventually I said, "OK, I'll see what I can do." They told me they would wait in the dressing-room until I came back.

'I hate to admit it, but there was no such meeting with Jock. I found a ladies' loo at the back of the stand and stayed out of sight for about 30 minutes. Then I came back to tell the players, "Sorry, lads, Jock is refusing to budge. He says the present contracts are the best the club can manage at the moment. You know how it is. Sorry about that." The players accepted the situation and filed past me. They knew, as I did, that they were chancing their arm and Jock wouldn't fall for that.'

Gemmell laughed as he recalled the day Celtic actually gave away free money to their players. He said, 'We were stuck in the Moscow Airport after our game against Dynamo Kiev in 1966. Desmond White, one of our directors at the time, suddenly became extremely generous. To be honest, that was most unlike him. He was a chartered accountant and every penny was a prisoner. He asked the players to form an orderly queue and he suddenly produced this massive wad of notes. Desmond had injured his right hand when he had been struck by a propeller during his days with the RAF during the Second World War. His hand was deformed, with the fingers pointing inwards, but it didn't stop him doing everything at incredible speed with his good left hand. Anyway, that day in Russia he played our kind benefactor. He put a wedge of cash under his right armpit and then fired out notes with his left at a speed that couldn't have been bettered by any ATM. Whoosh! Whoosh! The players were being handed bundles of cash by Desmond. "Thank you, Mr White," I said when I was handed my unexpected and more than welcome windfall.

'I looked at this pile of cash. It was in the local currency, roubles. Nobody in the squad had a clue how much a rouble was worth. We would soon find out. We went to one of the shops with our new-found wealth. It was there we discovered that all of our cash might cover the cost of a wee cheap wooden knick-knack. Some of the other lads thought it would be a good idea to hold on to the dosh and cash it in at the exchange when we got home. They were informed that the money wasn't worth the paper it was printed on. We should have known better. That was the one and only time Desmond White ever handed over cash to players.'

Bertie Auld smiled as he recalled, 'I thought Celtic were careful with their money, but they didn't come anywhere near Partick Thistle, as I discovered when I became their manager in 1974. One of the first things I did was telephone my old Celtic mate John Colrain to see if he was interested in doing some scouting work for us. Colly was in Ireland at the time and he agreed to help us out. I told him we couldn't spend too much. I think we agreed £10 per week with some expenses thrown in. Now, I know they were legitimate expenses. Colly could take in three games in one day, watching schoolboys, amateurs and juniors. I remember he submitted some receipts to our treasurer John Moynihan. He would always scrutinise everything and must have taken lessons from Scrooge. One day he called me over. "Look at this, Bertie," he said. "He's charged us for a fish supper!" Thank God Colly didn't have a pickle with it – that would surely have tipped old John over the edge.'

Harry Hood, bought for a club record £40,000 from Clyde in 1969, remained at Parkhead for seven years, scoring seventy-four goals from one hundred and eighty-nine games. Hood, a gifted performer, revealed, 'Actually, I could have joined Celtic about five years earlier than I did. I came into the Clyde team first time around in 1962 at the age of 18. I was enjoying my football and there were stories doing the rounds that Celtic – remember this was before Jock Stein – liked what they saw. They did make a move and I turned them down. Why? Money. I was part-time at Shawfield while working as a sales rep. I was picking up £26 per week. Celtic offered me 20 quid and I was told there would be no signing-on fee. Six pounds was a fair amount of cash back then and I couldn't afford to take the drop. So I stayed at Clyde and eventually moved to Sunderland. My time there was ravaged by injuries. I missed an entire season with a double hernia. I returned to Shawfield in 1966 and came back onto Celtic's radar in 1969. Jock shelled out what was his biggest-ever fee at the time to persuade me to make the short trip to Parkhead. They made it worth my while on that occasion.

'I take on board what Davie Hay says about the club winning more European honours and it's patently and painfully obvious that Davie, Lou Macari and Kenny Dalglish were never properly replaced. George Connelly, too.

'I was told a story from a good source about Leeds United making a £240,000 move for Kenny two years before he was sold to Liverpool in 1977. I was reliably informed that Jock was willing to pay a joint £100,000 fee for Dundee United's Andy Gray and Davie Narey with some of the transfer cash the club would be getting for Kenny. Look at the careers those lads had and think about what they might have achieved at Celtic. Andy was a bit of a Rangers fan, but I don't think that would have prevented him from going to Parkhead. He might tell you a different tale. In fact, neither of the United players might have even known about any proposed deal, because the players were often the last to discover these things. I was told that it looked as though everything was set to go ahead, but the Celtic hierarchy tried to get Jock to persuade Jim McLean, the United boss, to accept a total of £60,000 for his players. That was never going to happen and United got just about double that for Andy alone when he joined Aston Villa shortly afterwards in 1975, for £110,000.

'Whether the story is accurate or not, there was a definite lack of ambition from the powers that be at Parkhead at the time. Jock would never have allowed any meddling in team matters, of course, but he couldn't release the purse strings. The club started bringing in players such as Frank Munro from Wolves and Jimmy Smith from Newcastle. Both had been splendid players in their heydays, but, sadly, were past their best by the time they arrived at Celtic.'

Evan Williams, the goalkeeper who did so much to keep Celtic in the 1970 European Cup final when it looked as though Feyenoord might run amok, tells an amusing tale about signing a fresh contract at the club. 'I was informed Jock wanted to see me,' said Williams. 'I knew I was due a new deal, so I was happy to sign on again. Jock was sitting in his office when he pushed a contract in front of me. I was getting an extra fiver; that seemed to be the going rate at the time. Jock thought I was hesitating about signing when he suddenly grabbed the contract, opened a drawer and threw it in. "If it's not good enough for you, then that's it," he growled. I looked at him and said, "For God's sake give me a chance to get a pen, Boss!" That's the way it was in those days. I was almost out the door before I knew what I was doing. There were no such things as negotiations.

'Mind you, I did get my own back on him when we were playing Fiorentina in Italy on that run to Milan. We had won 3–0 in Glasgow, but they had pulled one back and we were under the cosh. Then they were awarded a free kick just outside our box. Their player sized up the situation and drilled in an effort. Big Jock was apoplectic about what happened next. I ducked under the Italian's shot and let the ball sail serenely into the net. Big Jock was up on his feet, arms waving all over the place and snarling at me. Thankfully, he simmered down when he spotted that the referee had awarded Fiorentina an *indirect* free kick. It was worth it just to see the look on Jock's face.'

Rather astonishingly, it was Stein and not one of the club directors who scrutinised the players' expenses. The Celtic manager did possess a sense of humour, but would never be famous for his flights of whimsy or genial buffoonery. Gemmell recalled a day when Stein hit the roof with some of his players over another cash issue. 'After a game, the club used to pick up the tab for the players at the Vesuvio Italian restaurant in Glasgow. One Saturday evening, the usual suspects – me, Big Billy, Bertie, Wispy and Jinky – decided to take our wives along with us. We didn't tell Celtic, of course, because we knew they would pay for us but our partners would have to settle their own bill. We grabbed one of the owners and told him to be careful with the receipt he would be handing in at Parkhead. We asked him to put the wives down as other players. Happily, he agreed to our wee bit of deception. As I remember, we had a few drinks that night. Maybe too many. Anyway, when we reported to Parkhead on the Monday, Big Jock was waiting for us.

'Jock would never have made it in stand-up comedy, but he looked sterner than usual on this occasion. We wondered what the problem was. It couldn't have been the result on Saturday, because we had won with a few goals to spare. Then he produced the receipt from the Vesuvio. "What's this?" he snapped. "Look at the drinks on this bill. Outrageous! We don't mind feeding you lot, but we're not going to pay for your boozing. It's coming out of your wages." We used to get paid in readies on a Tuesday and, sure enough, the drinks money had been deducted from our salaries. It was bad enough for the five players who were at the restaurant that night, but you had to feel for the five whose names had been used to cover the identities of our wives. Those players got hammered, too!'

Lou Macari can also laugh at another Stein rant after a night out at the Vesuvio. 'Jock looked livid. He was waving the bill in the air. "This is ridiculous," he said. We hadn't gone overboard on food or drink, so we wondered what all the fuss was about. Then he said, "OK, who ordered the cigar? We're not footing the bill for players smoking. It's not on." I don't know if he ever discovered who the "culprit" was, but it was so typical of the time. Every penny was a prisoner.'

Auld recalled, 'There was a day when Jock came into the dressing-room to announce we were going to either Bermuda or the Bahamas to play a local select. It was a wee five-day break in the sunshine during a typical Scottish winter and he thought it would freshen us up. One of our players, I think it was Jim Brogan, asked, "How much are we getting?" Jock turned round and said, "What do you mean?" Jim replied, "Well, presumably the club are getting something for making the trip, so how much are we getting? What's our cut?" Jock replied instantly, "You're getting nothing – the trip's off." And that was the end of it. We never got on that plane and I think our place was taken by Chelsea. Lucky sods!'

There was speculation at the time that the Celtic players took their eye off the ball while they thrashed out commercial deals before the 1970 European Cup final. 'Not so,' answered Hay. 'Yes, an agent had been appointed to look after those sorts of matters, but it certainly didn't interfere with our preparations for the game. A story broke around that time, but it was all a lot of baloney. No doubt lawyers would be brought in these days and writs would fly about, but back then we just shrugged our shoulders and thought no more about it.'

Despite possibly his best game for the club, Evan Williams was ultimately a loser in the 2–1 extra-time defeat against Feyenoord. He recalled, 'I thought I played well that night. It was maybe just as well, because I don't think I was ever worked so hard in any game for the club before or after. The Dutch just kept coming at us in waves and they were hammering in shots from all over the place. We were only about two minutes away from a replay – they didn't use penalty kicks in those days – when Ove Kindvall got their winning goal.'

Hay said, 'Believe me, if we had played them again we would have beaten them. We wouldn't have got caught cold again. They were a whole lot better than we anticipated. They were really well organised and had excellent players. Even Big Jock appeared to write them off. He told us their left-sided midfielder Wim van Hanegem was "a poor man's Jim Baxter". We were told he would tire and drop out of things after about half an hour. He was still pinging passes all over the place in extra time. Like Bobby Murdoch, Bertie Auld and George Connelly, he was a great exponent of making the ball do all the work. By the way, he was also good enough to make more than 50 appearances for Holland, including the 1974 World Cup final against West Germany. He was a player we never got to grips with in the San Siro, but he would never have had the luxury of time and space in any replay.

'Big Jock also changed the line-up of the side that had beaten Leeds United home and away, going with two midfielders, Bobby and Bertie, and dropping George to the subs' bench. Unfortunately, Feyenoord were extremely strong in that part of the pitch and it was virtually impossible for our two guys to dominate the way they had done against Inter Milan three years earlier.

'Kindvall, up front, had a fabulous turn of pace and was a constant threat when they got the ball forward. Wim Jansen, with whom I am still friendly after his one-season league-winning stint as Celtic manager in 1998, was in the middle of the park for them and he was a real dynamo. He was up and down the pitch all evening, tackling, passing and shooting. Bertie would later joke that Big Jock had assured him he would not see

Jansen in the final. "He was right," said Bertie. "One minute he was there, the next he was gone."

'Their manager was the astute Austrian Ernst Happel, who had done his homework on Celtic. Jinky was obviously pinpointed as a threat and, it must be admitted, Happel got his tactics spot-on. Jinky was shown inside all night, with Feyenoord double- and even treble-banked when facing him. He would simply run into a wall of bodies in a congested area and then van Hanegem would reverse the roles with one of his accurate long-range passes.

'There's no way anyone can point the finger at Big Jock when you consider what he did for the club. However, he seemed quite relaxed preparing for this game. The guys who had played in Lisbon told me he was really strict in 1967. He worried about how much pool time they should have, how long they could stay in the sun, what they were eating and drinking, when was the best time for meals, all that sort of stuff. He was meticulous. It was different, though, in the countdown for this one.

'Let's face it, we all thought we would win. We had beaten very good Italian champions Fiorentina 3–1 on aggregate in the quarter-final, with Bertie putting on a remarkable display in the first leg in Glasgow. I played that night and Bertie was exceptional. We had also taken care of Leeds United home and away in the semi-final. A goal from George in the opening moments was enough at their place and, after my wee Scottish mate Billy Bremner had levelled on aggregate with a fantastic strike at Hampden, John Hughes and then Bobby Murdoch netted in the second half to give us a 3–1 overall victory. We were already being hailed as European champions because the English media had assured everyone that Leeds were the best team in the world and not just Europe. You know, Big Jock wanted to play them in the final. That was his wish. He groaned when he heard the semi-final draw. He knew we could beat Leeds and he wanted to do it while the rest of Europe was looking on.

'I don't think we were complacent against Feyenoord, though. Confident, yes, but not complacent. They played really well at the San Siro. Yet we opened the scoring when Bobby Murdoch back-heeled a free kick to Tommy Gemmell and he fired a ferocious drive into the net from just outside the box.

'Bobby Lennox scored a perfectly legitimate goal, too, that was ruled out. We didn't make a fuss at the time. He cut in from the left to hit a right-foot shot across their keeper and into the corner of the net. The Italian referee, Concetto Lo Bello, ruled it out for offside. Later on, we saw film of the game and, amazingly, Bobby was played onside by three of their defenders. Not one or two, but three. That wee man was far too fast for his own good.

'To be honest, though, the Dutch played very, very well. They had a game plan and they stuck to it. We were asked to defend more often in that game than any other I can remember. Evan Williams was brilliant, probably his best-ever performance for us. They were solid at the back and they broke forward in numbers. We were out of sorts. Maybe if we had held our lead until half-time we might have done a whole lot better. As it was, they got a dodgy free kick on the right and, after a bit of ping-pong in our penalty area, the ball fell perfectly for their skipper Rinus Israël to head back across Evan high into the net. Our advantage lasted approximately three minutes.

'Their winning goal was downright bizarre but at least showed the sportsmanship of Bobby Murdoch. The referee awarded them a free kick in from the right about midway into our half. The ball was rolling away and Bobby, with all the innocence in the world, picked it up and handed it to his Dutch opponent. He could have let the ball run and the Dutch would have had to go and retrieve it for themselves. He could even have given it another nudge to send it further down the line. That would have given us time to erect a defensive wall and prepare for any threat. Bobby, though, actually picked up the ball and threw it to a Feyenoord player. The Dutchman didn't even have the good grace to say thank you. He planted it on the ground, looked up, spotted Kindvall lurking behind Big Billy and simply flighted the ball in the direction of his unmarked colleague.'

McNeill recalled, 'I still don't know why I did what I did. I didn't get the opportunity to organise the troops and, suddenly and without warning, the ball was dropping behind me. In normal circumstances, I would have set myself for a header, but, on this occasion, I was on the back foot. I threw up my hands and stunned the ball. It dropped behind me where Kindvall was waiting and it couldn't have sat up any better for him. He raced forward as Evan left his line and just managed to get his toe to the ball to lift it over our keeper into the net. The referee had played advantage and I am often asked what would have happened if Kindvall had missed. The letter of the law says the game would have remained 1–1. It should have been a penalty kick, of course, because of my handball, but the match official had waved play on, so, technically, he had overlooked that offence to play the advantage rule. You can't have it both ways. It's all conjecture now. He scored and we lost.

'Although I do agree with Davie that we would have beaten them in a replay. That would have been an entirely different game. We would have been better prepared.'

13

MIXED FORTUNES

Celtic strode out of the '60s and prepared to take the '70s by storm. The New Year's Day game of 1970 was against Clyde at Shawfield, where John Hughes and Lou Macari, already making a name for himself, helped themselves to the goals in a 2–0 triumph. The opening Old Firm game of the new decade, on the other hand, was a huge disappointment: a non-event goalless draw at Parkhead. Bertie Auld said, 'Obviously I didn't know it at the time, but that was my last appearance in a Glasgow derby against Rangers. After all the turbulent games since making my Celtic debut against them in 1957, this match was one of the most forgettable. Those games rarely passed without some sort of incident, but that one did. It would have been nice to have gone out on a winning note, but it wasn't to be.'

Auld, though, was bang on course to lift his fifth league championship medal, with eleven games still to play and Celtic in total command. They notched up eight successive triumphs before being derailed by Aberdeen, the team they would meet in the Scottish Cup final eighteen days later on 11 April. The swashbuckling Tommy Gemmell added to his growing total with another fabulous strike, but Celtic met with surprise 2–1 defeat by the Pittodrie outfit at Parkhead. It was the third time the club had lost on home soil that season, following reverses against Hibs and Hearts.

Rangers were still Celtic's main challengers, but new manager Willie Waddell was finding it impossible to unlock the secrets of a consistent winning formula. One of the first things this strict disciplinarian did was order Jim Baxter and Willie Henderson to shave off their Zapata moustaches! Baxter played only three games under the new regime before having his contract scrapped. His lack of fondness for hard training, plus excesses away from the pitch, didn't sit well with Waddell. A great talent dropped out of football and, somewhat ironically, he bought a pub on Paisley Road West, not far from Ibrox. Rangers, though, were never at the races as far as the title was concerned. Only 15,000 bothered to attend the last league match of the season at Ibrox, a 2–0 defeat by Morton. Rangers had endured another season in the wilderness.

Waddell's woes were none of Jock Stein's concern, of course, as Celtic steamed ahead stylishly towards flag number five. The championship was in the bag long before the 2–1 victory over Dundee at Dens Park, with Auld and Bobby Lennox scoring. Underlining the professionalism of Stein's players, they brought down the curtain with a hard-fought and well-earned 3–2 triumph over St Mirren at Love Street, where Harry Hood and Tommy Callaghan were on the mark. Vic Davidson, another gem from the Quality Street Gang, notched his first league goal for the club. Celtic completed the season with 57 points, an incredible 12 more than runners-up Rangers. In their championship-winning run since 1966, the club had walloped in 508 goals, more than 100 a term. Some shooting.

The Scottish Cup campaign kicked off at Parkhead against Dunfermline, who were no doubt dreaming of landing a quick knockout blow to repeat their considerable feat of two years previously at the same venue. John Hughes and Harry Hood netted in a 2–1 triumph to put an end to that notion.

Hughes was in one of his bring-'em-all-on moods in the next round against Dundee United in Glasgow a fortnight later. 'When Yogi was up for it, he was a one-man attack,' said Gemmell. 'There was just no stopping him once he got into his stride. This was one of those afternoons when the big man could do no wrong. As I recall, he was up against a very good right-back in Andy Rolland. Not too many wingers gave that guy the runaround, but Yogi was sheer dynamite that day. Rolland tried to push our guy further up the pitch, but that tactic didn't stop him. Yogi could run miles with the ball at his feet. He would beat the full-back on the halfway line and then simply take off. On days like that, I actually felt sorry for our opponents.' Hughes rammed in two and Macari and Hood also took advantage of a demoralised defence in a runaway 4–0 victory.

If the goalless Old Firm encounter in January had been a bit tedious, the Scottish Cup quarter-final collision between football's oldest foes was the exact opposite. It was a game that crackled with incident and excitement from the start. Celtic Park resembled a bog that February afternoon. The men from Govan took the lead when the unfortunate Jim Craig diverted a right-wing cross past the helpless Evan Williams. The Celtic right-back didn't look too chuffed when Willie Johnston patted him on the head as he ran away to join in the celebrations with his mates. Help was at hand, though, before the interval. Hay lofted one into the box from the right, the defence missed it completely and Lennox drove in from the left to hit it first time with his right foot. The ball zipped through the legs of Gerry Neef for the equaliser.

Hay, who then scored for Celtic to take the lead, recalled, 'I was never going to be noted for my goal-scoring prowess, so I have perfect recall of the ones that did hit the back of the opposition's net. The pitch that day was just a sea of mud, but that didn't prevent two committed sets of players piling into each other and giving it everything for ninety minutes. My magical moment arrived in the second half as I carried the ball forward from the old inside-left position. I made up my mind early on that I was going to give it some welly. As the Rangers defence backed off, I leathered the ball goalwards with all the power I could muster from about 25 yards. Their keeper made an acrobatic attempt to push it over the bar, but there was only one destination for that ball as soon as it left my boot and that was the roof of the net. Pinning medals on my own chest, I have to say it wasn't a bad goal. Wee Jinky added another as we won 3–1 on an afternoon when you had to be brave and courageous in monsoon conditions.'

It was a day to forget all round for Rangers, who also had Alex MacDonald ordered off. Apparently, he had been more than a little indiscreet in his remarks to referee Tiny Wharton while debating a decision – not particularly clever when dealing with that no-nonsense giant of a man who had in the past sent off Jimmy Johnstone on two occasions.

Hay added, 'Do you know how we celebrated that win? We went to a wedding reception in Castlemilk, the vast council housing scheme in Glasgow, for one of our young players, Tony McBride. These were the days before video recorders, so not one of that team saw the highlights on TV later that night. It was about 40 years before I saw my goal again!'

Macari and Lennox were the goal-scorers to end Dundee's Scottish Cup progress at the semi-final stage, Celtic winning 2–1. Aberdeen had earned the right to take on Celtic in the final with a 1–0 semi-final victory over Kilmarnock. Derek McKay's effort was enough to see them safely through to Hampden. Celtic had already dismissed the Pittodrie outfit from the League Cup and had also won at their place in the league. There was the hiccup of a 2–1 defeat in Glasgow, but Celtic were overwhelming favourites to win the trophy for the fourth time in Stein's five-year reign, following the triumphs over Dunfermline ('65), Aberdeen ('67) and Rangers ('69). The bookmakers priced it at 7–1 against Aberdeen and there weren't too many dissenting voices. They figured without match official Bobby Davidson's input.

'Easily the most diabolical piece of refereeing I have ever witnessed,' said Hay. 'In my playing days at Celtic, Bobby Davidson was, in my opinion, by far the worst referee to take charge of our games. I am not saying he was biased, but there seemed to be an awful lot of decisions against Celtic that would have to be filed under C for controversial. He was a constant irritant and when you saw he had been designated by the SFA to take charge of one of your games your heart sank. "What will he conjure up today? How can he annoy the players? How can he upset thousands of Celtic fans?" He was in charge against Aberdeen and that was when he really hit rock bottom. Some of his decisions that day definitely would not stand up to too much scrutiny in today's era. That game was only ten days after we had beaten Leeds United 1–0 at Elland Road and we were due to meet them again four days after the Dons final. Naturally, the players and the fans were still in a state of euphoria when Davidson blew to start the contest. It all went downhill after that.

'I knew there was never any love lost between Big Jock and Davidson, and you had to hope that personal feelings wouldn't come into play during a game of football. The referee first stepped into the spotlight when he awarded our opponents a penalty kick after the ball struck Bobby Murdoch in the midriff. Davidson signalled handball and would not be dissuaded even when Bobby went to him and showed him the mud-splatter on his jersey where the ball had struck him. Davidson was having none of it – a penalty it was. Joe Harper scored from the award.

'It was the first half and we still had plenty of time to get back into the game. We knocked the ball around in our usual fashion, probing and looking for an opening. Bobby Lennox, as a matter of course, harassed their keeper Bobby Clark when he was kicking the ball from hand. There was no six-second rule in those days for keepers to release the ball. Some goalies used to waltz around their area bouncing the ball for what seemed an eternity before deciding to heave it downfield. On this occasion, Clark flipped the ball up, but before he could kick it Bobby, with those astonishing reflexes, flashed in a foot, nicked it from him and, as the keeper watched open-mouthed, ran round him and plonked the ball in the net. It wasn't dangerous play because Bobby made his challenge from the side, so it wasn't studs up or a high boot. Once the ball has been released, it's up for grabs. Our player did what he was perfectly entitled to do and won it fairly and squarely.

'Not according to Davidson, though. He stifled the cheers from our support by immediately awarding the Dons a free kick. He motioned that our player had kicked the ball out of the keeper's hands. That wasn't the case. It's just a pity all the slow-motion replays we are treated to these days weren't available in 1970. Both of the referee's big decisions would have been seen to have been abominably wrong.

'Instead of being a goal ahead, we were one down. We were caught out in a breakaway after the interval when Derek McKay scored a second. We were forcing on play but making little headway when they got that goal. No complaints with that one; we left the back door open.'

There was a glimmer of hope for Stein's side when Lennox pulled one back near the end, a powerful close-range drive that left Clark motionless, but it wasn't to be Celtic's day and, after a low cross from the right, McKay knocked in number three from six yards.

Hay added, 'The outcome of the Scottish Cup had hinged on refereeing decisions and they had gone against us and for our opponents. It was a difficult defeat to accept. We always seemed to play 12 men when Davidson was in charge.'

Tommy Gemmell has a fascinating tale to tell about Davidson. He revealed, 'He made a strange decision that actually went for me, but I have to admit I was still left more than just slightly bemused. I was skipper of Dundee at the time. It was the League Cup final, being played in December 1973 against Celtic, and we were managed by former Rangers boss Davie White, who had brought me back to Scotland from Nottingham Forest. He thought I would be better deployed at centre-half that day. It was around the time of the miners' strike and power blackouts were crippling the country. The game was brought forward by a couple of hours to save electricity on the floodlights and, as I recall, it was a filthy day. A crowd of just over 27,000 turned up and the atmosphere was a bit surreal. It wasn't what I was used to at Hampden finals with Celtic, I can tell you that. The pitch was just a mess, draining the strength and stamina out of your body. We scored when a free kick from Bobby Ford fell to Gordon Wallace on the edge of the box and he swivelled before hitting a right-foot shot low past Ally Hunter.

'Now I knew better than most what would happen next. Celtic would come at us all guns blazing. I had been involved in a few of those cavalry charges myself over the years, so we braced ourselves. We were doing well enough until Big Jock put on my pal Wee Jinky as a substitute for Harry Hood, who had picked up an injury. My old boss knew what the Wee Man could do up against me. I was knackered and I thought, "Oh, God, how long to go?" I watched with interest as my wee pal came on. Would he go straight to the outside-right berth? Sadly, no. Jock gave him a roving role and that meant he would be coming at me. And he was fresh and raring to go. The game was coming to a close, my legs had just about gone, and Wee Jinky was driving straight in my direction. A shimmy and he was gone. He was running clear on goal, no defenders between him and our goalkeeper Thomson Allan. I can't recall any keepers being too successful against Jinky in a one-on-one situation. I would have put my money on the Wee Man scoring. He was about to pull the trigger, Hampden held its breath, I looked on from about 30 yards away, powerless to intervene, and then . . . Davidson blew the final whistle! Jinky put the ball in the net, anyway, as he assuredly would have done if the whistle hadn't gone.

'He looked at me, pointed at the ref and asked, "Whit dae ye think of that bastard noo?" I couldn't complain, but you can be certain if I had still been a Celtic player I would have been right in the ref's face. How on earth can you be so specific in timing a game? Another couple of seconds or so and Celtic would have equalised and taken the game to extra time. I wouldn't have had a clue what would have happened during another 30 minutes, but I can say with reasonable certainty that the casualty ward at nearby Victoria Infirmary might have had a visit from the Dundee captain later that day!

'Actually, I was quite embarrassed to go up and collect the League Cup. Of course, I was a professional and I was delighted for Dundee, the manager, my teammates, the fans and the city and, after all, the club paid my wages. However, as I made my way up the steps to the presentation area, I passed an awful lot of people I recognised as Celtic fans. I had met many during my years at the club and here I was now, captain of a team that had just beaten their favourites in a cup final. You couldn't make it up. I accepted the trophy, waved it for all of a second and passed it swiftly on to Thomson Allan, who was next in line behind me. I received my medal and made a beeline for the dressing-room. It had been a very interesting afternoon, to say the least. I appreciated that a lot of my old teammates, including Jinky, had the good grace to congratulate me afterwards. It reminded me of something I was already fully aware of: my old chums were good sports.'

There were contrasting fortunes in the finals of the Scottish Cup and the League Cup in season 1970–71, with Rangers the opponents on both occasions. Celtic failed to ignite on a rain-lashed day at Hampden in October 1970 when sixteen-year-old Derek Johnstone headed in the only goal past Evan Williams five minutes before half-time.

Davie Hay admitted, 'That was another hard one to take. It was even worse because it was our third successive cup final defeat, backing onto the losses against Aberdeen and Feyenoord. As in the previous two finals, we were favourites and we might just have relaxed a bit when we heard the news before the kick-off that Rangers skipper John Greig would be missing, sidelined by a flu bug. Greig was an immense player for them; he drove them on relentlessly. Obviously, he was their main source of inspiration. I played in central midfield that day while Big Jock was quietly rejigging things, with three others of the Quality Street Gang getting a game: Jimmy Quinn at left-back, George Connelly in midfield and Lou Macari in attack. They got the only goal with Big Derek's header and, although we had chances, we didn't put them away.

'It looked as though we might have blown it, too, in the Scottish Cup final six months later. Again, the bookies thought we would triumph and we were leading 1–0 through a typical goal from Bobby Lennox. His record against Rangers was phenomenal. There were only three minutes to go when one of their players hit a hopeful punt down the pitch. There looked absolutely no danger, with Evan and Big George appearing to be well in control of the situation. I think they left it to each other, the ball got caught up in the Hampden swirl and, all credit to Johnstone, he followed it in, got a touch with his head and his effort bounced into the empty net. Not again! Not another dreadful cup final experience.

'We won 2–1 in the replay, but once again we seemed determined to make life difficult for ourselves. Early goals from Lou Macari and Harry Hood (with a penalty kick) put us well in command. Near the end, we gifted them a lifeline when Jim Craig, unfortunately, deflected a high ball past Evan. Thankfully, there was no horrible ending this time around. The 2–1 scoreline didn't flatter us; we were well in control throughout. Could have done without the late flutters, though!'

That game threw up yet another fascinating football fact: Jim Craig scored two goals in the Scottish Cup during his career – and both were for Rangers!

The versatile Hay switched from midfield to right-back for the European Cup quarter-final against Ajax in Amsterdam in March. Celtic had knocked out Finnish champions Kokkola and Irish title-winners Waterford in the earlier rounds; the combined aggregate scores amounted to an astonishing 24–2. How they could have done with a couple of those goals against the Dutch, Johan Cruyff et al.

'We were handling exceptional opponents very well late in the game,' recalled Hay. 'It was goalless and I think there were about 15 or so minutes to play. Then – bang! – the ceiling fell in on us. They scored three goals in a devastating period. I got a close-up look at Cruyff that night. What a gifted player – great touch, fabulous movement, good pace and excellent strength. And he also scored into the bargain.'

A scrambled first-half goal from Jimmy Johnstone gave Celtic a 1–0 victory at Hampden in the return. It was no consolation that the club had lost for the third successive season to the eventual European Cup winners, with Ajax following Feyenoord and AC Milan.

The 1970–71 league season started enterprisingly enough with three successive victories without a goal being conceded, including a 2–0 victory over Rangers in which Bobby Murdoch and John Hughes netted. However, old favourite Joe McBride, allowed to leave the club on a free transfer, proved there were still goals in him by scoring both in a surprise 2–0 success for Hibs at Easter Road. Eight triumphs in a row followed before Celtic settled for a goalless draw with Falkirk at Brockville.

Tommy Gemmell recalled, 'We were in a good position and suddenly the talk was of six in a row. We hadn't set ourselves any targets that day back in Motherwell in 1966 when we'd won the first, but we were going strong and we knew we would take some stopping. At the same stage, after fourteen games, Rangers had lost four, to us, Aberdeen, Ayr United and Hibs. It didn't look as though they would prove to be any sort of threat unless we suffered an unforeseen collapse in form and they started to win every game.

'Clearly, Aberdeen were now our main danger. All eyes were on our home game against them in December. Big Jock wanted us to kill off the Dons' challenge as swiftly as possible. Some historian had mentioned that Celtic had last won six consecutive championships way back at the start of the century, kicking off the feat in 1905. A win against Aberdeen in front of a packed Celtic Park was a must. Jock had always insisted we should make our own history and we had been set another massive task.

'However, we lost 1–0 when their nippy little striker Joe Harper knocked a header past John Fallon. Jock thought the keeper should have come for the cross, with Harper scoring from about six yards. That was the end of the league campaign for Fallon, banished once more to the reserves. In came Evan Williams for the rest of the season.

'We made the trip across Glasgow for the Old Firm encounter on 2 January. That was the sad day of the Ibrox disaster, in which 66 football fans lost their lives. Tragedies like that put everything into sharp perspective. The game, which now seemed inconsequential, had ended 1–1 when there was a crush at the Rangers end. We were in the dressing-room while news was filtering through. The total of dead was growing by the minute. I remember Jock Stein going out to help the police and ambulancemen with the injured. It was a dreadful, awful day. All the players were numb by the time we left the ground. That was the one and only time I ever captained Celtic.'

Celtic travelled to Pittodrie in April knowing a loss against Aberdeen would almost certainly finish their hopes of achieving six in a row. Harry

Hood scored in a thrilling 1–1 draw, but the man the club had to thank for the precious point was skipper Billy McNeill. There wasn't long to go when Dons left-winger Arthur Graham, a boyhood Celtic fan, swept through the rearguard and rounded the exposed Williams. With the goal gaping, Graham fired the ball towards the net. Amazingly, McNeill hadn't given up hope of performing a miraculous rescue act. The centre-half, anticipating the movement of his Dons opponent, had positioned himself perfectly to deal with the finishing shot. McNeill hammered the ball off the line to safety and, in that precise instant, kept the championship dream alive.

McNeill said, 'I had always had the same outlook: it wasn't a goal until the ball was over the line and I would do my utmost until the situation was irretrievable. I had an idea what their player might do. I didn't think he would shoot or try to lob Evan. Graham had bundles of skill and would probably have bet on himself getting round our keeper. Thankfully, that's exactly what he did. He pulled a bit wide to his left and that gave me the opportunity to get back and just hack the ball anywhere. It probably ended up in Inverness!'

Three days later, Sir Robert Kelly, knighted for services to football in 1969, died after a long illness. He was 69 years of age. Kelly had been associated with the club for 39 years after being appointed to the board as a director in 1932. He became chairman 15 years later. He had been named president of the club shortly before his death. Desmond White replaced him as chairman.

With three games to go, Aberdeen, having lost the initiative, were deflated. Eventually, they would be two points adrift, with the six-time champions collecting fifty-six points. Celtic picked up the silverware with a 2–0 win over Ayr United, Bobby Lennox and Willie Wallace netting. The game was staged at Hampden Park while ground renovations were carried out at Parkhead.

14

FAREWELL TO THE LIONS

Celtic Park was awash with nostalgia on Saturday, 1 May 1971. After making certain of the championship, Stein had selected the final game of the season, against Clyde, as the last hurrah of the Lisbon Lions. A crowd of 35,000, paying 30 pence admission, turned up at the ground, minus a main stand, for the event. The players, delicately avoiding all sorts of rubble, made their way from the dressing-room down the steps and onto the pitch. Ronnie Simpson, of course, had already been forced into retirement by his recurring shoulder injury, but he took a bow before Evan Williams went into goal.

At kick-off time, there was hardly a dry eye in the house. Celtic followers realised they were watching the curtain come down on the club's most magical line-up, a collection of colourful characters it had been their privilege to witness through the spectacular turnaround during the turbulent '60s and into the '70s. It was the end of a golden era and, as you might expect, the players said cheerio to the adoring crowd with a fair degree of aplomb. Bobby Lennox fired in a hat-trick, Willie Wallace added two and, fittingly, Stevie Chalmers, the match-winner in Portugal four years earlier, added another. The Lions were paraded at the end of the 6–1 victory. If the old main stand hadn't already been razed to the ground, the raucous applause of the fans could have saved the demolition crew the bother of looking out the wrecking ball. The place rocked with raw emotion.

Bertie Auld was lifted onto the shoulders of Billy McNeill and five days later the thirty-four-year-old midfield man, who had typified the spirit of the club as it re-emerged as a genuine power in the game, was on his way to Hibs on a free transfer. In the summer, Chalmers, 34, and John Clark, 30, joined Morton and within a year Jim Craig, who had just turned 29, went to South African side Hellenic. Tommy Gemmell, at 28, moved to Nottingham Forest in December for £40,000, which would have been a down payment for his services only four-and-a-half years beforehand. John Hughes, 28, and Willie Wallace, 31, joined Crystal Palace two months ahead of him in a bargain £50,000 double deal.

Auld is among those who are of the belief that Jock Stein emptied the dressing-room too swiftly. He said, 'I often wonder what would have happened if we had won the European Cup in 1970. I ask because I believe Big Jock was just a bit too hasty in breaking up a team that had been good enough to reach soccer's summit, beating Leeds United twice along the way, but was dismantled a year later. Some of the lads were still young enough and in their prime to do a turn for the club. Look, I know when the time is right to make way for new players, and Jock had bought the likes of Harry Hood, Tommy Callaghan and Stevie Murray. There were the emerging talents of Kenny Dalglish, Davie Hay, Danny McGrain, George Connelly and Lou Macari, among others, coming through from the reserves. Time catches up with everyone, but I still find it difficult to get my head around the fact that so many left over such a short period of time. We hadn't all become duds in the space of 12 months or so.'

Hughes, popular with the support, doesn't hold back: 'Jock Stein wrecked my career. Like so many other players before me, I didn't want to leave Celtic. I was still young enough to finish my career at the club. That's what I wanted. Jock had other ideas. I was told I had to speak to Crystal Palace, but I didn't want to know. Frankly, Jock was pushing me out the door against my wishes. I believed I was being treated very badly, considering all the time I had been at the club. I had always given my very best and in fact I am still the seventh-highest-scoring player in the club's history with 188 goals. But Jock had made up his mind and that was the end of it.

'He told me that if I didn't sign for Palace he wouldn't pick me again for the first team and I would be in the stand for the next nine months. I have little doubt he would have carried out the threat. My basic take-home pay at the time was £33 after tax and other deductions and, without bonuses, it would have stayed that way. I was extremely hurt and I wanted the fans to know how I was being treated. I didn't go to Jock's funeral. That would have been hypocritical, because I didn't like what he had done to me.

'In 1971, I did move to the London side, but I was far from happy. One thing was certain, though, I was going to be professional at my new club. As I had done with Celtic, I would give my all for Crystal Palace. Their manager, Bert Head, still had faith in me and I was going to repay him.

'I discovered later that Everton had been interested, too, but I hadn't been told. They had lifted the English championship the previous season, but I'm sure it suited Jock better if I went to an unfashionable club that were unlikely to win anything and where I would be out of the spotlight.'

Hughes interrupted our interview to roll up a trouser leg and display a plainly visible scar on his right shin. 'I recall an incident when we were playing St Johnstone in Perth in February 1971. The Muirton Park pitch was cutting up fairly badly. I received a terrible injury during the first half. I got a gash down my leg that needed 12 stitches at the interval. As you can see, it's still a bit of a mess to this day. I couldn't possibly go out for the second half. The stitches would have burst, no doubt about it. I told Jock I couldn't cope with another 45 minutes. Stevie Chalmers was stripped and ready to go as a substitute, so it wasn't as though I was leaving the team a man short. Jock hit the roof. I was sitting there with a mangled leg and he wanted me to go out and play. We lost 3–2 and guess who got the blame? Me. There was little point in arguing with Jock when he was being so unreasonable.

'I don't think he ever forgave me for a miss I'd had against Feyenoord in the European Cup final the previous year. I was through early on in extra time, but their keeper made a save at my feet. Jock saw it as a sitter and told me I should have scored. Yes, it was an opportunity, but it was hardly a cert goal. I'll tell you this, if I had had a chance like that in a game where we were leading 1–0 or 2–0 and had missed, no one would have mentioned it. But I genuinely believe Jock never forgot it or forgave me.'

Hughes hit the headlines in England when he scored a sensational goal in one of his first games for the Palace. The giant forward raced about 50 yards down the left wing before cutting inside and thundering an unstoppable drive high past helpless Sheffield United keeper John Hope. *Match of the Day* featured the strike in their credits for the remainder of the campaign. Hughes recalled, 'It was in the running for Goal of the Season, but there was one reason it didn't win: Jock Stein was one of the judges on their panel. There's no way he would have voted for that goal. It would have had people querying his decision to sell me and he wouldn't have tolerated that. I really mean it. There's absolutely no way I would have got his vote.

'Actually, that goal for Palace was one of my fondest memories of my time in London. I received an injury after a couple of months or so that refused to heal and I signed for Sunderland to play alongside my brother Billy. I think I lasted about 15 minutes with them before I received another setback. That was my comeback over. Short and sharp. You look back and wonder if things would have been so much different if I had remained at Celtic. Until my injury at Palace, I always felt fit. I was an athlete at school and hadn't lost too much of my pace. I never wanted to leave Celtic; everyone should know that.'

That Jock Stein could be confrontational with his players should never be doubted. Another on the receiving end was Tommy Callaghan. He remembered, 'We were getting ready to travel to Seamill as we prepared for the second leg of the 1970 European Cup semi-final against Leeds United. Willie Wallace, who lived in Condorrat, agreed to pick up Tommy Gemmell in Kirkintilloch and then swing by Bishopbriggs and give me a lift to the ground. We hit all sorts of terrible traffic congestion and the situation wasn't helped when Tommy wasn't ready when we arrived at his place. Time dragged on and we knew we were going to be late for the coach. Eventually, we got to Parkhead about 45 minutes late and all the other players were on the bus and ready to go. Jock was raging and, unfortunately for me, he singled me out for his criticism.

'As Jock shouted and bawled, Big Tommy was honest enough to put his hands up. "Boss, it was my fault," he said. "I delayed us at Kirkintilloch." Jock wasn't listening. He turned to Tommy and Willie and shouted, "Get on the coach, you two." Then he looked at me and said, "You can get stripped. We've got a reserve game tonight and you're playing." It was unjust and unnecessary. Suddenly, through no fault of my own and with another player prepared to take the blame, I was out of a European Cup semi-final squad. I was totally embarrassed and, to be honest, I never forgave Jock for that. I had my pride and I didn't think I needed to be treated so harshly. I had so many happy times under Jock at Celtic, but that wasn't one of them.'

Evan Williams also has an interesting tale to tell about a run-in with Stein. The goalkeeper said, 'It was a winter's day and games were getting called off all over the place. The snow had been falling for about 24 hours and it looked as though there wouldn't be a game anywhere in Scotland. I can't remember who Celtic were due to play, but I received a telephone call to tell me that, as I'd expected, the game was off. My wife, Anna, was pregnant at the time and needed to use the family car that afternoon. Then I got another call to say Jock had arranged a bounce game with Raith Rovers and I was to get to the park. Easier said than done, unfortunately. I lived in Alexandria and I raced to the railway station and was amazed there was actually a train ready to head for Glasgow. I jumped on it, but we only got as far as Yoker when we were forced to stop. Continuing the journey was impossible in such treacherous conditions.

'The train reversed to another station, where we were told buses would be laid on to take us to Glasgow. A mobile phone would have been handy in those days. I trekked onto the bus and winced as I looked at my watch and realised I was going to be about an hour late, although still well in time for a 3 p.m. kick-off. Jock was a stickler for good timekeeping, but I knew I had a good reason for running late and, hopefully, he would be sympathetic. No chance. He was fuming. "What if it had been a cup final? Would you have been late then?" he demanded. I told him he could check with the railway and he would discover the train couldn't make it past Yoker. "I'll see you on Monday morning," he said. He was still ranting and raving 48 hours later. I was fined two weeks' wages. You could never argue with Jock.'

Hay, known as 'The Quiet Assassin' in his playing days, admitted Stein could strike fear into the heart of the strongest man. 'He had a considerable physical presence,' said Hay. 'He must have built up his muscles in his days working down the mines and, of course, he was a fairly rugged centre-half as a player. I remember Lou Macari and I were scared to tell him we wore contact lenses when we were just breaking through. We both believed it was tough enough trying to get into the first team, and if Jock had the hint of a suspicion you had a disadvantage of any kind, including weak eyesight, you could have been bombed out. We kept up our deception for years!'

Jim Craig said, 'I fully admit to making life difficult for Big Jock and I'm sure he found me a bit awkward. Right from the start, Jock could never get his head round the fact I had a job outside football. I was a qualified dentist – surely the only one who ever won a European Cup medal! – and he wasn't prepared to accept that I could concentrate 100 per cent on being a footballer while I had outside interests. I told him many times that I could indeed do both jobs equally well, but he was never convinced. It would be fair to say we had a few run-ins during our time together.

'Don't get me wrong, Big Jock was a very talented man, an exceptional, groundbreaking manager. But football to him was everything and if you weren't eating, drinking, sleeping football too, he believed there was something wrong with you. You got the impression you should park your brain at the door outside Celtic Park and pick it up on your way home. I had other interests, but I would defy anyone to say I wasn't committed to the Celtic cause. When I pulled on that green-and-white shirt, I was as ready to go as anyone. Jock and I had a problem, though, because of our differing attitudes. I'll admit I could be deliberately obstinate. I had an inquisitive mind – still do, I hope – and I would ask questions. This was something that was new to Big Jock and something he didn't embrace with any enthusiasm, believe me.

'I was the guy who would query this, that and the next thing while most of my colleagues bit their tongues and kept quiet. He would point to the tactics board and go through a lengthy routine. Some of us took it in and others didn't. How could you tell Jimmy Johnstone how to play? I would ask a few questions and make a point or two and our manager plainly didn't welcome such intrusions. He was a meticulous planner, probably the first of his kind. He would go through our line-up and tell us exactly what he expected us to do. He rarely dwelt on the opposition. He concentrated mainly on us and how we should perform. I thought it was only right and proper that I should ask a question or two just to clear up any possible misunderstanding. If Plan A wasn't working, what was Plan B? Jock didn't like that.

'He was a big fan of the master–servant relationship and, naturally, I didn't agree with that mode of thinking. For a start, I was halfway through my dental studies and that's a job where, quite literally, you have to think on your feet. You have to make decisions very quickly. You are very much your own man. So, I have to admit, when I turned up at Celtic Park and found I didn't have a mind of my own, it was extremely difficult to accept. Big Jock would wave you away with that big left hand of his. "Och, just do as you're told," he would say. OK, he was the boss, but that didn't mean I had to touch my forelock every time I spoke to him. In fact, I was never a massive admirer of authority figures. I'm afraid that still applies!'

One player who did blow his top at the Celtic manager and lived to tell the tale was Harry Hood. He remembered an incident at the end of a game, saying, 'I still don't know what came over me that day. I just lost it completely when Jock accused me of refusing to pass the ball to George Connelly on one occasion. Normally, things like that can sweep over you and the boss can make another observation to another player. I completely respected Jock Stein and he knew that. However, in an instant, I flared up and that, as everyone would no doubt tell you, was hardly my style. I would always like to think of myself as a level-headed individual who could take on board some criticism. I wasn't having this, though. I stood up and yelled, "How dare you accuse me of that! I wouldn't do such a thing. If I thought George was in a better position, then I would have passed the ball to him." And so it continued for another minute or so. Jock just looked at me and said nothing.

'I went to have a shower and Roy Aitken said to me, "Are you all right, Harry?" I was still shaking when I answered, "Yes, of course I am. Why?" Roy just laughed: "Because you're still wearing your kit!" In all the commotion, I had stormed off and forgotten to get stripped. It was the one and only time I raged at Jock Stein.'

Hood, though, was convinced that Stein had tried to get his own back before a Scottish Cup tie in 1971. 'We had drawn 1–1 with Dunfermline in the first game at our place and Jock was fizzing. We were due to face them in the replay four days later at East End Park, never the easiest of venues to visit. I had a pub at the time and Jock must have known his future son-in-law was having his stag night at my place 24 hours before the game in Fife. Obviously, it was impossible for anyone to reschedule and we had planned for a blank midweek. The replay put paid to that. I stayed until closing-up time about 2 a.m. and cleared the place before going home. I think I had one pint of lager all night. Jock might just have thought I was going to have a few and join in the revelries. No chance.

'Now, Jock rarely swore, so when he did utter an oath it made an impact and had the desired effect. As we were getting ready at East End Park, the manager opened up. "You bastards have got us into this mess!" he bellowed. "Now get us out of it! You were all hopeless on Saturday, the worst ever. Get out there and get the job done." I was sitting among the rest of the players when I was aware there was a giant shadow cast over me. I looked up and realised Jock was directing most of his diatribe in my direction. So I was the "bastard" who had got us into this mess? The only thing to do was go out there, perform and make sure Celtic's name was in the hat for the next round's draw.

'It was a very tough game as I recall and Jock might have wondered where all my stamina was coming from. On that score, he had nothing to worry about. I would never indulge a day, or even a couple of days, before a game. Thankfully, I got the only goal of the game and, equally satisfying, I scored a penalty kick in the 2–1 final replay win over Rangers later in the season.

'At the end of the East End Park encounter, Jock eyed me suspiciously as I came into the dressing-room. I'm sure I detected a slight smile. Mind you, it could have been wind!'

However, Stein did have the pleasure of a verbal blast at Hood some time later. 'We were playing Cowdenbeath,' said Hood. 'We were four goals up inside twenty minutes or so and were cruising. It was only a month after our win over Dunfermline and the manager saw his opening. "How dare you play like that?" came the roar from the touchline. OK, we were knocking the ball about at a rather leisurely pace, but, of course, the job was done. Jock, though, was on his high horse. "The punters want entertained. There's still over an hour to play and they've paid good money to watch you. Get your finger out." Eventually, we won 5–1 and I scored two goals. Jock was still growling on the team bus all the way back from Fife.'

Like Hood, Tommy Callaghan, bought from Dunfermline in 1968, was part of the revolution at Celtic. He remembered, 'I used to get ribbed by some of the Lisbon Lions, especially Bobby Lennox. "Where's your European Cup medal, Tommy?" I was asked on more than one occasion. I would always reply, "Just remember that Jock Stein bought me to *strengthen* this squad." That would shut them up. For a second or two!'

As the likes of Callaghan and Hood were brought in, Davie Hay was another who believed that the Lions still had an important part to play. He said, 'I think the young guys coming through would have actually benefited from a year or so mingling with and learning from those players in the first team. There was never any animosity between the experienced guys and the blokes like myself, Kenny, Lou or George coming through. It was never a "them-against-us" situation. Those guys were far too professional. So I don't think it would have done us any harm at all to have had some of them around. We all knew Yogi didn't want to go. People used to talk about his "horrendous" miss against Feyenoord. I didn't see the entire film of the game until years afterwards. I don't blame Yogi one bit. Yes, he might have scored, but give some credit to their keeper. He was pretty quick getting off his line to spread himself and block the shot. It's ridiculous to blame Yogi for that defeat. With the exception of Evan Williams, we were all to blame.'

Tommy Gemmell was in no rush, either, to turn his back on Celtic. 'Big Jock knew I didn't want to leave, even after I asked to go when I was dropped for the 1969 League Cup final against St Johnstone. He was well aware of my feelings for the club and my affection for the support. I was on the transfer list for two years! On a weekly basis, I would ask Jock if there had been any enquiries. He would just wave his big left paw at me and say, "Naw, naw, I'll let you know when there is."

'Actually, I knew Barcelona wanted to sign me. They were managed by an Englishman called Vic Buckingham at the time and he definitely wanted me to go to Barça. I could never reveal this to Jock because that would have meant that I would have been tapped and, of course, that was illegal. So, I had to stay mum and just accept getting waved away every week: "Naw, naw, I'll keep you informed."

'Then, when Jock thought the time was right, I was out the door. My argument was never about money, but Nottingham Forest had a £40,000 bid accepted and I was told to talk to them. After only a couple of minutes, they had made me an offer that trebled my basic wage of £65 and, on top of that, there was a bonus of £40 per point, appearance money and extra cash for being an international. I still didn't want to go!'

Stein, without doubt, would have raged long and loud if he ever thought one of his players had been tapped, but the Celtic manager wasn't beyond such skulduggery himself. Tommy Callaghan recalled, 'I was in the Dunfermline reserves at the time a local reporter got in touch. He told me Jock Stein wanted to sign me for Celtic. I couldn't believe it. Big Jock, of course, had been my manager at East End Park, so he had a fair idea what I could do. Excited? You bet! I may have been born in Fife, but I was a massive Celtic fan. A guy called Owen Moran used to be in charge of the Cowdenbeath Celtic Supporters Club and if I wasn't playing football the same day he would make sure I would get a place on the bus travelling through to Glasgow.

'So it was brilliant to believe Celtic were interested in actually signing me. The pressman asked me to come to his house late on a Friday night as he was expecting a phone call. It was all cloak-and-dagger stuff because, essentially, I was talking to one club while I was still under contract with another. That could have led to all sorts of ramifications. George Farm was our manager at the time and he and I rarely saw eye to eye. He was a real gruff character and I could imagine his reaction if he thought Celtic were making direct contact with one of his players. Sure enough, on the night, a call came through from Jock Stein.

'He told me, "I want you for Celtic. I've made a £30,000 bid, but Dunfermline are asking for £5,000 more. We'll need to wait and see." Now, I realise in this day and age that £5,000 is mere pocket money for some players, but back in 1968 it was a lot of money. In fact, £35,000 would have made me Jock Stein's record signing for Celtic at the time. Jock told me to check with George Farm to see if there was anyone interested in me. So, every morning, without fail, I would knock on the manager's door, wait to be told to enter and ask if there were any bids for me. I was out of the first team at the time, so obviously I was expendable, but I also knew our boss could be awkward. "No, nothing doing," I would be told. This went on for a few days until Farm blew up. "I've had enough of this," he said. "We'll sort this out." Shortly afterwards, I was on my way to Celtic and, yes, Dunfermline got their extra £5,000, so everyone was happy.'

Eventually, in 1976, Callaghan too would head for the exit. Despite the infamous run-in with Stein before the Leeds game, he said, 'It was absolutely wonderful playing for the club. I scored on my debut, a 4–0 win over Partick Thistle, and I picked up so many honours, including six league championship medals. I shared a dressing-room at Dunfermline for a few years with some excellent players and they never got anywhere near a league badge. Of course I was sad to go. But Jock pulled me aside one day and told me I should talk to Clydebank. I had to be philosophical.

When your time's up, that's it. Your tea's oot, as they say. I got in my car and headed for the Bankies' ground at Kilbowie. It was only when I reached Clydebank that I realised I hadn't a clue where Kilbowie was. I had never been there. I had to stop and ask a taxi driver for directions. When I got there, I thought, "What am I doing here?" It would be a bit of an understatement to say it was a culture shock.'

John Fallon, after 14 years at the club, was another player who had no desire to leave Celtic. However, he was on his way when Jock decided in February 1972 that he had served his purpose. Bertie Auld said, 'The story I heard was that John was actually given the news by a teammate after training. "I hear you're going to Motherwell," said the player. Fallon replied, "No, I'm not." After a meeting with Jock, the goalkeeper signed for the Fir Park side two days later.

'If Jock was ever hurt by having to release a player, then he hid it well. Maybe he did these things in private, but there was never a public show of emotion. Once a player was no longer considered good enough for Celtic, it was time to move on. Jock was never slow to inform you there were other players out there who could come in and do your job. Jock always insisted, "A manager is only as happy as his unhappiest player." So the boss would simply eliminate his unhappiest player.'

Kenny Dalglish took centre stage at the start of the 1971–72 campaign and played against Rangers three times in the opening weeks, Ibrox hosting the trio of confrontations because Celtic Park was still being rebuilt. He may have been a bit of a Rangers fan as a kid, but that didn't prevent a ruthless Dalglish putting his former favourites to the sword. He scored in each match. There were two League Cup triumphs (2–0 and 3–0) and a 3–2 victory in the league.

Tommy Gemmell had an interesting revelation about the new Bhoy wonder. He recalled, 'I had heard Kenny was about to get a free transfer in the summer. Back then, he wasn't anything like the player he would become, that's for sure. However, at the end of that season, Celtic were invited to play a testimonial match for a Kilmarnock player, Frank Beattie, at Rugby Park. Kenny had alternated between midfield and up front without, to be honest, being any great shakes. Jock played him as a striker against Killie and I think he scored five goals as we won 6–2. Jock saw him in a different light that night. Who knows what might have happened if Kenny hadn't performed so well at Rugby Park?'

Dalglish was also on the scoresheet in the final of the League Cup on 23 October 1971 but was as bewildered as the rest of his teammates to be on the receiving end of a shocker of seismic proportions against newly promoted Partick Thistle. It was one of the craziest outcomes of a game in Celtic's history, a 4–1 defeat, with 62,740 fans witnessing an impossibility become reality.

Harry Hood still groans at the memory. 'We were 4–0 down at half-time and we just could not quite take in what was happening all around us. By the time we reached the dressing-room at the interval, it would be accurate to say we were stunned. As the scoreline dawned on us, though, I can tell you this – we still believed we could beat them. Sounds daft now, I suppose, but that was the genuine belief. I remember Jock Stein being quite calm. "If they can score four against us in forty-five minutes, we can score five against them in forty-five minutes," he reasoned. By the time we went out for the second half, he had convinced us we would win. "Score a goal in the next five minutes and you'll be on your way," we were assured by our manager.'

The first period is better forgotten. Celtic were already without the injured Billy McNeill, with George Connelly taking over at centre-half, the main defensive position, in which he was never completely comfortable. Jimmy Johnstone took a sore one from Ronnie Glavin, a future Celtic teammate, early on and had to go off, with Jim Craig, the only allowed substitute, coming on in his place. It was an eventful early period. Remarkably, Thistle mustered four shots at Evan Williams – and all four eluded the green-jerseyed keeper.

First, Alex Rae beat him with an effort from the edge of the box that flew high into the net. No one seemed unduly worried because Celtic had gained a reputation for being quite generous in gifting opponents a goal's head start. Bobby Lawrie cut inside from the left to belt a screamer low past Williams for the second. Still, there was no anxiety on the terracings or, apparently, on the pitch. Denis McQuade smuggled in number three from almost under the crossbar, with the Celtic defence doing a fair impression of a display at Madame Tussauds. Frowns all round, except, of course, from the Firhill contingent, whose wildest dreams were heading for orbit. With Celtic in total disarray, Williams and his colleagues froze when a right-wing corner kick dropped into the penalty area and Jimmy Bone, who couldn't have been afforded more space if he had been rattling a big bell and yelling, 'Unclean . . . unclean,' just about walked the ball into the net.

Hood added, 'A friend of mine told me later he couldn't make it to the game and was tuning in to the BBC for an update. The half-time scores around the country were coming up on the old teleprinter and Frank Bough spluttered when the news came through from Hampden. My pal swears the presenter said, "Celtic 0, Partick Thistle 4. No, that's an obvious mistake. We'll get the correct scoreline for you in a moment."

Minutes later, Bough added, "That is the right half-time score in the Scottish League Cup final. I'll give it to you again: Celtic 0, Partick Thistle 4. That's incredible." If he didn't know what was going on, I can assure everyone the players in the Celtic dressing-room didn't have much of a clue, either.'

Williams recalled, 'I got the bulk of the blame for that defeat and I would be the first to hold up my hands if I thought it was solely down to me. I've watched film of that game and I don't accept it was all my fault. Certainly, it was a dreadful 45 minutes for everyone. We just could not get going and I don't mean to take anything away from our opponents by saying that. As Harry points out, every last Celtic player left the dressing-room at half-time utterly convinced we could turn things around. We had to accept we had been involved in a freakish performance in that opening 45 minutes and we would play like the real Celtic in the second period.

'As I recall, we peppered their goal right from the off and there was a typical Bobby Murdoch drive that looked like heading for the top corner. It just kept rising, though, and missed the target by inches. If that had gone in, who knows? Kenny Dalglish eventually scored when Alan Rough pushed out a Lou Macari shot, but we had left ourselves with too much to do. It was Thistle's day.'

Gemmell echoed Williams' words: 'I wouldn't want to take any credit away from Thistle, but we were an absolute shambles that day. Someone told me not that long ago that he had watched the entire 90 minutes again, which must have been painful because he was a big Celtic fan. He assured me our opponents had five shots on target that afternoon and we had more than twenty. They only count, though, if they hit the net.

'Jock immediately went out and bought a new goalkeeper, Denis Connaghan from St Mirren. Dixie Deans, an out-and-out striker, was also brought in from Motherwell. We played Thistle a month later in a league game at their place and gubbed them 5–1 just to let them know what it felt like!'

Stein set the move for Connaghan in motion only hours after the Thistle debacle. The keeper recalled, 'I had been linked with Celtic a couple of times and I was told that Saturday night that Jock wanted to sign me. I thought, "I've heard it all before." Sure enough, though, on Monday morning he telephoned me, we met at Love Street and the deal was struck. Of course, I was delighted at the time, but it was just a pity that my signing for the club arose from a cup final defeat.

'It was well known that Jock hated goalkeepers. He used to say to me, "When I die, Denis, I want to come back as a Celtic goalkeeper. It's the easiest job on earth." I suppose it was true. Celtic attacked in every game, but in that sort of situation your concentration had to be that bit sharper.'

The Scottish Cup final against Hibs in May, at the scene of the earlier crime, was a lot more pleasurable, a magnificent 6–1 triumph over an excellent Easter Road side that paraded six internationals in Jim Herriot, John Brownlie, Erich Schaedler, John Blackley, Arthur Duncan and skipper Pat Stanton, who would later join Celtic, but whose influence, sadly, would be cut short through injury. Without being cruel, Partick Thistle might have been perceived as mongrels in the earlier cup final, but Hibs had earned the right to be termed pedigrees.

Williams, after the October disaster, had won his way back into Stein's favour and into goal. The goalkeeper recalled, 'We had to banish the memory of that Thistle defeat and a game against Hibs was the ideal platform. Big Billy McNeill side-footed the opening goal past Jim Herriot after connecting with a long diagonal left-wing free kick.'

Incidentally, this was the same keeper beyond whom McNeill had sent a pulverising header to kick off the Celtic cavalcade seven years earlier. Alan Gordon knocked in a scrappy equaliser, but the day belonged to Celtic, and Deans claimed a memorable hat-trick, with Macari adding two.

It had been an interesting 17 days in Deans' career. His new club had reached the European Cup semi-final to face old rivals Inter Milan. Following a goalless draw in the first leg at the San Siro, Celtic were favourites to complete the job in Glasgow and reach a third final in five years in football's most prestigious tournament. The second tussle ended goalless, too, after extra time and the tie was decided on penalty kicks. Deans, who had replaced Dalglish during the game, elected to take the first. Unfortunately, he sent his shot flying over the bar and the Italians fired all five of their efforts beyond Williams to advance 5–4. They lost 2–0 to Ajax in the final.

However, there were celebrations for the seventh successive season in the league championship when Celtic took pole position with sixty points, ten clear of Aberdeen. Rangers were third, sixteen points adrift. The Ibrox men, after losing three times inside a month at the start of the campaign, succumbed again in the January fixture. The unlikely match-winner for Celtic was left-back Jim Brogan, who headed in the second goal in the last minute. Johnstone had claimed the opener.

The 1972–73 pursuit of the flag went right to the last game. Celtic, with a vastly superior goal average over Rangers, visited Easter Road to take on a Hibs team that had beaten them 2–1 in the League Cup final earlier in the season. On that occasion, Dalglish had scored for Celtic, but Pat Stanton and Jimmy O'Rourke had blasted two behind Williams. That game racked up an unwanted hat-trick: three straight defeats in three League Cup finals. However, that loss would pale into insignificance if the title was claimed for the eighth consecutive year. Stein's side were on 55 points and the Ibrox men on 54, so a draw in the capital would see Celtic take the championship irrespective of what their old foes achieved against East Fife in Glasgow.

Stein was at his bombastic best before the Edinburgh kick-off. 'We're not interested in playing for a point,' he said. 'That's not our style. I have complete belief in these players and we are looking for a victory. I'm sure we'll get it.' His players didn't let him down, Deans hitting two and Dalglish getting one in a 3–0 romp. Rangers beat East Fife 2–0 with goals from Cutty Young and Alfie Conn, who would later cause something of a stir by signing for Celtic. 'Who could say no to Jock Stein?' he queried reasonably at the time of his £65,000 transfer from Spurs in 1977.

Conn was on target for Rangers when they beat Celtic 3–2 in the 1973 Scottish Cup final. Dalglish thumped Stein's men ahead after a neat flick from Deans, but the Ibrox side were gifted a sloppy equaliser when Alex MacDonald was allowed too much time on the left wing before picking out Derek Parlane smack in front of goal. Even then, it looked as though Ally Hunter, yet another goalkeeper brought to the club by Stein, could have done better dealing with a powder-puff header, but it eluded him and it was 1–1. Conn then showed a flash of individual brilliance in the second half when he carried the ball about 30 yards before flicking it past the out-rushing Hunter. Connelly netted with a penalty kick after John Greig had punched a Deans shot off the line. In those days, it wasn't an automatic red card for the offence, so the Ibrox contingent's complement remained at 11. With the clock ticking down, Rangers got a massive break. Derek Johnstone headed a Tommy McLean free kick low past Hunter, again looking slow to react to the danger. The ball thudded against the inside of the right-hand post, ran along the line and eluded everyone until it found the unmarked Tom Forsyth at the back post. Not a known goal-scorer, the defender looked alarmed when he was presented with the opportunity. He stabbed at the ball and seemed to put his boot over it before having another go. This time he made contact and the ball trickled over the line. Not a brilliant finish, then, but it was sufficient to take the silverware to Ibrox.

'That was another of those games where you feel like asking, "Wait, can we start all over again, please?"' said Davie Hay. '"We won't make the same mistakes." Unfortunately, football doesn't work like that. If you make an error, you are normally punished and there are no second chances. I thought we were better than Rangers that day, but you can't argue with the facts. They scored three, we scored two, and they won the trophy.'

The European adventure had hardly gained momentum when Celtic were knocked out by the Hungarians of Újpest Dózsa in the second round. Celtic lost 2–4 on aggregate after being thrashed 3–0 away in the second leg.

Jimmy Johnstone scored the only goal as Celtic claimed the first Old Firm scalp of the 1973–74 campaign, and Bobby Lennox staged an action replay when Rangers came to Parkhead for the January fixture. The Ibrox side and Hibs were always there or thereabouts as Celtic targeted a world record of nine league titles on the trot. Jock Stein had freshened up the side, but the season also saw the sad exit of the truly wonderful Bobby Murdoch, given a free transfer at the end of an awesome fourteen years at the club that saw him win eight league championships, four Scottish Cups, five League Cups and, of course, a European Cup medal. He had made his debut against Hearts, scoring in a 3–1 win six days before his eighteenth birthday. He played 484 games for the club he adored all the way through childhood and into adulthood. Murdoch also racked up 105 goals, most of them unforgettable. It's difficult to recall him ever netting a tap-in. He joined Middlesbrough exactly a month after his 29th birthday on a free transfer. Murdoch was the eighth Lisbon Lion to move from the club, leaving Billy McNeill, Jimmy Johnstone and Bobby Lennox to carry on the good work.

Bertie Auld said, 'Bobby Murdoch was such a lovely guy. Speaking personally, he just left me with so many happy and treasured memories. He was an exceptional talent and everyone recognised that apart from one man: himself. He was just so down to earth.

'Do you know he had the nickname "Chopper" and Big Jock hated it? He earned that moniker during the Battle of the River Plate, our third game against Racing Club in Uruguay. Bobby had had enough of being spat on and kicked and he just lost it with about 20 minutes or so to go. He had seen his wee pal Jinky sent off and he had had enough of injustice. Bobby could look after himself and any Argentine who was daft enough to go near him late in the game was decked. The name "Chopper" was born in that Montevideo madhouse. When we talked about "Chopper" in the dressing-room, Big Jock would shout, "Don't call him that!" So, naturally, the nickname stuck.'

Stevie Murray, bought for £50,000 from Aberdeen, was in the position normally occupied by Murdoch when the league season kicked off with a 3–2 win over Dunfermline at East End Park. Whereas Murdoch made the ball do all the work, the latest acquisition was a runner who liked to come forward with the ball at his feet. It was an identical situation with Tommy Callaghan, who would be the first to admit he was never in Auld's class as a passer of the ball but who had an engine that could see him run from one penalty box to another all day, apparently without stopping for a breather.

Billy McNeill observed, 'I believe Jock thought a lot of teams had worked out how we played and he wanted to change things. He was eager to give them something else to think about. That's why the likes of Tommy Callaghan and Stevie Murray came into his thought process. This was a different Celtic team from the one the supporters were used to.'

The manager also introduced a teenager named Brian McLaughlin, a smooth running and passing midfielder, who possessed a combination of elegance and awareness startling in one so young. He played in the opening five League Cup ties of the 1973–74 campaign. He was paraded in the opening league day success at Dunfermline, but tragedy struck only a month into the season. McLaughlin was left horribly damaged after a coarse and brutal challenge by Clyde defender Willie McVie. Apart from one brief substitute's appearance in the second-last league game, with the title already won, that was the end of the youngster's season. By and large, it also put a stop to what should have been one of the brightest of careers at Celtic. McLaughlin never recovered properly from his cruciate ligament injury.

Hay recalled, 'Jock was distraught. He believed that Brian could have been the pick of all his young players. One look at Brian and you immediately understood why the manager had such high hopes. I had him at Motherwell for a spell when I was manager. After Celtic, he had gone to Sligo Rovers as part of his rehabilitation. But it was all over for him at Celtic; he wouldn't be able to perform at that level again. He went to Ayr United before coming to Motherwell. Sadly, he wasn't the same player. If he was bitter at the way things turned out for him, I never detected it.'

George Connelly added, 'Jock told me Brian would have been better than any of us if it hadn't been for that injury. I played that day against Clyde and once again it demonstrated just how fickle football can be. One bad tackle and that's your career over. As I recall, we won 5–0 in a canter, so there was no need for wild tackles flying around.'

Gemmell thought so much of the player he tried to sign him from Celtic in 1977 during his managerial stint at Dundee. He recalled, 'I was looking for a playmaker in the middle of the park and I thought Brian could still do a job for us. I was aware of his injury problems, but I was willing to take a chance. I put a call in to Big Jock. He wasn't available, but I got his assistant Davie McParland. I asked him, "Is there any chance of doing some business with Brian McLaughlin?" Davie replied, "I'll have a word with Jock. Can you phone back in the morning?" Now, you might have thought Jock would have done a former player, a Lisbon Lion, a wee favour. You would be wrong. I duly got back in touch early the next day. Imagine my surprise when I was informed McLaughlin had just signed for Ayr United!'

Going into his second full season, Danny McGrain, an ever-reliable performer, had made the right-back berth his own. His admiration for Jock Stein was obvious. 'I could never call our manager anything else other than Mr Stein,' recalled the player who would earn genuine world-class status. 'Let's face it, he deserved the utmost respect for his achievements in the game. Managing the club to success in Lisbon was simply awesome. He deserved to be held in the highest esteem, as far as I was concerned. I was 17 years old when I joined and could never think of calling him Jock. That may have been acceptable for the older players, but not for me. I remember Sean Fallon turning up at our home in Drumchapel to sign me. I immediately called him Mr Fallon. However, he told me to call him Sean, as everyone else did. Later on in my career, I would be an experienced player in my 30s and in the Scottish international set-up when Mr Stein was the manager and I still gave him his full title. Not once did he tell me to call him Jock.

'I was extremely fortunate to start my career with a manager such as Mr Stein around. Simply put, he was a winner and he wanted all his players to be winners, too. In fact, I was fairly lucky with all three of my Celtic bosses, because Billy McNeill and Davie Hay had the same outlook as Mr Stein. I had played alongside both, of course, and I called them by their Christian names, but that was not because of a lack of respect. It would have been very difficult to call them Mr McNeill and Mr Hay after calling them Billy and Davie throughout my playing career. I thought they were both excellent managers and I was also fortunate to be involved in so many memorable games. I don't have too many regrets, but one would be the lack of success in Europe during my time. I had arrived at a club that had conquered Europe, would reach another European Cup final three years later and always seemed to be there or thereabouts in these competitions.

'We reached the European Cup semi-final in 1974 before being kicked off the park by Atlético Madrid. In the main, though, we struggled to get past the quarter-final stages. I recall we were 2–0 up on Real Madrid in 1980 before we went down 3–0 at the Bernabéu. We got a good goalless draw with Brian Clough's Nottingham Forest in the UEFA Cup four years later but lost 2–1 in Glasgow. I don't think we did enough, though, in Europe back then. Not by Celtic's standards, anyway.'

As McGrain settled into the right-hand side of the defence, Roddie MacDonald, unfussy on the deck and excellent in the air, was given a few outings at centre-half. Pat McCluskey, a solidly built character, was being moved around the back four, although he was never played in the main central defensive position where his lack of inches would undoubtedly have created a problem in a team used to the aerial command of McNeill.

Dixie Deans wasn't particularly tall, but he had a wonderful leap and uncanny anticipation when he attacked the ball in the air. Former Scotland keeper Alan Rough would surely testify to his overall ability; Deans stuck six past him in a 7–0 rout of Partick Thistle at Parkhead on the team's unstoppable march towards title number nine. He also collected four in a 6–0 drubbing of Falkirk. Deans, like Jimmy Johnstone, was a free spirit whom Stein sometimes failed to understand. This colourful personality possibly didn't do anything to aid his cause in manager–player relations when he turned up one morning for training wearing a tuxedo, having come straight from a pal's wedding. He also enjoyed a cigarette or two and, while other players refrained from smoking in front of their manager, Deans would merrily puff away with the boss in attendance. 'Maybe I was the only one man enough to do it,' said Deans, adding, 'or mad enough.'

Looking back, Tommy Gemmell said, 'I'm sure Big Jock thought alcohol was the elixir of the Devil. He was teetotal and couldn't work out why anyone would take a drink. If we were on an away trip in Europe, down at Seamill or on tour, he would keep a wary eye on all the players. Some, of course, might have a vodka and Coke or a Bacardi and Coke. Jock knew full well what some of us were up to. He would come over, look at your glass and say, "I'm thirsty, let's have a sip of your drink." Then he would put it to his lips. Sometimes you got caught, sometimes you were fly enough to just have a Coke when you knew he was in the vicinity.

'Don't get me wrong. We were no angels and there were a few at Celtic who liked a drink, including me. We could have a bevvy on a Saturday night knowing we had the following day off. But if there was a game on Wednesday, that would be it. I never drank after Wednesday when we were playing on a Saturday. We all trained hard on Thursday and Friday, and by the time the game came around we were well up for it.

'The guys who really took the mickey out of Jock were the young blokes. He would bring a few of them down to Seamill when we were preparing for big games. Reasonably, he thought the experience would do them no harm. He would say to the first-team squad, "Look, I want you to set an example to these young lads. Watch what you're doing with alcohol." So, we would all be on our best behaviour and we would look over at some of the Quality Street Gang. Davie Hay and George Connelly were among them. We would spot George fumbling for something under the table and then coming up with a full glass. It certainly wasn't lemonade. Big Jock was too busy patrolling around and watching us to clock what the youngsters were getting up to.'

'Guilty as charged, m'lud,' laughed Hay. 'We would bring a couple of half-bottles of gin or vodka and then top them up with Coke or something when we sat around later in the evening. It wasn't a bevvy session or anything like that, but there was a wee bit of devilment in the youngsters back then. Of course, we realised Big Jock absolutely abhorred alcohol and we knew what we were doing. We did it for a laugh. God only knows what would have happened if we had been rumbled. It doesn't bear thinking about.

'Later on, I realised the lengths to which Jock would go to keep tabs on his players after their day's stint at the park was over. Of course, stories of Jinky and bevvy are legendary. You could say he liked to unwind after training. He used to go to a pub called Noggins – no longer there – in Uddingston and have a couple of drinks with some old mates. Then the telephone in the bar would ring.

'The barman would answer and shout, "Jimmy, that's your taxi."

'Jinky would pick up the receiver. "I never ordered a taxi," he would say.

'Then on would come the unmistakable tones of Big Jock. "Get out of there and get up the road!" he would growl.

'Jinky would look around the bar and wonder who was a spy for the boss. He never quite worked it out, but, unluckily for him, Celtic had a part-time scout who lived in a flat directly opposite Noggins. He had been instructed by Jock to keep an eye on the pub and if he saw Jinky he was to phone him immediately.'

Bertie Auld said, 'You might have thought with his mining background Big Jock would have fancied a foaming pint of ale after a day's hard graft down the pit. But I never once saw him take a drop of alcohol. The champagne corks could fly all over our dressing-room after an important victory, but Big Jock refused to indulge.

'I remember talking to him one day when we were travelling to an away game. "If we win with a couple of goals to spare, will you have a drink with us afterwards?" I queried, rather mischievously. Jock thought about it and surprised me when he answered, "OK, you're on – if you win by three."

'We duly went out and achieved the target set by our manager. On the way home, I asked Jock if he was coming for a drink.

'Again, he remained silent for a moment before replying, "Would you think any more of me if I went for a drink?"

'I answered, "I couldn't think any more of you than I do just now, Boss."

'He never went for that drink.'

Title number nine was in Celtic's sights when they travelled to meet Hibs only ten months after securing the eighth flag at the same venue. The club went into the match in the realisation that a win would put them five points clear of their opponents (who were also their main challengers for the title) and, at the same time, deal them a crippling blow. There was still a bit of the campaign to go, but the capital confrontation would be crucial to the destination of the flag.

The game was barely two minutes old when Deans stabbed the ball past Jim McArthur for the opener. Arthur Duncan equalised, but Dalglish restored the advantage after a neat piece of interplay on the edge of the box. Hibs came back defiantly once again and Jim O'Rourke beat Ally Hunter for the leveller. Paul Wilson, another to step off the conveyor belt, stuck number three past McArthur and it was all over when Deans, with that uncanny timing in the air, floated a header in for the fourth. Celtic would never lose top spot as they made history at the end of another marvellous campaign. Stein's machine notched up fifty-three points, four more than Hibs and five ahead of third-placed Rangers.

Dundee United arrived at Hampden for the 1974 Scottish Cup final in May wondering if they could follow the example of Dundee in the League Cup final earlier in the season and stage a Tayside double. The referee on this occasion was Willie Black of Glasgow and not the dreaded Bobby Davidson of Airdrie. Unhindered, Celtic won 3–0 in a canter. Hood nodded the first past Sandy Davie, Murray rifled in a second and, after the interval, Deans stroked in number three. In the vanquished Tannadice rearguard that day was a defender named Walter Smith, who would, of course, have some memorable jousts with Celtic in years to come during his two spells as manager of Rangers.

The European Cup journey ended in the most controversial and explosive of circumstances when Celtic, after dismissing Finland's TPS Turku 9–1, Denmark's Vejle 1–0 and Switzerland's Basel 6–5, faced Atlético Madrid (clearly not Danny McGrain's favourite team) in the semi-final. 'The goalless game in Glasgow was an absolute disgrace, an affront to the sport,' recalled Hay. 'The Spaniards didn't come to our place to even attempt to play football. They had three players sent off and another pile booked and it was just bedlam. Do you know we later discovered their manager had ordered his players not to shave for a week before the game so they would look more menacing?

'Big Jock had them sussed even before kick-off. He told us to expect to take some punishment and he warned us not to retaliate. Possibly it would have been better if we had let them know early in the game we could sort them out and weren't going to be used as punchbags. There were plenty of blokes in that Celtic team who could take care of themselves, believe me. But Atlético knew they were getting away with it and they just kept kicking us. They were obviously prepared to go to any length to get a good result at our place. The assaults on Jinky that night were obscene. Atlético would be thrown out of the tournament today if they acted like that.'

The Spaniards – managed by Argentine Juan Lorenzo, who had been his nation's manager during the infamous 1966 World Cup quarter-final against England at Wembley – had Ayala, Diaz and Quique sent off by an overworked and harassed match official who still found the time to book another seven of the thirteen players who were used by the Madrid side that night.

'Even at the end, they still wanted to kick us, particularly Jinky,' added Hay. 'It wasn't enough they had booted him up and down the park for 90 minutes, they now wanted to batter him in the tunnel. I lost it completely. I got a hold of one of them and he squealed. Retribution, I think it's called. Thankfully, the TV cameras didn't follow us down the tunnel or some of us might have been facing a custodial sentence! Did they seriously believe they would get away with it? What were we, a bunch of wimps? The police had to break up the fracas.'

Celtic rejected any thoughts of an official protest about the anti-football behaviour of their opponents, but neutral observers urged Europe's ruling soccer body to take action. The Spaniards received a slap on the wrist, a paltry fine and a tame warning.

Somehow, Atlético's support had become convinced that it was Celtic who had been the villains in Glasgow. The players got a hostile reception as soon as they touched down in Madrid and the intimidation continued until they got back on the plane to go home. Hay said, 'We were threatened with all sorts of violence and we didn't do a lot of sightseeing in Madrid, as I recall.

'Wee Jinky got a fright one night when he took a phone call in the hotel room he shared with Bobby Lennox. Apparently, the Wee Man's face went chalk white as he put down the phone. "Bobby, they're gonnae kill me! They're gonnae shoot me!" he cried. Someone had managed to get a direct line to Jinky's room to threaten him. I knew the Wee Man better than most and one thing he wasn't was a coward. He was never slow to stand up for himself. This was different, though. Some lowlife had told him he was going to be shot dead. Jinky went to see Big Jock to tell him about the threat. Jock said, "Ach, I received the same message about half an hour ago as well. They're going to shoot me too. You're the lucky one. At least, you can run about out there. I'm a sitting target!"

'We lost 2–0 and were happy to see the back of Atlético Madrid.'

There is, however, a happy ending to this sordid and sorry chapter. Atlético played Bayern Munich in the final in Brussels. They were leading 1–0 and precisely one minute away from being crowned European champions when, at last, justice kicked in. Giant West German centre-back Georg Schwarzenbeck, who would never be renowned for his goal-scoring exploits, went forward to take a direct free kick about 25 yards out. He took a mighty swipe at the ball and the leather was a blur as it hurtled high into the net for the equaliser. Celtic players and fans celebrated big style as they watched on television back home. Bayern wiped the floor with Madrid in the replay, humiliating them 4–0. It proved once again that there is no place in sport for cheats.

15

A TIME OF CHANGE

Alas, Celtic's grip on the nation's crown was loosened in season 1974–75. As they say, all good things must come to an end. However, a double success in the domestic cups went some way to consoling the fans. Celtic lost nine of their thirty-four league games, including home and away setbacks against Rangers, who claimed their first championship in eleven years. The Ibrox men completed the course with fifty-six points, Hibs were second on forty-nine and Celtic were a further four points behind them.

The drama of European competition wasn't quite as extreme as the previous season and the club failed to clear the first hurdle in the European Cup, losing 3–1 on aggregate to the Greeks of Olympiacos. To paraphrase Bob Dylan, the times they were a-changin'. Thankfully, though, there was normal service in the League Cup. In the final in October, Dixie Deans put on a repeat performance of his 1972 Scottish Cup hat-trick against Hibs. The chunky frontman rattled three behind Jim McArthur, and Jimmy Johnstone, Stevie Murray and Paul Wilson added the others in a fabulous, stirring 6–3 triumph. You would have had to possess a swinging brick disguised as a heart if you hadn't felt something for opposing striker Joe Harper. He claimed a hat-trick, too, yet finished on the losing side in a cup final. There can't be too many out there who have that on their CV.

Graham Barclay won't be a name most Celtic supporters will recognise, but he became another of the one-game goalkeepers when he played in the 4–1 Scottish Cup second-round win over Clydebank. Like Willie Goldie, Dick Madden, Jack Kennedy and Bobby Wraith in the '60s, he enjoyed his 90 minutes of fame and then vanished.

Celtic had already beaten Hibs 2–0 in the first round before dismissing the Kilbowie side and then Dumbarton 2–1 in the quarter-final. It took a goal from Ronnie Glavin, the prolific midfielder who cost £60,000 from Partick Thistle, to edge past Dundee in the semi-final.

Airdrie were the Hampden opponents and were written off by many, but Stein had three words for his troops before the game: 'Remember Partick Thistle.' The words might not have meant a lot to nine of the team; Kenny Dalglish and Harry Hood were the only survivors from the 4–1 debacle of three years before. Missing, for a variety of reasons, were Evan Williams, Davie Hay, Tommy Gemmell, George Connelly, Bobby Murdoch, Jim Brogan, Jimmy Johnstone, Tommy Callaghan and Lou Macari. Substitute Jim Craig had also been erased from the picture. In were Peter Latchford, Danny McGrain, Andy Lynch, Stevie Murray, Pat McCluskey, Ronnie Glavin, Bobby Lennox, Paul Wilson and Billy McNeill, who had missed the Thistle encounter through injury. Aye, the times they were a-changin', right enough.

Celtic eased to a relatively comfortable 3–1 victory over Airdrie, with Wilson notching two fine opportunist efforts and McCluskey claiming the other with a well-driven penalty kick. The only scare came when Airdrie's self-confessed Celtic fan Kevin McCann walloped an unstoppable equaliser high past Latchford, another keeper brought to the club by Stein as the search continued for a long-term replacement for Ronnie Simpson.

Former England Under-23 goalkeeper Latchford brought consistency to the number 1 position in his six years at the club, before making way for future Celtic legend Pat Bonner. It's interesting, then, to discover that Latchford wasn't even on Stein's wanted list initially. The Celtic manager, in pursuit of a recommendation, telephoned his good friend Don Revie, who had quit as boss of Leeds United to take over the England international post. Revie had bought a young Scot named David Stewart from Ayr United during his time in charge at the Yorkshire club. Stewart hadn't been able to dislodge Scotland international David Harvey and was stuck in the reserves. 'Is he worth a chance?' asked Stein. Revie, though, pointed him in the direction of West Brom. 'Latchford's a better bet,' Stein was told.

'I wondered what I was letting myself in for when I saw Glasgow for the first time,' admitted Latchford. 'Birmingham wasn't exactly Monte Carlo, but Glasgow took my breath away. It was an absolute mess. As we drove to Celtic Park I looked out the window and saw nothing but rubbish strewn all over the place. There were black bin bags everywhere. "What kind of city is this?" I asked myself. "Do I really want to play in this environment?" I had to ask the driver if this was normal. Thankfully, he put me right. "Naw," I was told. "The bin men are on strike just now. They'll be back soon enough, don't you worry." That explained everything.'

A swift £35,000 deal was agreed between the clubs and Latchford, relieved he wouldn't be living in what might have passed for a rubbish tip, made his debut in a 2–1 home defeat against Hibs in February. He did enough, though, to keep his place for the remainder of the season and Ally Hunter and Denis Connaghan joined the growing list of custodians handed a P45 by Stein.

The Celtic fans celebrating the victory over Airdrie didn't realise they were witnessing the last performance from skipper supreme Billy McNeill. The 35-year-old icon had decided to get out at the top after serving 18 years and making 790 appearances for his one and only club. It's maybe just as well the supporters in the 75,457 crowd hadn't a clue about their captain's momentous decision. It might have taken a day or two of encores from McNeill before they dispersed. At least now a loyal servant might have some spare time to visit Fort Knox and count his medals, all twenty-three of them – and, remember, he won the sum total of zilch in his first seven years as a top-team mainstay. Not bad for a late starter. McNeill collected nine league championships, seven Scottish Cups, six League Cups and, of course, the coveted and cherished European Cup. He also picked up twenty-nine international caps, turned out nine times for the Scottish League and made five appearances as a fresh-faced youth with the Under-23s. Any regrets? 'Actually, I do have one,' answered McNeill. 'I think I quit playing a bit too early. I felt fit enough to go on for at least another year, maybe two. I discussed it with Big Jock and he thought I should go out a winner. I took his advice. On that occasion, I wish I hadn't.'

A week before the Scottish Cup triumph, Jimmy Johnstone played in the final league game of the season, a 2–1 defeat by St Johnstone in Perth. It was the last time the famous green and white hoops would adorn his 5-ft-4-in. frame and, for a born entertainer who had thrilled the world with his exclusive box of tricks, it was hardly a fitting end to a spectacular career. The winger, at the age of 30, took his skills across the Atlantic to enthral a whole new appreciative audience at San Jose Earthquakes in the North American League. He left with a medal haul similar to his skipper's: 19 in all. He won nine leagues, four Scottish Cups, five League Cups and, of course, the precious prize from Lisbon. It's impossible to mention his name without smiling at the legacy he left behind. Wee Jinky was a complete one-off.

In July 1975, Jock Stein came close to losing his life when he was involved in a horrific car crash on the A74 at Lockerbie. He was returning from holiday in Menorca with his bookmaker friend Tony Queen and their wives when his Mercedes saloon was involved in a head-on collision with a vehicle driving in the wrong direction. He was taken to hospital in Dumfries and, suffering from head and chest injuries, deemed to be in a critical condition. Stein made a remarkable recovery, however, and within a week he was in good spirits and allowed to go home. He was ordered to recuperate away from football. He was expressly forbidden by doctors to go anywhere near a dugout on match day. Stein compromised. He would turn up at Celtic Park a couple of days a week while assistant Sean Fallon took charge of team matters. Without the enormous influence of Stein, Celtic endured their first trophyless season in 11 years.

Harry Hood gave his view on the barren campaign: 'To my mind, Sean Fallon's quality was not that of a team boss. I missed the influence of our manager that year. Like Danny McGrain, I always called our manager Mr Stein. I thought he had earned that respect. Other players may have called him Big Jock or whatever, but he was always Mr Stein to me. Some of my Celtic teammates had only known two managers in their careers, Jimmy McGrory and Jock Stein. They didn't really have too much to compare Jock with. When I arrived at Celtic in 1969, I had played under about ten different managers in my two stints at Clyde and my spell at Sunderland. I was hugely impressed by the man. Maybe some of the other players took him for granted and possibly didn't appreciate what he brought to the team and the club as a whole. But I did.

'I realised very quickly that he knew what he was talking about. He was by far the best manager I ever worked with. He looked at things in detail. He would work on all sorts of things. He would erect a defensive wall and tell me how he wanted me to take the free kick. He wouldn't tolerate anyone simply floating in a high ball. He demanded that you bent the ball round the corner of the wall at a lower level for players to come in at speed and try to get a head or a foot on the ball in the most dangerous of areas between the goalkeeper and the defenders. If you varied your delivery, you were made to do it again and again. I got dog's abuse every now and again for not following his instructions down to the letter. So if you didn't want an ear-bashing, you just kept doing it his way. Then he would be satisfied. It was normally the first-team defence who were in the wall, so they could get used to facing a different type of dead-ball situation. Heaven help them if they lost a goal after practising defending such a move all week.

'Jock was in a different class. Remember, I had been at Sunderland, where I thought the club was a disgrace, an utter shambles. Players were allowed to get away with murder. To come back to Glasgow and work with a professional such as Jock Stein was an absolute privilege. Certainly I never took his expertise for granted.

'Obviously, as I say, I missed him the year he wasn't in the dugout.

Sean Fallon left me out of the first team quite a lot and I got the impression I was a bit of a fall guy. I asked to play in the reserves rather than sit on a substitutes' bench. I thought I would be of more use to the team if I was match fit when I was called upon. Sean continually overlooked me and I admit it was frustrating. Then I was amazed when he pulled me aside and told me he wanted to play me in each of the three European away ties that season. He told me I was a big-game player and he could rely on me. I wasn't good enough to play in Scottish league games, but I was OK for Europe, apparently. I wasn't up to scratch to face Ayr United, St Johnstone or Motherwell, but I could be trusted against Valur in Iceland, Boavista in Portugal and Sachsenring Zwickau in East Germany. I never took a first-team place for granted. However, I had played the bulk of the games the previous campaign with Jock Stein in charge and, suddenly, I was mainly surplus to requirements.

'As I say, though, I didn't believe I should walk straight into the first team. Your feet were always on the ground at Celtic. I remember I scored a hat-trick in a 3–1 success against Rangers in the League Cup semi-final in 1973. I was delighted with that feat. I was in the Hampden bath afterwards when trainer Neilly Mochan congratulated me on my two goals. I thought he was winding me up. I had to convince him that I had in fact netted three. That was Celtic. You get three against Rangers and get credited with two. Back in season 1970–71, I'd finished as the club's top scorer with 31 goals. I was playing in my preferred position as main striker, although I could operate in midfield or on the wing. What happened the following season? I was put back to support striker, with Kenny Dalglish coming in as the main man. No, you never took anything for granted at Celtic.

'I thought I'd done reasonably well in the six years I'd played with Jock Stein in charge. Yes, he rarely complimented a player, but, as a professional, you accepted you were doing a job of work to the best of your ability. The attitude of the manager seemed to get through to some of the fans, too. I remember I was at a supporters function and was quite pleased with the way I was playing around that time. This bloke came over to my table and I was awaiting some sort of compliment. He looked at me and simply said, "Two good feet." And with that he walked away. So, that was me summed up as a Celtic player in three words: "Two good feet." Thanks, mate.

'By the end of the season when Jock Stein was missing, I did something I completely regretted: I asked for a free transfer. I was 32 years old at the time and, to be honest, I didn't think the manager would be back. It was difficult to believe he would ever overcome his injuries to recover fully and return to the dugout. To his eternal credit, he managed to do just that. Looking back, I think I could have had another two years at Celtic with him at the helm.'

Celtic were without Stein's tactical influence and they had no one to replace Johnstone as an out-and-out right-winger. Midfielders such as Jackie McNamara and Ronnie Glavin wore the number 7 shorts but were unlikely to hurtle down the flank and belt over inviting crosses. Paul Wilson was switched from left to right on a few occasions but without any notable success. Andy Ritchie came in, but was clearly not built for speed.

Eventually, in March, Celtic parted with £90,000 to buy Johnny Doyle from Ayr United. Doyle never attempted to disguise his affection for the club, as Billy McNeill recalled: 'When I was manager, the club were given three sponsored cars to present to some lucky players. It was up to me who would get the vehicles. I had a quick word with Danny McGrain and Peter Latchford before I called a team meeting.

'"OK," I said, "we've got some cars to hand out, but, unfortunately, I've only got three. I've got a green one, a red one and a blue one. I think it is only right that, as senior members of the first team, Danny and Peter get two. Danny, what colour would you like?"

'"The green one, boss," was the expected reply.

'"Fine. Peter, what about you? Which colour?"

'"I'll have the red one, please," answered Peter.

'"Right, that leaves the blue one. I think Johnny Doyle deserves one, too."

'However, before I could go any further, there was a high-pitched yell from the player. "I don't want a blue car, Gaffer! Give it to someone else!"

'He really meant it.'

Doyle did his best for the club so close to his heart. He had breathtaking pace, fought for every morsel and gave up on nothing. But, as one fan observed, 'If you opened the gates, he would keep on running and goodness knows where he would come to a halt.'

An effort from Alex MacDonald gave Rangers a 1–0 victory in the League Cup final while a 3–2 defeat by Motherwell in the first round of the Scottish Cup at Fir Park exposed all the flaws in the faltering line-up. Celtic were two goals ahead at the interval against Well with efforts from Kenny Dalglish and Andy Lynch. In the not-too-distant past, that would have constituted game over. Not in this particular season of torment. With lively forwards Willie Pettigrew and Bobby Graham upping the pace for the home side in the second half, the Parkhead outfit, to the dismay of the travelling support, capitulated. Rangers won the new-look 36-game Premier League with 54 points. Celtic settled for 48. Teams would play each other four times in the restructured top division. Rangers, with Jock Wallace in charge, helped themselves to six of the eight points available in the Old Firm games, winning two and drawing two. Interestingly, that was their points advantage at the end of a forgettable campaign. Meanwhile, the little-known East Germans of Sachsenring Zwickau put paid to interest in the European Cup-Winners' Cup at the quarter-final stage with a 2–1 aggregate victory.

Jock Stein was back for the start of the 1976–77 season, in which Celtic achieved a league and Scottish Cup double. With a bit of luck, he could have returned to celebrate a domestic clean sweep. Aberdeen downed Celtic 2–1 in extra time in the League Cup final, with a winner from Davie Robb from just about under the crossbar. Half-hearted appeals for offside by the Celtic players were waved away by the referee. Drew Jarvie got his side's other goal and Kenny Dalglish scored for the Parkhead side. Astoundingly, Dalglish had now netted in four cup finals – against Partick Thistle, Hibs, Rangers and now Aberdeen – and Celtic had lost the lot. It may have been a relief to some Celtic followers, then, that he didn't score in the Scottish Cup final against Rangers. The honour of the only goal on a wet and windy afternoon fell to left-back Andy Lynch, who flashed a low penalty kick wide of Stewart Kennedy after Derek Johnstone was adjudged to have handled a net-bound header from Jóhannes Edvaldsson, recruited that summer from Icelandic outfit Valur Reykjavik for a bargain £20,000. Former Ranger Alfie Conn turned out that day, but this time in the hoops to become the first player to win Scottish Cup medals with both Old Firm clubs.

The league title had been won, nine points ahead of Rangers, with only four losses in the thirty-six-game programme. The Ibrox side had been beaten twice and there had been two draws in Old Firm matches. One of the games, in Govan in November, was of particular significance. Joe Craig scored a pulverising winner, but unfortunately Bobby Lennox suffered a broken leg in a collision with John Greig. 'A complete accident,' Lennox said, exonerating his Rangers rival. 'Greigy was too slow, as usual!' Roy Aitken powered in two efforts in a 2–2 draw at Ibrox later in the season. The first Old Firm encounter of the campaign was also a 2–2 stalemate, with Paul Wilson getting Celtic's goals, and there was a 1–0 triumph in January when the unfortunate Colin Jackson put through his own goal while attempting to divert a Roddie MacDonald effort.

Overall, it had been a hugely successful comeback for Stein. The season saw Dalglish and Glavin joint top scorers on 26 goals each and Craig, an £80,000 purchase from Partick Thistle, on 22. The European excursion, however, was an unexpectedly short-lived one. Celtic didn't get past the first round, going out 4–2 on aggregate to the Poles of Wisla Kraków. Gone were the days when teams knocking Celtic out of Europe were of a calibre that they could be expected at least to get to the final.

Stein, at the age of 55, might have been entering the autumn of his extraordinary managerial career, but future prospects genuinely looked rosy. He knew he had two world-class performers in Danny McGrain and Kenny Dalglish. Pat Stanton, who arrived from Hibs in a straight swap for Jackie McNamara, was a steadying influence on the relatively inexperienced MacDonald in the heart of the defence. Ronnie Glavin was scoring goals from midfield and Joe Craig, a different type of player from Joe McBride, Willie Wallace or Dixie Deans, was a powerful attack-leader. There was the artistry of the flamboyant Alfie Conn, and teenager Roy Aitken was an emerging talent, in defence and midfield. Another youngster named Tommy Burns had been introduced in selected games during the previous season and had looked the part with a sweet left foot. All that and Peter Latchford was earning a reputation for being dependable between the sticks. And, of course, there was also the influence of the ever-popular Bobby Lennox, the last of the Lisbon Lions, who was still around to do his bit in cameo roles after recovering from a broken leg. Stein seemed to be preparing to turn back the clock to the mid-'60s and launch a new Celtic on the world of football.

It didn't take long for the expectation levels to be reduced to rubble. The season hadn't even kicked off when the first setback arrived. Liverpool, looking for a replacement for Kevin Keegan who was bound for the Bundesliga in a £500,000 move to SV Hamburg, turned their focus to Dalglish. Like Davie Hay and Lou Macari before him, Dalglish, as he was entitled to do, wanted what he thought he was worth. The English champions put a £440,000 cash offer on the table, a British record transfer fee at the time. Celtic accepted and yet another of the fans' favourites was spirited out of the door. Someone on Merseyside deserves a statue erected outside Anfield or at least a massive pat on the back. They got Dalglish and made a £60,000 profit into the bargain. A couple of months before Keegan's departure to Germany and Dalglish's to England, Stein was quoted as saying, 'Keegan is a fine player, but I don't rate him any more highly than Dalglish. They are different types of player, but I believe they have equal influence.' Why, then, did Celtic not demand an identical fee for their player? It was a brilliant bit of business from Liverpool's point of view and, without a shred of doubt, Dalglish contributed even more to their club's cause than Keegan managed.

Celtic spent £60,000 of the transfer cash on Dundee United striker

Tom McAdam, who would eventually do his best work for the club at centre-half, and £25,000 on unknown Fulham midfielder John Dowie, a one-time reject from Rangers. Presumably the balance of £355,000 was placed in a high-interest account that Celtic could unlock some time in the twenty-first century. As Harry Hood had so astutely observed the previous season, the warning signs were flashing. Stanton was seriously injured in the opening goalless draw against Dundee United. Dalglish made his debut for his new club in the Charity Shield match against Manchester United at Wembley. That, too, ended scoreless. Dalglish was the focal point of attention for the TV camera crews and interviewers afterwards. Before they could ask him a question, he had one of his own. 'How did Celtic get on? Anyone know the score from Parkhead?' asked Dalglish. He was informed it had ended 0–0. He reflected for a moment and said, 'Oh well, it's a point, at least.' Then, and only then, could the live interview continue. News filtered through that the injury to Stanton was so severe that there was no hope of a comeback that season. In fact, his playing career was over.

After a mere 90 minutes, the season had already started to disintegrate. A week later, Ayr United beat Celtic 2–1 at Somerset Park and following that Motherwell left Parkhead with a 1–0 victory. Edvaldsson gave Celtic a two-goal advantage at Ibrox, but Rangers came back to win 3–2. Dowie made his debut in that encounter and produced the sort of performance that stripped away any notion that Rangers might have made an error of judgement when they let him go for nothing. A lanky 6-ft-6-in. centre-half called Ian McWilliams, from Queen's Park, was drafted in beside MacDonald. It became the double act from hell. The cloud-scraping pair were unbeatable in the air, but, unfortunately, couldn't pass the ball six yards on the ground to anyone wearing the same colour of jersey. Celtic were using sticking plasters when major surgery was required. Aberdeen won 2–1 at Pittodrie to make it four losses and one draw from the first five league games.

Celtic struggled to overcome Clydebank 1–0 and worse was to follow. McGrain, after only seven league games, damaged an ankle so severely in a 2–1 win over Hibs that his season, like Stanton's, was over, his very career threatened. Dalglish transferred, Stanton finished and McGrain sidelined. All that was required to complete the bleak picture was a sudden outbreak of bubonic plague in the vicinity of Kerrydale Street. The team was falling apart.

Remarkably, it still managed to reach the League Cup final, where Rangers were lying in wait at Hampden in October. Davie Cooper thumped one past Latchford, but Celtic battled gamely throughout and

Edvaldsson outjumped Stewart Kennedy to head in a late leveller and force extra time. Fortune continued to ignore Celtic. Latchford mishandled a high ball, patted it straight onto the head of Gordon Smith and he nodded it into the net. Celtic couldn't come back a second time. Not this Celtic team, anyway.

Dowie was in the line-up, but, once again, contributed next to nothing. He would make nine appearances in total before being invited to leave the premises. The wretched Dowie would join the ranks of Hugh Maxwell, Bobby Craig and Paddy Turner as a colossal waste of money. When they first arrived at Celtic, the fans chorused, 'Who?' When they departed, the supporters cried, 'Why?'

After beating Luxembourg's Jeunesse d'Esch 11–1 on aggregate in the European Cup first round, Celtic surrendered meekly to Austria's SSW Innsbruck at the next hurdle. Conn and Craig scored in a 2–1 win in Glasgow, but the team, with another uninspiring new face in Jim Casey playing, flopped 3–0 in the second leg. Worse was to follow in the Scottish Cup. George McCluskey, skilful and clever, netted a hat-trick in a 7–1 demolition of Dundee in the first round, but some unwanted history was around the corner. Celtic toiled to a 1–1 draw against First Division Kilmarnock in the next stage at Parkhead. An out-of-sorts team relied on a goal from MacDonald to force a replay at Rugby Park. Roy Aitken was sent off in a night to forget when Celtic lost 1–0, humbled for the first time in the national tournament by opponents from a lower division. A miserable campaign – and one that had looked so promising in the summer – ended with a dismal 3–1 defeat against St Mirren at Love Street. Celtic finished fifth in the table on 36 points – 19 fewer than the previous campaign – with Rangers regaining the championship on 55. Aberdeen (53), Dundee United (40) and Hibs (37) all outperformed a poor Celtic team.

Giants such as Billy McNeill, Tommy Gemmell, Bobby Murdoch, Jimmy Johnstone, Bertie Auld, Davie Hay and Kenny Dalglish had been replaced by the likes of Ian McWilliams, Roy Kay, Jim Casey, Johnny Gibson, Peter Mackie, John Dowie and Jimmy Bone. The shift in quality was staggering, the downward spiral frightening. Older Celtic followers must have winced as they witnessed what looked like a restaging of the early '60s, with their club being sucked into a vortex of mediocrity and misery.

Unthinkable only a handful of years previously, it was now time for a change of manager. The whole sorry episode that came next was a black one in the history of a proud football club. Jock Stein discovered he was expendable. Frankly, though, the board were in a quandary about how to deal with the removal of their popular manager. After a month of negotiations, two things emerged: a post for Stein would be found on the board and Davie McParland, his assistant manager, would not be offered the job as his successor. The board turned to Stein for his thoughts. Without hesitation, he nominated Billy McNeill. The former captain was seen as Celtic manager material by his mentor, who, as well as shaping his playing career, had had an enormous influence on his first steps into management, possibly without McNeill's full knowledge.

McNeill, after quitting the game following the Scottish Cup final success over Airdrie in 1975, had tired of working on his own business interests and was persuaded to become manager of Clyde on 1 April 1977. A mere six weeks later, Stein received a telephone call from Dick Donald, the Aberdeen chairman. He was looking for a successor to Ally MacLeod, who had agreed to take over as manager of the Scotland international side. Donald had one name in mind: Bertie Auld. Stein nominated McNeill.

Auld, who was then team boss at Partick Thistle, said, 'Yes, I could have been Aberdeen's manager if it hadn't been for the intervention of Big Jock. Dick Donald approached Jock to seek his advice. This happened quite a lot. Jock had a massive influence and people listened to him. Now I don't know what went on in that private conversation between Jock and Dick, but I do know that Aberdeen immediately dropped their interest in me. For whatever reason, Jock didn't give me his recommendation. I'll never know why. Jock actually telephoned me to tell me what he had done. I was extremely hurt, as you might expect. But he insisted he was just being professional and honest. Actually, he also realised that I would have most certainly got to know all about his chat with the Aberdeen chairman. You don't keep things like that quiet for too long on soccer's grapevine. So, what had I done to be treated in such a manner after all the service I had given Jock and Celtic? Nothing, as far as I was concerned. I thanked Jock for the telephone call and we never mentioned it again. Not once.'

Stein informed Donald he believed McNeill would be 'more suitable' for the role of Aberdeen manager. Within hours, the Pittodrie supremo, with Stein's assistance, had made contact with McNeill and only a few days later the contract was signed, sealed and delivered. 'I didn't know anything about Bertie's situation at the time,' said McNeill. 'I was actually planning ahead for the new season with Clyde. The club had just won promotion from the old Second Division and I realised we would need to strengthen the squad. I was scouring the free-transfer lists, wondering, in fact, if I could get some youngsters in from Celtic. Then I received the call from Dick Donald. The Clyde directors were great. They realised I couldn't possibly turn down Aberdeen's offer. They wished me all the best for the future. In fact, I was able to do them a wee favour shortly afterwards. I knew they needed money and, in a short space of time, I had taken a liking to one of their players. I offered them something like £30,000 for Stevie Archibald. Not a bad bit of business for all concerned when you consider Spurs paid £800,000 for him a couple of years later.'

McNeill made an immediate impact on Aberdeen. In his only season, he took the club to runners-up position in the league, on fifty-three points, two adrift of Rangers and seventeen ahead of Celtic. They also reached the Scottish Cup final, where they were beaten 2–1 by the Ibrox side. No silverware in the Pittodrie trophy cabinet, but Stein was impressed. He advised the board to waste no time in moving for McNeill and they left it to Stein to make contact.

McNeill recalled, 'I was at the Scottish Football Writers' Association Player of the Year dinner at the Macdonald Hotel in Newton Mearns. Actually, I was picking up the Manager of the Year award, so Big Jock knew I would definitely be in Glasgow that evening. Jock took me aside at one stage and told me he wanted to have a word in private. He told me he would drive his Mercedes to a quiet spot just down the road and I was to meet him there in a few minutes. I was more than a little intrigued. I got into my car, drove to the nominated place and jumped into Jock's car. He smiled and said, "I think it's time you came back to Celtic Park." Just like that. There was no preamble. Before I could ask in what capacity, he quickly added, "Would you take the manager's job?" I was a little stunned by the offer and I listened to him as he laid out the reasons why he thought Celtic and I were made for each other. As ever, he was very persuasive.'

McNeill has a remarkable confession to make: 'I'll tell you this, if the Celtic board had approached me to take the job instead of Jock I would have rejected it. I wouldn't have gone back. My wife, Liz, and I were extremely happy with our new environment in Aberdeen. We had a lovely home in Stonehaven, we had made new friends, the board were great to work with, especially Dick Donald, I had good players and we were getting good results. It was the perfect setting. But I couldn't bring myself to say no to Big Jock. I just couldn't face turning him down. He had been such a huge influence in my life as well as my career. If it hadn't been for Jock, I would never have returned to Celtic.'

Dick Donald told those arranging a farewell party for McNeill that he would not be in attendance, too emotional over his manager's departure. Instead, he passed on a message: 'Tell Billy thanks for everything, but tell him I don't think he'll enjoy working with that board as much as he did with this one.'

On 20 April 1978, Celtic held a meeting at the North British Hotel in Glasgow. A section of the minutes of the get-together makes interesting reading:

> In the view of Mr Stein's long and valued service with the club, it was agreed that at the time a new manager was appointed, Mr Stein be offered an executive directorship with the club as recognition and compensation by the club for these services. Mr Stein indicated that he would be very pleased to accept such a directorship.

On the surface, it appeared to be a seamless changeover. Stein admitted, 'I am more than pleased to be going on the board at Parkhead.' A week or so later, the picture changed dramatically when it was revealed exactly what his role overseeing a new commercial enterprise at the club would entail. He could hardly comprehend what the board were proposing. Stein, the manager who had won 25 trophies at Celtic and made them the best team in Europe in 1967, was being asked to take over a new lottery venture. Stein told friends, 'You'll never believe what they want me to do – they want me to sell pools tickets!'

A proud man, Stein never did agree to that offer. Wily to the last, however, he did not go public with his intention to leave the club. Celtic were due to play Liverpool in his testimonial match at the beginning of August and Stein thought it better to remain silent. A crowd of 60,000 rolled into Celtic Park, generating something in the region of £80,000 for the club's former manager. The following day, Stein met Leeds United chairman Manny Cussins and agreed to become team boss of the Elland Road outfit. He remained in the post for only forty-four days, involved in only ten games, before coming back to take over as international boss in October when Ally MacLeod was finally sacked in the aftermath of a dreadful World Cup finals performance in Argentina in 1978. Stein would remain in the post for just under seven years before his untimely death at the end of a World Cup qualifying tie in Wales on 10 September 1985. He was 62 years old. A giant passed away that evening in Cardiff.

16

PARADISE REGAINED

Billy McNeill was furious and in no mood for taking prisoners. He had just watched Celtic tamely surrender 4–1 in his eighth league game in charge. The team that had inflicted the damage was Aberdeen, at Pittodrie. Alex Ferguson had taken over from McNeill and had guided what was basically McNeill's team to a one-sided victory stroll over the Parkhead side on an October afternoon in 1978.

'I was very, very angry,' recalled McNeill. 'What I had just watched was unacceptable. It was a dire performance and, on a personal level, it was a sore one. However, it was not about me – it was about Celtic Football Club and their supporters. I watched as the players trooped in, got cleaned up and prepared themselves for the trip back to Glasgow. I wanted to detect the mood in the camp. I wasn't about to start throwing teacups around. However, I would make certain I would have my say on the coach on our return. I went to the front of the bus and got their attention. "Do you think displays like that will be tolerated by anyone at this club?" I asked. "Do you want to remain Celtic players? If that's the best you can do, there is no place at Celtic for you." It went on in a similar vein most of the way back to Glasgow. I told them, "A reporter has just asked me if any of you picked up an injury. Do you know what I told him? I said, 'What do you mean? By falling out the bath? That's the only way any of that lot could get hurt.'"

'I wanted them to have a good look at themselves and, at the same time, be honest with themselves. That was very important. Did they think they were good enough to play for Celtic? Obviously, I was looking for a response. I wanted the players to know how much Celtic meant to me. I was determined to get across all the good things Jock Stein had instilled in me. I had a clear vision of what I desired for the club and what I hoped to achieve. I couldn't accept Celtic teams playing like that in front of the best set of supporters in the world. If the players hadn't known what it meant to pull on that green-and-white jersey before the game at Pittodrie, then they certainly did by the time we reached Glasgow. A few of them looked relieved to get off that coach. I had given them plenty to think about over the weekend, that's for sure. I had plenty to think about myself.'

McNeill's managerial reign had got off to a good start in the league with four straight wins, starting with a solid 2–1 victory over Morton at Cappielow. The ITV network were so intrigued as to how the new man would perform that they sent a camera crew from London and one of their top commentators at the time, Martin Tyler, to cover the game in Greenock. Highly unusual, but indicative of the interest generated by McNeill's return to Celtic. Goals from Roddie MacDonald and Ronnie Glavin secured the win. Former Ranger Alfie Conn netted two in a 4–0 victory over Hearts in Glasgow and repeated the feat in a 5–1 triumph over Motherwell at Fir Park. McNeill, viewed from the outside, was fitting perfectly into the dugout once commandeered by mentor Stein. The new manager, though, was having to prove himself on a match-by-match basis in the early days.

'Look, I realised what I was letting myself in for,' McNeill admitted. 'Jock had laid it out, warts and all, from day one. I knew what to expect. The fourth league game of the season was against Rangers and was at our place. No one needed to tell me how much these games meant to everyone connected with the club. Actually, looking back, it was quite strange because they had a new manager too, in John Greig, who had taken over from Jock Wallace. We seemed to be mirroring each other in our career paths. He had played for Rangers as a teenager, had captained the club, had won a European medal, had known the good times and the bad times and had taken over as manager maybe a lot earlier than he might have expected. Whereas he came straight to management from playing, I had had a spell away from Celtic and a full season as boss at Aberdeen. It wasn't a case of me playing with the guys one minute and then becoming their gaffer the next. I think that helped.'

McNeill hadn't added to a fairly threadbare squad in the summer, concentrating completely on what he already had at his disposal. Rangers arrived at Parkhead as champions and were slight favourites with the bookies. Over 60,000 were in the ground to see if McNeill's team could achieve what Stein's side couldn't in five games the previous season: beat their oldest foes. McNeill delivered the goods, with goals from Tom McAdam (2) and George McCluskey in a 3–1 victory.

'That was a big win for me,' recalled McNeill. 'Actually, I sensed the support wanted me to do well. I knew they were on my side and I had to prove worthy of that backing. There had always been an affinity between me and the fans when I was a player. It was reassuring it was still there when I was manager.

'As a matter of fact, I had realised that the previous season when I'd returned for the first time as manager of Aberdeen. I'd wondered how they would receive me in the opposite dugout from Jock Stein. You've no idea how I felt when they started singing my name. That was a truly amazing experience.'

A week after the Rangers victory, McNeill, with only one change in the line-up, Conn replacing Johnny Doyle, lost 1–0 to Hibs in Glasgow. It was an unexpected reverse and the new boss persuaded his board to part with £125,000, a Scottish record transfer fee, to bring in Davie Provan, the elegant outside-right from Kilmarnock. 'I had always liked the look of Davie,' said McNeill. 'He was such a nice striker of a ball and his crosses into the box were of the highest quality. Celtic fans had been looking for the "new Jimmy Johnstone" as soon as the Wee Man left, but that was a burden that shouldn't have been placed on anyone. I told Davie I expected him to play his natural game for us, go out and do what he did so well for Kilmarnock. He delivered OK.' Provan made his debut only a few days after signing and goals from defenders Andy Lynch, Roy Aitken and MacDonald pushed Celtic to a 3–2 win over Partick Thistle at Firhill. This was followed by a nervy 2–1 home success over St Mirren, with Lynch and Conn on target. Six wins from his first seven league games looked perfectly acceptable for the new manager.

Then came the nosedive in Aberdeen. 'That's why I was so angry,' added McNeill. 'Expectation levels were now high, there was a bit of optimism about the place and I knew exactly what we would face at Pittodrie that day. I went into detail on everything, so there was no room for anyone not knowing what was required of them. I didn't want to hand the advantage to Alex Ferguson or Aberdeen. I knew they would be extremely dangerous rivals when it came to any thoughts I had of winning any sort of silverware in my first season at Celtic. You can only do so much as a manager. You can prime your team and then it's up to them once they cross that white line and go onto the field. It's often been said that your best days in football are when you are playing. I wouldn't disagree with that.'

Four days after Pittodrie, Celtic took on Motherwell in the second leg of a League Cup third-round tie at Fir Park (the group sections had been scrapped the previous season). McNeill had seen his players slump to a 1–0 first-game defeat against the same opponents in Glasgow the previous week. How would they respond to the tongue-lashing they had received on the way back from Aberdeen? 'I got exactly what I was looking for,' said McNeill. 'We won 4–1 and I couldn't have asked for more. The response was excellent. It was like watching a different team.' McAdam (2) and Aitken netted and there was a goal, too, from substitute Bobby Lennox, back from a brief stint in America with Houston Hurricane. The last of the Lisbon Lions was proving he could still roar. Celtic had reached the third round after eliminating Dundee, 6–1 on aggregate, and Dundee United, 4–2, in the previous stages.

In the championship, though, a worrying sequence of results was about to begin. Celtic went six games without a win, losing to Dundee United (0–1), Hearts (0–2) and Motherwell (1–2) and drawing with Morton (0–0), Rangers (1–1) and Hibs (2–2). 'Doesn't look much like championship-winning form, does it?' asked McNeill. 'Thankfully, teams around about us were spilling points, too. However, I wasn't interested in what was happening outside the walls of Celtic Park. It was what we did that would count in the end. I had a few heart-to-heart talks with the players. Once more, everything was laid on the line. "Do you think results like that are acceptable to Celtic?" I let them know I was only interested in sharing a dressing-room with winners. Anyone prepared to be second best would be out the door. Players with that attitude were no use to me.'

McAdam halted the landslide of mediocrity with the only goal of the game against Partick Thistle, but, alarmingly, Celtic began haemorrhaging results again. Aberdeen gained a point in a goalless draw on 9 December at Parkhead and four days later a record number of consecutive appearances in the League Cup final came to an abrupt halt at the semi-final stage. McNeill had been hoping to guide his team to their 15th successive grand finale in the tournament, a remarkable run that had kicked off in season 1964–65, when he was only 25 years old.

Rangers were the team to interrupt the procession and one of Celtic's own players, who shouldn't have been on the pitch, got the touch to extinguish the hopes of early silverware for the new Celtic manager. The game was deadlocked at 2–2 in extra time, with McAdam and Doyle on the mark for the Parkhead side and Sandy Jardine (pen.) and Colin Jackson replying. McNeill threw on substitute Jim Casey for the injured Mike Conroy. The fates had made their decision, and unfortunately the newcomer was to have the deciding say in the dramatic outcome. Casey, in truth a very ordinary player who had been signed as a schoolboy, inexplicably toe-poked the ball past the grounded keeper Roy Baines, who had just pushed out a header from Derek Johnstone. Casey panicked in the resultant melee and propelled the ball into his own net. There were only seven minutes remaining before the game would have gone to a penalty-kick decider. It was one of the player's last actions in a Celtic shirt and he eventually signed for American outfit Phoenix Inferno.

Desperately, McNeill tried to galvanise the troops for the visit of Dundee United three days later. The best his team could offer was a 1–1 draw, left-back Lynch sinking a penalty kick past Hamish McAlpine.

Murdo MacLeod, known as 'Rhino' because of his robust midfield play, had been bought the previous month for £100,000 from Dumbarton. 'I reckoned we needed a ball-winner in the middle of the park and I knew Murdo would give us that bit of steel,' said McNeill. 'It also helped that he could cover the ground at speed, could pass a ball and possessed a shot that terrified goalkeepers. In actual fact, I watched him a couple of times and there was another lad at Dumbarton who also caught my eye. He was a big frontman with a reasonable first touch and good in the air. For whatever reason, I just couldn't believe Dumbarton could unearth two such fine players at the same time. I thought I had maybe just been seeing him on his good days. What a mistake. The youngster was Graeme Sharp who went to Everton and also played beside Murdo in the Scottish international team. Lesson learned.'

Celtic came back from a stumble against Morton, a 1–0 defeat at Cappielow, to string together three important victories. McNeill enjoyed his first win over his old team Aberdeen. It was 1–0, with McAdam getting the goal. That was followed by back-to-back victories over Motherwell (2–1) and Morton (3–0).

The Motherwell triumph was notable for the introduction of a young Irish goalkeeper from Keadue Rovers called Pat Bonner. He had been Jock Stein's last signing for the club. Davie Hay had been the first in 1965, and in 1985 the two combined to bring the Premier League to Celtic. Hay was the manager who masterminded the late surge that saw Celtic win 5–0 at St Mirren, while Hearts, leaders on the last day, went down 2–0 to Dundee. 'OK, we won it on goal difference, but, as everyone knows, the best team always wins the league,' said Hay. 'Remember we won every one of our last eight games when the pressure was on and that told you everything about my players.'

Back in season 1978–79, Celtic were searching for an inspirational succession of victories such as that. Peter Latchford returned to goal in a 2–1 defeat against Hibs. In March, the club relinquished any hopes of Scottish Cup glory when they lost 2–1 in a third-round replay to Aberdeen at Parkhead. The first game had ended 1–1, but two breakaway goals put paid to any thoughts of a Hampden appearance in May.

A 4–3 victory over Motherwell at Fir Park was just the start of eight exhausting league games in the month of April. A 2–0 win over Partick

Thistle was followed by a 2–1 defeat by Dundee United at Tannadice. McNeill urged his players to concentrate. 'There were 11 games to play,' said the manager. 'Unfortunately, we had no other distractions. The League Cup had gone, we were out of the Scottish Cup and, for the first time since 1962 when I was just a laddie, there had been no involvement in Europe. So I told the players to treat these remaining games as cup finals. I didn't think it was too much to ask.'

Celtic won five, drew one and lost one of their next seven fixtures. The defeat came at Ibrox when Alex MacDonald netted the game's only goal, and a point was dropped – or won – in a 1–1 draw at Aberdeen, where Lynch again scored with an expertly taken penalty kick. However, there were victories over St Mirren (1–0 and 2–1), Hearts (3–0), Dundee United (2–1) and Hibs (3–1). Nine players shared the eleven goals: Mike Conroy (2), Roy Aitken (2), Murdo MacLeod, Tommy Burns, Jóhannes Edvaldsson, Andy Lynch, Davie Provan, George McCluskey and Danny McGrain. That was the right-back's second strike of the campaign – his other was in the 4–3 triumph over Motherwell – and he would score another five over the next eight years!

'Actually, it was marvellous to see so many players pitching in just when we needed them most,' observed McNeill. 'The last thing you ever want to be is a one-man band, because if anything happens to that individual then you are in big trouble. It was more than pleasing to see the goal threat coming from so many different angles. With four games to go, I was getting a good feeling.'

The manager then made an astonishing decision on the run-in. He took striker Tom McAdam out of the firing line and put him into central defence. It was a bold move that must have puzzled even the player, who had performed throughout his career at Dumbarton, Dundee United and Celtic as a target man up front. The one person who didn't believe it was such a gamble was McNeill himself. 'I had watched Tom with interest throughout the season,' he said. 'He got up to good heights in the air and was a good header of the ball. You would be surprised at the amount of players who possess a fabulous leap and are then weak when it comes to actually doing something with the ball. He was decent on the deck in link-up play, but I fancied he could provide even more when the play was coming towards him, rather than him chasing balls placed in front of him. I played him against Partick Thistle in defence, he did well and we won 2–1. I decided to keep him there for the next three games. Hardly the right time to experiment with the team, but I was convinced he wouldn't let us down.'

With Love Street undergoing a facelift, St Mirren elected to play their 'home' game against Celtic at Ibrox on 11 May. The match was played on a Friday night to prevent a clash with the Scottish Cup final, which was due the following day at Hampden between Rangers and Hibs. Old favourite Bobby Lennox, on as a substitute, shared the goals with George McCluskey as the Paisley side were undone 2–0. 'Ibrox always was one of my favourite grounds,' grinned Lennox afterwards.

Two to go and the tension was reaching fever pitch. A stubborn and determined Hearts team arrived in Glasgow and it was down to a severe test of nerve. Stein would have been proud of McNeill, who did his best to ease the tension, saying, 'I didn't expect us to be in this challenging position and I still say if we make it to Europe next season we will have done very well all things considered.' That was for public consumption; inside the dressing-room was a different matter. Murdo MacLeod said, 'He wanted that title, you can be sure of that. All season he had driven us towards it.' The Tynecastle side had everything to play for in Glasgow. They had slipped into the relegation dogfight and it was between them and Partick Thistle as to who would join Motherwell in the First Division. They battled for every ball, ran harder than ever and strained every sinew to get something from this encounter. A goal from Conroy settled it for Celtic. It set up the club's last game of the season against Rangers, a title decider.

Rangers had been relentless in their pursuit. The situation for McNeill's team was clear cut: a triumph would take the Premier League championship to Parkhead. A win or a draw would suit Rangers, who still had two more games to play, against Partick Thistle and Hibs. In that case, Celtic, in McNeill's return season, would have to settle for second best. McNeill was never comfortable with that mantle.

The manager recalled, 'I talked to the players as a team unit before the game. I didn't pick out individuals, as I didn't think that would be fair. Jock, of course, did that every now and again, particularly with Jinky, but then he was exceptional, world class, and could handle anything thrown at him. On this occasion, I just wanted to remind the players what we had all been through to get the club into this position. We were 90 minutes away from winning the league. I said, "Listen to that crowd. That's your fans out there. They're worth a goal of a start." I sensed a very determined mood in the camp.'

The hottest ticket in town was for Parkhead on the evening of Monday, 21 May, when football's greatest and most ancient foes would lock horns. The scramble for tickets had been more frantic than ever because a union strike would be keeping TV cameras away from Parkhead. If you wanted to see this one, you had to be there. Only flickering images shot by a fan from the terracing still exist. A thriller of epic proportions was, sadly, never witnessed by millions. As kick-off time approached, Celtic Park throbbed and pulsated, the old ground's foundations heaving and rocking, as a capacity 52,000 frenzied fans, engulfed in wild emotion, prepared to watch a spectacle that would unfold in the most dramatic of circumstances. It was a night for the strong of heart.

In the ninth minute, a deadly hush swept over the Celtic end. Rangers were a goal to the good after Alex MacDonald had knocked one wide of Peter Latchford. That goal was to trigger off a remarkable series of events as Celtic desperately tried to respond. There was no change in the scoreline, though, by the time the interval arrived. Ten minutes after the turnaround, McNeill winced as he saw his side go down to ten men. Johnny Doyle and MacDonald, both fiery characters, were involved in a scuffle and the referee dismissed the Celt for retaliation. He sobbed uncontrollably as he raced off the pitch. The game restarted at a punishing pace during this rawest and most rumbustious of Old Firm confrontations, a rollicking roller-coaster, one of the most nerve-shredding derbies in memory.

Breathtakingly, Celtic drew level midway through the half as Roy Aitken surged forward to belt one past Peter McCloy. In the 74th minute, the roar that went up from the East End of Glasgow must have registered on the Richter scale. Celtic were ahead. George McCluskey, wily and skilful, got through on the blind side to thump the ball low into the net. Two minutes later, it was 2–2, with Bobby Russell scrambling one past Latchford from close range.

This pulverising confrontation was going all the way to the wire. Rangers sat in, obviously more than satisfied to take a point. Celtic, driven on by McNeill from the touchline, had other ideas. Six minutes were left when McCluskey fired in a dangerous low effort from the wing. It was an awkward one for McCloy to deal with. The towering keeper got down to parry the ball up and away, but it struck the inrushing Colin Jackson. The defender could only look on in horror as the clearance bounced off him into the net. Cue bedlam on the terracings. Parkhead became a rhapsody in green and white. Could there possibly be anything left to witness in this no-holds-barred, shuddering conflict?

'I remember picking the ball up in midfield,' said Murdo MacLeod. 'I knew it was late in the game, but I didn't know how late. There was a pass on to either side of me with teammates breaking forward. I just kept going. In an instant, I knew I was going to shoot, there was no chance of me passing. I thought to myself, "Hit this as hard as you can and, even if you miss, the ball will go away into the Celtic end and it will waste time." But I struck the shot really well and it went high and dipped over the keeper's right hand into the top corner. I still had no idea how long there was to go. We all geared up to go again when the referee blew for time up seconds after Rangers had kicked off. I must have been the last Celtic player to touch the ball that evening. It was my best-ever night in football. I had a few memorable ones, but nothing ever touched that. No team could have stopped us even when we were down to ten men.'

A jubilant Celtic crowd brought the house down with their frenzied celebrations, a wall of noise enveloping the stadium. No one had a thought of dispersing until their heroes emerged for a lap of honour. 'The boys deserved it,' recalled McNeill. 'It was simply fantastic. I have never seen a game like it. When George McCluskey scored to make it 2–1 for us, I just couldn't believe it. Then they came right back. One minute you're up there, the next you're down here. My players would climb a mountain and then find there was another waiting for them. Our ten men did extraordinary things. To score four goals in just over half an hour with only ten men against Rangers was just incredible. Unbelievable. John Greig was one of the first to congratulate me and I really appreciated that. He was as proud a Rangers man as I was a Celtic man and he must have been hurting, but he still sought me out to shake my hand. A great gesture from a genuine sportsman. I was overjoyed for my players and I even had to persuade Johnny Doyle to go out there and take a bow. He didn't want to go because he thought he had let us down. Eventually, I think I threw him onto the pitch! All of my players, including Johnny, were heroes.'

On a monumental evening, as the blare of acclaim and the pounding racket of applause reverberated around Celtic Park, the din rising to puncture the rapidly darkening skies above the East End of Glasgow, there could not have been a more electrifying contrast with the drab occasion back on the first day of January in 1960 at the same venue against the same opponents. Then, with hardly a murmur, the desolate Celtic support had drifted away after witnessing a further loss to Rangers, the defeat the result of yet another dull and tedious performance by an indifferent or inferior bunch of bedraggled individuals who, with the odd exception, were blindingly inadequate in skill, guile and craft. The cast of hundreds of performers in the green and white hoops saw too many understudies and not enough leading men. The crestfallen Celtic fans had every reason to be apprehensive about the future. Loyally and stubbornly, they followed a club that was bankrupt of leadership, bereft of guidance, destitute of direction and starved of inspiration. The board, during those difficult times, appeared to be hypnotised into apathy. The diversity between the emotions inspired by the two games nineteen years apart couldn't have been more stark, the extremes bordering on the incredible. Celtic's odyssey from the awful to the awesome had been as improbable as it was captivating, as implausible as it was compelling.

Until the arrival of a full-blown tempest in the shape of one remarkable individual in 1965, the entire football club had been locked in a labyrinth of hopelessness. Unburdened of meddlesome and antiquated interference from above, the new manager, Jock Stein, smashed his way through the barricades of the mundane, obliterating all obstacles as he single-mindedly drove Celtic towards the zenith. It was an extraordinary expedition through the emotions, an adventure often fraught with anxiety, punctuated by the spectacular, dominated by ambition, laced with drama, sprinkled with disappointment and, ultimately, rewarded with accolades and triumphs. A team that had been routinely turned over by substandard opposition in the early part of the '60s had aspired to such an exalted position that the rest of Europe cast envious glances towards an illuminating little corner of Scotland, so often a cold, dank place in the past. This was a team that ripped away the suffocating cloak of negativity and let football breathe again. It was a victory for the beautiful game when Celtic lifted the European Cup in 1967, burying the belief that success could be achieved only by the denial of flair, the prohibition of flamboyance, the absence of exhibitionism. An honourable club had restored romance and razzmatazz to football. Supporters throughout the globe were reassured that enterprise and enjoyment had returned once more to their beloved sport. Celtic joyously sprinkled stardust everywhere their travels took them, to the gratification of a worldwide audience who appreciated the finer arts of the game.

The Lisbon success was no rare spontaneous combustion of attacking aggression allied with pomp and elegance. Those who witnessed Celtic's classy pioneers on a consistent basis would have testified to that fact. The importance of what this club achieved, and how it was accomplished, should never be overlooked. The mere fact that so many sought to plagiarise their style could be accepted as a massive compliment. Celtic cannot be denied their place in the pantheon of football. A manager and his 11 players, all born within a 30-mile radius of Parkhead, earned the right to be paraded among the privileged, to stride alongside the colossi. Lisbon, ablaze with colour on an unforgettable May day in 1967, was, of course, the pinnacle of their achievement. The storm clouds, angry and persistent, had at last been banished to the darkest recesses of the gloomiest domain. Painful recollections of a team aimlessly and laboriously bumbling through the wilderness years were extinguished in a glowing eruption and fusion of talent. That was the glorious gift Celtic bestowed upon the game. They put the smile back on the face of football.

Celtic Park was no longer a place where dreams went to die.

APPENDIX
THE HONOURS LIST

SEASON 1959–60
Honours: none
League position: ninth

PLAYED	WON	DRAWN	LOST	FOR	AGAINST	POINTS
34	12	9	13	73	59	33

SEASON 1960–61
Honours: none
League position: fourth

PLAYED	WON	DRAWN	LOST	FOR	AGAINST	POINTS
34	15	9	10	64	46	39

SEASON 1961–62
Honours: none
League position: third

PLAYED	WON	DRAWN	LOST	FOR	AGAINST	POINTS
34	19	8	7	81	37	46

SEASON 1962–63
Honours: none
League position: fourth

PLAYED	WON	DRAWN	LOST	FOR	AGAINST	POINTS
34	19	6	9	76	44	44

SEASON 1963–64
Honours: none
League position: third

PLAYED	WON	DRAWN	LOST	FOR	AGAINST	POINTS
34	19	9	6	89	34	47

SEASON 1964–65
Honours: Scottish Cup
League position: eighth

PLAYED	WON	DRAWN	LOST	FOR	AGAINST	POINTS
34	16	5	13	76	57	37

SEASON 1965–66
Honours: First Division Championship, League Cup

PLAYED	WON	DRAWN	LOST	FOR	AGAINST	POINTS
34	27	3	4	106	30	57

SEASON 1966–67
Honours: European Cup, First Division Championship, Scottish Cup, League Cup

PLAYED	WON	DRAWN	LOST	FOR	AGAINST	POINTS
34	26	6	2	111	33	58

SEASON 1967–68
Honours: First Division Championship, League Cup

PLAYED	WON	DRAWN	LOST	FOR	AGAINST	POINTS
34	30	3	1	106	24	63

SEASON 1968–69
Honours: First Division Championship, Scottish Cup, League Cup

PLAYED	WON	DRAWN	LOST	FOR	AGAINST	POINTS
34	23	8	3	89	32	54

SEASON 1969–70
Honours: First Division Championship, League Cup

PLAYED	WON	DRAWN	LOST	FOR	AGAINST	POINTS
34	27	3	4	96	33	57

SEASON 1970–71
Honours: First Division Championship, Scottish Cup

PLAYED	WON	DRAWN	LOST	FOR	AGAINST	POINTS
34	25	6	3	89	23	56

SEASON 1971–72
Honours: First Division Championship, Scottish Cup

PLAYED	WON	DRAWN	LOST	FOR	AGAINST	POINTS
34	28	4	2	96	28	60

SEASON 1972–73
Honours: First Division Championship

PLAYED	WON	DRAWN	LOST	FOR	AGAINST	POINTS
34	26	5	3	93	28	57

SEASON 1973–74
Honours: First Division Championship, Scottish Cup

PLAYED	WON	DRAWN	LOST	FOR	AGAINST	POINTS
34	23	7	4	82	27	53

SEASON 1974–75
Honours: Scottish Cup, League Cup
League position: third

PLAYED	WON	DRAWN	LOST	FOR	AGAINST	POINTS
34	20	5	9	81	41	45

SEASON 1975–76
Honours: none
League position: second (Premier Division)

PLAYED	WON	DRAWN	LOST	FOR	AGAINST	POINTS
36	21	6	9	71	42	48

SEASON 1976–77
Honours: Premier Division Championship, Scottish Cup

PLAYED	WON	DRAWN	LOST	FOR	AGAINST	POINTS
36	23	9	4	79	39	55

SEASON 1977–78
Honours: none
League position: fifth

PLAYED	WON	DRAWN	LOST	FOR	AGAINST	POINTS
36	15	6	15	63	54	36

SEASON 1978–79
Honours: Premier Division Championship

PLAYED	WON	DRAWN	LOST	FOR	AGAINST	POINTS
36	21	6	9	61	37	48

SEASON 1979–80
Honours: Scottish Cup
League position: second

PLAYED	WON	DRAWN	LOST	FOR	AGAINST	POINTS
36	18	11	7	61	38	47

TOTAL HONOURS

Twenty-seven: one European Cup, eleven League Championships, nine Scottish Cups, six League Cups